Victimology

CU00649598

"*Victimology: Research, Policy and Activism* iden
analysis and exploration, extending the field of vi   ...e frontiers of
justice-focused reform. This book brings together diverse authors that set the
pace for change in a world increasingly aware of the need for justice activism
that includes the voice of the victim as a significant constituent of justice. Victim
interests are addressed across a full range of fora, from women's rights and gendered violence to cyber abuse to the emergence of the victim-survivor through
narrative victimology. The book is essential reading for anyone interested in
victimology, criminal justice and social change."

—Tyrone Kirchengast, Associate Professor, *The University of Sydney
Law School, Australia*

Jacki Tapley • Pamela Davies
Editors

Victimology

Research, Policy and Activism

Editors
Jacki Tapley
University of Portsmouth
Portsmouth, Hampshire, UK

Pamela Davies
Department of Social Sciences
Northumbria University
Newcastle upon Tyne, UK

ISBN 978-3-030-42287-5   ISBN 978-3-030-42288-2   (eBook)
https://doi.org/10.1007/978-3-030-42288-2

This Palgrave Macmillan imprint is published by the registered company Springer Nature Switzerland AG.
The registered company address is: Gewerbestrasse 11, 6330 Cham, Switzerland

Acknowledgements

To my parents, Alf and Margaret Tapley, for teaching me the value of education, hard work and always having the courage to pursue what you believe in!

Contents

Notes on Contributors

Oona Brooks-Hay is Senior Lecturer in Criminology at the Scottish Centre for Crime and Justice Research (Sociology), University of Glasgow, Scotland, UK.

Michele Burman is Professor of Criminology and head of the School of Social and Political Sciences at the University of Glasgow, Scotland, UK.

Elizabeth Cook is an ESRC post-doctoral research fellow, Centre for Criminology, Faculty of Law, University of Oxford, UK.

Pamela Davies is Professor of Criminology in the Department of Social Sciences, Northumbria University, UK.

Edna Erez is Professor of Criminology in the Department of Criminology, Law, and Justice, University of Illinois at Chicago, US.

Simon Green is a reader in Criminology and Associate Dean for Research in the Faculty of Arts, Culture and Education, University of Hull.

Matthew Hall is Professor of Law & Criminal Justice and Director of Research, Lincoln Law School, University of Lincoln, UK.

Jize Jiang is an assistant professor in the School of Law at Shanghai University of Finance and Economics, China.

Ndumba J. Kamwanyah is a lecturer and deputy director, Centre for Professional Development, Teaching and Learning Improvement, University of Namibia.

Kathy Laster is Professor of Law and director of the Sir Zelman Cowen Centre at Victoria University, Melbourne, Australia.

Ruth Lewis is an associate professor at the Department of Social Sciences, Northumbria University, UK.

Kate Mukungu is Lecturer in Social Sciences, Department of Business, Law, Policing and Social Sciences, University of Cumbria, UK.

Nicola O'Leary is Lecturer in Criminology, Department of Criminology and Sociology, University of Hull.

Antony Pemberton is Professor of Victimology and director INTERVICT, Tilburg University.

April Smith is Senior Lecturer in Criminology and Penology, Institute of Criminal Justice Studies, Faculty of Humanities and Social Sciences, University of Portsmouth, UK.

Lisa Sugiura is Senior Lecturer in Criminology and Cybercrime, Institute of Criminal Justice Studies, Faculty of Humanities and Social Sciences, University of Portsmouth, UK.

Jacki Tapley is Principal Lecturer in Victimology and Criminology, Institute of Criminal Justice Studies, Faculty of Humanities and Social Sciences, University of Portsmouth, UK.

Jemma Tyson is Principal Lecturer in Criminology, Institute of Criminal Justice Studies, Faculty of Humanities and Social Sciences University of Portsmouth, UK.

Valeria Vegh Weis is Professor of Criminology and Transitional Justice at Buenos Aires University and Quilmes National University, Argentina.

Alexander von Humboldt is a post-doctoral fellow at Freie Universität Berlin, Germany.

Rob White is Professor of Criminology in the School of Social Sciences at the University of Tasmania, Australia.

Clare Wiper is a post-doctoral researcher and lecturer, Department of Social Sciences, Northumbria University, UK.

List of Tables

1

Victimology: A Conversion of Narratives

Jacki Tapley and Pamela Davies

The criminal justice landscape has evolved significantly during the last four decades, with its predominant focus on the offender shifting to the background, while the role and experiences of the victim have emerged as centre stage, rhetorically at least. The focus of this book is to examine the range of complex factors that have impacted upon and altered this landscape. In particular, the interplay between victimology as an academic discipline, the role and activism of individuals and special interest groups, and the subsequent impact upon policy making and professional practices. The merger of narratives, from the basic tenets of the early positivist victimologists to the challenges of radical, critical and cultural approaches,

J. Tapley (✉)
Institute of Criminal Justice Studies, Faculty of Humanities and Social Sciences, University of Portsmouth, Portsmouth, UK
e-mail: jacki.tapley@port.ac.uk

P. Davies
Department of Social Sciences, Northumbria University, Newcastle upon Tyne, UK
e-mail: pamela.davies@northumbria.ac.uk

© The Author(s) 2020
J. Tapley, P. Davies (eds.), *Victimology*,
https://doi.org/10.1007/978-3-030-42288-2_1

have altered the trajectory of the criminal justice process, influencing political rhetoric and policy responses, challenging professional cultures and gradually changing perceptions of the crime victim and their treatment. This chapter will provide a brief overview of the historical, social and political contexts that have subsequently shaped the criminal justice landscape. In particular, it will explore the emergence of *Victimology* as a valid and credible academic discipline, its origins, influence, impact and potential for the future.

Victimology—A Theoretically Informed Humanist Endeavour?

The roots of victimology have been traced back to the theoretical musings of unconventional male scholars in the 1940s and 1950s. Often referred to as a sub-discipline of criminology, victimology was viewed with suspicion by some criminologists within academia, one critic describing their endeavours as 'the lunatic fringe of criminology' (Becker 1981, cited by Rock 2018: 35). Undeterred, early theorists challenged the offender-centric focus of criminology by questioning the absence of the victim in debates about crime and offenders. Commenting on this omission, Rock (2018: 32) observes: 'There was almost no place there for the pathos and pains of individual victimisation or the personal and communal costs of everyday crime.'

Following in the methodological footsteps of positivist criminology, Hans von Hentig (1948), an early pioneer of victimology, was keen to identify why some people became victims of crime, whilst others did not. Introducing the concept of 'victim proneness', von Hentig identified typologies from the characteristics that appeared to make some people more prone to victimisation than others. Later work by Mendelsohn (1956) focused on 'culpability', introducing a sixfold typology of victims' culpability ranging from the completely innocent to the guiltiest, which also included the criminal who became the victim.

Whilst such typologies, by their very nature, have been challenged and criticised for being anecdotal and lacking in empirical ratification, it was the later, more sophisticated work within this conventional perspective that successfully translated victim culpability into the powerful concept of 'victim precipitation'. Such perspectives tended to place responsibility upon the individual to avoid behaviour that may result in their own victimisation, as indicated by Wolfgang's (1958) study of homicide and Amir's (1971) controversial study on rape. Again, as observed by Rock (2018: 34), there was a general sense of unease and otherness about victims and a desire to distance oneself from those stigmatised by misfortune:

> Their very existence is disturbing because it can challenge the belief in a just world where people simply cannot incur harm unless they have somehow earned their suffering through their own misdeeds or foolishness... To think otherwise would turn the moral order quite upside down.

Whilst this early thinking was later criticised for focusing purely on the role of the victim and for failing to acknowledge the wider social structures and constraints that may contribute to victimisation, these perspectives became and remain highly influential, determining 'what might be considered reasonable and rational behaviour for a victim' (Walklate 2001: 28). In particular, these early conventional theories were criticised for failing to acknowledge the social factors that contribute to increasing individuals' and groups' vulnerability and risk to specific types of victimisation, such as, class, race and gendered power relations. In part inspired to redress this, radical and critical theories emerged in the 1970s and 1980s. These perspectives started to examine the wider social contexts in which crime and victimisation occurred, and the impact of crime as it affects different social groups (Goodey 2005: 101). With a particular focus on the gender order, MacKinnon (1989: 161) observed:

> The state is male in the feminist sense: the law sees and treats women the way men see and treat women. The liberal state coercively and authoritatively constitutes the social order in the interest of men as a gender—through its legitimating norms, forms, relations to society, and substantive policies.

As such, it has been recognised that the agencies administering and implementing criminal justice are part of a wider traditional system operating within a deeply embedded patriarchal framework that privileges men (Mawby and Walklate 1994: 185). Essentially, 'in everyday life, victim status depends upon wider historical, social and cultural processes and their relationship to human action' (Spalek 2017: 5), rather than the sole actions of an individual.

In response to the criticisms of the early conventional theories, later positivist theories emerged which focused on lifestyle and routine activities (Hindelang et al. 1978; Gottfredson 1981; Cohen and Felson 1979, all cited by Spalek 2017: 62), arguing that differences in lifestyle impact on the risk of victimisation, based upon particular locations, at certain times and contact with potential offenders. As observed by Goodey (2005: 71) 'where you go, what you do, and who you are, as determined by the limited choices in your routine daily activities, determines your victimisation proneness'. However, these routine activity theories remain focused on the individual, rather than acknowledging the impact of wider social structures that govern peoples' routine activities and their ability to change them, if they so wish. Consequently, they continue to fail to recognise the power differentials that exist between social groups, created by socio-economic status, gender, race, culture and age, thereby rendering some groups more prone to certain types of victimisation than others (Tapley 2020). (For a fuller exposition of the early contributor perspectives on victimisation and critiques of these, see Francis 2007; Mawby and Walklate 1994; Rock 2018.)

Despite these criticisms, victim blaming has become a common default position and it is often left for victims themselves to demonstrate their legitimate status as an 'ideal victim' (Christie 1986). However, attaining this status may prove problematic for many individuals and groups; social and legal processes often requiring them to go to some lengths to prove their 'ideal' status (Duggan 2018). It can be argued that the obstacles encountered in achieving any sense of justice and the dissatisfaction felt by many victims and victim advocates, has provided the motivation and momentum to challenge some of the myths and assumptions associated with victimisation, through activism and the mobilisation of campaigns often targeted at specific types of offence and victims.

Academia, Advocacy and Activism

A fundamental aspect of the critical and radical theories emerging in the 1970s was their link to wider social movements, the questioning of grand theories and challenges to the wider post-war social and political consensus of the 1950s and 1960s. This was a distinctive feature of the emerging discipline of victimology. Developing in parallel—and sometimes in tandem—with academic theorising and research was an identifiable, if not cohesive, 'victim's movement' (van Dijk 1988).

The 1960s and 1970s witnessed the activities of increasingly well-organised groups who set themselves up specifically to assist or campaign on behalf of victims and advocate their rights, particularly in the United States. Whilst commonly and conveniently referred to as a 'movement' by many commentators, this term implies a misleading impression of unity and has been more accurately described by van Dijk (1988) as 'ideologically heterogeneous'. For the 'movement', as such, remains a loose association of individuals and groups representing a diverse range of motivations and agendas, ranging from far right political movements, single-cause interest groups and more radical grassroots and critical perspectives. One key element of the movement had an agenda that became particularly aligned to the concerns of victims and victimology—second-wave feminism. Whilst first-wave liberal feminism in the late 1800s had out of necessity campaigned for women's rights as citizens to education, politics, employment and finance; second-wave liberal, socialist, radical and post-modern feminisms challenged the conventional victimological agenda (Davies 2018: 109). In particular, past and present feminist perspectives challenge patriarchal structures that tolerate and condone the oppression of women through hidden forms of violence and abuse, and the failure of criminal justice agencies to recognise these forms of violence (often within a domestic context) as 'real crime' (Tapley 2010: 138; Tapley and Jackson 2019).

The significant contribution of feminist thought and activism to victimology as an academic discipline has been well documented (Davies 2018), but it also created tensions within the discipline of victimology. In particular, concerns about the erosion of victimology as a theoretical endeavour and fears it was becoming a humanist movement. Fattah (1997) warned of the dangers of creating a false contest between the rights of offenders and victims. He later reflected on what he viewed as the transformation of victimology 'from an academic discipline into a humanistic movement, the shift from scholarly research to political activism' and the serious implications of this 'metamorphosis' on the negative impact on criminal policy (Fattah 2000: 25). Whilst Fattah (2000) is prudent to caution against the use of emotive language relating to victims where it is used to enhance political rhetoric promoting punitive political agendas, it is equally important to recognise the inability of some to achieve legitimate victim status. The dissatisfaction caused by a criminal justice process that fails to acknowledge the crucial role victims have, and which fails to afford them specific rights to protect their interests and assist in their recovery, is not a hallmark of an effective criminal justice system (Wedlock and Tapley 2016).

There is no doubt that the growth in populist politics and the immediacy of sound bite politics (Garland 2001) assisted in propelling the extraordinary ascendance of crime victims on the political agenda from the 1990s. A plethora of reforms aimed at modernising criminal justice ensued with political rhetoric pledging to *'rebalance the system in favour of victims, witnesses and communities and to deliver justice for all'* (Home Office 2002, cited by Tapley 2005: 250). The aim of this book is to reflect upon the development of victimology and its contribution to these reforms. Victimology has been described as a discipline consisting of three strands: 'research, activism and policy' (Goodey 2005: 94). The chapters in this volume examine the influence of these three strands on criminal justice practices, policies and professional cultures in the twenty-first century. They variously explore, through theoretically informed debate, the past, present and future potential of the discipline of victimology and its capacity to impact upon and ameliorate the tendency for criminal justice processes to evoke secondary victimisation and incur further harm for both victims and offenders.

Victimology—Present and Future

The politicisation of crime victims is a central focus of this book, but more specifically, this book examines how victimology, as a theoretically informed humanist endeavour, has shaped the political and criminal justice landscape during the last half of the twentieth century and continues to do so in the early decades of the twenty-first century. This is what we mean by a 'conversion of narratives'. What has victimology as a discipline achieved, given its diversity and competing aims, mix of ideas and agendas? Can it contribute to the development of policies and practices that help to temper the negative impact of adversarial criminal justice processes for both complainants and defendants; victims and offenders? (See Chapter 13 for more on the challenges that an adversarial system poses for victims' rights.) This book emphasises and explores the influence of the humanist and activist arm of victimology on the subsequent development of policy and legislation. Much of the victimological enterprise has sought to challenge the domain assumptions of early positivist thinking and more latterly the impact of prevailing neoliberal ethos evident in many jurisdictions as the socio-political climate changes. Many are involved in the emancipation of specific groups of victims or forms of victimisation and, as the chapters within this book will demonstrate, activism has championed victims of specific offences and attention is drawn to alternative forms of offending and different forms of victimisation created by new forms of technology. Whilst entrenched and persistent attitudes sustained by old power structures remain stubbornly persistent to erosion, the contributors to this volume illustrate that the efforts to address these deep-seated historical and cultural practices are edging forward. Does this indicate a failure of victimology or highlight the continued need for the discipline to develop further as a theoretically informed humanist movement, utilising activist strategies as a tool to persuade and influence social change? The remainder of this book allows the readers to form their own conclusions to these questions.

We now set out how the remainder of this volume is organised. The following chapters demonstrate the links between theoretical perspectives and their influence upon activism, policy and professional practice.

Chapters 2, 3, 4, and 5 provide a foregrounding of activism with an emphasis on victim advocacy, with a particular focus on gender-based violence (GBV) and abuse, demonstrating the influence of feminist and critical perspectives, which robustly challenge the early positivist narratives of victimisation.

In Chapter 2, Clare Wiper and Ruth Lewis examine the history of activism against violence against women (VAW), which has been informed by and helped shape a feminist victimology. The authors analyse how feminist principles have influenced the activism and how the activism has shaped policy and service provision for victim/survivors of VAW. They consider the challenges posed by the contemporary landscape of neoliberalism and austerity economics and what challenges this presents for feminist activist victimology around VAW in the future. Despite rising levels of VAW and diminishing resources for service delivery and prevention in both the UK and beyond, they contend that new forms of feminist organising are extending the scope of gender politics towards an anti-capitalist and anti-austerity critique. Their optimism for the future points towards ongoing resistance efforts across the generations and they argue that critical feminist victimology thrives amongst those committed to upholding a feminist analysis of all forms of violence against women and girls.

In Chapter 3, continuing with the theme of the harm incurred within neoliberal regimes, but with a similarly optimistic tone about the state of online activism, Lisa Sugiura and April Smith explore the practices of victim blaming, responsibilisation and resilience in the context of online sexual offending through trolling and harassment, 'revenge pornography' and 'upskirting'. Though they acknowledge there are gaps in knowledge which require examination—online abuse towards non-binary, intersex and transgender persons—the authors explore how victim resilience is mobilised via online activist movements including #MeToo and #EverydaySexism, and they contemplate the positive role of digital technologies in enabling feminist activism and advocacy to empower victims, challenge and raise awareness of not only online sexual abuses, but also wider societal sex-based harms.

The next chapter to explore gender-based violence and activism does so in the context of Namibia where the country's dual justice systems are examined. In Chapter 4, Kate Mukungu and Ndumba Kamwanyah take pains to articulate the two separate justice systems Namibia inherited at the point of independence in 1990. The formal statutory system and an informal or traditional system. In a bid to protect its traditions and customary law, the constitution now recognises both systems, making improving the response to women violated by GBV challenging. A coalition against gendered and sexual violence is discussed and their multimedia campaigning, which encompasses a variety of activities and events including a 'Mini-Skirt' protest, marches and vigils. These authors are also upbeat in their conclusions about GBV in Namibia where they suggest that substantial progress has been made in developing progressive legislation to address GBV in the criminal justice system. They explore how activists have been important in advocating for such improvements and highlight where responses have fallen short.

Foregrounding the topic of bereaved family activism after violent death, and drawing on her own research (interviews and participant observations) on Mothers Against Violence—an anti-violence charity—Elizabeth Cook maintains the thread established in the chapters that precede it on advocacy and GBV. Chapter 5 explores the attempts by bereaved families to manage and address their experiences of violent death through public campaigns, which confront injustices, raise awareness and promote the acknowledgement of harms that may have previously gone unheard. She demonstrates the significance that stories of suffering can hold in public life and what can be learned from the experiences of bereaved families. Illustrating her points with reference to Doreen Lawrence and the practice of sharing experiential stories, the author discusses how bringing personal experiences out of the private and out of the isolated can encourage victims to make sense of lethal violence, reclaim control, and gain recognition. Her conclusions highlight the importance of victims' voices in creating communities of solidarity and recognition of injustices.

Chapters 6, 7, 8, 9, 10, and 11 have a distinct focus on the politicisation of victims and the development and impact on policy making, notwithstanding the significant contribution of the news and social media representations of victimisation and who the victims are. In Chapter 6, Michele Burman and Oona Brooks-Hay trace the histories of victim advocacy as a prelude to sharing their research on the provision of support to report rape. Within an adversarial context, victim-survivors of GBV find themselves in the midst, but not in control, of what can be a protracted and bewildering process. Whilst there has been a proliferation of advocacy services to support victims, there are important questions concerning where services are physically located and how they are delivered, along with their level of (financial, operational) autonomy. The authors argue that the role advocates can play in terms of 'institutional advocacy'—within the criminal justice process, within police stations, within examination suites and within prosecutor offices—is significant and they conclude on the merits of multifaceted advocacy work.

Chapter 7 explores victim activism and its relationship to the politics of justice suggesting the nature of the journey has been one from invisible to conspicuous. Nicola O'Leary and Simon Green do so with reference to the role of the media and with the aid of three case studies of high-profile victim campaigns. The first is the campaign for justice pursued by the parents of Stephen Lawrence. The second is the tabloid-led campaigns for various offender registers (Megan's Law, Sarah's Law, and Clare's Law) and the third is the #MeToo campaign on Twitter and its influence on public debates about sexual harassment in the workplace. The authors use these case examples to show how such victim activism can be both extremely controversial and extremely effective at challenging the status quo. As with several of the other chapters in the volume, there are losses—exacerbated suffering and misrepresentations of the needs of crime victims—and gains—victim campaigns that have held governments and criminal justice agencies to account—in terms of this approach to victim activism. Overall, however, the authors end on a note of optimism by concluding that whilst victim-driven activism can bring forth the potential for social division and political misrepresentation, they can also drive changes in public attitudes, criminal justice policy and the law. They can also provide crime victims, and indeed all of us, with a genuine opportunity for moral debate and democratic engagement.

The tragic murder of Stephen Lawrence in 1993 features again in Chapter 8 which recognises this case, and the subsequent inquiry, as the catalyst for change in how hate crime is defined and reported, allowing for the victim, or any other person, to define their victimisation as a hate crime. For Jemma Tyson, this also served to draw attention to the victimisation of other communities subject to hate crimes motivated by prejudices and hostility beyond race. Whilst the focus for academics and politicians has primarily been on racially motivated hate crimes, the author concentrates on disablist hate crime and the challenges faced in recognising this type of victimisation. How social processes define disablist hate crime is explored, alongside the role of activists and advocates in raising awareness of the impact on individuals and wider communities. The role of identity politics in shaping responses to disablist hate crime is considered and her critique of a perceived hierarchy to hate crime is used to illustrate where efforts to drive change might be directed.

In Chapter 9, Jacki Tapley examines politics, policies and professional cultures in the context of the Crown Prosecution Service (CPS). The chapter considers the impact of the reforms aimed at improving victims' experiences of the criminal justice system and reflects on this from the perspective of an 'academic' and 'humanist' victimology. The evolving legal culture of the CPS, necessitated by the introduction of victim-centred reforms, begs the question of whether the CPS's increasing responsibilities to engage directly with victims and witnesses compromises its role as an independent prosecuting authority, and threatens the integrity of the service at a time of escalating political and public pressure to improve performance under increasing scrutiny. In order to better understand the challenges now being faced by the CPS, the chapter starts by considering its historical origins and examines periods of resistance and reform, before discussing the opportunities for creating space for a victim perspective in the prosecution decision-making process to assist in bridging the gap between professional and victims' discourses.

In Chapter 10, Matthew Hall examines the significant changes to the commissioning of local victim support services in England and Wales. The new commissioning model places responsibility for the commissioning upon Police and Crime Commissioners and these developments, Hall suggests, represent a significant watershed in the long-running transportation of victim services from being activist driven to market driven. Despite this, once again, there are grounds for optimism in respect of improving support and services for victims in that many PCCs have found creative ways to gather data on victims' needs in their local area and are commissioning services in accordance with the best data they have. Furthermore, the commissioning framework has also opened potential opportunities for the victim's movement to further its work, especially in the area of sexual violence, though as Hall stresses, larger charities still tend to dominate this new 'marketplace' of supply for victim services. This bias curbs the ability of the more activist-based support organisations for victims of crime to challenge the government and criticise the criminal justice system, including the PCCs themselves, on victim policies. There are also gaps in knowledge, meaning there is little proof of the economic effectiveness of this commissioning system, the quality of the services available or their genuine impact on victims. We also know very little about the service providers who might have lost out because of local commissioning. The important question of the politicisation of victims of crime bubbles to the surface in this chapter. PCCs being politicians, the line between using this role as a platform to advocate on behalf of crime victims at the regional or national level, and exploiting them for political gain, is often a grey one.

Chapter 11 focuses on multi-agency partnerships as a means of exploring the ways in which activism manifests in safeguarding victims. Pamela Davies critically reviews twenty-first-century pluralised multi-agency approaches to tackling crime, preventing harm, responsibilising perpetrators and supporting victims, drawing on a case study example: Tackling serial perpetrators of domestic abuse through Multi-Agency Tasking and Co-ordination (MATAC) and the subsequent Domestic Abuse Whole Systems Approach (DAWSA), both pioneered in the North East of England, UK to reflect on developments in community safety. New partnerships such as these appear less wedded to the traditional criminal justice paradigm that has so far failed so many victims of domestic abuse and more committed to a holistic approach. The spur to recent developments in the policing of domestic abuse is seemingly a complex mix of political—including diverse feminist influenced—drivers pushing for change. A key message from this chapter is that healthy scepticism from partners means that collaboration is hard work, but can be effective in preventing victimisation and supporting victims. Stakeholders from charities and statutory bodies alike are finding ways of working, such that they are 'critical allies' in the drive for change.

Chapters 12, 13, and 14 harness a collection of theoretically informed thought-provoking arguments and ideas that reflect on concepts of justice, victim's participation and conceptual thinking about the role of victims and future dynamics and controversies around activism, protest and consumerism.

In Chapter 12, Valeria Vegh Weis and Rob White discuss the intersection of environmental activism and victimisation. Broadly based on radical victimology and climate change criminology, they examine different actors involved in the struggle against green crimes and environmental harms, using the student movements for climate justice as a case study of the evolvement from victims-to-be to activists in the here-and-now. From an activist student movement perspective, bottom-up strategies built upon the involvement of those living and working at the grassroots appears as the best way to tackle top-down harms. On the one hand, victims' voices are powerful and integral to social change movements. On the other hand, their involvement might also represent a useful way to channel their own anger and grief into meaningful outlets that hold out the promise of change. The students' movement also exposes existing obstacles within environmental activism. Essentially, their experience shows that in order to sustain the movement and enhance its impact, building up social environmental movements and engaging in spectrum politics might be desirable further steps to confront backlashes. From an academic perspective, the movement encourages us to follow up different case studies in order to learn 'what works', 'what does not work' and 'what sometimes works' in different circumstances, while to also study corporate and state responses to activism—learn what most disturbs, annoys and unsettles the powers that be.

In Chapter 13, Edna Erez, Jize Jiang and Kathy Laster trace the changing role of victims in an adversarial criminal justice system predominantly from a US perspective. Adopting a historical perspective, they examine the impact of victim-centred reforms aimed at improving victim participation in a criminal process not designed to accommodate them. The chapter considers why these reforms have not fully realised their intended objectives and examines alternative ways in which the interests of victims can be integrated within a system of criminal justice. The authors contend that in the digital age, reconceptualising victims as 'consumers' of criminal justice services could yet provide a metaphoric shift in thinking, allowing victims to be better integrated into the system. In support of their argument, they refer to other areas of public and private service delivery where they maintain that a new consumerist perspective has made organisations more respectful, accountable and responsive to the needs of their increasingly empowered 'customers'. They suggest that, at the very least, a 'customer focus' approach, including the use of 'customer satisfaction surveys', and 'user-centred design' approaches will make victims' experiences more central, as well as enhance accountability for the way they are treated. Ending on a note of optimism, the authors suggest that revisiting a consumerist approach could still yet address the crisis of trust in criminal justice systems, which are falling short of changing public expectations about the need for greater transparency, accountability and community engagement.

In Chapter 14, Antony Pemberton develops a 'theory of injustice'. This he argues will provide the basis for a victimological perspective on justice processes. He commences by reflecting on the consequence of viewing justice and injustice as poles of one dimension. Exposing his theory of injustice, the issue at stake is the manner in which this theory connects to victims' participation in justice processes and criminal proceedings. Acknowledging that victims need to communicate their experience in justice processes, Pemberton casts doubt on the extent to which this is best understood in terms of reducing their stress symptoms, becoming less anxious, or changing the sentence. He proposes that the justice process itself can be an important site for reconnection: of victim experience with society, and with important symbols of shared values. This critical stance has some degree of synergy with the restorative justice perspective and central to his proposition is the need to understand that injustice concerns a relationship of victim with his or her self, rather than a relationship with other persons. The second requirement is to appreciate that this self is only accurately understood if it is conceived as being-in-the-world. Only then does the experience of injustice come into its own—when it amounts to an ontological assault. Pemberton's theorising requires a fundamental rethink about the way we experience our victimisation and by implication, the traditional ways in which we have come to think about activism.

Chapter 15 is the concluding chapter where we, as editors, take stock, reflect and proffer our final thoughts about victimology: research, policy and activism.

References

Amir, M. (1971). *Patterns in Forcible Rape*. Chicago: University of Chicago Press.

Christie, N. (1986). The Ideal Victim. In I. Fattah (Ed.), *From Crime Policy to Victim Policy*. London: The Macmillan Press.

Davies, P. (2018). Feminist Voices, Gender and Victimisation. In S. L. Walklate (Ed.), *Handbook on Victims and Victimology* (2nd ed., pp. 107–123). London: Routledge.

Duggan, M. (Ed.). (2018). *Revisiting the 'Ideal Victim'*. Bristol: Policy Press.

Fattah, E. A. (1997). Toward a Victim Policy Aimed at Healing, Not Suffering. In R. C. Davis, A. J. Lurigio, & W. G. Skogan (Eds.), *Victims of Crime*. London: Sage.

Fattah, E. A. (2000). Victimology: Past, Present and Future. *Criminologie, 33*(1), 17–46.

Francis, P. (2007). Theoretical Perspectives in Victimology. In P. Davies, P. Francis, & C. Greer (Eds.), *Victims, Crime & Society: An Introduction* (2nd ed., pp. 82–107). London: Sage.

Garland, D. (2001). *The Culture of Control: Crime and Social Order in Contemporary Society*. Oxford: Oxford University Press.

Goodey, J. (2005). *Victims and Victimology: Research, Policy and Practice*. London: Longman.

Home Office. (2002). *Justice for All Cm5563*. London: HMSO.

MacKinnon, C. A. (1989). *Toward a Feminist Theory of the State*. Cambridge, MA; London: Harvard University Press.

Mawby, R. I., & Walklate, S. L. (1994). *Critical Victimology*. London: Sage.

Mendelsohn, B. (1956). Une nouvelle branche de la science bio-psycho-sociale: victimologie. *Revue Internationale de Criminologie et de Police Technique*, 10–31.

Rock, P. (2018). Theoretical Perspectives on Victimisation. In S. Walklate (Ed.), *Handbook on Victims and Victimology* (2nd ed., pp. 30–58). London: Routledge.

Spalek, B. (2017). *Crime Victims: Theory, Policy and Practice*. London: Palgrave.

Tapley, J. (2005). Confidence in Criminal Justice: Achieving Community Justice for Victims and Witnesses. In F. Pakes & J. Winstone (Eds.), *Community*

Justice: Issues for Probation and Criminal Justice. Collumpton: Willan Publishing.

Tapley, J. (2010). Working Together to Tackle Domestic Violence. In A. Pycroft & D. Gough (Eds.), *Multi Agency Working in Criminal Justice* (pp. 137–153). Bristol: Policy Press.

Tapley, J. (2020). Crime, Victimisation and Criminology. In P. Davies & M. Rowe (Eds.), *An Introduction to Criminology*. London: Sage.

Tapley, J., & Jackson, Z. (2019). Protection and Prevention: Identifying, Managing and Monitoring Priority Perpetrators of Domestic Abuse. In A. Pycroft & D. Gough (Eds.), *Multi Agency Working in Criminal Justice: Theory, Policy and Practice* (2nd ed., pp. 137–153). Bristol: Policy Press.

van Dijk, J. (1988). Ideological Trends Within the Victims' Movement: An International Perspective. In M. Maguire & J. Pointing (Eds.), *Victims of Crime: A New Deal?* Milton Keynes: Open University Press.

Von Hentig, H. (1948). *The Criminal and His Victim*. New Haven: Yale University Press.

Walklate, S. L. (2001). The Victim's Lobby. In M. Ryan, S. Savage, & D. Wall (Eds.), *Policy Networks in Criminal Justice*. Basingstoke: Palgrave.

Wedlock, E., & Tapley, J. (2016). *What Works in Supporting Victims of Crime: A Rapid Evidence Assessment*. London: Victims' Commissioner. Ministry of Justice.

Wolfgang, M. E. (1958). *Patterns in Criminal Homicide*. Philadelphia, PA: University of Pennsylvania Press.

2

Violence Against Women and Girls: Feminist Activism and Resistance

Clare Wiper and Ruth Lewis

Introduction

At the time of writing, we are in a moment of intense, unprecedented attention to violence against women[1] (VAW). Accusations of sexual assault by dozens of women working in the film industry against the leading Hollywood film producer, Harvey Weinstein, have been followed by similar accusations against many other leading figures in the entertainment, political and other sectors (Hudson and Milne 2018; Krook 2018). At the same time, ongoing investigations into abuse in sport (Mergaert et al. 2016) and the Christian church (Aune and Barnes 2018), as well as video footage of men's violence against women on the street (Cosslett 2018), receives more media coverage than ever before. These events have sparked the #MeToo movement,[2] a hashtag used on social media to reveal the widespread prevalence of sexual assault and harassment, especially in the workplace, highlighting the extensive activism against VAW. This new attention may suggest such activism is a new phenomenon; in fact, it has

C. Wiper (✉) • R. Lewis
Department of Social Sciences, Northumbria University,
Newcastle upon Tyne, UK
e-mail: clare2.wiper@northumbria.ac.uk; ruth.lewis@northumbria.ac.uk

© The Author(s) 2020
J. Tapley, P. Davies (eds.), *Victimology*,
https://doi.org/10.1007/978-3-030-42288-2_2

a long history. This chapter examines this history of activism against VAW, which has been informed by and helped shape a feminist victimology. In outlining this history, it analyses how feminist principles have influenced the activism and how the activism has shaped policy and service provision for victim/survivors of VAW, with a particular focus on the UK context. It will also consider the challenges posed by the contemporary landscape of neoliberalism and austerity economics and will consider the future for feminist activist victimology around VAW. First, we set out the empirical evidence of VAW.

The Nature and Extent of Violence Against Women

VAW is now recognised globally as a significant harm, affecting large proportions of women with potentially devastating consequences for them and their wider networks of family and friends. Global estimates published by the World Health Organisation (WHO) reveal that approximately one in three women worldwide have experienced physical and/or sexual intimate partner violence or non-partner sexual violence in their lifetime (WHO 2013). The same report also predicts that as many as 38% of all murders of women are committed by a male intimate partner. In the UK, in 2017, according to the Femicide Census (Long et al. 2018), at least 139 women were killed by men, the majority (76%) of whom were killed by a man known to them.[3] Walby, Towers, and Francis' (2016) analysis of Crime Survey of England and Wales data (a victimisation survey which produces the most reliable national prevalence data[4]) reveals that '82% of domestic violent crimes are against women' (p. 18), 87% of domestic violent 'high frequency' (more than ten crimes in a year) crimes are committed against women, and 91% of domestic violent crimes resulting in injury are against women.

Sexual harassment on the street and at work is currently receiving renewed attention, in comparison to the relative dearth of scholarly and media coverage since the 1970s. Everyday Sexism, a website (https://everydaysexism.com/) and book (Bates 2015) contains thousands of accounts of sexual harassment experienced by the women who posted their accounts online. Vera-Gray (2016) examines the impact of public intrusions by unknown men on women's everyday lives and finds that, while they are experienced by women of all ages, they are virtually ubiquitous in the lives of adolescent girls. Violence against students and sexist cultures in universities has also received considerable media and scholarly attention recently (see, e.g., Anitha and Lewis 2018; Batty et al. 2017). In addition, recent attention has also been paid to the variety of ways in which technology is used to perpetrate VAW through online abuse (see Jane 2016; Lewis et al. 2016), sexual violence (Powell and Henry 2017) and image-based abuse (McGlynn et al. 2017; see also Chapter Three in this volume).

The impacts of VAW are also more widely recognised now than in earlier eras, although this violence is still normalised and overlooked (Gurrieri et al. 2016; Nayak et al. 2003). As well as injuries, including fatal injuries and suicide, VAW causes myriad emotional and psychological harms. Pain (2014: 531) likens intimate partner violence to war and to terrorism, arguing that they are 'attempts to exert political control through fear' and Stark's (2007) concept of 'coercive control', incorporated into a new offence in English law in 2015, highlights the ways in which intimate partner violence 'traps women in personal lives'. The impacts of VAW are felt disproportionately by marginalised women, such as those who are working class or living in poverty, from ethnic minorities, and/or living in rural areas, due to the complex and intersecting nature of the structural oppressions (i.e. racism, classism, sexism, xenophobia) that characterise their lived experiences (Siddiqui 2018; Crenshaw 1991).

The knowledge about VAW outlined above has been generated over the last 50 years or so, since VAW emerged as a social problem. The next section outlines this history of activism against VAW. Following sections examine how activism and scholarship intertwined to produce a feminist activist victimology about VAW, and consider tensions between a feminist activist victimology and the contemporary mainstream approach to VAW.

The Emergence of VAW as a Social Problem and of VAW Activism

It was the 1960s and 1970s in the UK and US that saw the emergence of the modern movement against men's VAW,[5] as part of the wider women's liberation movement. However, important activism, which has often been overlooked, precedes this development. Alison Phipps (2018: 43) notes that '[r]adical feminists were not the first to politicise rape'. Drawing on research by McGuire (2011) and Davis ([1981] 2011), Phipps (2018: 43) shows that 'the US Civil Rights movements was rooted in a powerful (and now largely obscured) strand of anti-rape resistance, which prefigured many of the insights of second-wave feminism'. This reminds us that the histories told are partial accounts, which can reflect the power dynamics at the time of events, and at the time of the telling of the events.

Similarly, today, certain kinds of activism receive greater attention than others; for example, disclosures of sexual victimisation made by white women with a high public profile (such as actors and 'celebrities') gain greater coverage than do incidents of sexual violence, including lethal violence, against Black women (Williams 2016).

In the UK, the modern movement against men's violence developed through women's activism, generated and influenced by developments in theoretical explanations and knowledge. Activism often focused on either intimate partner violence (or what was then called 'wife battering', 'domestic violence' or 'family violence'), *or* sexual violence. Dobash and Dobash (1992) describe the founding of the first refuge for 'battered wives', in Chiswick, London in 1972. In a changing wider culture in which 'women's issues' were being spoken of in public, and women were forming consciousness-raising groups to understand their experiences in the context of patriarchal power, one such group persuaded their local council to provide as a meeting place a derelict, four-roomed house with outside toilet, which was due for demolition. First one, and then many more women arrived, seeking refuge from violent husbands. This building became the UK's first refuge—Chiswick Women's Aid—and the start of a national organisation as other refuges for women and children fleeing men's violence became established across the country.[6]

The first Rape Crisis Centre (RCC) in Britain, also based in London, emerged from the action of a group of women influenced by growing agitation about sexual violence in the US, who came together because of their desire to do something about rape (Bowen in *Trouble and Strife* 1987). It was from the activism of this group that the Centre was established in 1976, rapidly followed by others around the country. Centres provided telephone helplines (originally, operating a 24-hour service) and face-to-face support, practical information about the police and court systems, sexually transmitted infections, pregnancy testing, abortion, non-sexist doctors and self-defence classes (Jones and Cook 2008).

From these beginnings, services for victim/survivors of men's violence have developed significantly. What is most significant about these developments is that they were developed by women for women, as no other services existed. The state had not acknowledged the need for these services and had not taken any responsibility to provide them or address the causes that necessitated them. Women's Aid Federation of England (WAFE) and Rape Crisis have had to adapt, but have survived as campaigning and service-providing organisations, despite a lack of sufficient and sustainable funding from governments (see Hall, Chapter 10 in this volume). Organisations for Black and minority ethnic (BME) women also emerged since the recognition in the 1980s that such women were ill-served by mainstream VAW services due to their failure to recognise the intersecting oppressions of ethnicity, gender and class (Mama 1989). London-based Southall Black Sisters (SBS) were particularly influential in demonstrating the need for alternative support structures and culturally sensitive services for victim/survivors. They successfully campaigned for refuges led by and for BME women; advocated for a bi-lingual domestic violence helpline; demanded more funding for language provision to enable BME women to communicate without relying on translation by perpetrators or family members; and demonstrated how poverty, racism, language barriers, insecure immigration statuses, childcare responsibilities, fear of the police, of shaming their families, and of further violence, intersect in ways that create numerous barriers for BME women attempting to escape violent men and situations (see Gupta 2003).

Social Change, the State and Grassroots Organisations

The services outlined above, designed to support women victim/survivors of men's violence, developed frameworks for practice rooted in feminist theoretical understandings. The development of a feminist victimology made significant contributions in terms of conceptualisations of VAW, practice to support women who experienced it, and policy developments.

These contributions emerged in the midst of fraught and often hostile relationships with the state. The feminist aspects of WAFE and RCC detailed above were at odds with statutory ways of addressing social problems. Statutory agencies tend to adopt hierarchical structures, based on ideas of professionalism and the notion that expertise is held by the professionals rather than those who use their services, and have a narrower focus that precludes wider social change. Furthermore, the modern state supports the status quo rather than the radical social change sought by the VAW movement, and so 'very real hurdles [are] imposed by institutional priorities and constraints' (Dobash and Dobash 1992: 100). The state, then, was a strange bedfellow for WAFE and RCC, and, while they sought to influence the state and hold it responsible for its role in VAW, the organisations were cautious about losing their independence by relying on state funding and other charitable grants that often demand a bureaucratic structure. The history of feminists' engagement with the state is one in which feminists have been reverently tied to the liberal project while simultaneously seeking to escape it (Charles and Campling 2000). At once, feminists make claims upon the state to deliver women's rights and broader societal demands while also criticising it as enforcer of patriarchal relations, as they intersect with other forms of power and oppression, such as capitalism and colonialism. On the one hand, states can play an integral role in promoting accountability for tackling VAW, coordinating prevention efforts, developing policies and legal reforms, establishing funding commitments for services and directing strategies for social change (Weldon and Htun 2013). On the other hand, feminists have acknowledged 'how the Liberal discourse of reform accepts hierarchy and inequality within the overall society and attempts simply to allow each group to compete "equally" for the unequal distribution of resources, power and rewards' (Dobash and Dobash 1992: 23). The tensions presented by this strained relationship between feminists and the state are discussed in the following sections, which address how feminists have conceptualised and articulated VAW, how this has informed their work with victim/survivors, and the policy directions that they have pursued.

Historical and Contemporary Feminist Conceptualisations of VAW

As the modern movement developed in the 1960s and 1970s in the UK, it conceptualised men's violence as a widespread phenomenon and a cause and consequence of women's wider oppression, challenging earlier theoretical perspectives which often blamed women for their own victimisation (see Amir 1971). This framing of VAW also contrasted with earlier misguided conceptualisations of it as rare, usually committed by crazed pathological strangers (in the case of sexual violence), or as a private problem stemming from 'marital difficulties' (in the case of IPV). The seventh demand of the Women's Liberation Movement (WLM), adopted in 1978 reflects the new feminist conceptualisation:

> Freedom from intimidation by threat or use of violence or sexual coercion, regardless of marital status; and an end to all laws, assumptions and institutions which perpetuate male dominance and men's aggression towards women. (Dobash and Dobash 1992: 25)

The WLM and feminist activists and scholars located the problem of VAW firmly in the public, political domain demonstrating that 'the personal is political', an assertion made about a range of issues, from contraception and childcare to employment and housework. The conceptualisation of VAW as a form of men's oppression and power has influenced the discourse about the problem since the 1970s, although there has also been considerable resistance to it. Donaldson et al. (2018) outline the different approaches developed more recently within the countries of the UK, with Scotland and Wales adopting a gendered approach which recognises that it is mostly perpetrated by men against women and girls, and Northern Ireland and UK governments adopting a gender-neutral approach (see below).

A key element of the feminist conceptualisation of VAW identified that, rather than being at risk from strangers, women were most likely to be victimised by the men closest to them—their partners, husbands, fathers and other relatives, friends and acquaintances. This has been borne out by the empirical evidence collected since the 1970s (Walby et al. 2016). Recognition that women were most at risk from the men closest to them also demanded a radical reassessment of the gendered nature of the family, education, the workplace, the social environment, sexual relations and notions of romance. If women are most likely to be assaulted by men whom they know rather than by strangers, what does this say about normative relations between women and men?

The fundamental re-conceptualisation of VAW was further developed through Liz Kelly's concept of the 'continuum' of violence (1987). First applied specifically to sexual violence, it has been adapted to refer to all forms of VAW in order to demonstrate the connections between different experiences—intimate partner violence, sexual harassment on the street and in the workplace, sexual violence, and behaviours which normalise sexism and sexual objectification. The 'continuum' refers to the conceptual connections between acts that constitute the wallpaper of violations—the behaviours and expressions so commonplace that they often recede into the minutiae of everyday life—and the less common 'sledgehammer' events (Stanko 1985) that are more widely recognised as harm, which are both underpinned by and reinforce gendered power hierarchies. The everyday expressions and behaviours scaffold a culture of gender inequalities that sustains and enables the rarer acts (Anitha and Lewis 2018: 1).

The 'continuum' concept has been fundamental to the feminist victimology of VAW, capturing the subjective experiences of violations, rather than relying on legal categories which have reflected a masculine interpretation of men's behaviours[7] or on dominant discourses which limit what counts as rape (Walby et al. 1983). The concept also draws attention to the ways in which VAW is sustained through forms of structural and state-sanctioned violence, including institutionalised discriminations in policy, culture, media, education and law.

Since the late 1980s, dominant approaches to VAW at the international level have been set within the context of human rights. The slogan 'women's rights are human rights'—first coined at the World Conference on Human Rights in Vienna in 1993—has been used by feminist activists to demonstrate the ways in which VAW violates women's human rights and fundamental freedoms, including, among others, their 'right to equality' and their 'right not to be subjected to torture, or other cruel, inhumane or degrading treatment or punishment' (UN General Assembly, 1993). Walby notes that this framing of VAW has been 'strategically utilized by collectively organized women, in the context of developing powerful transnational political institutions' (2002: 549) and Kelly demonstrates how it has been used at local levels as a 'source of universal values for a globalised world' (Kelly 2005: 476). Deploying UN machinery and international human rights law has enabled feminists from different nations to bridge their diverse priorities and conceptual framings of VAW, and hold their governments to account for tackling all forms of VAW—though not without challenge and contestation, as discussed further below.

Anti-Feminist Conceptualisations of VAW

At the heart of a feminist victimology of VAW, both in the UK and internationally, is a recognition of the gendered nature of such violence; it is perpetrated predominantly by men against women, and it constitutes both a cause and a consequence of patriarchal oppression, and a violation of women's human rights. By contrast, competing approaches that frame this violence as 'gender-neutral' claim that the focus on women as victims of men's violence is misguided because men are also, or equally, victims of violence, and conceive of it instead as a form of 'bullying' or problematic relationships. Dragiewicz (2012) argues that this latter approach is favourable to those who benefit from patriarchy, as it ensures that the systemic causes of VAW as embedded in patriarchal relations are less visible, less understood by society at large and thus rarely addressed in ways that threaten the status quo. Gender-neutral analyses of VAW must be understood in the broader context of a 'backlash' against (perceived) feminist advances. Sylvia Walby (1993: 79) sees the anti-feminist backlash as 'a recurring feature in the history of feminism', which tends to manifest most acutely when the powerful perceive a threat to existing hierarchies of power and privilege. Considered through this historical approach, it becomes clear why an anti-feminist backlash has become more forceful as VAW has been mainstreamed and accepted as a legitimate public policy issue. Collier (2008) argues that 'gender symmetry' arguments started out as a marginally relevant form of anti-feminist backlash, but have become increasingly threatening as efforts to prevent VAW have been taken more seriously by governments and international institutions, such as the UN.

Yet some scholars have questioned the seriousness of government action around VAW prevention. Reflecting on the new 'gender-aware governmentality' deployed by the UK New Labour governments of the late twentieth and early twenty-first centuries, McRobbie (2009: 46) argues that feminism was 'taken into account' at local, national and international levels in ways that successfully appropriated feminist discourse and demands, but without implementing the transformation that early feminist calls sought. According to Genz (2006: 335), although feminism appeared to have achieved the status of 'common sense' in contemporary culture and politics during this period, it was actually deployed 'through an acknowledgement/repudiation dynamic that simultaneously includes and excludes, accepts and refutes feminism'. In other words, the neoliberal politics of New Labour had succeeded in producing a spectral version of feminism, which it began using for its own ends. Several scholars have constructed this 'disarticulation' (McRobbie 2009) of the feminist imaginary as pivotal to the development of post-feminist thought. For instance, Baker (2008) notes how some young women have rejected the reviled 'victim' status to the extent that they take responsibility for the sexual violence they experience rather than be associated with ideas of weakness and vulnerability. Stringer argues this has much to do with neoliberal discourses 'that derogate and pathologise complaints about inequality' in order to promote a 'rejection of victimhood as a worthy place from which to forge personal identity and wage political struggle' (2014: 7).

That gender-neutral and victim-blaming approaches to VAW are now increasingly adopted by people working in the VAW sector is highly problematic for feminist practice. For example, in a US study of VAW movement activists, Nichols (2013) found some VAW service providers did not identify as feminist or recognise gender inequality as both a cause and consequence of this violence, which is reflected in one participant's assertion 'that domestic violence services should not focus more on women than on men' (2013: 186). Lehrner and Allen (2009) reported similar findings in their study of the domestic violence sector in a US state. They found 'a deflated movement, lacking urgency and fervor that has become unmoored from initial visions of a changed society' (Lehrner and Allen 2009: 6). They attribute this to an increase in gender-neutral and individual-level (non-structural) analyses of VAW among service providers. Other scholars have constructed this de-politicisation of the VAW movement as a consequence of the movement's preoccupation with criminal justice solutions to domestic and sexual violence (Stark 2007; Finley 2010), which is discussed further below. Overall, this scholarship demonstrates that it is not only the material implications of neoliberal policies and forms of governance, but also their discursive power that regulate politics at the levels of culture and agency (Larner 2000).

While neoliberalism evidently poses new challenges for feminist conceptualisations of VAW, it is important to remember that language has long been used to trivialise or make VAW invisible. Euphemisms such as 'a lovers' tiff', 'flashing', 'interfered with' and 'bullying' minimise behaviours and the harms they can do, and gain a currency which contributes to the cultural denial of VAW. With the emergence of the VAW movement in the 1960s and 1970s, new ways of thinking and theorising about VAW generated a new language to describe it. 'Battered wives' and 'raped women' suggest 'a permanent status, a master identity that can never be escaped' (Dobash and Dobash 1992: 4) and so were replaced with 'women who experience violence'. Similarly, 'victim' suggests a master identity and, more recently, has become highly loaded, as discussed above. Feminists working with women who experienced men's violence adopted the term 'survivors' or, in recognition that not all women *do* survive, 'victim/survivors'. However, we argue that there is value in reclaiming the term 'victim' as it does describe the actions experienced by the woman, and her lack of responsibility for them.

In WAFE and RCC, there was also a concern that the 'victim' label made a crude distinction between the women using their services and the women providing their services. Many service providers are also survivors of this violence, and given the idea of the continuum that reveals the prevalence of these behaviours, women came to be referred to not as 'cases' or 'clients' but as 'women'. At the same time, WAFE and RCC named the problem as 'men's violence' and 'men who use violence' to forefront the gendered nature of it, and to position perpetrators as agents of their own actions rather than as haplessly caught up in physiological, instinctive responses to 'the red mist'. The paradigmatic shift in understanding and naming men's violence can also be seen in campaigns (see Sugiura and Smith, Chapter 3). For example, a recent campaign by Scottish Women's Aid—'Ten Top Tips to End Rape'—humorously turns on its head the safety advice so often given to women which makes them responsible for avoiding rape, and includes tip 10, 'Don't rape' (see https://www.rapecrisisscotland.org.uk/10-top-tips-to-end-rape/).   The earlier Zero Tolerance campaign, which first ran in Edinburgh in 1992, contained the strap-lines 'no man has the right' and 'violence against women and girls is a crime' (Jones and Cook 2008: 91). These campaigns reflect the language and conceptualisations of a feminist victimology of VAWG; it is a fundamental cause and result of men's control of women, it is criminal, and responsibility for it lies with the men who perpetrate it.

Feminist Practice: Working with Victim/ Survivors

With the VAW movement, a new feminist practice developed, informed by and informing the re-conceptualisation of men's violence. This feminist practice has several key features. As the emerging feminist victimology of VAW identified the violence as a form of power and control that is overwhelmingly perpetrated by men against women, feminist VAW services in the UK and US prioritised women-only environments. The focus on creating women-only services stemmed from their birth in women's consciousness-raising groups which equipped the organisations to respond to women's experiences, not men's, their commitment to feminist principles, and their response to women's preferences for women-only space. This commitment to women-only environments has been challenged by men hostile to the work of the organisations (see Bowen, in *Trouble and Strife* 1987, for accounts of men attacking Rape Crisis Centres in the UK), by funders seeking to fund services for men who are victims and, more recently, by those who argue for services to be extended to trans people.[8]

In the UK, both WAFE and RCC prioritised a victim-/woman-centred approach which started from the premise that women were believed, in contrast to the powerful traditional views that women made up stories about their own victimisation. Moreover, the woman's own account of her experiences was accepted, rather than seeking to fit the experiences into legal definitions of offences; this was part of attempts to challenge the primacy of legal definitions, attempts which have been further developed through scholarship and implemented in policy (e.g. Stark's (2007) concept of coercive control). A crucial aspect of the Rape Crisis approach was based on the premise that 'rape takes away a woman's control of her life, [so] everything we did in our counselling was about helping her regain control' (Bernadette Manning in *Trouble and Strife* 1987). The approach adopted was non-directive and designed to empower; information rather than advice was offered, although women's self-blame and myths about sexual violence were challenged in careful, non-confrontational ways. Recognising that most women experience some or many forms of the continuum of men's violence, and that the professions of social work, medicine, and the law have not served victim/survivors well, WAFE and RCC emphasised self-help, as part of women's 'absolute need for self-determination' (Rape Crisis Centre, 2nd report in *Trouble and Strife*: 52). The aim was not only to support a woman with her immediate material needs and ongoing emotional needs but also to help her develop a politicised understanding of her circumstances and of the violence she experienced.

To provide this kind of support to women, WAFE and RCC sought to adopt egalitarian, co-operative approaches to organising, forming as collectives rather than as hierarchies (discussed further in Dobash and Dobash 1992; Jones and Cook 2008). Recognising that VAW is an expression of men's power and that all institutions have been dominated by men, the VAW movement sought to enable different ways of being that would avoid the damaging power dynamics of most organisations. There was an emphasis on consensual decision-making and on changing roles and responsibilities so that there were not 'leaders' or 'heads of' organisations. This presented various challenges for funders and the media, who typically want to know who is 'in charge', and for workers and volunteers who may experience the limitations of this mode of organising, or what Freeman (1972) called 'the tyranny of structurelessness'.

For both organisations, their work was much more than 'service delivery'. The organisations were committed to social change in terms not only of VAW, but also wider gendered relations and inequalities. As Dobash and Dobash (1992: 29) put it, the refuge movement had three goals—'assisting victims, responding to male violence and changing women's position in society'. For Bernadette Manning, long-term member of Rape Crisis (in *Trouble and Strife* 1987: 50), the organisation had three levels—direct support work with women, 'a commitment to working collectively in a women-only environment', and public education to 'effect social change' about sexual violence. The work of Women's Aid and Rape Crisis reflected their understanding of VAW as a cause and consequence of wider male domination; VAW could not be ended without addressing this pervasive male power.

In these ways, the feminist activist victimology of VAW—represented by organisations such as Women's Aid and Rape Crisis—reflected a fundamental break with the traditional, mainstream perspective—reflected in state approaches. These different approaches have very real consequences. Amrit Wilson, one of the founders of Awaz, a women's collective that campaigned to set up amongst other things, refuges for South Asian women experiencing domestic violence in the 1970s, recalls the requirement that, once it had achieved charitable status, the organisation 'keep clear of anything that could be considered political' (Wilson 2006: 164). Awaz had developed as 'an openly political organisation' (ibid.: 56), influenced by the anti-racism and women's movements, but in frustration at the sexism and racism in each of these. The organisation collapsed after being taken over by South Asian social workers whose politics did not align with the organisation's feminist or anti-racist politics, but who were 'the "preferred" representatives of South Asian women within the emerging multiculturalist framework of the state' (ibid.: 59). An organisation with aims of radical social transformation that directly challenged the state's patriarchalism and racism was replaced with a more acceptable version of services for South Asian women. Similar outcomes were also reported by Women's Aid and Rape Crisis Centres during the 1980s and

1990s. Gaddis (2001) describes a process whereby the women who initially founded and developed these services were increasingly undervalued and pushed into submission by newly qualified healthcare professionals and social workers who were less concerned about identifying and eradicating the root causes of VAW and more interested in 'making it better' for abused women. Similarly, Dobash and Dobash (1992) note that many of these professionals were preoccupied with assessing survivors for 'treatment' rather than empowering them to understand and challenge the structures that facilitate male violence. These approaches were at odds with the liberational, empowering self-help approach adopted by feminist organisations as described above.

Feminism and Policy Approaches

Globally, VAW movements have aimed for radical social transformation to bring an end to all forms of patriarchal oppression, including VAW. To this end, as well as supporting victim/survivors, activists have also engaged in protests, campaigns, consciousness-raising and awareness-raising initiatives and lobbied their governments for adequate service delivery, effective legal protection and more attention to the root causes of violence, including women's structural societal inequality. However, many governments' ambitions, particularly in Western countries such as the UK and US, have been considerably more modest and narrowly focused on policy developments in discrete sectors, such as, housing, health care, and the criminal justice system. Undoubtedly, there have been positive developments in these countries over the last 60 years, so that a woman who experiences violence from a man in the twenty-first century can expect a very different response to a woman in the 1960s. However, as governments have become increasingly involved in conceptualising and responding to VAW and providing partial financial support to a range of VAW organisations, scholars and activists in both the UK and US have expressed concern about the co-optation of VAW activism from its 'founding goals of widespread social change toward a more constrained, less political emphasis on social service provision' (Lehrner and Allen 2009: 2).

This change is due, in part, to developments that accompanied the shift towards neoliberal capitalism. In the UK, this shift occurred during Thatcher's Conservative governments (1979–1991) and was continued, to a significant extent, by Blair's New Labour governments (1997–2007) and governments since then. These governments sought to decrease public expenditure by outsourcing state service provision to private sector and voluntary and community sector (VCS) organisations, including services for VAW victim/survivors. Fyfe (2005) argues that this strategy sought to heighten competition between and among VCS organisations and the private sector, and increase government's competitive control over community-based organisations. New Labour introduced specific targets, performance indicators and quality controls for VAW service delivery, and those VCS organisations reliant on government funding now had to comply or risk losing their service contracts to private sector organisations. Numerous scholars have documented how this neoliberal restructuring of the VCS led to the institutionalisation and professionalisation of VAW services in the UK and in particular, to a preoccupation with individual-level service delivery at the expense of direct political action and structural critique (Wiper 2018; Ishkanian 2014; Gupta 2012). Similar depoliticising trends have also been reported in the US, Australia and Canada, where the neoliberalisation of VAW services has also occurred (see INCITE! 2006; Lehrner and Allen 2009; McDonald 2005; Collier 2008).

As feminists have begun working more closely with the state, a significant area of policy focus has been the criminal justice system. From the 1980s onwards, feminist activists and scholars expended much energy trying to hold the state and the criminal justice system to account for their failure to protect and provide justice for women experiencing violence (see, e.g. Dobash and Dobash 1992). Achieving recognition that VAW constituted criminal behaviour was seen as an important break from the long history in which VAW had been ignored, minimised, and conceived as a personal trouble rather than a criminal offence. In terms of police practice, this was reflected in the non-intervention approach, which meant arrest was rarely used (Lewis 2004). Scholarly and activist attention was paid first to the police, and then to prosecutorial decision-making and court processes (Hester 2006). Progress in making changes in criminal justice responses was slow and hard fought but, to a significant extent, these efforts have been impactful and VAW has come to be conceived of primarily as a criminological matter. New Labour's broader crime reduction programme positioned the criminal justice system—not education, or public health, for example—as central to crime prevention efforts in the UK (Sudbury 2006). Through a focus on crime reduction, accompanied by a set of audit measures—targets and performance indicators—VAW came to be constructed as a matter of criminal justice policy. Phipps' (2010: 367) analysis of sexual violence policy documents shows that, since the turn of the century, sexual violence had been constructed 'as first and foremost a criminal justice issue'.

While criminal justice responses to VAW have undoubtedly produced some important benefits over the years (including improvements in multi-agency collaboration between voluntary and statutory services attempting to meet the complex needs of victim/survivors of VAW) reliance on a criminal justice solution presents several problems. Only a minority of incidents of VAW come to the attention of the criminal justice system due to significant under-reporting by victim/survivors (Beckford 2012). A range of cultural, economic and social factors, including shame, fear of victim-blaming and lack of faith in the criminal justice system, contribute to non/under-reporting. The majority of victim/survivors remain outside the criminal justice apparatus. Complainants are treated as victims who constitute a 'case' rather than survivors; conceptualisations that are far from the liberatory feminist approaches adopted by the early VAW movement, as discussed above. Criminal justice responses deal with individual offenders and victims and so individualise what has been shown to be a *social* problem, produced by intersecting social, structural forces, such as patriarchy, capitalism and colonialism. Lehrner and Allen (2009: 12) argue that this reflects an increasing difficulty for VAW activists:

> to maintain a macro-level movement analysis of the problem in the face of concrete pressures to intervene (and thus conceptualize) at the individual level. As resources are directed toward individual services for victims, a myopic analysis of the issue as "that individual's problem" becomes possible.

Reliance on a criminal justice response also tends to neglect the important matter of preventing VAW. While prevention might be considered in terms of, for example, equipping individual women with personal alarms, prevention in terms of collective social change is largely neglected in a criminal justice framing of VAW. This would require initiatives, such as public health and educational campaigns, amongst others, that pursue structural, attitudinal and cultural change in order to transform entrenched patriarchal institutions, cultures and gender roles. The failure to transform these structures arguably accounts for the failure to reduce the prevalence of VAW (Walby et al. 2016).

These shortcomings raise questions about the value of adopting a criminal justice approach to VAW; questions that scholars and activists who initially welcomed the criminalisation of VAW are asking of themselves. Weissman (2013) argues that many feminists, who pursued a law and order agenda because they saw this as the best way of ensuring VAW was established as central to policy development, have become reliant on a response that is often disempowering for its victims, fails to address the causes of their oppression and will not protect them from further violence in the future. Sudbury (2006) is more critical; feminists calling for domestic violence and rape to be criminalised have unwittingly helped the government shift resources away from social welfare programmes and towards the profitable prison-industrial complex (see also Bumiller 2008). The recent criminalisation of forced marriage under English law in 2014 was controversial among VAW activists, including BME women's organisations that have long feared the problem would be driven underground because victim/survivors are often reluctant to criminalise their families, or that criminalisation would create a racist and xenophobic backlash against minority communities. Siddiqui (2018: 366) argues that while making forced marriage a criminal offence sends out an important message, '[c]uts in specialist BME women's VAWG services' and the 'proposed abolition of the Human Rights Act' are currently undermining its purpose, as are 'wider austerity measures'. The next section discusses the contemporary austerity context in the UK and outlines some of the main implications of austerity measures for feminist anti-VAW activism.

Contemporary Feminist Practice and UK Austerity Policies

In the UK, feminists have historically relied on the political spaces opened up by the welfare state in order to transform responses to and services for survivors of domestic and sexual violence. The ongoing encroachment of neoliberal policies into these political spaces—especially since the implementation of austerity measures in 2010—has therefore had a significant impact on feminist anti-VAW organising in Britain, restricting the space for community-based organising and political participation (Ishkanian 2014). The UK Coalition government (2010–2015) executed over £21 billion in social security cuts during their time in power (Emmerson 2017) leading to significant disinvestment in policies and services for race and gender equality (Emejulu and Bassel 2015) and resources for preventing VAW (Towers and Walby 2012). Women are now at greater risk of continuing violence due to not only these cuts in services and resources (Sanders-McDonagh and Neville 2017), but also due to poverty and the degradation of their positions in social and political life. Walby and Towers (2018) show that having fewer economic resources is associated with higher rates of domestic violent crime. VAW, specifically domestic violent crime, has increased since the 2008 recession (Walby et al. 2016).

For poor, BME and immigrant women, austerity has generated a particularly 'hostile environment' (McIntyre and Topping 2018). Narratives that depict BME and immigrant communities as inherently patriarchal and violent are now frequently used to justify restrictive immigration policies and in some instances the British government's own approaches have conflated violence against BME women—particularly honour-based violence, forced marriage and female genital mutilation—with violent extremism (Imkaan 2017). Cuts to funding for specialist VAW services led by and for minority ethnic women, the removal of housing benefits for those attempting to access refuges, and cuts to Legal Aid are, among a number of other austerity policies, restricting victim/survivors' access to safety and social justice (Siddiqui 2018). In addition, feminist activists face significant challenges in this austere, racist and xenophobic environment, as they attempt to respond to increasing levels of VAW with fewer resources than were available in previous decades (Wiper 2018).

Yet despite this bleak landscape for feminist anti-VAW activists, there is evidence of significant resistance to these developments. Resistance to neoliberal economics and ideologies and to racist policies and rhetoric is also blossoming. Women's organisations such as Southall Black Sisters, the Nia Project, the Angelou Centre and Saheli have engaged in protests against austerity policies while highlighting their disproportionate impact on women, and poor, minority ethnic women in particular. Sisters Uncut, a feminist direct action group, is currently fighting against domestic, sexual and state-sanctioned violence against women, and the government austerity cuts that continue to destroy VAW services across the country (http://www.sistersuncut.org/). Wiper's (2018) study of women's VAW services in North East England reveals how activists within them are resisting the harmful effects of the government's austerity programme by building solidarity between their organisations, resisting mergers and the centralisation of VAW services, and refusing to implement gender-neutral definitions of domestic violence or provide services for men where this contravenes the organisations women-only policy. Despite diminishing funding and resources, Wiper (2018: 146) demonstrates that VAW activists continue to fight against structural and interpersonal forms of male violence, as one participant noted:

> Austerity, the cuts, women being disproportionately affected [by the cuts], survivors left destitute; that's violence in my eyes but funders [of VAW services] see violence as something much more narrow, they aren't adopting this kind of definition which is about structural violence … That's what we're all about understanding here, we'll not give up on that.

Concluding Thoughts

VAW as a social problem emerged due to the efforts of activists and scholars who developed a feminist victimology of VAW, a feminist response to victim/survivors, and feminist efforts to end VAW, all of which marked a radical shift from the previous social and political neglect of VAW. In this chapter, this shift has been considered in terms of UK and global contributions to the conceptualisation of VAW, practice in supporting women abused by men, and state policy approaches. While the efforts of the VAW movement have had significant impacts on public awareness of the issue and state responses to it, they have also met with resistance, as discussed above. Backlashes against feminist successes (Walby 1993), the simultaneous institutionalisation and marginalisation of feminism (McRobbie 2009), together with neoliberal austerity economics and ideologies create significant challenges for a feminist victimology of VAW. However, there is also evidence that the UK austerity context has generated new forms of feminist organising that are extending the scope of gender politics towards anti-capitalist and anti-austerity critique. Furthermore, the tremendous burst of attention to VAW in light of revelations about the widespread nature of sexual harassment, abuse and violence in the workplace and elsewhere, bears witness to the ongoing resistance efforts across the generations. Not least of these are efforts amongst activists, scholars and activist-scholars to develop a feminist critical analysis of contemporary forms of VAW and the structures, cultures and policies which fail to prevent it. Thus, in spite of rising levels of VAW and diminishing resources for VAW service delivery and prevention in both the UK and beyond, critical feminist victimology appears not only to have survived these difficult setbacks, but thrives amongst those committed to upholding a feminist analysis of all forms of violence against women and girls.

Notes

1. There are several terms to describe violence against women. More recently 'gender-based violence' has been used to refer to the wide range of behaviours, directed not only at women but also LGBT+ people. However, for the purposes of this chapter, which examines the history of feminist victimology and activism, we use the term violence against women.

2. Tarana Burke, an African-American civil rights activist, initiated the phrase 'Me Too' in 2007 when she developed Just Be Inc, an organisation to support victims and survivors of sexual harassment and assault. In 2017, it was later popularised on Twitter by American actor, Alyssa Milano.

3. The Femicide Census builds on the 'Counting Dead Women' campaign by Karen Ingala-Smith, which attempts to fill the gap in official data about femicides. It recommends that national data collection about homicide 'reflects the gendered nature of these crimes, by collecting comparative data on the sex and age of the perpetrator and victim, on their relationship, on any previous convictions relating to abuse or violence' (Brennan 2017: 27).

4. However, Walby et al. (2015) highlight a significant flaw in its methodology—the 'capping' of high-frequency victimisation, which under-counts intimate partner victimisation.

5. We refer to the 'movement against men's violence' and 'the VAW movement' to refer to the people and organisations involved in challenging men's violence against women. While there is no formal, centralised movement to which people can sign up, at different times and in different locations, these groupings have been more—or less—organised, have involved coalitions across national boundaries and with various state, voluntary sector and independent actors, as well as with other movements (such as the women's liberation movement), and have included victim/survivors, their advocates, activists, scholars, practitioners, politicians and policy-makers.

6. The National Women's Aid Federation (NWAF) began in 1974 but without the Chiswick refuge, which, represented by Erin Pizzey, wished 'to maintain central control, power publicity and exclusive access to funds donated by the public' while the NWAF wished 'to form a democratic, egalitarian organization (Dobash and Dobash 1992: 33).

7. For example, it was not until 1989 that Scottish law, and 1991 that English law classified marital rape as a crime; men's lethal violence to their partners has long been treated more leniently than women's lethal violence in self-defence, partly because in law women's behaviour (such as 'nagging') was accepted as provocation while men's (such as violence) was not (see Burton 2008).

8. For further consideration of this debate about women-only spaces and trans people's access, see, for example, Browne (2009), Lewis et al. (2015), and Roestone Collective (2014).

References

Amir, M. (1971). *Patterns in Forcible Rape*. Chicago: University of Chicago Press.

Anitha, S., & Lewis, R. (2018). *Gender-Based Violence in University Communities: Policies, Prevention and Educational Initiatives*. Bristol, UK: Policy Press.

Aune, K., & Barnes, R. (2018). In Churches Too: Church Responses to Domestic Abuse – A Case Study of Cumbria. Coventry: Coventry University and Leicester: University of Leicester. Retrieved from https://restored.contentfiles.net/media/resources/files/churches_web.pdf.

Bates, L. (2015). *Everyday Sexism*. London: Simon & Schuster.

Batty, D., Weale, S., & Bannock, C. (2017, March 5). Sexual Harassment at 'Epidemic' Levels in UK Universities. *The Guardian*. Retrieved July 2018, from https://www.theguardian.com/education/2017/mar/05/students-staff-uk-universities-sexual-harassment-epidemic.

Beckford, M. (2012, March 12). 80% of Women Don't Report Rape or Sexual Assault, a Survey Claims. *The Telegraph*. Retrieved August 2018, from https://www.telegraph.co.uk/news/uknews/crime/9134799/Sexual-assault-survey-80-of-women-dont-report-rape-or-sexual-assault-survey-claims.html.

Brennan, D. (2017). *The Femicide Census: 2016 Findings*. Retrieved August 2018, from https://1q7dqy2unor827bqjls0c4rn-wpengine.netdna-ssl.com/wp-content/uploads/2017/12/The-Femicide-Census-Report-published-2017.pdf.

Browne, K. (2009). Womyn's Separatist Spaces: Rethinking Spaces of Difference and Exclusion. *Transactions of the Institute of British Geographers, 34*(4), 541–556.

Bumiller, K. (2008). *In an Abusive State: How Neoliberalism Appropriated the Feminist Movement Against Sexual Violence*. Durham: Duke University Press Books.

Burton, M. (2008). *Legal Responses to Domestic Violence*. New York: Routledge-Cavendish.

Charles, N., & Campling, J. (2000). *Feminism, the State and Social Policy*. Basingstoke: Palgrave.

Collier, C. N. (2008). Neoliberalism and Violence against Women: Can Retrenchment Convergence Explain the Path of Provincial Anti-Violence Policy, 1985–2005? *Canadian Journal of Political Science, 41*(1), 19–42.

Cosslett, R. L. (2018, July 31). The 'Paris Harasser' Video Shows Why Women Fear Male Violence. *The Guardian*. Retrieved from https://www.theguardian.com/commentisfree/2018/jul/31/paris-harasser-video-men-rejected-women-fear-violence.

Crenshaw, K. (1991). Mapping the Margins: Intersectionality, Identity Politics, and Violence Against Women of Color. *Stanford Law Review, 43*(6), 1241.

Davis, A. Y. [1981] (2011). *Women, Race, & Class*. New York: Knopf Doubleday Publishing Group.

Dobash, R. E., & Dobash, R. P. (1992). *Women, Violence and Social Change*. London: Routledge.

Donaldson, A., McCarry, M., & McCullough, A. (2018). Preventing Gender-Based Violence in UK Universities. In S. Anitha & R. Lewis (Eds.), *Gender-Based Violence in University Communities*. Bristol: Policy Press.

Dragiewicz, M. (2012). Antifeminist Backlash and Critical Criminology. In W. S. DeKeseredy & M. Dragiewicz (Eds.), *Routledge Handbook of Critical Criminology* (pp. 279–288). London: Routledge.

Emejulu, A., & Bassel, L. (2015). Minority Women, Austerity and Activism. *Race & Class, 57*(2), 86–95.

Emmerson, C. (2017). Two Parliaments of Pain: The UK Public Finances 2010 to 2017. *Institute for Fiscal Studies*. Retrieved August 2018, from https://www.ifs.org.uk/publications/9180.

Finley, L. (2010). Where's the Peace in This Movement? A Domestic Violence Advocate's Reflection on the Movement. *Contemporary Justice Review, 13*(1), 57–69.

Freeman, J. (1972). The Tyranny of Structurelessness. *Berkeley Journal of Sociology, 17*(1), 151–164.

Fyfe, N. R. (2005). Making Space for "Neo-communitarianism"? The Third Sector, State and Civil Society in the UK. *Antipode, 37*(3), 536–557.

Gaddis, P. (2001). In the Beginning…: A Creation Story of Battered Women's Shelters. *Off Our Backs, 31*(9), 14–15.

Genz, S. (2006). Third Way/ve. *Feminist Theory, 7*(3), 333–353.

Gupta, R. (2003). *From Homebreakers to Jailbreakers*. London: Zed Books Ltd.

Gupta, R. (2012, January). Has Neoliberalism Knocked Feminism Sideways? *Open Democracy*. Retrieved from https://www.opendemocracy.net/5050/rahila-gupta/has-neoliberalism-knocked-feminism-sideways.

Gurrieri, L., Cherrier, H., & Brace-Govan, J. (2016, September 13). Why Is the Advertising Industry Still Promoting Violence Against Women? *The Conversation*. Retrieved from http://theconversation.com/why-is-the-advertising-industry-still-promoting-violence-against-women-64086.

Hester, M. (2006). Making It Through the Criminal Justice System: Attrition and Domestic Violence. *Social Policy and Society, 5*(1), 79–90.

Hudson, D., & Milne, T. (2018). Workplace Harassment After #MeToo. *Queen's University Industrial Relations Centre (IRC).* Retrieved from https://irc.queensu.ca/sites/default/files/articles/workplace-harassment-after-metoo.pdf.

IMKAAN. (2017) 'Tallawah: A briefing paper on black and 'minority ethnic' women and girls organising to end violence against us'. Available at: https://www.newwomens.net/publication/tallawah-briefing-paper-black-and-'minority-ethnic'-women-and-girls-organising-end [Accessed 23 March 2020]

INCITE! Women of Color Against Violence. (2006). The Revolution Will Not Be Funded: Beyond the Non-Profit Industrial Complex. Retrieved from https://collectiveliberation.org/wp-content/uploads/2013/01/Smith_Intro_Revolution_Will_Not_Be_Funded.pdf.

Ishkanian, A. (2014). Neoliberalism and violence: The Big Society and the changing politics of domestic violence in England. *Critical Social Policy 34*(3), 333–353

Jane, E. A. (2016). *Misogyny Online: A Short (and Brutish) History.* London: Sage.

Jones, H., & Cook, K. (2008). *Rape Crisis: Responding to Sexual Violence.* Lyme Regis: Russell House.

Kelly, L. (1987). The Continuum of Sexual Violence. In J. Holmes & M. Maynard (Eds.), *Women, Violence and Social Change* (pp. 46–60). London: Macmillan.

Kelly, L. (2005). Inside Outsiders: Mainstreaming Violence Against Women into Human Rights Discourse and Practice. *International Feminist Journal of Politics, 7*(4), 471–495.

Krook, M. L. (2018). Westminster Too: On Sexual Harassment in British Politics. *The Political Quarterly, 89*(1), 65–72.

Larner, W. (2000). Neo-liberalism: Policy, Ideology, Governmentality. *Studies in Political Economy, 63*(1), 5–25.

Lehrner, A., & Allen, N. E. (2009). Still a Movement After All These Years?: Current Tensions in the Domestic Violence Movement. *Violence Against Women, 15*(6), 656–677.

Lewis, R. (2004). Making Justice Work: Effective Legal Interventions for Domestic Violence. *British Journal of Criminology, 44*(2), 204–224.

Lewis, R., Sharp, E., Remnant, J., & Redpath, R. (2015). 'Safe Spaces': Experiences of Feminist Women-Only Space. *Sociological Research Online, 20*(4), 1–14.

Lewis, R., Rowe, M., & Wiper, C. (2016). Online Abuse of Feminists as an Emerging Form of Violence Against Women and Girls. *British Journal of Criminology, 57*(6), 1462–1481.

Long, J., Harper, K., & Harvey, H. (2018). The Femicide Census: 2017 Findings. Annual Report on UK Femicides 2017. Retrieved from https://1q7dqy2unor827bqjls0c4rn-wpengine.netdna-ssl.com/wp-content/uploads/2018/12/Femicide-Census-of-2017.pdf.

Mama, A. (1989). *The Hidden Struggle: Statutory and Voluntary Sector Responses to Violence Against Black Women in the Home*. Nottingham: Russell Press.

McDonald, J. (2005). Neo-liberalism and the Pathologising of Public Issues: The Displacement of Feminist Service Models in Domestic Violence Support Services. *Australian Social Work, 58*(3), 275–284.

McGlynn, C., Rackley, E., & Houghton, R. (2017). Beyond 'Revenge Porn': The Continuum of Image-Based Sexual Abuse. *Feminist Legal Studies, 25*(1), 25–46.

McGuire, D. L. (2011). *At the Dark End of the Street: Black Women, Rape, and Resistance – A New History of the Civil rights Movement from Rosa Parks to the Rise of Black Power*. London: Vintage Books.

McIntyre, N., & Topping, A. (2018, 16 August). Abuse Victims Increasingly Denied Right to Stay in UK. *The Guardian*. Retrieved August 2018, from https://www.theguardian.com/uk-news/2018/aug/16/abuse-victims-increasingly-denied-right-to-stay-in-uk?CMP=Share_iOSApp_Other.

McRobbie, A. (2009). *The Aftermath of Feminism: Gender, Culture and Social Change*. London: SAGE Publications Ltd.

Mergaert, L., Arnaut, C., Vertommen, T., & Lang, M. (2016). *Study on Gender-Based Violence in Sport*. Luxembourg: Publications Office of the European Union. Retrieved December 2018, from https://ec.europa.eu/sport/sites/sport/files/gender-based-violence-sport-study-2016_en.pdf.

Nayak, M. B., Byrne, C. A., Martin, M. K., & Abraham, A. G. (2003). Attitudes Toward Violence Against Women: A Cross-Nation Study. *Sex Roles, 48*(7), 333–342.

Nichols, A. J. (2013). Meaning-Making and Domestic Violence Victim Advocacy: An Examination of Feminist Identities, Ideologies, and Practices. *Feminist Criminology, 8*(3), 177–201.

Pain, R. (2014). Everyday Terrorism: Connecting Domestic Violence and Global Terrorism. *Progress in Human Geography, 38*(4), 531–550.

Phipps, A. (2010). Violent and Victimized Bodies: Sexual Violence Policy in England and Wales. *Critical Social Policy, 30*(3), 359–383.

Phipps, A. (2018). 'Lad Culture' and Sexual Violence Against Students. In S. Anitha & R. Lewis (Eds.), *Gender Based Violence in University Communities.* Bristol: Policy Press.

Powell, A., & Henry, N. (2017). *Sexual Violence in a Digital Age.* London: Springer.

Roestone Collective. (2014). Safe Space: Towards a Reconceptualization. *Antipode, 46*(5), 1346–1365.

Sanders-McDonagh, E., & Neville, L. (2017). Too Little, Too Late – Domestic Violence Policy in the Age of Austerity. *Discover Society.* Retrieved from https://discoversociety.org/2017/05/02/politics-and-policy-too-little-too-late-domestic-violence-policy-in-the-age-of-austerity/.

Siddiqui, H. (2018). Counting the Cost: BME Women and Gender-Based Violence in the UK. *IPPR Progressive Review, 24*(4), 362–368.

Stanko, E. (1985). *Intimate Intrusions.* London: Routledge and Kegan Paul

Stark, E. (2007). *Coercive Control: The Entrapment of Women in Personal Life.* Oxford: Oxford University Press.

Stringer, R. (2014). *Knowing Victims: Feminism, Agency and Victim Politics in Neoliberal Times.* London: Routledge.

Sudbury, J. (2006). Rethinking Anti-Violence Strategies: Lessons from the Black Women's Movement in Britain. In INCITE! (Ed.), *Color of Violence.* Durham: Duke University Press.

Towers, J., & Walby, S. (2012). Measuring the Impact of Cuts in Public Expenditure on the Provision of Services to Prevent Violence Against Women. *Report for Northern Rock Foundation and Trust for London.* Retrieved from http://eprints.lancs.ac.uk/55165/1/Measuring_the_impact_of_cuts_in_public_expenditure_on_the_provision_of_services_to_prevent_violence_against_women_and_girls_Full_report_3.pdf.

Trouble and Strife. (1987). Writing Our Own History: Romi Bowen and Bernadette Manning Interviewed on Ten Years of London Rape Crisis. *10,* 49–56.

UN General Assembly. (1993). *Declaration on the Elimination of Violence against Women.* Available at: https://www.un.org/en/genocideprevention/documents/atrocity-crimes/Doc.21_declaration%20elimination%20vaw.pdf [Accessed: 23 March 2020]

Vera-Gray, F. (2016). *Men's Intrusion, Women's Embodiment: A Critical Analysis of Street Harassment*. London: Routledge.

Walby, S. (1993). Backlash in Historical Context. In M. Kennedy, C. Lubelska, & V. Walsh (Eds.), *Making Connections: Women's Studies, Women's Movements, Women's Lives* (pp. 79–89). London: Taylor & Francis.

Walby, S. (2002). Feminism in a Global Era. *Economy and Society, 31*(4), 533–557.

Walby, S., & Towers, J. (2018). Untangling the Concept of Coercive Control: Theorizing Domestic Violent Crime. *Criminology & Criminal Justice, 18*(1), 7–28.

Walby, S., Hay, A., & Soothill, K. (1983). The Social Construction of Rape. *Theory, Culture & Society, 2*(1), 86–98.

Walby, S., Towers, J., & Francis, B. (2016). Is Violent Crime Increasing or Decreasing? A New Methodology to Measure Repeat Attacks Making Visible the Significance of Gender and Domestic Relations. *British Journal of Criminology, 56*(6), 1203–1234.

Weissman, D. M. (2013). Law, Social Movements, and the Political Economy of Domestic Violence. *Duke Journal of Gender Law and Policy*. Retrieved August 2018, from http://scholarship.law.duke.edu/djglp/vol20/iss2/1/.

Weldon, S. L., & Htun, M. (2013). Feminist Mobilisation and Progressive Policy Change: Why Governments Take Action to Combat Violence Against Women. *Gender & Development, 21*(2), 231–247.

WHO | World Health Organisation. (2013). Global and Regional Estimates of Violence Against Women: Prevalence and Health Effects of Intimate Partner Violence and Non-partner Sexual Violence. Retrieved December 2018, from http://apps.who.int/iris/bitstream/handle/10665/85239/9789241564 625_eng.pdf;jsessionid=3110608285D8A1884F1FE805CED46445?sequence=1.

Williams, S. (2016). # SayHerName: Using Digital Activism to Document Violence Against Black Women. *Feminist Media Studies, 16*(5), 922–925.

Wilson, A. (2006). *Dreams, Questions, Struggles: South Asian Women in Britain*. London: Pluto Press.

Wiper, C. (2018). *Feminist Anti-Violence Activism in Austerity Britain: A North East of England Case Study*. Unpublished Doctoral Thesis, University of Northumbria.

3

Victim Blaming, Responsibilization and Resilience in Online Sexual Abuse and Harassment

Lisa Sugiura and April Smith

Introduction

An unintended consequence of the expansion of digital technologies has been the growth of criminal activity shaping traditional offences in new and diverse ways. In particular, digital technologies have been used as tools to facilitate sexually based harms. Such harms are further exacerbated via the amplified responses to victimization that often accompany online sexual abuses, which are indicative of similar patterns of victim blaming to what has traditionally occurred offline. This chapter provides a conceptual exploration of how victims of sexual abuse and harassment online have been blamed or responsibilized, before considering the positive role of digital technologies in enabling feminist activism and advocacy to challenge and raise awareness of not only online sexual abuses, but wider societal sexually based harms. The practical implications of

L. Sugiura (✉) • A. Smith
Institute of Criminal Justice Studies, Faculty of Humanities and Social Sciences, University of Portsmouth, Portsmouth, UK
e-mail: lisa.sugiura@port.ac.uk; april.smith@port.ac.uk

© The Author(s) 2020
J. Tapley, P. Davies (eds.), *Victimology*,
https://doi.org/10.1007/978-3-030-42288-2_3

activism are then examined in regard to the extent to which it can influence changes in attitude, policy and legislation. The chapter aims to establish the links between theoretical perspectives, activism and the development of policy via an exploration of gendered online sexual abuse and harassment.

The harassment and abuse by online trolls, the advent of 'revenge pornography', and the phenomena of 'upskirting' are explored within the context of cybercrime. These are examples of harmful online behaviours that have elicited not only victim blaming (Eigenberg and Garland 2008; Grubb and Harrower 2008; Hayes et al. 2013; Moor 2010; Suarez and Gadalla 2010; Ullman 1996; Williams 1984b) and responsibilization (Garland 1997) responses towards the victims, but have also inspired victim resilience in the form of social media campaigns and social movements, resulting in the development of new legislation and the potential to influence substantive structural change.

As digital technologies become ever more pervasive and interconnected, so cybercrime expands as a criminal activity, creating both new forms of offences and victims. Online behaviour is often associated with exposure to risk, constituting new vulnerabilities, but also new ways of connecting people. This is an especially pertinent issue with increasing concern about online safety and the ever-growing threat of cybercrime dominating global media and government policy, such as the UK National Cybersecurity Strategy 2016–2021, and eliciting increased responses from Europol[1] and Interpol.[2] Cybercrime encompasses a multitude of offences, including frauds such as phishing, romance scams and social engineering; victims can be from any background, ethnicity, socioeconomic status, gender, age or geographical locale (Jaishankar 2010). However, the majority of victims of interpersonal cybercrimes, such as cyberstalking and sexual exploitation, are women and girls, who experience a greater adverse effect as opposed to men (Halder and Jaishankar 2012), due to the nature of the abuse inflicted upon them. Research has shown that responses to certain groups—those who are oppressed or marginalized—and certain types of cybercrime involving harassment and abuse are gendered. They appear to follow similar patterns of victim blaming and responsibilization techniques that pre-existed the Internet and continue to remain problematic offline, thereby maintaining and exacerbating existing structural gendered inequalities (Powell and Henry 2017). Certainly, women encounter similar constraints and commentary on their behaviour online as offline. Following the standard myths associated with rape and sexual violence, whereby certain behaviours precipitate victimization, they are expected to police their own conduct offline; such as not drinking alcohol to excess, not wearing revealing clothing and not being alone after dark in public, otherwise they risk the consequences of being blamed for any victimization incurred (Burt 1998). Online, women should refrain from engaging in provocative discussions, only utilise their 'safe spaces' and, in some cases, should not disclose their gender (e.g. when online gaming), for fear of inciting abuse. This sends a message that women are not welcome, are not entitled to engage in the cyber world; as such, it is a male domain. This exposes misogynistic views, expectations and practices similar to offline physical 'men only' spaces. Web spaces, including social media platforms like Twitter, are renowned for a myriad of sexual violence and abuse undertaken by abusers online against women who dare to engage in provocative, political and gender-related topics, or who champion different causes or demonstrate alternative opinions (Banet-Weiser and Miltner 2016; Henry and Powell 2015; Jane 2016; Mantilla 2013; Megarry 2014). Research by Amnesty International reveals the exponential scale of abuse against women, particularly journalists and politicians on Twitter, highlighting how 1.1 million offensive tweets were sent to women in the US and UK in 2017, averaging 1 every 30 seconds (Amnesty 2018).[3] Notably, such abuse is also exacerbated for women of colour (Citron 2014), with 1 in 10 tweets directing abuse towards black women, compared to 1 in 15 for white women (Amnesty 2018). Furthermore, black and minority ethnic women were 34% more likely to be cited in abusive tweets than white women (Amnesty 2018). Those whose appearance does not meet the capitalist, mediatized societal ideal of being white, heteronormative, slim and able-bodied are more vulnerable to online abuse (Gigi Durham 2004; Hardin 2003; Parker et al. 1995; Wykes and Gunter 2004). Homophobia and transphobia are also endemic online, with lesbian, gay, bisexual, transgender, intersex and queer (LGBTIQ+) communities more susceptible to abuse (Jaffe 2016), in which hostility or prejudice based on sexual orientation or transgender identity is perpetuated. The form the abuse takes is very much centred upon homophobic or transphobic hate, with offensive slurs and comments alluding to sexual orientation, sex and gender. It is not necessarily the case that marginalized people are always targeted for abuse online, but when they are subjects of abuse, the abuse invariably involves those facets of their identity being denigrated. The Internet has enabled those with prejudice and hate to practice this more freely, as the technology provides them with greater anonymity (Suler 2004). Digital technologies have assisted those who perhaps would not physically engage in such abuse in the real world to express their hateful views using more distant and anonymous channels. The same technologies have also enabled those groups, previously silenced, to be equally bold in speaking out against such abuse, disclosing levels of abuse and challenging it.

Technology can be both a reproducer of inequalities and harmful practices; however, it can also be a tool to challenge and change those discriminations and systems. Social media movements such as #Fem2 (in 2008); to #EverydaySexism and #GirlsLikeUs (in 2012); to #SafetyTipsforLadies and #MasculinitySoFragile (in 2013); to #RapeCultureIsWhen, #YesAllWomen, #BeenRapedNeverReported, #AskHerMore and #WhyIStayed (in 2014); to #BlackWomenMatter and #SayHerName (in 2015), to #WhyWomenDontReport and #NotOkay (in 2016), to #MeToo and #TimesUp (in 2017) demonstrate the power in using technology to bring victim/survivor experiences and accounts to the forefront of public attention and advocacy, with the potential to impact on meaningful cultural and social change. Such campaigns have facilitated the rise of a renewed public narrative around violence against women and girls (VAWG), aligned with widespread disclosures of women's experiences of sexual violence and abuse, and inspired a revival in feminist discourse. This enables the voices of the victims to be more accurately heard. Whereas previous coverage in the media has tended to reinforce myths and stereotypes that place blame on the victim (Ardovini-Brooker and Caringella-MacDonald 2002), social media enables an alternative narrative to be spoken underpinned by a new wave of feminism that can be understood through theoretical perspectives such as Kelly's (1987) continuum of sexual violence and Stanko's everyday violence (1985, 1990).

The UK government's current VAWG strategy (2016–2020) includes the strategic aim of *'making VAWG everyone's business'*, with specific emphasis on the accountability of *'men, boys and bystanders'* to challenge VAWG and *'further social change'* (Home Office 2016). With the emergence of #AskMoreofHim and #ManEnough (in 2018), what have previously predominantly been women-centric movements are now acquiring support from men. The Internet has also proven to be empowering in providing a critical resource for transgender persons, via increased access to information, resources and community, as such, they are themselves increasingly becoming active producers of online knowledge about transgender issues and identity via social media and blogging (Heinz 2012).

This chapter explores such online activism, and how, by empowering victims, it offers opposition to the usual responses of victim blaming and responsibilization informed and perpetuated by patriarchal norms and male privilege. In particular, it is situated within the context of gendered and sexually orientated online abuse and harassment. The chapter proceeds as follows: first, online harassment and abuse is situated within the wider context of cybercrime. The discussion then examines in more detail how victim blaming and responsibilization are directed towards victims of online offences through the use of trolling and harassment, so-called revenge pornography and upskirting. The chapter then explores how some victims are challenging such abuse by developing resilience. This is through the mobilization of support in the digital age via online activist movements including #MeToo #EverydaySexism and the anti 'upskirting' campaign, which can be understood via Kelly's (1987) continuum of sexual violence and Stanko's everyday violence (1985, 1990). This is followed by an examination of the impact such campaigns have had upon the development of new legislation and policy (primarily within the context of England and Wales, and the US), and the potential to effect wider social change.

Cybercrime: Online Harassment and Abuse

Cybercrime remains a topic of considerable attention within criminology; however, most of the focus remains on high-level organized crimes, in particular, fraud and financial crimes, rather than the everyday online behaviours between individuals that are likely to cause harm. Wall (2007) has discussed how the web has created new opportunities for criminal activity. The Internet Society (Castells 1996) has transformed criminal behaviour, enabling new conduits for criminal action. Castells (1996) claimed that the information age has altered relationships of power, production and consumption. In much the same way that criminal law categories obfuscate the lived reality of crime (Christie 1986), so discussions of cybercrime tend to do the same. The victim perspective is often overlooked, which in turn, minimises the impact upon victims. Online harassment is a particular type of cybercrime fraught with such complexities whereby the very definition, behaviours and resulting harms suggest wider influences from traditional lines of patriarchal power and male privilege impacting upon perpetrator motivation and conduct and victim reactions. Moreover, it encompasses acts that may not necessarily be deemed a criminal offence, yet are nevertheless harmful. All of these areas of neglect have consequences upon professional and public responses, and effective courses of action to tackle such harms and abuses.

Online harassment, of which there are different abuses via digital technologies, typifies this blurring of crime, deviance and harms; giving rise to competing debates and legal complexities. For example, hate speech, intertwined with hate crime, is a difficult concept to define although there are a number of UK laws that address hate speech.[4] An example is S4.A of the Public Order Act (1986), whereby expressions of hatred towards someone on account of that person's colour, race, disability, nationality, ethnic or national origin, religion, gender identity, or sexual orientation is forbidden. Furthermore, the Criminal Justice and Public Order Act 1994 states any communication that is threatening or abusive, and is intended to harass, alarm or distress someone is an offence. Certainly, scholars tend to view hate crime as a social construct without a clear meaning, yet having defining characteristics (the victims, the form the hate takes) which are central to its commission (Chakraborti 2017).

In broad terms, online harassment is a form of interpersonal cyberviolence victimization which can leave victims feeling fearful or distressed, as would victims of offline stalking and harassment (Bossler et al. 2012; Bocij 2004; Finn 2004; Wall 2001). Online harassment can involve unwanted contact, trolling, character assassinations and cyberbullying, as well as sexual harassment and threats of physical violence, rape and death. The problem lies in identifying what constitutes harassment and attempting to demarcate between speech and behaviour that is merely offensive or persistent, as opposed to that which is evidentially hostile and impacting negatively upon individuals. In August 2018, the Crown Prosecution Service in England and Wales produced guidelines on prosecuting cases involving communications sent via social media. S.43-46 of the 'Cyber-enabled VAWG offences' note that cyberstalking and online harassment are often conducted with other forms of traditional stalking or harassment. Prior to the implementation of the Stalking Protection Act in March 2019, which addresses stalking and harassment in England and Wales; stalking was not a specific offence and was governed by legislation such as the Protection from Harassment Act 1997 and the Protection of Freedoms Act 2012. The lack of a clear definition in the previous laws as to what constituted stalking meant that there was vagueness as to the offence. Although the wording of the 2019 Act does not currently make particular reference to social media or the use of digital technologies, restrictions or requirements on offender's behaviours are expected to incorporate cyber as well as traditional stalking.

Although there is an abundance of abhorrent commentary online; sexist, racist and homophobic speech is overwhelmingly present (Bartow 2010; Citron 2014). Online harassment is not restricted to gender (Foxman and Wolf 2013). Studies suggest that men encounter some forms of online abuse at comparable rates to women (Powell and Henry 2017). However, there is nevertheless evidence to show that online harassment is related to traditional power structures based upon patriarchal norms; women, sexual minorities and people of colour are more likely to be victims (Citron 2014). Furthermore, the language perpetuated during the abuse does appear to be gendered—both men and women receive abuse online; however, the abuse that women experience involves both physical and sexual violence, such as rape threats (Jane 2016). Men suffer abuse in the main related to sexual identity and/or their perceived sexuality. They experience homophobic and/or feminine slurs, which intertwine with masculine role conformity involving constructed hegemonic ideals of what it is to be a 'man' (Connell 1987).

Statistics from the non-profit organization Working to Halt Online Abuse (WHOA) show that of almost 4000 cyber harassment and cyber-stalking cases, the majority of victims were female (72%), and 48% of the known perpetrators were male (WHOA 2013). Due to the potential to remain anonymous online, the identity of many abusers may be undis-coverable; however, these may also include women. A high number of cases have involved female political activists experiencing abuse (see in particular Caroline Criado-Perez,[5] the journalist Laurie Penny,[6] the UK Labour MPs Stella Creasy[7] and Jess Phillips[8]), and female victims in other traditionally male-dominated environments, such as technology and gaming (Anita Sarkeesian, BriannaWu and Zoe Quinn).[9]

Online harassment as a punishable offence is often subject to opposi-tion by freedom of speech advocates, impacting how victims are viewed and treated. Freedom of speech and the right to freedom of expression are significantly important in protecting the articulation of ideas and opin-ions; however, these are not completely ubiquitous rights. In certain cir-cumstances restrictions can and should be placed upon speech by governments, for example, where hate speech is concerned. Free speech and concerns of an overabundance of policing the Internet are often pro-vided as a justification to mask threats and abuse as mere opinion thereby affording lacklustre responses (Herring et al. 2002). However, respond-ing to harassment with blanket-ban censorship is not necessarily the solu-tion either and risks controlling online speech overall.

As discussed previously, online harassment as a type of interpersonal cybercrime is complex and difficult to define. What is apparent is that the same marginalized persons who are more prone to abuse offline are also more vulnerable online. Hence, there is a need to move beyond the false dichotomy of on and offline, and understand that, as our lives are increas-ingly involving digital technologies, behaviours on and offline are inter-twined and occurring simultaneously. The web provides an unprecedented opportunity to share knowledge and information (Webster 2003), though freedom of speech is not devoid of responsibility. The line between expressing opinion and perpetrating abuse is regularly crossed, with the same groups oppressed prior to the pervasiveness of the web receiving the majority of it. Victims of online harassment are told not to 'feed the trolls', refrain from speaking about certain subjects or to go offline to mitigate their abuse, the same patterns of blaming and responsibilization are apparent. It is often the behaviour of persons who have experienced victimization that is subject to more scrutiny and judgement, not just from those in authority but from the wider public. This is especially the case where rape and sexual violence are concerned.

Victim Blaming and Responsibilization

Rape and Sexual Violence

Rape Crisis, in their headline statistics for England and Wales 2017–2018 (Rape Crisis 2018), claims that approximately only 15% of victims of sexual violence report it to the police. This reporting rate has been stable since 2013, when the Ministry of Justice (MoJ), Office for National Statistics (ONS) and the Home Office published *An Overview of Sexual Offending in England and Wales*, the first ever joint official statistical bulletin on sexual violence. Reasons for non-reporting of rape may include many different factors, such as privacy, fear of reprisal, internalizing blame and concerns about the criminal justice process, for example, how they will be treated (Cohn et al. 2013; Felson et al. 2002; Thompson et al. 2007), not being believed and being blamed (Ahrens 2006; Lizotte 1985; Williams 1984a). It is also worth noting that the majority of sexual offences are committed by someone known to the victim (Bachman and Saltzman 1994; Burt 1998), as opposed to the purported 'stranger', commonly portrayed in media narratives. These reasons are not exhaustive and they have a damaging compounding effect, silencing victims and creating barriers to reporting rape and other forms of sexual violence. Furthermore, Crown Prosecution Service (CPS) figures for 2016–2017 indicate that only 1 rape in every 14 reported in England and Wales ended with a conviction. Fewer than 3000 people were convicted of rape in 2016–2017, despite 41,150 people reporting the offence to the police (CPS 2018). Victim blaming towards those who have experienced sexual violence has a detrimental effect upon how the crimes committed against them are responded to. Victims are blamed or disbelieved and the persistence of stereotypes and rape myths silences victims (Jones 2012). With clear criminal justice failures not serving the best interests of victims, digital technologies provide new means to seek one's own version of retribution and justice, via online disclosures and the opportunity to share experiences and garner support.

Online Sexual Harassment

The extent of online sexual harassment (Henry and Powell 2016; Powell and Henry 2017) is a signifier of wider gender inequality and discrimination, whereby the acceptance of rape culture is perpetuated and patriarchal norms reinforced. As with offline gendered harassment, power and control are embodied online to repress and limit behaviours that challenge the hegemonic masculine status quo. In cases where feminists have dared to voice their opinions on a public platform, they have received misogynistic abuse online by trolls, attempting to silence them through the use of intimidation and threats. Marginalized social groups are already underrepresented in the public sphere; further attempts at exclusion demonstrate processes of silencing or invisibilizing. Traditionally, women's voices have been silenced to the extent that their absences are barely acknowledged (Houston and Kramarae 1991). In regard to barriers to reporting rape, masking the visibility of rape and the inability to procure successful rape prosecutions, Jordan (2012) identified six silencing agents. These are the self and the difficulty for the victim in acknowledging what has happened to them, fear of police reaction,[10] the courts and the potential for secondary victimization and finally reactions from others, and a lack of adequate support from those such as family and friends, academics and researchers and the media (Davies 2017). These factors are enduring and indicative of persistent patriarchal attitudes, continuing to silence women's voices, thus rendering their experiences invisible.

Research conducted by the digital security firm Norton (2016) indicates that the harassment of women online is at risk of becoming '*an established norm in our digital society*', with women under 30 particularly vulnerable and, as a consequence, they are being encouraged to seek out feminist-only 'safe spaces'. Such behaviour not only affects individual freedoms, but also democracy, with women who have the courage to raise their head above the parapet increasingly exposed to vile threats and abuse. In the virtual world, as in the real world, women's individual attributes, their attitudes and behaviour are judged as contributing to their victimhood, and the solutions proposed only suggest restrictions upon their movements and environment, reinforcing a wider victim blaming rhetoric traversing on and offline.

Rape Culture and Normalization

The term 'rape culture' has been embraced by academics, commentators and activists, drawing on Dianne Herman's (1984) description of the cultural association between violence and sexuality in America. It is a concept that is used to critique the incessant responsibilization of women and girls for their sexual victimization. Garland's (1997) responsibilization thesis considers how responsibility for one's own, or indeed the security of those around us, is being shifted from the criminal, via the corporation to the victim. Responsibilization is intertwined with judgement, which in turn becomes blame and impacts how victims are perceived. The British Social Attitudes Survey (BSA 2015), based on figures from the Office of National Statistics (ONS), revealed that more than one-third of the UK public—from whom rape trial juries are obtained—are of the opinion that sexual assault victims bear partial responsibility for their attack if they have been 'flirting heavily' beforehand. More than one-quarter perceives them to be partially responsible if they are drunk. There is a perpetual message that it is an individual's responsibility to avoid being raped, rather than the responsibility of the perpetrator not to rape. Such entrenched norms reinforce a victim-blaming culture that arguably has repercussions in the online world. Note, for example, the swathe of judgemental comments that accompany media reports of sexual assault on news sites and social media. The severity of sexual violence has also been minimized by the very institutions entrusted with attending to criminal behaviour. For example, in 2015 the Merseyside police Twitter account contained 'banter' about rape between themselves and members of the public, further fuelling the reluctance to report sexual assault.

Rape culture has been further utilized in understanding the normalization and acceptance of sexual violence in digital society. Powell and Sugiura (2018) describe rape culture as the collection of highly gendered norms, behaviours, attitudes, beliefs, values, customs, artefacts, symbols, codes, language and institutions that tolerate, condone or celebrate sexual aggression. In addition, though rape culture is especially related to cis-gender women's experiences of heterosex (as per Herman's original thesis; Herman 1984), it is also a useful concept for unpacking the unequal power relations ingrained within the sexual violence, abuse and harassment directed at LGBTIQ+ persons.

Powell and Henry (2017) describe the copious ways that digital technologies facilitate sexually harmful behaviours; for example, dating apps and online trading sites are used to set up rape or sexual assault, 'revenge pornography', online sexual harassment (such as repeated, unwanted sexual requests and receiving unsolicited sexual images), 'socio-cultural support rape' (in the form of rape memes, pro-rape websites), online gaming containing sexual violence against women and other rape-promoting content in online platforms and communities. There is a banal-like quality to the portrayal of sexual violence, normalizing rape culture and desensitizing such behaviours, which devalues the harms experienced by victims.

Blame and Revenge Pornography

The media generated term 'revenge pornography' has been used to describe the growing problem relating to the distribution of nude, semi-nude, sexual or sexually explicit images without consent. This has involved the use of dedicated websites where such images can be displayed to publicly shame and humiliate the victim on a global scale. These have proven extremely popular and lucrative, along with social media platforms. However, the term itself has problematic connotations for victims, with the inclusion of 'revenge' implying their fault or misconduct, synonymous with someone else wanting to exact retribution. Fuelling the notion of the rejected, 'heartbroken' ex, who is lashing out due to their hurt at the relationship ending and aside from the fact that people are entitled to break-up, not all perpetrators are driven by revenge (Powell and Henry 2017). Furthermore, not all instances involve parties that have been in a romantic relationship; on occasions the parties may not personally know each other at all (see 'celebgate').[11] Additionally, not all images are intended for pornographic purposes (Henry and Powell 2016). Hence, scholars such as Clare McGlynn and Erika Rackley (2016) argue that 'image based sexual abuse' is a more accurate term, such that it does not minimize the harms experienced by victims.

Certainly, image-based sexual abuse is shrouded in a social and cultural context, whereby blame is attributed to victims and they are denied the label of the 'ideal victim' (Christie 1986). Having shared images with a once 'trusted' intimate partner, taking the pictures in the first place, or having been gullible enough to have enabled the pictures to have been taken, the victim is seen as culpable or in part responsible. Certain beliefs, attitudes and values about gender and sexuality are prevalent, especially in relation to women's bodies and how they are governed. The same structures of power, control and privilege are enacted online, whereby male heteronormative inclination is favoured (Connell 1987; Connell and Messerschmidt 2005).

'Upskirting'

Just as image-based sexual abuse must be accepted and acknowledged as significant sexual harm, so too must other forms of technologically facilitated abuse, such as the growing trend of 'upskirting' (colloquially known online as 'creepshots'), facilitated by the ubiquity of smartphones (McGlynn and Rackley 2017). Similar to image-based sexual abuse, images may also end up on dedicated websites. Gina Martin was at a UK festival in 2017 when she realized that the photo on a phone two men were looking and laughing at was of her crotch. One of the men, unbeknownst to Martin, had surreptitiously used his phone to take a photo up her skirt. Despite reporting the incident immediately to the police, and having the evidence of the image in her possession, Martin was horrified to discover that no law had been broken, thus no recourse could be taken against her violator. Upon turning to social media to tell her story, Martin found that whilst there was support and empathy for her plight, not least from other women who had experienced the same, she also became the subject of hate. Abuse involved the old adage of attributing blame on wearing too short a skirt, as well as criticisms of publicity, attention seeking and the banality of the cause *'cops are killing people and she is worried people will see the colour of her panties…damn, go to the beach and get over it!'* Martin was also turned into a figure of public ridicule online, with memes utilizing her original Facebook post created and circulated online, comprising of additions such as *'Viva la upskirters!'* and crying-laughing emojis. This highlights how the focus of attention is placed upon the victim and the policing of their behaviour to avoid the abuse simply by not wearing a skirt, rather than on the people committing the acts. In order to have her incident reopened, Martin harnessed the power of online support via an online petition (obtaining over 50,000 signatures) and employed the hashtag #stopskirtingtheissue, whilst also being instrumental in raising awareness about 'upskirting', such that there were campaigns to amend the law in England and Wales to reflect this behaviour. Despite the interventions of the Conservative MP Christopher Chope in initially delaying the passage of the Bill,[12] specific legislation addressing 'upskirting' has now been implemented.[13] Martin challenged the condoning of unacceptable behaviour, and is just one example of the myriad of activism and resilience against sexual violence and harassment visible online.

Resilience—Activism and Advocacy

There has been an expansion of digital platforms and online communities utilized for feminist activism; presenting an intriguing juxtaposition whereby misogynistic sexual violence and feminism coexist simultaneously in shared digital media (Keller et al. 2018). Technology has a dual cause-and-effect role; it can be both a reproducer of gender inequalities and sexually violent practices, whilst also being used as a tool (Markham 1998) to challenge discriminations and harmful practices. Sexual violence is reinforced via abusive language and threats online, whilst concurrently the same web spaces are used to collate and share everyday instances of sexism and misogyny, with a view to preventing and reducing such abuse. The digital renders the global scale of oppression visible and traverses national borders, bringing together feminist collective movements, connecting local anecdotes and experiences of individual women to broader structural inequalities (Baer 2016). It is impossible to ignore the unprecedented scale of women's experiences of sexism and abuse. However, it is not just about sharing stories, but also readdressing the balance. For example, those victimized online are turning the tables on their abusers by deploying tactics, which include retweeting/sharing the offensive posts, in an effort to publicly shame and garner support from others. For instance, Stella Creasy regularly retweets her trolls:

> **stellacreasy** stellacreasy*RT @Hannah2001Hd: @stellacreasy I don't want to see your face, I might just die, so I would rather do it over twitter< lovely! * thumbs up * ▶* (sourced from Sanghani—The Telegraph*, 20 October 2014)

More people are harnessing digital technologies to assemble and denounce the normalization of rape culture, misogyny and everyday sexism. This has been acknowledged as a form of digital feminist activism, whereby the ubiquity and affordances of digital media have impacted upon contemporary feminism, especially in relation to communication and innovative forms of global activism, bridging both the on and offline (Baer 2016; Clark 2016; Horak 2014; Keller et al. 2018; Nuñez Puente 2011; Rentschler 2014; Thrift 2014; Williams 2015).

Some feminist scholars have argued that digital feminist activism deviates from traditional approaches of undertaking feminist politics in a number of ways, which signals a turning point for contemporary feminism. Thrift (2014) considers how digital feminist activism has reinvigorated interest and mobilized new engagement with feminism. In comparison, Thelandersson (2014) views the aggregation of diverse feminist communities on digital platforms as an opportunity to appreciate intersectional oppression, and encourage new dialogues on intersectionality (Crenshaw 1991). Salime (2014) discusses how digital feminist activism highlights that conventional legal responses to gendered sexual violence are viewed as ineffective; instead, such movements are seeking their own technologically facilitated remedies. It appears that a paradigm shift in relation to the digital administration of feminist action is transpiring. The spotlight on individual instances of sexism and misogyny, as emphasized by digital feminist activism, is fuelled by policy and practice concerns, relating to sexual and gender-based violence, such that Hanisch's '*the personal is political*' is actualized online (Hanisch 1969), rather than dichotomizing politics and culture. As Clark (2016) posits, the corroboration of the customary power structures, infiltrating everyday life, is fundamental to feminist activism, highlighting the importance of the political in online and offline articulations. Experiences are not necessarily exclusive and unique; the various forms of conscious raising digital technologies encourage the discovery of commonalities whilst revealing structural inequalities at the same time. Digital feminism can move beyond the political, academic and structural echo chambers to engage with different people, and their experiences, to embrace what on the surface appears unfamiliar. The acknowledgement of repetitive sexual abuse, which is often routine and part of day-to-day life, highlights discrimination in the form of human stories, providing a voice to those previously disempowered by such behaviours.

There are multiple ways of conducting activism online and utilizing digital technologies as resistance techniques; these range from the documenting of micro-aggressions to larger scale direct actions. Such forms of activism highlight the refusal to accept rape culture; the acts of resistance that are synonymous with contemporary feminism. As an example, in April 2012, Laura Bates set up the #everydaysexism project online. This was a precursor for the manifestation of the #MeToo viral campaign, exposing the endemic sexual abuse in Hollywood. However, Tarana Burke established the original Me Too movement over a decade ago to support women of colour who had been abused. The Everyday Sexism project documents both the micro- and macro-aggressions that are occurring in an unremarkable way every day. The second-wave feminists first raised such issues in the late 1960s and 1970s, demonstrating the lack of progression in tackling sexist culture. For example, in 1979 Catharine MacKinnon's influential book *Sexual Harassment of Working Women* helped to shape the understanding of how women experienced harassment.[14] Furthermore, the extent of hostility exhibited towards these women, both in the 1970s and 50 years on, is also not new, though there are key distinctions with what is occurring with current activist movements, associated with the online experience.

Online Activism

The instantaneous exponential global reach of living in an 'information age' (Webster 2003) was not possible before the implementation of the web. This has enabled various forms of digital feminist activism, which have reframed how women and girls participate in feminist politics and embrace technological opportunities, to challenge patriarchal and rape culture. Scholars have explored the use of online feminist communities (Harris 2008a, b), blogs (Keller 2015), and participation on social media platforms, as counter public spaces that directly oppose sexism (Sills et al. 2016). The field has notably been impacted by the rise of 'hashtag feminism' (Williams 2015), most prominently associated with #MeToo. Hashtags, especially on Twitter, have been used to inform and encourage action to counteract injustice for individuals (#JusticeForJada, #RememberRenisha), empower the marginalized and oppressed (#WhyWeCan'tWait, #WhyIStayed), and call out pervasive sexist practices (#rapecultureiswhen). Modern media provides the opportunity to coordinate unified movements, exposing the endemic sexual violence and harassment that continues to pervade society, in order for it to be absorbed into collective recognition. The power of online disclosures of sexual victimization, when supported by others with economic and cultural privilege (such as celebrities in the case of #MeToo or #TimesUp), can be harnessed to create tenable and extensive tangible outcomes, challenging the embedded gender discrimination dynamics still prevalent in society.

Inevitably, there have been pejorative insinuations levelled towards these digital feminist movements, much like the backlash encountered after second-wave feminism (Faludi 1991). However, unlike the diminished support for feminism, especially from young women following the powerful backlash in the 1990s, contemporary digital activism appears to be reinvigorating feminism (Powell and Sugiura 2018). Nevertheless, when women make substantial gains in their efforts to obtain gender equality and diminish discrimination, we often witness a media-driven counter-narrative, presenting the advances as hostile ideology; except, the retaliation today is conducted via both traditional forms of media, such as the press, as well as social media. The criticisms that #MeToo is totalitarian and a dangerous form of censorship links to the earlier discussion about threats to freedom of speech, with an example in the form of an open letter denouncing it, provided by the actress Catherine Deneuve (Safronova 2018). An article in the New York Times claims the cause reduces women to Victorian Housewives lacking agency and overtly fragile (Merkin 2018), whilst the director Terry Gilliam views it as creating *a world of victims'* (Anderton 2018). These stories support the #NotAllMen, aiming to counteract campaigns such as #MeToo.

The incredulity that women are unable to deal with instances of sexual harassment as they occur shows the framing of the harassment itself is misunderstood. In the first instance, situations of power and control are disregarded, especially where it might not be safe for a woman to refuse unwanted sexual advances. A victim-blaming rhetoric comes into play whereby victims are less deserving of sympathy, and have their status as an 'ideal' victim (Christie 1986) questioned. Women are considered at fault for not diffusing their victimhood. Digital feminist activist movements, such as #MeToo and #TimesUp, in cataloguing instances of abuse and providing solidarity, are challenging the blame culture so often associated with victims of sexual abuse, so that there is a destigmatizing effect. However, victims may find themselves doubly damned if they attempt to own their experiences, and are subjected to victim-blaming tropes (see Chapter 13, Erez, Jian and Laster, for more on blame and victim myths). The 'snowflake' narrative has received a great amount of traction in regard to the millennial generation (Fox 2016), whereby it is not the action that is problematic, rather it is the (over)sensitive reaction, with women in particular viewed as overreacting to forms of objectionable sexual behaviour (Jane 2016). However, there is a lack of distinction between appropriate and inappropriate sexual conduct, which in turn suggests that there is a spectrum of behaviour, and accordingly, a spectrum of subjective responses should be reasonably expected in return. Sexual harassment and sexual violence are not unrelated and exist on a continuum (Kelly 1987). The micro-sexisms—the catcalling and comments—occur so regularly that they are largely unacknowledged. They are embedded into our everyday lives, and the acceptance of smaller incidents leads to the more serious acts of sexual abuse and harassment. Kelly (1987) also took into account the importance of women being able to define their own experiences as sexual abuse, which is what we see materialising online today. Elizabeth Stanko's persuasive work on everyday violence also deconstructed women's fear from a feminist perspective (Stanko 1985, 1990). When women do feel afraid, this is justified in the context of the significant number of sexual crimes and domestic violence that they suffer that go unreported or unrecorded (Stanko 1985, 1990). More recently, Vera-Gray (2018) has written about the safety work women employ to avoid sexual violence. Her illuminating study shows how current rape prevention and safety measures negatively affect women and girls' ability to speak out about their experiences (Vera-Gray 2018). The importance of language is meaningful, with women being able to own and articulate what is happening to them, conveying the severity and the impact, and in doing so, removing guilt.

These forms of digital feminist activism demonstrate a cultural shift is underway; every instance of sexism, harassment and sexual abuse, from the small to the large needs to be investigated, with perpetrators held accountable. Digital feminist activism is doing more than simply offering evidence of the problems, it is forcing a rethink of how to tackle the broader gender power imbalances and causes underpinning them. As discussed earlier, these issues are not new or unique to the web; rather they are continuing outcomes of patriarchy and male privilege, impacting upon individual and state power, which contributes to a broader rape acceptance culture. This chapter now directs focus to the criminal justice response and the development of new legislation to tackle online harassment and sexual abuse, demonstrating the tangible impact that campaigns and social movements can have upon policy development, before considering how such expressions of resilience connect to challenging repressive societal structures.

The Impact on Legislation and Policy

Traditionally, the law has struggled to keep up with the rapid developments and pervasive use of digital technologies and the injuries and harms it facilitates. This is further evidenced by the inability of the criminal justice system in England and Wales to enact justice for the victims of online harassment and sexual abuse, which still continues to fail victims of offline harassment and sexual/physical abuse, despite new policies and reforms. However, the awareness raised by online social movements and campaigns have demonstrably begun to impact upon legislation. This includes the application of existing laws, as well as the implementation of new laws, to prosecute perpetrators.

Responses towards trolling and online harassment have seen increasing advancements. Utilizing Ministry of Justice (MoJ) figures, *The Telegraph* (2015) claimed that five people a day are convicted in England and Wales for trolling and online abuse. These numbers are a tenfold increase over the last decade, with 1209 people found guilty of offenses under S.127 of the Communications Act 2003, equivalent to 3 every day in 2017, compared to 143 in 2004. A similar increase in the number of convictions, under the Malicious Communications Act 1988, is also highlighted in the figures from the MoJ. In 2017, 694 individuals—the equivalent of 2 a day—were found guilty of offences under this Act. This is the highest number for at least a decade, and more than 10 times higher than the 64 convictions recorded in 2004.

Although this might demonstrate a worrying rise in abusive behaviour online, coinciding with the surge in social media use, this could also indicate the readiness of the criminal justice system to take instances of offensive, indecent or obscene messages online seriously, with perpetrators now less able to evade prosecution. Whilst S.127 had scarcely been used, it has come to prominence in recent years, following a string of high-profile cases of abuse on social media, such as those discussed earlier, including Caroline Criado Perez and Stella Creasy. In a further display of solidarity for victims of online harassment, the UK government, in October 2017, announced measures to increase the maximum sentence for trolls convicted under the Malicious Communications Act from

6 months to 2 years, and extend the time limit for prosecutions under S.127 to 3 years from the commission of the offence. There have also been increased calls for social media companies to take more legal liability, in regard to the online abuse that takes place on their platforms, with proposals afoot for the UK government to establish a new social media code of conduct,[15] outlining new rules for social media platforms (Bienkov 'Business Insider', 2018). Currently, organisations are not especially candid about the extent of abuse and problematic behaviours occurring on their platforms, thus, there are plans within this proposed code of conduct for social media companies to deliver annual transparency reports, which will track their progress in mitigating online harassment.

When considering the impact of online campaigns upon the criminal justice response, finding prosecutable #MeToo cases, for example, has proven difficult. Los Angeles police said in December 2017 that they were investigating 27 entertainment figures, but none have yet resulted in arrests. LA County prosecutors launched a task force in November 2017 to evaluate cases, but so far it has brought no charges (Dalton 2018). The biggest obstacles by far are statutes of limitations, which have had special prominence amid the #MeToo and #TimesUp movements. This is because so many of the incidents involve women working up the courage to come forward after years of silence. Prolonged period between the incident and reporting it is also something used against victims, who are forced to provide justifiable explanations for not having reported their experience when it occurred. California, joining other states, recently eliminated its statute of limitations for rape, making the law a closer match for the #MeToo era, but most cases reported before the changes are unaffected. Nevertheless, this signifies a landmark moment in the digital activist age. There are indications that sexual crimes are being taken more seriously by prosecutors, with Harvey Weinstein sentenced to 23 years in prison for rape and sexual assault in New York.[16]

Image-Based Sexual Abuse

In 2015, a new law relating to revenge pornography was introduced in England and Wales—S.33 of the Criminal Justice and Courts Act 2015. Under this legislation, perpetrators can be sentenced to up to 2 years in prison for the offence of disclosing private sexual photographs or films without the consent of an individual who appears in them, and with intent to cause that individual distress. Previously, a number of laws were used in attempts to prosecute these offences, such as the Communications Act 2003 S.127, Malicious Communication Act 1988 or Protection from Harassment Act 1997. However, the activities particularizing revenge pornography (or as more accurately termed 'image-based sexual abuse', which the law erroneously does not use) are not explicitly considered within such legislation, hence the need for legislative reform to ensure recourse or justice for the victims.

The implementation of the new legislation saw more than 200 cases ending in prosecution in the first year since its implementation (CPS VAWG Report 2016). Notwithstanding this, the harms experienced by the direct and indirect victims are often overlooked and the focus is on the motivations of the perpetrators. The law only applies where private sexual images are shared without consent, and the perpetrator intended to cause distress to the victim. Therefore, if the motive was for financial gain (such as selling to a revenge pornography website), sexual gratification or for humorous purposes, no offence would deem to have been committed in the eyes of the law. The same applies to the production and distribution of 'fake' sexual images, despite those who view them being convinced of their authenticity. Such images involve digital manipulation via photoshopping, where without consent, pornographic images are superimposed onto a person's head/body, so that it appears as if they are participating in the sexual activity (McGlynn et al. 2017). Technological advancements mean that the image quality is often so realistic that it is impossible to tell that edits have been undertaken. There is evidence to suggest that what McGlynn et al. (2017) term 'sexualised photoshopping' contributes to a large proportion of the non-consensually distributed image-based sexual abuse online (Gander 2016; Gladstone and Laws 2013).

The impact upon the victim is undermined and any resulting secondary harms that can arise from audience reactions are overlooked, which occur regardless of what drove the act, or whether it was truly the victim in the image. In addition, threats to disseminate images are not covered by the law. Furthermore, it is questionable whether the legislation and the sanctions available offer a sufficient deterrent, with maximum sentences of only 2 years. Legal sanctions tend not to adequately reflect the distress experienced by victims. The law is constructed as such that it is concerned with the violation of privacy, rather than addressing the act as a sexual offence, and victims are not granted automatic anonymity. Nonetheless, there are third sector support services campaigning to raise awareness of the harm caused by these abuses and offering support to the victims, such as the UK national organizations Suzy Lamplugh Trust and Paladin. Following such campaigns, the Sentencing Council has issued new guidelines[17] and doubled the sentences for stalking and harassment. Most recently, the Stalking Protection Act 2019 introduced Stalking Protection Orders (SPOs) in an effort to improve the safety of stalking victims. The SPOs provide law enforcement with greater authority to restrict and monitor perpetrators' actions, including online activity. Certainly, any breach of these orders can result in up to 5-year imprisonment.

Non-consensual Pornography and Distribution

In the US, there are 38 states that have laws for what they term 'non-consensual pornography'. Although the implication is that these images are for pornographic purposes, which is not always the case (Powell and Henry 2017), the addition of consent is a step in the right direction away from the victim-blaming narratives outlined earlier. Canada has introduced legislation titled 'Non-Consensual Distribution of Intimate Images', acknowledging that not all private images distributed online are for pornographic reasons.

In Britain, Members of Parliament and Police and Crime Commissioners called for a change in the law in response to a campaign started by Gina

Martin, discussed previously, highlighting that the existing legislation in England and Wales did not apply to most forms of 'upskirting'. Introduced in 2003, the law on voyeurism is designed to capture those 'peeping toms' who spy on people in private for sexual gratification, and therein lies the problem. The majority of 'upskirting' cases, such as that of Martin's, occur in public spaces like festivals and on public transport, rather than in private areas, such as changing rooms or toilets. The old common law 'outraging public decency' could apply to 'upskirting'; however, victims and law enforcement are typically unaware of or unable to apply such an archaic piece of legislature. In addition, the issue of demarcating sufficiently between the public and private is unclear and no more established than within the law on voyeurism. According to the Human Rights Act Article 8, we have the right to private life; however, it seems as if this right is not automatically extended to our bodies and undergarments, whilst in a public place. Feminists such as Catharine MacKinnon (1989) have long argued the supposed distinction between the public and private, claiming that women have no privacy and are essentially public property. Australia already had legislation to address this activity—the Summary Offenses Amendment ('upskirting') Bill 2007—which criminalises all non-consensual creation and/or distribution of intimate sexual images, including threats to do so, as well as modified images.

Previous opportunities to reform the law and address 'upskirting' were missed, for example, when the law relating to revenge pornography was implemented in 2015. 'Upskirting' could also have been included, but was not due to the then public outcry and the resulting focus being solely on that problem. This highlights how political will to change can sometimes be impacted by public demand and attention to the particular issue. The attention that this issue received from the campaigns, discussions and media attention—both press and social media—demonstrate the support to recognize this behaviour as a serious sexual offence, and the failure of the existing law to capture all instances of 'upskirting'. The Voyeurism Offences Act, more commonly known as the 'Upskirting' Bill, was introduced on 21 June 2018, and despite initial delays, came into force on 12 April 2019. Distinct from the sentencing for 'revenge pornography', offenders will automatically receive a 2-year imprisonment. Where it is proven to have been committed for sexual gratification purposes, the most serious offenders may be placed on the sex offenders register. Unlike victims of 'revenge pornography', victims of 'upskirting' are also entitled to automatic protection from being identified in the media. This of course does not negate the possibility of other individuals releasing identifying information online, as the preservation of anonymity is often compromised in the digital age.

Law reforms are crucial in regard to cybercrime involving harassment and sexual abuse. This is so that the criminal justice system is able to take necessary action against perpetrators and protect victims, commensurate with the seriousness of such offences. The outcomes of campaigns such as #MeToo and #stopskirtingtheissue, harnessing the voices and unifying experiences of victims, from Hollywood celebrities to public individuals, signifies the potential generation of a cultural shift. These developments highlight the power that can be mobilized through feminist inspired online activism. The examples explored in this chapter show how the assembly of shared collective responsibility can address the problem of online harassment and abuse.

Conclusion

As innovative digital communications, technologies and developments create new forms and experiences of victimization and a proliferation of victims, there is a greater need to explore victims and activism in the context of cybercrime. This chapter has examined how conceptualisations of victimization that facilitate victim blaming are evident in the criminal justice system. It has also explored how victimization is resisted and the capacity for resilience using digital technologies. The technology is an enabler of abuses that have traditionally occurred offline and perpetuates structural inequalities, though it is also being utilized as a promising solution. Prevention is the key to reducing the escalating harms caused by cyber abuse and this demands a strategy that moves beyond victim blaming. This emphasis on prevention and individual responsibility relates to both victims and offenders, yet this raises dilemmas, especially in relation to victim safety and safeguarding. Legislation, policies and strategies need to hold accountable not only the offenders, but also to encourage and enforce Internet giants such as Facebook, Twitter and Google to take responsibility for the way their platforms are being used and monitored. What longevity, practical outcomes and justice for the victims such campaigns as #MeToo will have are unknown; however, there is already emerging evidence as examined in this chapter. From this and other forms of activism and resilience, we might be optimistic. What appears to be materializing is something powerful in itself—a societal cultural shift, whereby the voices of victims are heard and advocated. However, within this rapidly developing field there are gaps in knowledge, such as the prevalence of online abuse towards non-binary, intersex and transgender persons, and in turn, the voices and experiences of such groups and their resistance to it, which require additional exploration. What occurs online has effective repercussions offline, and though in the digital domain silence is less common, voices are being reclaimed and the invisibilized brought back into public consciousness.

Notes

1. European Cybercrime Center https://www.europol.europa.eu/about-europol/european-cybercrime-centre-ec3.
2. https://www.interpol.int/Crime-areas/Cybercrime/Cybercrime.
3. See examples of Diane Abbott and Mary Beard. Dianne Abbott is a UK Labour MP who has suffered from a multitude of harassment online, including racism sexism and insulting comments about her weight and looks. Of any UK MP, irrespective of gender, she has received the most abuse: https://www.theguardian.com/politics/2017/sep/05/diane-abbott-more-abused-than-any-other-mps-during-election. Mary Beard is a Professor of Classics at Cambridge University. After appearing on UK television in a debate about immigration, she received misogynistic online abuse with comments disparaging her appearance and crude sexual images created involving her picture: https://www.theguardian.com/media/2013/jan/21/mary-beard-suffers-twitter-abuse.
4. The UK also has hate crime laws. For England, Wales and Scotland, the Crime and Disorder Act 1998 makes hateful behaviour towards a victim based on the victim's membership (or presumed membership) in a racial group an 'aggravating factor' for the purpose of sentencing in respect of specified crimes. A 'racial group' is a group of persons defined by refer-

ence to race, colour, nationality (including citizenship) or ethnic or national origins. The specified crimes are assault, criminal damage, offenses under the Public Order Act 1986, and offenses under the Protection from Harassment Act 1997. http://www.opsi.gov.uk/si/si2003/uksi_20032267_en.pd.

5. Caroline Criado-Perez is a British feminist activist who received an onslaught of abuse on Twitter, including rape threats, after she campaigned to have a woman on UK banknotes. A man and a woman were jailed for making extreme threats towards her: https://www.theguardian.com/uk-news/2014/jan/24/two-jailed-twitter-abuse-feminist-campaigner.

6. Laurie Penny is a UK feminist author and journalist who has received misogynistic and anti-Semitic abuse online https://www.independent.co.uk/news/people/unspeakable-things-feminist-author-laurie-penny-subjected-to-vile-sexist-and-anti-semitic-abuse-over-9617744.html.

7. Stella Creasy is a UK Labour MP who was subjected to death and rape threats online after supporting Caroline Criado-Perez https://www.telegraph.co.uk/news/uknews/crime/10227486/Man-arrested-over-Twitter-abuse-of-Stella-Creasy-MP.html.

8. Jess Phillips is a UK Labour MP who after receiving online abuse has publicly shared examples to highlight the issue. She is campaigning for an end to anonymity on social media, in that users should have to declare their true identities to social media companies in order to use the platforms: https://www.theguardian.com/society/2018/jun/11/labour-mp-jess-phillips-calls-for-end-to-online-anonymity-after-600-threats.

9. See 'GamerGate', a harassment campaign conducted against several women in the video gaming industry, involving the hashtag #GamerGate, which was ostensibly concerned with ethics in game journalism and identity, yet involved rape and death threats https://www.ibtimes.com/what-gamergate-scandal-female-game-developer-flees-home-amid-online-threats-1704046.

10. Hester (2013) reports that the police now have a belief in the victim approach, with the emphasis on the victim's credibility as a witness.

11. On 31 August 2014, private pictures of celebrities, mostly women, and many containing nudity, were leaked on 4chan after being hacked from the iCloud https://www.bbc.co.uk/news/technology-45354309.

12. https://www.theguardian.com/world/2018/jun/15/tory-mp-christopher-chope-blocks-progress-of-upskirting-bill.

13. https://www.gov.uk/government/news/upskirting-know-your-rights.

14. The harassment of women at work in the 1970s seemed to come as a surprise to some when the extent of Jimmy Saville's abuse (see: https://www.theguardian.com/media/2014/jun/26/jimmy-savile-sexual-abuse-timeline) started to become clear along with an examination of the culture that facilitated it.
15. https://www.gov.uk/government/news/making-britain-the-safest-place-in-the-world-to-be-online.
16. https://www.bbc.co.uk/news/world-us-canada-51840532.
17. https://www.sentencingcouncil.org.uk/news/item/sentencing-council-publishes-new-guidelines-on-intimidatory-offenses-and-domestic-abuse/.

References

Ahrens, C. E. (2006). Being Silenced: The Impact of Negative Social Reactions on the Disclosure of Rape. *American Journal of Community Psychology, 38*(3/4), 263–274.

Amnesty International UK. (2018, December 18). *Women Abused on Twitter Every 30 Seconds – New Study*. Retrieved January 1, 2019, from https://www.amnesty.org.uk/press-releases/women-abused-twitter-every-30-seconds-new-study.

Anderton, J. (2018, March 17). Monty Python's Terry Gilliam Likens MeToo Movement to "Mob Rule." *Digital Spy*. Retrieved March 20, 2018, from http://www.digitalspy.com/showbiz/news/a852536/monty-python-terry-gilliam-likens-metoo-movement-to-mob-rule/.

Ardovini-Brooker, J., & Caringella-MacDonald, S. (2002). Media Attributions of Blame and Sympathy in Ten Rape Cases. *The Justice Professional, 15*(1), 3–18.

Bachman, R., & Saltzman, L. E. (1994). *Violence Against Women* (Vol. 81). Washington, DC: US Department of Justice, Office of Justice Programs, Bureau of Justice Statistics.

Baer, H. (2016). Redoing Feminism: Digital Activism, Body Politics, and Neoliberalism. *Feminist Media Studies, 16*(1), 17–34.

Banet-Weiser, S., & Miltner, K. M. (2016). # MasculinitySoFragile: Culture, Structure, and Networked Misogyny. *Feminist Media Studies, 16*(1), 171–174.

Bartow, A. (2010). Portrait of the Internet as a Young Man. *Michigan Law Review, 108*(6), 1079–1106.

Bienkov, A. (2018, February 6). Theresa May Calls for New Laws to Ban the Abuse of Politicians on Social Media. *Business Insider.* Retrieved August 13, 2018, from http://uk.businessinsider.com/theresa-may-abuse-politicians-social-media-twitter-facebook-bullying-laws-2018-2.

Bocij, P. (2004). *Cyberstalking: Harassment in the Internet age and how to protect your family.* Westport, CT: Praeger.

Bossler, A. M., Holt, T. J., & May, D. C. (2012). Predicting Online Harassment Victimization Among a Juvenile Population. *Youth & Society, 44*(4), 500–523.

British Social Attitudes Survey. (2015). National Centre for Social Research. Retrieved January 3, 2019, from http://www.bsa-data.natcen.ac.uk.

Burt, M. R. (1998). Rape myths. In M. E. Odem & J. Clay Warner (Eds.), *Confronting Rape and Sexual Assault* (pp. 129–144). Lanham, MD: Rowman & Littlefield.

Castells, M. (1996). *The Information Age: Economy, Society, and Culture. Volume I: The Rise of the Network Society.* Cambridge, MA: Blackwell.

Chakraborti, N. (2017). *Hate Crime: Concepts, Policy, Future Directions.* Cullompton: Willan.

Christie, N. (1986). The Ideal Victim. In E. A. Fattah (Ed.), *From Crime Policy to Victim Policy* (pp. 17–30). London: Palgrave Macmillan.

Citron, D. K. (2014). *Hate Crimes in Cyberspace.* Cambridge, MA: Harvard University Press.

Clark, R. (2016). "Hope in a Hashtag": The Discursive Activism of# WhyIStayed. *Feminist Media Studies, 16*(5), 788–804.

Cohn, A. M., Zinzow, H. M., Resnick, H. S., & Kilpatrick, D. G. (2013). Correlates of Reasons for Not Reporting Rape to Police: Results from a National Telephone Household Probability Sample of Women with Forcible or Drug-or-Alcohol Facilitated/Incapacitated Rape. *Journal of Interpersonal Violence, 28*(3), 455–473.

Connell, R. W. (1987). *Gender and Power.* Cambridge: Polity.

Connell, R. W., & Messerschmidt, J. W. (2005). Hegemonic Masculinity: Rethinking the Concept. *Gender & Society, 19*(6), 829–859.

Crenshaw, K. (1991). Mapping the Margins: Intersectionality, Identity Politics, and Violence Against Women of Color. *Stanford Law Review, 43*(6), 1241–1299.

Crown Prosecution Service (CPS). (2016). *Violence Against Women and Girls Crime Report 2015–2016.* Retrieved January 3, 2019, from https://www.cps.gov.uk/sites/default/files/documents/publications/cps_vawg_report_2016.pdf.

Crown Prosecution Service (CPS). (2018) *Social Media – Guidelines on Prosecuting Cases Involving Communications Sent Via Social Media*. Retrieved January 3, 2019, from https://www.cps.gov.uk/legal-guidance/social-media-guidelines-prosecuting-cases-involving-communications-sent-social-media.

Dalton, A. (2018, October 7). One Year on from #MeToo, Sexual Misconduct Prosecutions Are Still Rare in Hollywood. *The Independent*. Retrieved February 4, 2019, from https://www.independent.co.uk/news/world/americas/me-too-hollywood-sexual-misconduct-prosecutions-weinstein-cosby-spacey-a8572066.html.

Davies, P. (2017). Feminist Voices, Gender and Victimization. In S. Walklate (Ed.), *Handbook of Victims and Victimology* (2nd ed., pp. 107–123). Oxon: Routledge.

Eigenberg, H., & Garland, R. (2008). Victim Blaming. In L. J. Moriarty (Ed.), *Controversies in Victimology* (pp. 21–36). Newark, NJ: Elsevier Press.

Faludi, S. (1991). *Backlash: The Undeclared War Against American Women*. New York: Crown.

Felson, R. B., Messner, S. F., Hoskin, A. W., & Deane, G. (2002). Reasons for Reporting and Not Reporting Domestic Violence to the Police. *Criminology, 40*(3), 617–648.

Finn, J. (2004). A Survey of Online Harassment at a University Campus. *Journal of Interpersonal Violence, 19*(4), 468–483.

Fox, C. (2016, June 4). Generation Snowflake: How We Train Our Kids to Be Censorious Cry-Babies. *The Spectator*. Retrieved March 20, 2018, from https://www.spectator.co.uk/2016/06/generation-snowflake-how-we-train-our-kids-to-be-censorious-cry-babies/.

Foxman, A. H., & Wolf, C. (2013). *Viral Hate: Containing Its Spread on the Internet*. New York: Palgrave Macmillan.

Gander, K. (2016, October 13). The People Who Photo Shop Friends and Family onto Porn. *The Independent*. Retrieved January 3, 2019, from http://www.independent.co.uk/life-style/love-sex/porn-photoshopping-4chan-family-friends-superimposed-into-sex-scenes-world-a7358706.html.

Garland, D. (1997). Governmentality and the Problem of Crime: Foucault, Criminology, Sociology. *Theoretical Criminology, 1*(2), 173–214.

Gigi Durham, M. (2004). Constructing the "New Ethnicities": Media, Sexuality, and Diaspora Identity in the Lives of South Asian Immigrant Girls. *Critical Studies in Media Communication, 21*(2), 140–161.

Gladstone, B., & Laws, C. (2013, December 6). Why One Mom's Investigation Might Actually Stop Revenge Porn. *WNYC*. Retrieved January 3, 2019, from http://www.wnyc.org/story/why-one-moms-investigation-might-actually-stop-revenge-porn/#transcript (transcript).

Grubb, A., & Harrower, J. (2008). Attribution of Blame in Cases of Rape: An Analysis of Participant Gender, Type of Rape, and Perceived Similarity to the Victim. *Aggression and Violent Behavior, 13*(5), 396–405.

Halder, D., & Jaishankar, K. (2012). *Cyber Crime and the Victimization of Women: Laws, Rights and Regulations*. Hershey, PA: Information Science Reference.

Hanisch, C. (1969). The personal is political. Radical feminism: A documentary reader, in *Radical Feminism: A Documentary Reader*, 113–116. New York: New York University Press.

Hardin, M. (2003). Marketing the Acceptably Athletic Image: Wheelchair Athletes, Sport-Related Advertising and Capitalist Hegemony. *Disability Studies Quarterly, 23*(1), 108–125.

Harris, A. (2008a). *Next Wave Cultures: Feminism, Subcultures, Activism*. New York: Routledge.

Harris, A. (2008b). Young Women, Late Modern Politics, and the Participatory Possibilities of Online Cultures. *Journal of Youth Studies, 11*(5), 481–495.

Hayes, R. M., Lorenz, K., & Bell, K. A. (2013). Victim Blaming Others: Rape Myth Acceptance and the Just World Belief. *Feminist Criminology, 8*(3), 202–220.

Heinz, M. (2012). Transmen on the Web: Inscribing Multiple Discourses. In K. Ross (Ed.), *The Handbook of Gender, Sex, and Media* (pp. 326–343). Chichester, UK: John Wiley & Sons.

Henry, N., & Powell, A. (2015). Beyond the 'Sext': Technology-Facilitated Sexual Violence and Harassment Against Adult Women. *Australian & New Zealand Journal of Criminology, 48*(1), 104–118.

Henry, N., & Powell, A. (2016). Sexual Violence in the Digital Age: The Scope and Limits of Criminal Law. *Social & Legal Studies, 25*(4), 397–418.

Herman, D. (1984). The rape culture. In J. Freeman (Ed.), *Women: A Feminist Perspective* (pp. 45–53). Mountain View, CA: Mayfield.

Herring, S., Job-Sluder, K., Scheckler, R., & Barab, S. (2002). Searching for Safety Online: Managing "Trolling" in a Feminist Forum. *The Information Society, 18*(5), 371–384.

Hester, M. (2013). Who does what to whom? Gender and domestic violence perpetrators in English police records. *European Journal of Criminology, 10*(5), 623–637.

Home Office. (2016). *Ending Violence Against Women and Girls Strategy 2016–2020.* London: HM Government.

Horak, L. (2014). Trans on YouTube: Intimacy, Visibility, Temporality. *Transgender Studies Quarterly, 1*(4), 572–585.

Houston, M., & Kramarae, C. (1991). Speaking from Silence: Methods of Silencing and of Resistance. *Discourse & Society, 2*(4), 387–399.

Jaffe, M. (2016). Social Justice and LGBTQ Communities in the Digital Age. In J. Frechette & R. Williams (Eds.), *Media Education for a Digital Generation* (pp. 103–118). New York: Routledge.

Jaishankar, K. (2010). The Future of Cyber Criminology: Challenges and Opportunities. *International Journal of Cyber Criminology, 4*(1/2), 26–31.

Jane, E. A. (2016). *Misogyny Online: A Short (and Brutish) History.* London: Sage.

Jones, I. (2012). A Problem of the Past? The Politics of "Relevance" in Evidential Reform. *Contemporary Issues in Law, 11*(4), 277.

Jordan, J. (2012). Silencing Rape, Silencing Women. In J. M. Brown & S. L. Walker (Eds.), *Handbook on Sexual Violence* (pp. 253–286). Abingdon: Routledge.

Keller, J. (2015). *Girls' Feminist Blogging in a Postfeminist Age.* London: Routledge.

Keller, J., Mendes, K., & Ringrose, J. (2018). Speaking 'unspeakable things': Documenting digital feminist responses to rape culture. *Journal of gender studies, 27*(1), 22–36.

Kelly, L. (1987). The Continuum of Sexual Violence. In J. Hanmer & M. Maynard (Eds.), *Women, Violence and Social Control* (pp. 46–60). London: Macmillan.

Lizotte, A. J. (1985). The Uniqueness of Rape: Reporting Assaultive Violence to the Police. *Crime & Delinquency, 31*(2), 169–190.

MacKinnon, C. A. (1989). *Toward a Feminist Theory of the State.* Cambridge, MA; London: Harvard University Press.

Mantilla, K. (2013). Gendertrolling: Misogyny Adapts to New Media. *Feminist Studies, 39*(2), 563–570.

Markham, A. N. (1998). *Life Online: Researching Real Experience in Virtual Space* (Vol. 6). Lanham: Rowman Altamira.

McGlynn, C., & Rackley, E. (2016). Not 'Revenge Porn,' But Abuse: Let's Call It Image-Based Sexual Abuse. *Inherently Human: Critical Perspectives on Law, Gender & Sexuality, 41.*

McGlynn, C., & Rackley, E. (2017, August 15). Why 'Upskirting' Needs to Be Made a Sex Crime. *The Conversation*. Retrieved January 20, 2019, from https://theconversation.com/why-upskirting-needs-to-be-made-a-sex-crime-82357.

McGlynn, C., Rackley, E., & Houghton, R. (2017). Beyond 'Revenge Porn': The Continuum of Image-Based Sexual Abuse. *Feminist Legal Studies, 25*(1), 25–46.

Megarry, J. (2014). Online Incivility or Sexual Harassment? Conceptualising Women's Experiences in the Digital Age. *Women's Studies International Forum, 47*(Part A), 46–55.

Merkin, D. (2018, January 5). Publicly, We Say #MeToo. Privately, We Have Misgivings. *New York Times*. Retrieved March 13, 2018, from https://www.nytimes.com/2018/01/05/opinion/golden-globes-metoo.html.

Moor, A. (2010). She Dresses to Attract, He Perceives Seduction: A Gender Gap in Attribution of Intent to Women's Revealing Style of Dress and Its Relation to Blaming the Victims of Sexual Violence. *Journal of International Women's Studies, 11*(4), 115–127.

Norton. (2016, October 10). Online Harassment: Halting a Disturbing 'New Normal'. *Norton*. Retrieved June 12, 2018, from https://community.norton.com/en/blogs/norton-protection-blog/online-harassment-halting-disturbing-new-normal.

Nuñez Puente, S. (2011). Feminist Cyberactivism: Violence Against Women, Internet Politics, and Spanish Feminist Praxis Online. *Continuum: Journal of Media & Cultural Studies, 25*(3), 333–346.

Parker, S., Nichter, M., Nichter, M., Vuckovic, N., Sims, C., & Ritenbaugh, C. (1995). Body Image and Weight Concerns Among African American and White Adolescent Females: Differences That Make a Difference. *Human Organization, 54*(2), 103–114.

Powell, A., & Henry, N. (2017). *Sexual Violence in a Digital Age*. Basingstoke: Palgrave Macmillan.

Powell, A., & Sugiura, L. (2018). Resisting Rape Culture in Digital Society. In W. S. DeKeseredy, C. M. Rennison, & A. K. Hall-Sanchez (Eds.), *The Routledge International Handbook of Violence Studies* (pp. 469–479). Milton: Routledge.

Rape Crisis. (2018). *Rape Crisis England and Wales Headline Statistics 2017–18*. Retrieved January 19, 2019, from https://rapecrisis.org.uk/get-informed/about-sexual-violence/statistics-sexual-violence/.

Rentschler, C. A. (2014). Rape Culture and the Feminist Politics of Social Media. *Girlhood Studies, 7*(1), 65–82.

Safronova, V. (2018, January 9). Catherine Deneuve and Others Denounce the #MeToo Movement. *New York Times*. Retrieved March 20, 2018, from https://www.nytimes.com/2018/01/09/movies/catherine-deneuve-and-others-denounce-the-metoo-movement.html.

Salime, Z. (2014). New Feminism as Personal Revolutions: Microrebellious Bodies. *Signs: Journal of Women in Culture and Society, 40*(1), 14–20.

Sanghani, R. (2014, October 20). Online Abuse: How to Live a Happy Troll-Free Life on the Internet. *The Telegraph*. Retrieved June 6, 2018, from https://www.telegraph.co.uk/women/womens-life/11174222/Troll-jail-sentences-how-to-live-a-happy-troll-free-life-on-the-internet.html.

Sills, S., Pickens, C., Beach, K., Jones, L., Calder-Dawe, O., Benton-Greig, P., & Gavey, N. (2016). Rape Culture and Social Media: Young Critics and a Feminist Counterpublic. *Feminist Media Studies, 16*(6), 935–951.

Stanko, E. (1985). *Intimate Intrusions: Woman's Experience of Male Violence*. London: Routledge & Kegan Paul.

Stanko, E. A. (1990). *Everyday Violence: How Women and Men Experience Sexual and Physical Danger*. London: Pandora.

Suarez, E., & Gadalla, T. M. (2010). Stop Blaming the Victim: A Meta-analysis on Rape Myths. *Journal of Interpersonal Violence, 25*(11), 2010–2035.

Suler, J. (2004). The Online Disinhibition Effect. *Cyberpsychology & Behavior, 7*(3), 321–326.

The Telegraph. (2015, May 24). Five Internet Trolls a Day Convicted in UK as Figures Show Ten-Fold Increase. *The Telegraph*. Retrieved June 6, 2018, from https://www.telegraph.co.uk/news/uknews/law-and-order/11627180/Five-internet-trolls-a-day-convicted-in-UK-as-figures-show-ten-fold-increase.html.

Thelandersson, F. (2014). A Less Toxic Feminism: Can the Internet Solve the Age Old Question of How to Put Intersectional Theory into Practice? *Feminist Media Studies, 14*(3), 527–530.

Thompson, M., Sitterle, D., Clay, G., & Kingree, J. (2007). Reasons for Not Reporting Victimizations to the Police: Do They Vary for Physical and Sexual Incidents? *Journal of American College Health, 55*(5), 277–282.

Thrift, S. C. (2014). # YesAllWomen as Feminist Meme Event. *Feminist Media Studies, 14*(6), 1090–1092.

Ullman, S. E. (1996). Social Reactions, Coping Strategies, and Self-blame: Attributions in Adjustment to Sexual Assault. *Psychology of Women Quarterly, 20*(4), 505–526.

Vera-Gray, F. (2018). *The Right Amount of Panic: How Women Trade Freedom for Safety.* Bristol: Policy Press.

Wall, D. S. (2001). Cybercrimes and the Internet. In D. S. Wall (Ed.), *Crime and the Internet* (pp. 1–17). New York: Routledge.

Wall, D. (2007). *Cybercrime: The Transformation of Crime in the Information Age* (Vol. 4). Cambridge: Polity.

Webster, F. (2003). Information Warfare in an Age of Globalization. *War and the Media: Reporting Conflict, 24*(7), 57–69.

Williams, L. S. (1984a). The Classic Rape: When Do Victims Report? *Social Problems, 31*(4), 459–467.

Williams, J. E. (1984b). Secondary Victimization: Confronting Public Attitudes About Rape. *Victimology, 9*(1), 66–81.

Williams, S. (2015). Digital Defense: Black Feminists Resist Violence with Hashtag Activism. *Feminist Media Studies, 15*(2), 341–344.

Working to Halt Online Abuse (WHOA). (2013). *Comparison Statistics 2000–2012.* Retrieved from http://www.haltabuse.org/resources/stats/Cumulative2000-2012.pdf.

Wykes, M., & Gunter, B. (2004). *The Media and Body Image: If Looks Could Kill.* London: Sage.

4

Gender-Based Violence: Victims, Activism and Namibia's Dual Justice Systems

Kate Mukungu and Ndumba J. Kamwanyah

Introduction

The Constitution of Namibia promotes a wide range of fundamental human rights for all Namibians. This is in complete contrast to the colonial regime of South Africa, from which Namibia obtained independence in 1990. The advancement of women's rights and the increase in Namibian women's participation in the public sphere are among the many positive benefits of Namibian independence. Successive post-independence governments under the Swapo Party have shown support for these goals by developing a raft of relevant policies and declarations through the United

K. Mukungu (✉)
Institute of Business, Industry and Leadership, University of Cumbria, Carlisle, UK
e-mail: kate.mukungu@cumbria.ac.uk

N. J. Kamwanyah
Centre for Professional Development, Teaching and Learning Improvement, University of Namibia, Windhoek, Namibia
e-mail: nkamwanyah@unam.na

© The Author(s) 2020
J. Tapley, P. Davies (eds.), *Victimology*,
https://doi.org/10.1007/978-3-030-42288-2_4

Nations (UN), the African Union (AU) and the Southern African Development Community (SADC). However, gains achieved are overshadowed by high levels of Gender-Based Violence (GBV) in relationships and non-partner sexual violence (WHO 2013). This chapter contextualises GBV in Namibia and considers the experiences of GBV victims who, through activism and amidst the dual justice system, seek to access justice.

Namibia inherited two separate justice systems at independence: the formal statutory system based on Roman Dutch law and an informal, or traditional, system. The constitution recognises both systems, although neither may contravene the constitution as the supreme law of the land (Amoo 2008). This means that although the responsibility to enforce the rights of victims of GBV primarily falls on the state's criminal justice system, in effect victims may engage with either or both systems. It is therefore important that this chapter locates victims of GBV in the context of the state and traditional justice.

Namibia's criminal justice responses to rape and domestic violence stem from the Combating of Rape Act 8 of 2000 and the Combating of Domestic Violence Act 4 of 2003. Our analysis will set out key points from both these acts and consider their implementation. In exploring GBV victims' experiences of traditional justice, we will focus on the processes and penalties in customary law for the gendered crime of rape. We will detail key contributions from victim-led and victim-focused activism in Namibia. Finally, we will conclude with recommendations about responding to victims of GBV in Namibia, from a victimology perspective.

In Namibia, as in many African countries, Traditional Authorities oversee everyday life, mainly in rural communities, including the allocation of land, and uses of natural resources (Keulder 2010). The Traditional Authorities Act 25 of 2000 sets out Traditional Authorities' roles, including to 'promote peace and welfare' and 'supervise and ensure the observance of customary law' (Republic of Namibia 2000b: 4). Traditional Authorities have predominantly patriarchal structures, although notable examples of authorities with strong female leadership and participation are also in evidence (Ubink 2011). Methods of ascending into traditional leadership vary. Whilst elections take place in some communities, family succession, or appointment from within the leadership network are more common processes (Hinz 2016).

The term GBV is used here in recognition of its widespread usage in Namibian discourse. However, we recognise that GBV and Violence Against Women (VAW) are often used interchangeably, most notably in the UN Declaration on the Elimination of Violence Against Women (see UN General Assembly 1993). To clarify, this chapter exclusively considers women's experience of justice systems following violence perpetrated by men. Doing so does not diminish the importance of men and children who experience GBV; people who experience violence perpetrated by women; or hate crime such as homophobic and transphobic violence. In stating our interest in the experience of victims, we acknowledge that victims of GBV are not a homogenous group and experiences of justice may be influenced by a range of factors, including the context of the GBV perpetrated. By paying attention to women's experiences, we are responding to the reality highlighted by the Legal Assistance Centre (2017) that the vast majority of GBV victims in Namibia are women.

Namibia in Context

Namibia's 824,292 sq. km mass (almost four times the size of the United Kingdom) is one of the least densely populated countries in the world, with a population of 2.1 million in the 2011 census (Namibia Statistics Agency 2016). The vast size, small population and inaccessibility of rural areas make the administration of justice a challenge: a void that is, in the main, filled by the traditional justice system. Courts in the statutory justice system are mainly restricted to large towns and cities, where Namibia's 400 lawyers are based (Solli 2013). Although English is the official language, Namibia is a diverse country with around 30 local spoken languages and 13 ethnic groups (Amoo 2014). Formal Criminal Courts rely on interpreters to function, unlike Traditional Courts, which are usually operated in locally understood languages.

As German South West Africa, the country was controlled by Germany from 1884 to 1915, a period that included Germany's perpetration of genocide against Ovaherero and Nama people, from 1904 to 1908. South

African occupation commenced in 1915, during the First World War, following which policies of apartheid entrenched widespread racial subjugation and separation until Namibia's independence in 1990. Since independence, Namibia has successfully introduced multi-party democracy and has largely been enjoying peace and stability. Namibia ranks highly in Africa in relation to good governance, democracy and human rights (Melber 2009). Namibia has a national police force, NamPol, which is approximately two-thirds male and one-third female (Legal Assistance Centre 2017).

The World Bank raised Namibia's economic classification to an upper middle-income economy in 2011 (World Bank 2013, cited in Cairney and Kapilashrami 2014). However, Namibia is one of the most economically unequal countries in the world with widespread absolute poverty. The wealthiest 5% of people control 70% of the Gross Domestic Product, with only 3% controlled by the poorest 55% of people (World Bank 2016). The gender pay gap is smaller than elsewhere in the region, as women's Gross National Income (GNI) is estimated to be 68% that of men in Namibia, compared to 63% in sub-Saharan Africa (United Nations Development Programme 2016, cited in the Legal Assistance Centre 2017). Unemployment in 2016 was estimated at 36%, though broken down by gender and geography show women's unemployment as being 44% rural and 34% urban, and men's as 34% rural and 27% urban (Legal Assistance Centre 2017). Female students in the University of Namibia outnumber males by two to one (University of Namibia 2018).

Urban and rural differences as well as regional variations permeate many aspects of life in Namibia, including educational attainment, access to support services, cultural norms, poverty levels and HIV prevalence. HIV is a significant problem in Namibia, which peaked in 2002 at an estimated prevalence rate of 21.3% among 15–49 year olds (UNAIDS 2004). The most recent estimate of HIV prevalence among the 15–49 age range is 14.5% for women and 9.5% for men (UNAIDS 2017).

GBV Against Women in Namibia

The problem of GBV against women is a global pandemic (Bennett et al. 2000) and therefore not uniquely Namibian or African. In Namibia, over one-third (35.9%) of women who ever had a partner report being subjected to violence by their partner, which includes 31% of women having experienced physical violence and 16.9% having experienced sexual violence (Garcia-Moreno et al. 2005). Several groups are identified as being at risk of GBV and vulnerable to intimate partner violence, including unemployed women and women with lower levels of education than their partners (Ministry of Health and Social Services 2013). Matthews and von Hase (2013) recommend addressing GBV against sex workers as a priority, not least because of sex workers' testimonies that this problem is compounded by physical and sexual violence being meted out by police officers. It has also been noted that GBV against older women is under-researched in Namibia (Legal Assistance Centre 2017).

Explanations for the various manifestations of GBV against women in Namibia are at an early stage. Current perspectives suggest a range of complex and interlinked socio-economic and political factors including:

- **Deeply held patriarchal power across cultures.** All ethnicities in Namibia have varying and entrenched levels of gender inequality in the form of patriarchy (Amoo 2014; Ruppel 2010). Manifestations range from the 'patriarchal system of gender subordination' on white Afrikaner farms (Sylvain 2001) to a range of harmful cultural practices towards women in communities across several different ethnic groups (see McFadden and !Khaxas 2007; !Khaxas 2009; !Khaxas 2010). Namibia is ethnically and culturally diverse, and the relative paucity of research on how to address GBV across the range of different contexts warrants in-depth attention (see Ambunda and de Klerk 2008).
- **The impact of colonial rule.** Patriarchal power is exacerbated by protracted colonial rule, firstly by Germany from the late 1800s, and then South Africa from 1915 to 1988. South Africa's method of dealing with so-called tribal authorities in Namibia reduced the levels of female leadership previously in place. This increased women's dependence on

men and the subjugation of women (Becker 1998, 2000). In addition, the violence of colonialism shaped pervasive violent masculinities in Namibia (Edwards-Jauch 2016; Scully 1995).

- **Gender-based violence arising from militarism and conflict.** Feminist scholarship has placed a spotlight on the use of rape to exert control in conflict contexts (Scanlon 2008). This occurred during the Namibian liberation struggle prior to independence in 1990 as military forces on both sides committed atrocities, including rape (Akawa 2014; Britton and Shook 2014). Felton and Becker (2001) correlated high levels of gender-based violence with Namibian communities in which male gender roles had been strongly influenced by militarisation. Psychological effects of militarisation can include a process of moral exclusion and resultant destructive behaviours, especially towards those deemed as enemies (Opotow et al. 2005). Feminists warn of 'a post conflict backlash', where women may experience new forms of violence (Britton and Shook 2014; Sjoberg 2009).

- **Masculine anxiety and insecurity.** A range of factors contributing to this angst are identified by Edwards-Jauch (2016). She argues that the traditional image of male success, the ownership of land and cattle, has been fused with global capitalist expressions of wealth and luxury. The combined ideals of traditional and modern hegemonic masculinity contrast with a harsh reality for most Namibian men living amidst the structural violence of poverty and inequality. Hardship and social exclusion in Namibia contribute to men's 'existential doubt' (Tersbøl 2006: 403).

Studies about attitudes to GBV in Namibia point to some significant changes in recent years. For example, the acceptance of the justification of wife beating in certain circumstances by 35% of women and 41% of men in 2008 reduced to 28% of women and 22% of men by 2013 (Ministry of Health and Social Services 2008, 2013). The comparatively slower change in women's attitudes could be attributed to entrenched patriarchy. In 2008, the opinion that domestic violence is a family matter which should not be shared with others in the community was expressed by 45% of research interviewees (Social Impact Assessment and Policy Analysis Corporation 2008). This appears to be an ongoing issue, as in

2013, only 21% of women who experienced GBV disclosed it, and almost half of these turned to family members, rather than other figures in the community (Ministry of Health and Social Services 2013).

Disbelief in the concept of marital rape among urban and rural men and rural women was highlighted by LeBeau and Spence (2004). Another study capturing attitudes about rape by Iipinge et al. (2004) found that almost one quarter of research participants blamed the victim for rape, whilst a further 13% said the fault is shared between the rapist and the victim. Research with imprisoned male perpetrators of GBV revealed that the majority held the view that they are entitled to discipline female partners for disobedience (Van Rooy and Mufune 2013). In a study by Chiremba (2015), imprisoned rapists expressed the misogynistic opinion that women enjoy sex, even when they resist, and the pervasive view that women were objects for sexual gratification was widely expressed by male prisoners of all offence types.

Victims' Experiences in Namibia's Dual Justice Systems

Prior to independence, the two justice systems not only operated in isolation but also treated people, and therefore women subjected to GBV, completely differently. Now that both systems are required to uphold the supremacy of the Namibian constitution, they must implement measures to protect the human rights set out in the constitution. Significant progressive reform has undoubtedly been made, a process that has witnessed the introduction of progressive statutory GBV legislation, as well as the placing of the customary laws of various Traditional Authorities on written record for the first time. Despite such progress, challenges remain for women victims of GBV in both justice systems. In the criminal justice system there are gaps between the letter of the law, how it is interpreted and its implementation. Furthermore, distance and inadequate resources restrict victims' access to support services. The remainder of this section summarises the key findings relating to each system.

Namibia's State Justice System

Two major pieces of legislation, the Combating of Rape Act 8 of 2000 and the Combating of Domestic Violence Act 4 of 2003, were introduced to respond to GBV in Namibia. In the first decade following independence in 1990, women's groups, non-governmental organisations (NGOs) and several female politicians internally lobbied for improved laws to address GBV. During the same period, the Namibian government repeatedly expressed commitment to address GBV in international discussions in SADC, the AU and the UN.

The Combating of Rape Act 8 of 2000 was seen as ground-breaking, not just within SADC but on a global scale. The Act diverges from the old colonial technical description of rape as penetration by a penis without consent. Instead it carries a minimum sentence of 5 years' imprisonment for a wide range of sexual acts defined as rape, including vaginal, anal and oral penetration, by a penis, other human or animal body part or any other object, under coercive circumstances (Republic of Namibia 2000a). In so doing, the Act recognises various forms of degradation in the crime of rape, and fully recognises male victims of rape. The Act prohibits marital rape. Bohler-Muller (2001) argues that a key quality of the Act is that it implicitly recognises rape as a crime of violence and power. It is also lauded for containing measures that minimise the re-victimisation of complainants in the criminal justice system, including closed court proceedings and restrictions on questioning the complainant about her sexual history in court.

Several reviews have taken place of the 2000 Combating of Rape Act since 2006, mainly of services involved in responding to rape (see Ministry of Gender Equality and Child Welfare 2012 below). The most comprehensive review was undertaken by the Legal Assistance Centre in 2006. This review, which tracked several hundred rape case files, noted that conviction rates in Namibia rose steadily since the legislation was introduced in 2000. Tracked files had a conviction rate of 18% (Legal Assistance Centre 2006), which, even allowing for variations in recording methods, is higher than in European countries (see Jehle 2012).

Two main concerns uncovered by the 2006 review relate to ineffective and negative responses from criminal justice agencies and attrition caused by complainant withdrawal in one-third of reported rape cases (Legal Assistance Centre 2006). Specific negative feedback about the police included unsympathetic attitudes towards women victims, the discouragement of reports of marital rape, and delayed responses to reports of rapes (Legal Assistance Centre 2006). Additional problems included insufficient application of special measures in the Combating of Rape Act, such as not complying with closed court proceedings requirement, reduced reliability of trial evidence due to lack of language translation, and a lack of victim support, especially social work follow-up (Legal Assistance Centre 2006).

Delayed police responses particularly affected rural complainants, thus preventing some women victims from accessing medical examination, emergency contraception and post-exposure prophylaxis to reduce the risk of HIV transmission within the effectivity deadline (Rose-Junius and Kuenzer 2006). Beyond the serious health risks of pregnancy and HIV infection, these delays also have legal implications in terms of gathering forensic evidence for court. Recognising the distance rural complainants may be from police stations, both the Legal Assistance Centre (2006) and Rose-Junius and Kuenzer (2006) recommended ensuring that Women and Child Protection Units or WCPU (multi-sectoral teams now known as GBV Investigation Units) have dedicated vehicles to provide a timely response.

Statutory agencies have acknowledged shortcomings in their own services. The Ministry of Gender Equality and Child Welfare undertook a review of WCPU in 2012. This review highlighted a range of problems in WCPU responses to all forms of GBV, not just rape. The Ministry of Gender Equality and Child Welfare (2012) highlighted that WCPU staff made good use of the support services of local NGOs, where they existed. However, referrals between different sector staff in WCPU, such as from the police to social workers, or from either party to introduce victims to prosecutors, were not effectively carried out. The review did not identify why internal referrals were so weak but did highlight the lack of dedicated funding and other resources for WCPU as problematic. In another study on service responses to GBV, police officers in areas without access to social work support felt ill-equipped to provide the level of support required by victims of GBV (Mgbangson 2015). The Legal Assistance Centre (2017) cited an interview with Inspector Zimmer from Windhoek WPCU in 2013, where she reportedly stated that WPCU were only dealing with cases of rape and serious assaults resulting in hospitalization. This goes against the vision that WPCU operates as a one-stop service for all GBV cases. Shifting eligibility criteria are likely to confuse victims in the immediate aftermath of a crime and risks shaking their confidence to report and seek support.

Returning our focus to withdrawal of rape cases, a follow-up to the 2006 review by the Legal Assistance Centre (2009) found that the most cited reason for withdrawal was the arrangement whereby the alleged perpetrator would compensate the complainant in lieu of proceeding in the criminal justice process. This finding was based on the perceptions of informed community members in different parts of Namibia. However, there were regional variations as to whether this arrangement was thought to be reached in the Traditional Court (see the next section), or, directly and discreetly between the families of the complainant and alleged perpetrator.

In the absence of firm data on family-only negotiated arrangements, it is not possible to analyse the compensatory approach in depth, other than to highlight a concern that complainants may feel pressurised to accept financial compensation. We have already mentioned the stark levels of prevailing economic inequality in Namibia, which has the effect of compounding the risk that economically active perpetrators of rape would be able to buy their way out of facing the consequences of their actions. To overcome this, the Legal Assistance Centre (2009) recommended amending the Combating of Rape Act 8 of 2000 to explicitly prohibit coercive compensation. This measure would send out a strong message from the state that the perversion of justice will not be tolerated. However, it would be critical that criminal justice agencies have mechanisms in place to effectively detect and address coercive compensation at every stage in the criminal justice process for such an amendment to be impactful. Given the shortcomings in implementing the 2000 Act already identified, the desired impact of the suggested amendment could not be assumed.

We now turn to some challenging issues affecting women victims of domestic violence. Namibia introduced the Combating of Domestic Violence Act 4 of 2003, which radically changed the definition of domestic violence. The 2003 Act is assessed as progressive because it recognises a range of violations that may be inflicted in the context of a domestic relationship, not just physical assault. It means that abusive acts such as harassment including stalking, threats, sexual assault, intimidation, and economic and psychological abuse can be addressed in legal proceedings under the Act (Beninger 2014). A key component of the Act is the emphasis placed on protecting victims, and, as such, the Act grants complainants the right to seek and be issued with a protection order by the Magistrates Court against the alleged perpetrator. The protection order process is not contingent on prosecution and around nine out of ten complainants who apply for protection orders, opt not to prosecute (Beninger 2014).

A major review of the implementation of the 2003 Combating of Domestic Violence Act was conducted by the Legal Assistance Centre in 2012. The review notes the steady increase of the use of the Act since it became law but that 92% of complainants are from urban areas (Legal Assistance Centre 2012). Low reporting of domestic abuse by rural women (in contrast to rape) is attributed to the predominance of customary law in rural areas, as well as lack of awareness of rights under the Act among rural women. The lack of visibility of rural women in relation to domestic abuse is a theme to which we will return. Key issues from the 2012 Legal Assistance Centre review are summarised as follows:

- **Difficulties with interim and final protection orders.** Victims experienced difficulties with the process of applying for protection orders on complicated forms. Court staff were overstretched, and many were not trained in the protection order process. Police ineffectiveness in serving and enforcing protection orders; and occasional unsympathetic police attitudes were also identified.
- **High rates of attrition.** Two key aspects of attrition were highlighted: the withdrawal of one in five complainants between the interim and final protection order stages and, the extremely poor follow-up of complainants who failed to appear at court. Poor follow-up was

attributed to the courts for failure to notify the police of most non-attendances, and to the police, for failing to follow up when notified of non-attendances by the courts.

- **Shortage of victim support services.** Findings here are similar to those already covered in relation to rape. The review recommended setting up volunteer run victim support services to guide domestic abuse complainants through the justice system.

Examples of ineffective criminal justice responses provided by survivors of GBV were provided by Matthews and von Hase (2013). One survivor highlighted a number of failings that prolonged her GBV victimisation including WCPU being unable to send somebody out following violent incidents, the police stating they could not find her husband to arrest him, and not being told about refuge provision until her fifth encounter with WCPU.

Testimonies from police officers provide insight into the problems faced by victims. These include having to place a victim in a custody area for her safety due to lack of refuge provision. Furthermore, officers report their inability to intervene when men are violent towards partners who are unwilling to prosecute or seek a protection order (Mgbangson 2015). Given the reliance on the victim to cooperate with the police, it is crucial to have clear measures to protect victims who are unwilling, or perhaps too frightened, to cooperate. This need has been identified and addressed in other countries. In 2001, the police in England and Wales were guided to exercise their powers of arrest to prevent further violence towards victims unwilling to cooperate with an investigation (Hester 2006). Such approaches may be appropriate for NamPol.

In summary, there are several barriers that negatively impact on the experiences of women victims of GBV in the criminal justice system. These comprise: unsympathetic encounters with inadequately trained criminal justice professionals, challenges in dealing with bureaucracy, language and literacy barriers, delays in criminal justice responses, low reports from rural women affected by domestic violence, lack of support to victims through the criminal justice process and the risk of being pressured to drop criminal proceedings by being offered compensation. Not only is there a gap between legislation and social transformation pertaining to GBV (Britton and Shook 2014), but also there is a gap between the aims of the existing legislation and how it is interpreted and implemented. GBV disproportionately affects women, and women often find it more difficult than men to access justice (Stevens 2001). Understanding how best to overcome these barriers in the Namibian context is imperative and gender-wise approaches to justice are crucial to the safety of women in Namibia.

Namibia's Traditional Justice System

Having considered the implementation of GBV law in the state justice system in Namibia, we now turn our attention to customary law in traditional justice. As already mentioned, in contrast to Magistrates Courts, Traditional Courts are locally accessible in rural communities and the business of these courts is conducted in local languages. The number of Traditional Court sessions that take place annually is unknown, but Hinz (2008) estimates that it runs into several thousands. As with Criminal Courts, Traditional Courts place a fundamental emphasis on telling the truth, although the method of establishing the truth is distinct from Criminal Courts. Each Traditional Court has its own conventions, although they usually provide space for a wide variety of people to participate in the hearing proceedings including the involved parties, Traditional Court leaders, and the wider community (Ubink 2011). The offence or conflict issue is discussed in depth, either until consensus is reached, or a referral to a higher level of traditional authority is required, due to lack of consensus (Peters and Ubink 2015).

Traditional justice has an overarching emphasis on restorative justice and reparation rather than retribution. Omale (2012) argues that reconciliation and restoration of harmony in community relationships lie at the heart of the traditional African dispute settlement processes, rather than punishment for offences. Victim-focused qualities of restorative justice include enabling victims to voice their feelings and opinions, have their experiences validated and participate actively in proceedings (Zehr 2004). These qualities feature in customary proceedings in Namibia and Traditional Courts have been applauded for their 'flexible, negotiable and participatory character' and for taking into account 'the needs of victims, perpetrators and the community' (Peters and Ubink 2015: 300). Whilst acknowledging the positive features of restorative justice, its suitability in cases of GBV is contentious. Feminist and victim advocates in Europe highlight that placing emphasis on restoration in violent relationships may increase the risk for further victimisation (Gavrielides and Artinopoulou 2013).

The approach to reparation in Traditional Courts in Namibia is similar to elsewhere in Africa. In addition to a public apology by the perpetrator, the sentencing procedures in Traditional Courts usually require the perpetrator to pay compensation to the victim (Solli 2013). This is similar to the approach in western civil courts. This similarity between the Namibian traditional and western civil legal process does not extend to the profile of the participants. In Namibia, the vast majority of Traditional Court users are impoverished people from rural areas, with limited access to other courts.

There is a diverse range of customary laws in Namibia reflecting the various Traditional Authorities and ethnicities that operate Traditional Courts (Stewart 2008; Visser and Ruppel-Schlichting 2008). Thus, there is no single uniform response to GBV in this complex, heterogeneous system, as shall be demonstrated. Furthermore, there are now two tiers of Traditional Court in Namibia, since the Community Courts Act 10 of 2003 set out the conditions by which some Traditional Courts may be granted the status of state-funded Community Courts. Such conditions include having customary law ascertained (set out in a clear, specific and explicit manner), ensuring court recording processes are in place and undertaking to refer unresolved cases to Magistrates Courts, rather than to a higher level of the Traditional Authority as would have previously been the case (Ruppel and Ambunda 2011). A total of 43 Traditional Authorities from 10 Namibian ethnicities went through the ascertainment process between 2010 and 2016. Researchers from University of Namibia documented the customary laws as provided by the Traditional Authorities. The ascertainment project lead, Hinz (2016), explains that although the ascertainment process makes most customary laws clear and certain in written form for the first time, it is within the gift of a Traditional Authority to change its customary law at any point it so decides.

Amoo (2008) notes that Community Courts have both civil and criminal jurisdiction, provided they do not impose custodial sentences. As already stated, the minimum sentence for rape in criminal law is 5 years' imprisonment. It would therefore follow that Community Courts, which are lower than Magistrates Courts, should not be a setting for criminal proceedings for rape. This is because, in line with Article 66 of the Constitution, the application of customary law is only valid so long as it does not conflict with the Constitution or statutory law (Ruppel and Ruppel-Schlichting 2011). In support of this point, it is the expressed opinion of the Legal Assistance Centre that Traditional Courts do not have jurisdiction to oversee criminal proceedings for rape, which must be addressed by the state under the 2000 Combating of Rape Act (Legal Assistance Centre 2006). However, the Legal Assistance Centre contends that compensation proceedings for rape may be addressed in Traditional Courts. This must be in addition to, not in lieu of, state proceedings.

Below is a precis of the individual ascertained customary laws on rape from Nama, Ovaherero, Ovambanderu and San people. This represents 17 of the 43 Traditional Authorities that had their laws ascertained and is the most recent group to do so (see Hinz and Gairiseb 2016). We have organised details of the customary laws on rape into six classifications:

1. Not qualified to prosecute due to severity of crime, but with no further instruction.
2. Does not mention rape.
3. Various minimum and maximum amounts of compensation (usually described as heads of cattle or money equivalent) with a referral to the criminal justice system.
4. Various minimum and maximum amounts of compensation to be paid after the convicted perpetrator had served their state justice sentence.
5. Various minimum and maximum amounts of compensation with no mention of the state criminal justice system.
6. Distinct processes in place according to aspects of the victim's demography, which applied to two authorities. One authority had a compensation payment in place, except in relation to the rape of minors, which resulted in an automatic referral to the Magistrates Court.

Another authority had an automatic referral to the police, except when rape was alleged within marriage. In this instance, customary law stated the spouse was to be provided with information about counselling and would have to decide for herself whether to take further action.

The first classification cannot be confidently interpreted due to lack of detail. In other words, because the stated customary law does not explicitly instruct complainants to take their case to the criminal justice system, it is not possible to determine whether somebody victimised by rape will receive enough guidance to report the crime to NamPol with a view to a proceeding in a state criminal court. Similarly, the second classification does not provide insight into the likely response a rape complainant may receive, because no detail is provided.

The third and fourth classifications suggest that a twin process of traditional compensation and criminal justice is being followed, as per the recommendation of the Legal Assistance Centre. It is difficult to interpret why the fifth category of response sets out traditional justice compensation arrangements without also signposting to criminal justice. Mindful of the risk highlighted by the Legal Assistance Centre (2009) that compensation may be exchanged for dropping criminal proceedings, this failure to signpost to the criminal justice system is worrying as regards justice for victims of GBV.

The sixth classification alerts us to a duplicitous process that facilitates a criminal justice referral for some—in these cases minors and single women and denies a referral to others—adult women and married women. This suggests that some Traditional Authorities explicitly operate in ways that deny access to criminal justice to some women based on their age and marital status, contrary to the Namibian constitution which enshrines rights for all. Following the ascertainment process of the first group of Traditional Authorities to do so in 2010, Horn (2011) critiqued the lack of willingness of some authorities to relinquish hearing cases of rape. Based on the 2016 process summarised here, the issue appears ongoing and requiring action.

It is not clear why the state recognises Community Courts that operate contrary to criminal law. The Government of Namibia, according to its democratic mandate, is at the forefront of determining the exact circumstances and purpose for which customary law *may* be used and when criminal law *must* be used. The case for governmental oversight of the latter is clear and relates to the minimum sentence of 5 years for rape in criminal law. Additionally, given the low numbers of women from rural communities seeking justice via the Combating of Domestic Violence Act 2003, and the lack of explicit procedures for domestic violence in customary law, there is just as much need for clarity about the boundaries between customary and criminal law in relation to domestic violence. At present, routes to effective justice for rural women who seek justice following domestic violence are unclear. The relationships between the government, the state system of criminal justice and traditional courts are complex and the boundaries between them are blurred. What is evident is that women are unsupported in this complex mix of routes to justice and many fall between these systems.

Having considered the wording of customary law, we now move to the gendered practices of Traditional Courts. In most Traditional Authorities, women are as equally entitled as men to bring a case to be heard in court. However, in some instances, the practice of requiring the approval of a male family member of the complainant, before proceeding with a case, has also been identified (Ubink 2011; Becker 1998). In one Traditional Authority, the required male relative was specified as the woman's father, if unmarried, or her husband, if married (Peters and Ubink 2015). The patriarchal restrictions of this procedure make access to justice for women victims impossible, especially when violence has been perpetrated by fathers or husbands.

Before the introduction of Community Courts, Becker (2006) argued that there were many examples of gender-balanced Traditional Courts in some authorities that competently hear rape cases and that rape survivors often feel more comfortable in traditional than in criminal proceedings. More recently, the female-led Traditional Court run by Uukwambi Traditional Authority has been highlighted as demonstrating the potential for change in gendered practices within traditional systems (Ubink 2018). These reports of gender-balanced courts are encouraging. Peters and Ubink (2015) observe variations in levels of gendered participation across a range of Traditional Courts regarding levels of active participation in discussion, court leadership and knowledge of the methods of negotiating compensation. They do however conclude that, where gender imbalances exist, they usually favour men (Ubink 2011; Peters and Ubink 2015). The gendered power differentials within Traditional Courts arguably reflect relationships in the communities where they operate. All of this reinforces our earlier point about the heterogeneity of the traditional system. Given that most gender imbalances in the system disadvantage women, the requirement on some women to have a male family member's approval to engage with the system and the questionable practice of some courts in responding to rape, we conclude that there are sections of the traditional system that deny access to justice for women victims of GBV.

Before moving on from traditional justice, we wish to address the role of culture in the quest to promote gender-wise justice in rural Namibia. Culture can be (mis)used as a reason for preventing change and it can be too easy to dismiss culture as being the antithesis of women's rights. We support the contention that:

> Most of what is understood as 'culture' in contemporary Africa is largely a product of constructions and (re)interpretations by former colonial authorities in collaboration with African male patriarchs (Tamale 2008: 51).

In so doing, we recognise the fluidity of culture and the responsibility to support traditional authorities and communities in developing new traditions and customary laws. Traditional justice is the system of choice for most rural people, therefore it is incumbent on all who wish to promote women's rights in Namibia to view culture as the pathway rather than the barrier to women's justice. Justice is unlikely to be achieved otherwise. To that end, the importance of grassroots debate and activism to achieve change from the bottom up is pivotal.

Activism to Address GBV

In this section, we highlight notable achievements in respect of collaborative activism whilst acknowledging challenges that remain for GBV activists. Our experience and history of working with NGOs and GBV networks in Namibia to address human rights and GBV inform our review of activism to address it. As with many African countries seeking freedom from colonial rule in the mid- to late twentieth century, issues such as GBV were placed at the periphery of the struggle for independence (Hubbard and Solomon 1995; Becker 1995). Indeed, during the Namibian Independence Struggle, SWAPO (South West Africa's Peoples Organisation, the liberation movement that became the Swapo Party after independence) curtailed women's activism, which had grown in the 1980s, out of concern that it might detract attention from the ultimate goal of national independence. The opposing views between those who remained loyal to SWAPO and those who challenged the movement from a gendered perspective, resulted in a divided women's movement by the time Namibia became independent in 1990 (Akawa 2014). This division continued in the years immediately following independence despite efforts to unify the women's movement across party political lines and between political parties and the NGO sector (Becker 1995). These underlying tensions make the subsequent achievements of female activists working towards the development of legislation to address GBV especially significant.

Feminist Activist Groups and NGOs Addressing Violence Against Women

Given the side-lining of gender equality issues prior to independence, it is perhaps no surprise that Namibia's first organisation with a sole focus on violence against women—Women's Solidarity—was formed only in 1989. This was after the agreement was reached in December 1988 to implement UN Resolution 435, for Namibia's independence. Women's Solidarity, alongside other NGOs set up at this time, the Legal Assistance Centre in 1988, and Sister Collective (which publishes the feminist magazine, *Sister Namibia*) in 1989, have been key in the response to violence against women since the formation of Namibia in 1990. Women's Solidarity was originally intended to be the Namibian centre of the international Rape Crisis movement. Instead, it became a service supporting women affected by all forms of GBV. As a feminist organisation directly supporting women victims of violence, Women's Solidarity has been vocal at highlighting instances when women have not been in receipt of legal redress. The organisation temporarily closed in 2004, due to lack of funding, and although it re-launched in 2006, the scale of activity was smaller than previously.

Although Women's Solidarity is the only explicitly feminist GBV victim support NGO in Namibia, other specialist NGOs provide support and therapeutic services for victims of GBV. These include Friendly Haven, a shelter for women and children fleeing violence run by the Ecumenical Social Diaconate Action and Regain Trust, an NGO providing psychological interventions for both victims and perpetrators of GBV. Counselling NGOs Philippi Trust Namibia and Lifeline/Childline Namibia are both active in supporting people affected by GBV. Lifeline/Childline coordinates MenEngage Namibia, working with men and boys to campaign against GBV.

Based on global level research, Htun and Weldon (2012) argue that autonomous, non-governmental feminist mobilisation is pivotal to ensure effective policy and practice to address violence against women within individual countries. Outside of providing direct support services, several feminist groups address GBV issues. The Women's Leadership Centre regularly works with women victims to share their experiences and publishes collections of women's stories and poems as part of their commitment to challenging harmful cultural practices and oppression in communities (Andima and Tjiramanga 2014). The feminist magazine *Sister Namibia* also provides a platform to women to share their experiences of victimisation and survival (see Feris 2014). These groups recognise that victims of GBV are bearers of knowledge and can be powerful agents for social change (Stringer 2014). A range of groups have contributed significantly to policy and practice developments in Namibia through their activism, as highlighted in examples below.

The Multi-Media Campaign on Violence Against Women and Children

The Multi-Media Campaign on Violence against Women and Children (hereafter the Campaign) had NGO members from a wide variety of sectors such as women's rights, children's rights, HIV and AIDS, LGBT rights and those engaged in counselling. The Legal Assistance Centre, Women's Solidarity and the Sister Collective were particularly active NGO participants. Statutory members included representatives from the Law Reform and Development Commission, NamPol, and the Ministry of Women Affairs and Child Welfare (now the Ministry of Gender Equality and Child Welfare).

The Campaign was active in the 1990s and early 2000s advocating for laws on rape and domestic violence. Britton and Shook (2014) argue that NGO input was pivotal in informing the comprehensive, progressive and tough anti-rape content of the 2000 Combating of Rape Act. NGOs were aligned with international networks addressing GBV with access to information on good practice developments from other countries, which strengthened their lobbying of the Namibian government. When the Combating of Rape Bill was circulated for consultation in 1999, the Campaign took out adverts in the national newspapers and brought 20 NGOs together to provide a single set of recommendations for improvement, which were mostly incorporated into the 2000 Act (Legal Assistance Centre 2007).

In 2003, the Campaign organised a demonstration to coincide with the opening of Parliament, calling for urgency in pushing through domestic violence legislation. Although a member of the Campaign, NamPol would not permit the Campaign to demonstrate directly outside Parliament and the High Court refused the Campaign's urgent application to overturn NamPol's decision. When the women and children protesting opted instead to gather outside the nearby Supreme Court, a stand-off with armed NamPol officers ensued. Legal Assistance Centre (2012) noted the irony that this tense situation was taking place, whilst President Nujoma was addressing Parliament and making positive statements about the forthcoming domestic violence legislation. The Campaign ceased soon after the 2003 Act was introduced, having achieved its goal to change the law. However, with hindsight, the ending of the Campaign may have been premature, given the gap between GBV laws and their implementation, as detailed earlier in the chapter. Changing attitudes about GBV is a longer term process than changing laws, a point which is borne out in relation to a significant series of events that started in 2013.

The 'Mini-Skirt' Protest

Women's activism in Namibia has been responsive to issues pertaining to GBV, a recent notable example being activists' responses to the so-called mini-skirt ban in 2013. In January 2013, one newspaper reported that a large group of around 40 girls and young women in Rundu, in the north of Namibia, were arrested over the Christmas holidays for wearing 'hot-pants'. There were conflicting media reports about whether they were in custody for breaching public decency or for their own safety. Media reports of a follow-up interview with the head of NamPol, Police Inspector General Sebastian Ndeitunga, magnified the attention focused on this incident (see Shinovene 2013). Although the Inspector General later said he was misquoted, he was reported to have said that young people should dress in line with tradition by wearing modest clothes, and as well as linking modern revealing clothing to the upsurge of GBV, suggested that further arrests for public indecency could follow.

Women's Solidarity made contact with individual women who expressed their anger at this example of victim blaming and together they set about organising a protest to denounce it. The 'mini-skirt protest' took place in Zoo Park in the capital city, Windhoek on 23 February 2013 and was attended by several hundred members of the public. The event was widely supported by a range of NGOs and political representatives and extensively covered by newspaper, broadcast and social media. The speechmakers denounced victim blaming and challenged Namibians to level the blame for sexual violence with the perpetrators. The similarity between the 'mini-skirt protest' and SlutWalk is notable. This transnational protest movement started off as a single event in Canada on 3 April 2011, following comments by a Toronto Police officer to students that to deter sexual assault they should avoid dressing like sluts. Although sparked by similar attitudes, both protests are distinct from each other. An informal coalition emerged from the initial protest gathering, which became the Coalition Against Gender-Based and Sexual Violence. The Zoo Park protest turned out to be the first in a series of events that both continued and extended beyond the mini-skirt issue.

The Coalition Against Gender-Based and Sexual Violence

The Coalition Against Gender Based and Sexual Violence (hereafter, the Coalition) is made up of Women's Solidarity, Sister Namibia, as well other groups not previously mentioned. These are Victims 2 Survivors (a GBV self-help group), Namibian Women's Health Network (a women's HIV self-help organisation), Her Liberty Namibia (a female student group challenging GBV), the Media Institute for Southern Africa (an organisation promoting democracy through independent media) and individuals from the arts and media. The purpose of the Coalition is to raise awareness of the need to address GBV.

The Coalition organised a mini-skirt themed fashion show and the funds raised were used to run GBV awareness sessions with women. Throughout 2013 and 2014, the Coalition organised an extensive range of events including a 'Take Back the Night March', which set off from the home of Eleanor Diergaardt, a young woman who was killed by her step-father (see Tibinyane 2014). Other events: a flash mob to address the issue of bystander intervention, testimonies of GBV survivors and a prayer vigil for imprisoned perpetrators, also received positive media coverage. The Coalition set itself an ambitious goal of organising a monthly event, with all members expected to lead on a rotational basis. However, by 2015 the Coalition's momentum was negatively affected by a lack of resources to sustain collective activism, in addition to the core work of each member group. The Coalition's main achievements include bringing activists together across groups, organisations and generations, and impacting national conversations about GBV, particularly rape. Although currently less active in relation to events organising, the cross-organisational structure of the Coalition still exists.

Challenges Facing Activism Against GBV

We highlight the two main challenges facing activism against GBV, which are lack of sustainable funding for GBV support services and the challenge of maintaining and developing collective activism against GBV. The closure of Women's Solidarity in 2004 demonstrates the precarious situation of GBV support services in Namibia. NGOs, and indeed many government programmes are heavily reliant on international funding, making them vulnerable to changes in the priorities of international donors (Britton and Shook 2014). These changes may be because donors opt to prioritise GBV elsewhere, particularly in highly indebted poor countries. Major international donors prioritise funding for HIV programmes in Namibia because of the devastating impact of this problem. Funding for GBV interventions are incorporated into donor led HIV programme plans (see, e.g., President's Emergency Fund for AIDS Relief 2018). On the one hand, this is purposeful given that HIV is an outcome of GBV (Jewkes et al. 2010). However, it is important to provide funding to address GBV and its causes in their own right, not just because of their impact on HIV prevalence.

We now turn to the challenges of sustaining collective activism as experienced by the Coalition. The problem of burnout is not unique to women's collective GBV activism in Namibia and can affect all social movements (Della Porta and Diani 2006). It does however point to the need for infrastructure support for collaborative victim-led and victim-focused activism by women's groups. Not only could it help strengthen collective activism, but potentially increase its reach across the 14 regions of Namibia. Although various multi-agency GBV action planning meetings are coordinated by Ministry of Gender Equality and Child Welfare, this does not address the problem of burnout for women's activism groups. This is because attending coordination meetings is time- and resource-intensive for women's groups, an outlay for which they are not reimbursed. Furthermore, given the earlier cited benefits of autonomous feminist activism, it is important that grassroots activism sets its own agenda and organises its own campaigns, such as the events organised by the Coalition. In the early post-independence phase, Hubbard and Solomon (1995) noted the challenges of conceptualising the women's movement in Namibia, due to the loose and fluid connections between actors. Given that this is a key feature of both past and present activism in Namibia, Hubbard and Solomon's analysis appears to have ongoing relevance.

The Potential Contribution of Victimology: Challenges and Possibilities

This chapter has shown that the content of state legislation addressing rape and domestic violence is victim focused and has detailed the implementation gap between the letter of the law and its application. We have problematised the low numbers of rural domestic violence cases in the formal criminal justice system. Whilst acknowledging the significance of the traditional justice system, we have drawn attention to the need for clarity from the state about the legal scope of Traditional Courts, particularly in relation to rape. We have argued that the gendered practices of some Traditional Courts are counterproductive to the application of gender-wise justice. We have shown that culture, often used to justify such unequal gendered practices, is fluid, and does not need to stand in the way of gender justice. We have presented examples of how activism has contributed to formal law making in Namibia, and the national conversation about GBV, particularly by challenging victim blaming.

We begin our reflection on the potential contribution of victimology by advocating for up-to-date victim-centred primary research on the experiences of women victims of GBV in both justice systems. Previous research by the Legal Assistance Centre informs our understanding of issues in the formal justice system, such as delayed responses following rape and inadequate enforcement of protection orders demanding action. Primary research with victims would enhance insight into the implications of these problems from victims' perspectives. It would also ensure that pertinent issues, like complainant withdrawal, are informed by those with the most expertise, the complainants. Resultant research findings would thus have the potential to improve the responsiveness of future victim-focused measures to victims' needs.

There are several important methodological considerations to be taken on board in conducting primary research with victims in Namibia. Firstly, victimology researchers need to be completely open to engaging with state criminal law, customary law, and the systems that administer both. Otherwise, victimology would be restricted to a partial application and relevance in Namibia. Thus, complex issues around accessing victims in both systems need to be worked through sensitively and ethically. The dearth of primary research with GBV victims in the traditional justice system particularly needs to be addressed. A bespoke approach is needed to research such a complex, varied and localised traditional justice system. We suggest that training and utilising peer researchers could be a useful way to address this challenge.

Next, it is crucial that victimological enquiry is approached in a way that is appropriate to Namibia as a place. The reality that the modern discipline of victimology is dominated by theoretical perspectives from Europe and North America (Saponaro 2013) prompts scholars, such as Peacock (2013), to argue for an African victimology that is culturally and contextually relevant. We argue that, as a minimum, it is vital to engage openly and sensitively with peoples' world views and be cognisant of how views are influenced by place. There are practical challenges to undertaking large-scale victimology research in Namibia. Criminology, and therefore victimology, is not a core discipline in Namibian higher education. The subject of criminal justice is taught at higher level alongside correctional services studies and policing studies. This is not insurmountable but is important to bear in mind when drawing on human and academic resources. A further constraint, which causes concern, is the earlier mentioned shortage of resources to respond to the needs of victims of GBV in Namibia. Researchers must approach their task with this ethical consideration in mind, to guard against building false hope of increased provision, whilst recognising that research *may* help build a case for increased resource allocation.

An enabling factor for victimology research in Namibia is that the sharing of testimonies by women who have been harmed by GBV already takes place in women's organisations and groups. This means there is a foundation on which to build. Such powerful testimonies need to be told, as Kirchhoff (2013: vii) attests; 'avoiding silencing is part of "victim truth"". We recommend that the expertise of organisations such as Women's Solidarity, the Women's Leadership Centre and Victims 2 Survivors are utilised and remunerated in future endeavours. This will require political will and a long-term commitment to tackling and resourcing GBV from both government and, importantly, international donors. The precedent exists in relation to HIV programming in Namibia and GBV should be addressed with similar urgency and resource allocation.

We contend that victimology insights can contribute to practice improvements in Namibia and recommend the introduction of victimology as a core subject in the training of criminal justice practitioners. Doing so would underscore the importance of addressing the earlier mentioned shortcomings in criminal justice practice that increase risks to the safety of GBV victims. Whilst victim-focused training should not be an alternative to ensuring the services are resourced to meet the demands they face, it is important that practitioners are able to understand the human cost to victims when denied the processes promised by law.

Our final recommendation is to set up an observation scheme covering GBV court proceedings in both the state and traditional hearings in Namibia. There are precedents for this approach from academia (see Smith and Skinner 2012) and from practice, utilising members of the general public as observers, by Durham et al. (2017). Such a scheme has the potential to benefit several areas, as it would address the prevailing lack of knowledge about GBV processes in various Traditional Courts and would identify when processes promised by legislation are not being implemented in formal state courts. The expertise to oversee such a scheme in Namibia exists in the Legal Assistance Centre, should resources be allocated.

In conclusion, substantial progress has been made in developing progressive legislation to address GBV in the criminal justice system, even though further implementation improvements are required. Activists have been important in advocating for such improvements and highlighting where responses have fallen short. Although a young country, in terms of independence, democracy, and constitutional law-making, Namibia has chosen to protect its traditions and customary law. The ascertainment of various customary laws should be the start of a process to ultimately ensure that Traditional Courts deal with GBV in line with the constitution, which also requires addressing both the legal scope and gendered practices in the traditional system. Set against this backdrop, if victimology was embraced as a discipline in Namibia, it has the potential to contribute to the overall goal of improving the response to women violated by GBV, by informing victim-centred research processes and practice in both justice systems in Namibia.

References

Akawa, M. (2014). *The Gender Politics of the Namibian Liberation Struggle.* Basel: Basler Afrika Bibliographien.

Ambunda, L., & de Klerk, S. (2008). Women and Custom in Namibia: A research Overview. In O. C. Ruppel (Ed.), *Women and Custom in Namibia: Cultural Practice Versus Gender Equality?* Macmillan Education Namibia: Windhoek.

Amoo, S. K. (2008). The Structure of the Namibian Judicial System and Its Relevance for an Independent Judiciary. In N. Horn & A. Bösl (Eds.), *The Independence of the Judiciary in Namibia.* Windhoek: Macmillan Eduction.

Amoo, S. K. (2014). *Property Law in Namibia.* Pretoria: Pretoria University Law Press.

Andima, L., & Tjiramanga, A. (2014). The Oppression of Women in Selected Narratives by Namibian Female Authors. *NAWA Journal of Language and Communication, 8*(2), 76–91.

Becker, H. (1995). *Namibian Women's Movement, 1980 to 1992: From Anti-colonial Resistance to Reconstruction.* Frankfurt: IKO-Verlag für Interkulturelle Kommunikation.

Becker, H. (1998). Gender Aspects of Traditional Authorities and Customary Courts in Northern Namibia. In F. M. D'Engelbronner-Kolff, M. O. Hinz, & J. L. Sindano (Eds.), *Traditional Authority and Democracy in Southern Africa.* Wndhoek: New Namibia Books.

Becker, H. (2000). A Concise History of Gender, 'Tradition' and the State in Namibia. In C. E. Keulder (Ed.), *State, Society and Democracy; A Reader in Namibian Politics.* Gamsberg Macmillan: Windhoek.

Becker, H. (2006). 'New Things After Independence': Gender and Traditional Authorities in Postcolonial Namibia. *Journal of Southern African Studies, 32*(1), 29–48.

Beninger, C. (2014). The Effectiveness of Legislative Reform in Combating Domestic Violence: A Comparative Analysis of Laws in Ghana, Namibia and South Africa. *Netherlands Quarterly of Human Rights, 32*(1), 75–108.

Bennett, L. R., Astbury, J., & Manderson, L. (2000). *Mapping a Global Pandemic: Review of Current Literature on Rape, Sexual Assault and Sexual Harassment of Women*. Melbourne: Global Forum for Health Research / Consultation on Sexual Violence against Women / Key Centre for Women's Health in Society.

Bohler-Muller, N. (2001). Valuable Lessons from Namibia on the Combating of Rape. *South African Journal of Criminal Justice, 14*(1), 71–80.

Britton, H., & Shook, L. (2014). "I Need to Hurt You More": Namibia's Fight to End Gender-Based Violence. *Signs: Journal of Women in Culture and Society, 40*(1), 153–176.

Cairney, L., & Kapilashrami, A. (2014). Confronting 'Scale-Down': Assessing Namibia's Human Resource Strategies in the Context of Decreased HIV/AIDS Funding. *Global Public Health, 9*(1–2), 198–209.

Centre, L. A. (2006). *Rape in Namibia: An Assessment of the Operation of the Combating of Rape Act 8 of 2000*. Windhoek: Legal Assistance Centre.

Centre, L. A. (2007). *Advocacy in Action: A Guide for Influencing Decision Making in Namibia*. Windhoek: Legal Assistance Centre.

Chiremba, W. (2015). Understanding Sex Offending in Namibia: A Preliminary Analysis. *Acta Criminologica: Southern African Journal of Criminology* (Special Edition 1), 62–81.

Della Porta, D., & Diani, M. (2006). *Social Movements: An Introduction*. Oxford: Blackwell.

Durham, R., Lawson, R., Lord, A., & Baird, V. (2017). Seeing Is Believing: The Northumbria Court Observers Panel Report on 30 Rape Trials, 2015–2016. Retrieved November 6, 2018, http://www.northumbria-pcc.gov.uk/v2/wp-content/uploads/2017/02/Seeing-Is-Believing-Court-Observers-Panel-Report.pdf.

Edwards-Jauch, L. (2016). Gender-Based Violence and Masculinity in Namibia: A Structuralist Framing of the Debate. *Journal for Studies in Humanities and Social Sciences, 5*(1), 49–62.

Felton, S., & Becker, H. (2001). *A Gender Perspective on the Status of the San in Southern Africa: Regional Assessment of the Status of the San in Southern Africa*. Windhoek: Legal Assistance Centre.

Feris, L. (2014). My Name Is Lizette. *Sister*. Retrieved November 6, 2018, from https://sisternamibiatest2014.files.wordpress.com/2014/07/2014-vol-26-1rev.pdf.

Garcia-Moreno, C., Jansen, H. A., Ellsberg, M., Heise, L., & Watts, C. (2005). *Multi-country Study on Women's Health and Domestic Violence Against Women: Initial Results on Prevalence, Health Outcomes, and Women's Responses.* Geneva: World Health Organisation.

Gavrielides, T., & Artinopoulou, V. (2013). Restorative Justice and Violence Against Women: Comparing Greece and the United Kingdom. *Asian Journal of Criminology, 8*(1), 25–40.

Hester, M. (2006). Making It Through the Criminal Justice System: Attrition and Domestic Violence. *Social Policy and Society, 5*(1), 79–90.

Hinz, M. O. (2008). Traditional Courts in Namibia – Part of the Judiciary? Jurisprudential Challenges of Traditional Justice. In N. Horn & A. Bösl (Eds.), *The Independence of the Judiciary in Namibia.* Macmillan Education: Windhoek.

Hinz, M. O. (2016). The Ascertainment of Namibian Customary Law Completed: What Has Been Done and What Lies Ahead. In N. Horn & M. O. Hinz (Eds.), *Beyond a Quarter Century of Constitutional Democracy: Process and Progress in Namibia.* Windhoek: Konrad Adenauer Stiftung.

Hinz, M. O., & Gairiseb, A. (2016). *The Customary Law of the Nama, Ovaherero, Ovambanderu and San Communities of Namibia.* Windhoek: UNAM Press.

Horn, N. (2011). Review of Customary Law Ascertained Volume 1. *Namibia Law Journal, 3*(1), 133–140.

Htun, M., & Weldon, S. L. (2012). The Civic Origins of Progressive Policy Change: Combating Violence Against Women in Global Perspective, 1975–2005. *American Political Science Review, 106*(3), 548–569.

Hubbard, D., & Solomon, C. (1995). The Women's Movement in Namibia: History, Constraints and Potential. In A. Basu & C. E. McGrory (Eds.), *The Challenge of Local Feminisms: Women's Movements in Global Perspective.* Boulder, CO: Westview Publishers.

Iipinge, S., Hofnie, K., & Friedman, S. (2004). *The Relationship Between Gender Roles and HIV Infection in Namibia.* Windhoek: UNAM.

IKhaxas, E. (2009). *Cultural Practices, Women's Rights, HIV and Aids: A case study of the Caprivi Region in Namibia.* Windhoek: Women's Leadership Centre.

!Khaxas, E. (2010). *Violence Is Not Our Culture: Women Claiming Their Rights in Caprivi Region.* Windhoek: Women's Leadership Centre.

Jehle, J. M. (2012). Attrition and Conviction Rates of Sexual Offences in Europe: Definitions and Criminal Justice Responses. *European Journal on Criminal Policy and Research, 18*(1), 145–161.

Jewkes, R. K., Dunkle, R., Nduna, M., & Shai, N. (2010). Intimate Partner Violence, Relationship Power Inequity, and Incidence of HIV Infection in Young Women in South Africa: A Cohort Study. *The Lancet, 376*(9374), 41–48.

Keulder, C. (2010). Traditional Leaders. In C. Keulder (Ed.), *State, Society and Democracy*. Windhoek: Macmillan Education Namibia.

Kirchhoff, G. F. (2013). Foreward. In R. Peacock (Ed.), *Victimology in South Africa*. Pretoria: Van Schaik.

LeBeau, D., & Spence, G. J. (2004). Community Perceptions of Law Reform: People Speaking Out. In J. Hunter (Ed.), *Beijing+ 10: The Way Forward: An Introduction to Gender Issues in Namibia*. Namibia Institute for Democracy: Windhoek.

Legal Assistance Centre. (2009). *Withdrawn: Why Complainants Withdraw Rape Cases in Namibia*. Windhoek: Legal Assistance Centre.

Legal Assistance Centre. (2012). *Seeking Safety: Domestic Violence in Namibia and the Combating of Domestic Violence Act 4 of 2003*. Windhoek: Legal Assisance Centre.

Legal Assistance Centre. (2017). *Namibia Gender Analysis 2017: Prepared by the Legal Assistance Centre for the Delegation of the European Union to Namibia*. Windhoek: Legal Assistance Centre / European Union.

Matthews, J., & von Hase, I. (2013). *Gender-Based Violence (GBV) in Namibia: An Exploratory Assessment and Mapping of GBV Response Services in Windhoek*. Windhoek: Victims 2 Survivors / UNAIDS.

McFadden, P., & !Khaxas, E. (2007). *Research Report on Patriarchal Repression and Resistance in the Caprivi Region in Namibia*. Windhoek: Women's Leadership Centre.

Melber, H. (2009). One Namibia, One Nation? The Caprivi as Contested Territory. *Journal of Contemporary African Studies, 27*(4), 463–481.

Mgbangson, A. (2015). Gender-Based Violence: Systems Response Versus Personal Agency. In A. Mgbangson (Ed.), *Gender Based Violence in Namibia: A Response Driven Approach*. Windhoek: UNAM Press.

Ministry of Gender Equality and Child Welfare. (2012). *Assessment of the Woman and Child Protection Services in Kavango, Karas, Khomas, Omusati and Omaheke Regions in Namibia: Synthesis Report*. Windhoek: MGECW.

Ministry of Health and Social Services. (2008). *Namibia Demographic and Health Survey 2006–07*. Windhoek; Namibia and Calverton, Maryland, USA: MoHSS Namibia and Macro International Inc..

Ministry of Health and Social Services. (2013). *Namibia Demographic and Health Survey 2013*. Windhoek: MoHSS Namibia and ICF International.

Namibia Statistics Agency. (2016). Namibia Social Statistics 20/15/2016, Quarter 1, Windhoek. Retrieved November 14, 2018, from https://cms. my.na/assets/documents/Namibia_Statistical_Abstract_Report.pdf.

Omale, D. J. O. (2012). *Restorative Justice and Victimology: Euro-Africa Perspectives.* Oisterwijk: Wolf Legal Publishers.

Opotow, S., Gerson, J., & Woodside, S. (2005). From Moral Exclusion to Moral Inclusion: Theory for Teaching Peace. *Theory into Practice, 44*(4), 303–318.

Peacock, R. (2013). Victimology in South Africa: Some Concluding Remarks. In R. Peacock (Ed.), *Victimology in South Africa*. Pretoria: Van Schaik.

Peters, E. A., & Ubink, J. M. (2015). Restorative and Flexible Customary Procedures and Their Gendered Impact: A Preliminary View on Namibia's Formalisation of Traditional Courts. *The Journal of Legal Pluralism and Unofficial Law, 47*, 1–21.

President's Emergency Plan for AIDS Relief. (2018). Namibian Country Operational Plan 2018. Retrieved November 6, 2018, from www.pepfar.gov/documents/organization/285857.pdf.

Republic of Namibia. (2000a). Combating of Rape Act 2000 (Act 8 of 2000). Retrieved November 18, 2018, from https://laws.parliament.na/annotated-laws-regulations/law-regulation.php?id=370.

Republic of Namibia. (2000b). Traditional Authroties Act 2000 (Act 25 of 2000). Retrieved November 18, 2018, from https://laws.parliament.na/annotated-laws-regulations/law-regulation.php?id=393.

Rose-Junius, H., & Kuenzer, E. (2006). *An Investigation into the Functioning of WCPU's and Police Stations with Regard to the Protection of Abused Women and Children in the Country.* Windhoek: UNICEF.

Ruppel, O. C. (2010). *Women's Rights and Customary Law in Namibia: A Conflict between Human and Cultural Rights?* Basel: Basler Afrika Bibliographien.

Ruppel, O. C., & Ambunda, L. (2011). *The Justice Sector and the Rule of Law in Namibia.* Windhoek: Namibia Institute for Democracy.

Ruppel, O. C., & Ruppel-Schlichting, K. (2011). Legal and Judicial Pluralism in Namibia and Beyond: A Modern Approach to African Legal Architecture? *The Journal of Legal Pluralism and Unofficial Law, 43*(64), 33–63.

Saponaro, A. (2013). Theoretical Approaches and Perspectives in Victimology. In R. Peacock (Ed.), *Victimology in South Africa*. Pretoria: Van Schaik.

Scanlon, H. (2008). Militarization, Gender and Transitional Justice in Africa. Feminist Africa 10 Militarism. *Conflict and Women's Activism, 10*, 31–49.

Scully, P. (1995). Rape, Race, and Colonial Culture: The Sexual Politics of Identity in Nineteenth-Century Cape Colony, South Africa. *American Historical Review, 100*(2), 335–359.

Shinovene, I. (2013). Top Cop Says Miniskirts Are Not African. *The Namibian.* Retrieved November 18, 2018, from https://www.namibian.com.na/index.php?id=105372&page=archive-read.

Sjoberg, L. (2009). Introduction to Security Studies: Feminist Contributions. *Security Studies, 18*(2), 183–213.

Smith, O., & Skinner, T. (2012). Observing Court Responses to Victims of Rape and Sexual Assault. *Feminist Criminology, 7*(4), 298–326.

Social Impact Assessment and Policy Analysis Corporation. (2008). *Knowledge, Attitudes and Practices Study on Factors That May Perpetuate or Protect Namibians from Violence and Discrimination.* Windhoek: SIAPAC for Ministry of Gender Equality and Child Welfare.

Solli, J. (2013). *The Traditional Courts of Namibia: A Forum for Consumer Protection, If Not Actual Redress?* London: Consumers International.

Stevens, J. (2001). *Access to Justice in Sub-Saharan Africa: The Role of Traditional and Informal Justice Systems.* New Models of Accessible Justice and Penal Reform. London: Penal Reform International.

Stewart, J. (2008). Intersecting Grounds of (Dis)advantage: The Socioeconomic Position of Women Subject to Customary Law – A Southern African Perspective. In O. C. Ruppel (Ed.), *Women and Custom in Namibia: Cultural Practice Versus Gender Equality?* Windhoek: Macmillan Education Namibia.

Stringer, R. (2014). *Knowing Victims.* London: Routledge.

Sylvain. (2001). Bushmen, Boers and Baasskap: Patriarchy and Paternalism on Afrikaner Farms in the Omaheke Region, Namibia. *Journal of Southern African Studies, 27*(4), 717–737.

Tamale, S. (2008). The Right to Culture and the Culture of Rights: A Critical Perspective on Women's Sexual Rights in Africa. *Feminist Legal Studies, 16*(1), 47–69.

Tersbøl, B. P. (2006). 'I Just Ended Up Here, No Job and No Health…' – Men's Outlook on Life in the Context of Economic Hardship and HIV/AIDS in Namibia. *SAHARA-J: Journal of Social Aspects of HIV/AIDS, 3*(1), 403–416.

Tibinyane, N. (2014). Misa Namibia and Coalition of NGOs Work with Namibian Youth to Tackle Gender Based Violence. Retrieved November 6, 2018, from http://misa.org/media-centre/press-releases/misa-namibia-and-coalition-of-ngos-work-with-namibian-youth-to-tackle-gender-based-violence/.

Ubink, J. M. (2011). Gender Equality on the Horizon: The Case of Uukwambi Tradtional Authority, Northern Namibia. In E. Harper (Ed.), *Working with Customary Justice Systems: Post-Conflict and Fragile States.* Rome: International Development Law Organization.

Ubink, J. M. (2018). Customary Legal Empowerment in Namibia and Ghana? Lessons About Access. *Power and Participation in Non-state Justice Systems. Development and Change, 49*(4), 1–21.

UNAIDS. (2004). 2004 Report on the Global AIDS Pandemic: 4th Global Report. Retrieved October 4, 2018, from http://files.unaids.org/en/media/unaids/contentassets/documents/unaidspublication/2004/GAR2004_en.pdf.

UNAIDS. (2017). Namibia Country Fact Sheet 2017. Retrieved October 4, 2018, from http://www.unaids.org/en/regionscountries/countries/namibia.

United Nations General Assesmbly. (1993). Declaration on the Elimination of Violence Against Women, 20 December 1993, A/RES/48/104.

University of Namibia. (2018). Enrolment by Academic Year and Gender 1992–2018. Retrieved October 10, 2018, from http://www.unam.edu.na/about-unam/statistics.

Van Rooy, G., & Mufune, P. (2013). Psycho-social Characteristics of Male Perpetrators of Intimate Partner Violence in Namibia. *Acta Criminologica: Southern African Journal of Criminology, 26*(2), 1–14.

Visser, W., & Ruppel-Schlichting, K. (2008). Women and Custom in Namibia – The Legal Setting. In O. C. Ruppel (Ed.), *Women and Custom in Namibia: Cultural Practice Versus Gender Equality?* Windhoek: Macmillan Education Namibia.

World Bank. (2016). Namibia: Poverty Alleviation with Sustainable Growth. Retrieved October 4, 2018, from http://web.worldbank.org/WBSITE/EXTERNAL/TOPICS/EXTPOVERTY/EXTPA/0,,contentMDK:2020458 3~menuPK:435735~pagePK:148956~piPK:216618~theSit ePK:430367,00.html.

World Health Organisation. (2013). *Global and Regional Estimates of Violence Against Women: Prevalence and Health Effects of Intimate Partner Violence and Non-partner Sexual Violence*. Geneva: World Health Organisation, London School of Hygiene and Tropical Medicine and South African Medical Research Council.

Zehr, H. (2004). Commentary: Restorative Justice: Beyond Victim-Offender Mediation. *Conflict Resolution Quarterly, 22*(1, 2), 305–315.

5

Bereaved Family Activism

Elizabeth A. Cook

Introduction

In the aftermath of lethal violence, victims are confronted with a conflict of uncertainties and demands placed upon them by communities, criminal justice agencies and wider society. As Gadd (2015: 1032) writes, 'when people are seriously harmed or murdered, it is often difficult to discern where the violence ends and the aftermath begins'. For victims, responses to violence emerge in efforts to rebuild relationships, restore meaning, and to 'be heard', 'even if it threatens to break the order of the known world for those who listen', as well as responses that can stifle recovery (Stauffer 2015: 80). While some argue that the retelling of these experiences threatens to incite further violence, the practice of sharing these stories out of isolation can also encourage victims to make sense of lethal violence, reclaim control, and gain recognition from a wider community.

With the rise of mass media culture and a relentless stream of images of violence, the private grief of victims has become subject to commodification and public consumption (McEvoy and Jamieson 2007;

E. A. Cook (✉)
Centre for Criminology, Faculty of Law, University of Oxford, Oxford, UK
e-mail: elizabeth.cook@law.ox.ac.uk

© The Author(s) 2020
J. Tapley, P. Davies (eds.), *Victimology*,
https://doi.org/10.1007/978-3-030-42288-2_5

Evans and Giroux 2015; O'Leary 2018). Critical and, more recently, cultural victimologists have noted the importance of an increasingly influential contemporary media culture in publicising victims' experiences and there is now an increased recognition of the varied ways that lethal violence can impact upon not only individuals, but also families, communities, and even cultures. The effects of lethal violence are shared across different collectives by virtue of identity, kinship, and social bonds, while spectators are encouraged to imagine and invest in the experience of others from a safe bystander distance. Amid this contemporary culture of public suffering, victims' voices have been formalised and professionalised through the emergence of victims' movements and have become the concern of politicians, policy makers, and the public. A number of collectives now make normative claims on behalf of the wider collective concerning the nature of victim needs and how the criminal justice system should respond.

This chapter explores the above through the phenomenon of bereaved family activism: namely, the attempts by bereaved families to manage and address their experiences of violent death through public campaigns. The chapter is organised in three parts. First, the growing importance of victims' voices in public debate and policy making is considered before relating this more widely to how victims' voices feature in the wider landscape of criminal justice. Second, bereaved family activism is introduced within this wider context and used to highlight the efforts of bereaved families in confronting injustices, raising awareness, and promoting acknowledgement of harms that may have previously gone unheard. A number of examples from a national context are discussed to illustrate the varied shapes and forms that bereaved family activism takes. The third part of this chapter draws upon interviews and participant observation conducted by the author during doctoral research to investigate the efforts of one such campaign, *Mothers Against Violence*: an anti-violence charity that emerged in response to an intense period of gun violence and ensuing community outcry nearly two decades ago. The chapter concludes by highlighting the importance of victims' voices in creating communities of solidarity and gaining acknowledgement of injustices and considering what can be learned from, as Shute (2016: 174) asks, a 'victimological engagement with those that speak for the dead'.

The Rise of Victim Movements and Victims' Voices

As a number of scholars have noted, victims in both national and international criminal justice have, until recently, been somewhat absent (Zedner 2002; Walklate 2006; Karstedt 2010). Historically, victims have held little substantive legal or procedural rights in the criminal justice system and the full effects of victimisation have been overlooked. If victims were acknowledged in any way besides as a 'trigger' for State justice, they were pitted as individuals desperately seeking revenge (Christie 1977). Victims, therefore, were seen as a 'hazard' to the solutions that formal justice offered and, as Rock (2002: 4) notes, 'if they did appear, they were spoken about or spoken for but they were rarely allowed to speak, and they acquired a correspondingly fantastic appearance'. Victims in many cases were relegated to being purely instrumental and secondary to the criminal justice system, merely instigating the claims necessary for the State to proceed. An unusual paradox arose here, as both Shapland (1984) and Christie (1977) noted. While cases in the criminal justice system largely relied on the reports and experiences of victims, much early research highlighted a disregard within the criminal justice system for victims' needs and a lack of support and sympathetic treatment of victims in the aftermath of violence. As Christie (1977: 3) explains in his oft-cited essay *Conflict as Property*:

> ...the one party that is represented by the state, namely the victim, is so thoroughly represented that she or he for most of the proceedings is pushed completely out of the arena, reduced to the triggerer-off of the whole thing. She or he is a sort of double loser; first, vis-a-vis the offender, but secondly and often in a more crippling manner by being denied rights to full participation in what might have been one of the more important ritual encounters in life. The victim has lost the case to the state.

However, as first submitted in Garland's (2001: 11) landmark study of *The Culture of Control*, the criminal justice system has witnessed a 'return of the victim'. Victims' issues have moved out of the shadows and towards the centre stage in part due to the efforts of a politically active victims' movement. During the 1960s and 1970s, the plight of crime victims in the United States became the centre of a punitive criminal justice policy and law-and-order regime, sparking the formalisation of the victim movement. The movement has quickly expanded to accommodate a range of different political interests, from feminists to right wing law-and-order advocates (Elias 1993; Rentschler 2011; Hoyle 2012; Goodey 2005: 102). Commenting on the participation of crime victims in the criminal justice system, Barker (2007) argued that the moral claims of victims are in various ways shaped and constrained by the political contexts and systems in which they develop. A number of factors such as a history of civic engagement, strong civilian participation, coercive public policies, and social polarisation characterise the nature of victims' movements as retributive or restorative. Barker (2007: 623) argues, there is a 'politics of pain' within each system which influences the expressions of anger, compassion, and empathy.

A number of commentators have stressed their concerns over the risk of political exploitation of victims' rights in the climate of punitive populism and against the backdrop of neoliberalism, where concern for victims has become the product of economic rationales (Duggan and Heap 2014: 2; Christie 2010; Harper and Treadwell 2013). With the acceleration of victim advocacy and policy, the politicised nature of victimhood remains topical. Speaking first on the 'politicisation of the victim', Miers (1978: 51) described this as a process in which 'victims of crimes of violence were converted into an identifiable and coherent group, with evident political potential'. According to Garland (2001) and others (Elias 1993; Christie 2010; Duggan and Heap 2014; Lawther 2015), this politicisation of victimhood persists in a number of contexts raising concerns of ownership, representation, and voice when public victims speak on behalf of others and have taken on a 'much more representative character' (Garland 2001: 11).

Departing from earlier notions of the victim as marginal and suspect, criminal justice policy has instead sought to formalise victims' voices through victim impact statements, national charities, and victim champions (McGarry and Walklate 2015). Victim movements serve endless personal and political purposes for those involved. Each represents a diversity of voices, needs, and strategies, emerging at one historical and cultural moment in time, in response to a particular form of violence and, as

Pemberton (2009) argues, is perhaps characterised by diversity rather than uniformity. Despite these caveats, victim movements have come to represent valuable opportunities for social justice advocacy, state accountability, and a renewed confidence in policy making with victims deploying personal experiences to engage political responses. Sharing experiences often by virtue of collective identity, relationships, and intimate ties of kinship, bereaved families emerge at the forefront of these public responses in the aftermath of violence.

Bereaved Family Activism After Violent Death

Death, dying, and bereavement are widespread and common experiences that all of us in our lifetimes will be challenged and unsettled by in some form. However, violent death raises a distinctive set of experiences for the bereaved and creates a complicated blend of the distress of loss and the overwhelming and disruptive experience of trauma. The effects of lethal violence reverberate widely, manifesting in the consequences of physical death, emotional injury, and the harms experienced through communal ties. Spalek (2006: 88) draws upon the notion of 'spirit injury' to highlight the experiences of women in black and ethnic minority communities and the effects of victimisation that resonate in self-identity and shared experiences. Violent death runs the risk of complicating the already severe emotional and social consequences of bereavement, compounding the problems of powerlessness, vulnerability, and feelings of loss of control that bereaved families experience. However, the rise of victim movements speaks to the potential of bereaved families in confronting and harnessing their experiences for the purpose of gaining acknowledgement of injustices and raising awareness. Describing the attempts by bereaved families to confront their experiences of lethal violence, Shute (2016: 173) first proposed the term 'bereaved family activism' to explain:

> the effects of violent bereavement on family members—defined as any self-identifying relation by blood or partnership—and attempts, among the normal range of responses, to understand the organised attempts of some to address publicly aspects of their experience.

Shute's (2016: 174) use of the term appeared in the context of organised mass violence and reflections on what could be learned from a 'victimological engagement with those who search and speak for the dead'. Drawing upon the efforts of the Mothers of Plaza de Mayo in Buenos Aires in Argentina and the Mothers of Srebrenica in Bosnia-Herzegovina, Shute (2016) argued that, while violent death under any circumstance is potentially debilitating, the nature of organised mass violence places demands upon bereaved families which are different to those bereaved during peacetime violence. Families bereaved by mass violence must also contend with the absence of a body to grieve. For example, in Argentina, victims were 'disappeared' in clandestine executions and, in Bosnia-Herzegovina, victims' remains were buried and scattered across different grave sites. However, bereaved families in both contexts became driving forces in recovering and identifying victims' remains and driving commemorative rituals, shaping international criminal justice responses and prompting acknowledgement from states in denial (Cohen 2001). Depending upon the context, victim movements must contend with different barriers to recognition.

Bereaved family activism is a phenomenon which draws upon the collective defiance of a strong kinship, imagined or otherwise, to confront and sometimes reverse the effects of lethal violence. Such effects are typically rooted in private experiences yet have increasingly become the subject of shared curiosity and commodified for the purpose of public consumption through mainstream media. O'Leary (2018) explores this in her analysis of stigma, community identity, and the Dunblane school shooting and warned against the effects of the conflation between private and public grief. On 13 March 1996, Thomas Hamilton shot and killed 16 children and one teacher at a Dunblane Primary School near Stirling in Scotland, UK. The massacre prompted an outcry of collective grief across the country and an inquiry into gun control policies, which have since been reformed. Based on qualitative interviews with members of the wider community, O'Leary (2018) argues that acts of extreme violence, such as those that occurred in Dunblane, become subject to amplification and commodification by the media in the aftermath. Dunblane became known as a 'tragic town', stigmatised by the acts of extreme violence that had unfolded there and commodified further for the public to participate in and respond to.

This conflation between public and private grief has also been the focus of much cultural victimological work, which has recognised the varied ways that the experience of lethal violence can be shared across society. This 'increasingly visual nature of social life', as McGarry and Walklate (2015: 17–18) describe, 'constantly and consistently places us beside the victim, encouraging us to feel what they feel'. To provide another example, consider 'Columbine'. In the United States on 20 April 1999, at Columbine High School in Littleton, Colorado, 2 students armed with guns entered the school and shot 12 students and 1 teacher dead. The shooting prompted a similar response of public mourning to that in Dunblane. In the aftermath of the shooting, a collection of commemorative rituals to remember the victims emerged, including memorial websites, building shrines at the abandoned cars of victims and sites of remembrance, which prompted people across the country to join in a 'community of bereavement' (see Fast 2003). Such communities provide a sense of belonging where violence has brought change and uncertainty. As Greer (2004: 117) points out when discussing crime, media, and the community response to high-profile child sexual murders:

> By vicariously participating in the suffering of those affected or afflicted by child sexual murders—by sorrowing with their loss, and sharing in the anger that loss may invoke—people garner a sense of community, a sense of membership and belonging, in a world where the notion of community and community membership has changed fundamentally.

Violent death is often an intimate and vivid experience, suffered privately and out of sight of others. Greer (2004) continues to explain how such experiences can also become part of a public consciousness when shared for various reasons with a wider collective of activists, politicians, judges, juries, journalists, researchers, and virtual and 'imagined communities' when such deaths are high profile. For example, the deaths of Milly Dowler, a 13-year-old girl who was abducted and murdered in 2002 by Levi Bellfield in Surrey, and Holly Wells and Jessica Chapman, two 10-year-old girls murdered by Ian Huntley in Soham in the same year, provoked outrage and public mourning across the United Kingdom. Condolences poured in from across the country as both cases became the focus of sustained media campaigns and triggered wider discussions about the safety of children in the community. Personal experiences of harm and injustice are therefore inevitably public and political issues—as Carol Hanisch's (1970) much-used feminist phrase alludes to, 'the personal is political'. However, this erosion between private and public also allows victims' stories to engage a wider community of concerned onlookers and to raise awareness of suffering to public audiences. Bereaved family activism provides an opportunity to build dialogue and create communities of empathy and solidarity for those bereaved through violent death. The following section illustrates this phenomenon through a number of notable examples.

Contemporary Examples of Bereaved Family Activism

Bereaved family activism has emerged in response to a broad spectrum of harm, injustice, and violence in different contexts and for different reasons. Bereaved families may become involved to share their experiences; to provide a service they felt they should have had access to; to voice concerns that they believe others need to hear; to share information; or to make sense and give meaning to their experiences. Perhaps one of the most influential bereaved family activists in criminal justice policy and practice in the United Kingdom is Doreen Lawrence, the mother of teenager Stephen Lawrence who was murdered in a racially motivated attack in East London in April 1993. Writing 13 years after the death of her son, Doreen Lawrence (2006) begins the preface for her book, *And Still I Rise*:

> Two lives ended one chilly April night thirteen years ago. One was the life of my eldest son. You don't have to be a mother to understand what that means, but perhaps only the parents of children can truly imagine what the loss is like…The second life that ended was the life I thought was mine. Since my son Stephen was killed with such arrogance and contempt I've had a different life, one that I can hardly recognise as my own.

In the aftermath of the murder, the anguish of Doreen has become subject to public display and expression through political exchanges and media interest. Over the past quarter century, she has campaigned against institutional failures, racial injustices, and police violence and has become a public icon in the long-standing fight for racial equality. Her role in campaigning for victims of racist crimes during this time has established investigations, charitable trusts, and public inquiries changing the course of criminal justice policy. Doreen Lawrence has sustained a lengthy and compelling campaign against the structural injustices of the state and has prompted a host of policy changes (see Rock 2004). Nearly three decades after her son's death Doreen Lawrence now sits as Life Peer in the House of Lords and has been awarded an OBE for her services to the community, continuing her public campaign against racism, and hate crimes. The prolonged campaign launched by Lawrence prompted a change in policy debates on police reform and responses to racially motivated crimes and continues today to raise awareness of continuing issues of social injustice.

Strong matriarchal figures have often emerged as the public figure-heads of these movements, representing symbols of peace, dignity, and resilience in the aftermath of violence, speaking to the often gendered nature of these movements. A similar observation can be made of the Hillsborough Families, where strong matriarchal figures such as Margaret Aspinall and the late Anne Williams have been driving forces in fighting for truth and justice in the aftermath of the Hillsborough Tragedy. On 15 April 1989, Liverpool Football Club were scheduled to play Nottingham Forest at Sheffield Wednesday's Hillsborough Stadium in the North West of England. That day, 96 supporters of Liverpool Football Club died at Hillsborough Stadium in a human crush. The public grief that materialised following the tragedy emerged through a sense of shared place and 'localized feeling of suffering, the collective identity of the football club and its supporters, and the shared experience of traumatic loss (Hughson and Spaaij 2011: 284; Brennan 2017). Shortly after the event, the Hillsborough Family Support Group and Hillsborough Justice Campaign emerged representing the interests of the bereaved families (see Scraton 2016). Various lines of scrutiny of the Hillsborough Tragedy were pursued in the following years, taking the form of civil litigations, public inquests, judicial reviews, independent panel reports, and private prosecutions. Such sustained scrutiny has been driven unreservedly by the bereaved families and survivors and, as Brennan (2017) argues, is perhaps intimately linked with the resolution of and recovery from suffering. Sudden death is unexpected and disturbs the assumption that we have basic protections and safety in the world. However, it can be further complicated by the series of investigations, trials, and extensive media coverage that follows in the aftermath.

The stories of families bereaved in the Grenfell Tower disaster represent another example of the importance of bereaved family activism in the aftermath of violence. On 14 June 2017, a fire broke out in Grenfell Tower, a 24-storey block of flats located in North Kensington, an area which highlights the stark juxtaposition of the most wealthiest and most impoverished communities, where housing, pay, and health inequalities are at their most severe (see Macleod 2018). The fire spread rapidly from the fourth floor throughout the building leading to the deaths of 72 people and leaving scores more homeless. In the aftermath of the tragedy various concerns surfaced from the residents of Grenfell Tower over its structure and construction in combustible cladding, faulty equipment and lighting, and a lack of fire safety policies. Many demanded charges of corporate manslaughter against the local authority responsible. As Cooper and Whyte (2018) argue, the tragedy at Grenfell highlights the culmination of a stream of ideological policies on austerity, the deregulation of health and safety, and the disenfranchisement of working class voices. Many have been quick to point out the ill-co-ordinated and slow response of government to the bereaved families, commenting on the institutional neglect of authorities and dangerous disregard for the living conditions of particular communities at a time of insecurity and housing precarity (see, e.g., Cooper and Whyte 2018).

As Tombs (2017) describes, for families and survivors of the Grenfell Tower, the fallout of the fire has surfaced in the effects on physical and mental health, traumatic loss, post-traumatic stress disorders, loss of homes, destroyed possessions, and emotional distress. In an effort to manage the harms of this violence, the bereaved have since become engaged in a number of public campaigns with the aim of achieving accountability, remembrance, and, more broadly, to attain safer housing and prevent such a tragedy from happening again. Campaigns such as Grenfell United, Justice4Grenfell, and Grenfell Speak represent just a few of the campaigns that have emerged to support the victims and their families (Grenfell United 2019; see Grenfell Speaks 2019; Justice4Grenfell 2019). Families and survivors have been at the forefront of these campaigns, working to rehome those affected, contributing to an ongoing public inquiry, organising peaceful demonstrations, and establishing symbolic reminders through public commemorations. Bereaved family activism offers a valuable insight into how the interests of particular victims can be communicated to the wider collective and bridge divides between otherwise unfamiliar communities. By organising, sharing stories, and mobilising these issues, these campaigns can communicate personal experiences to engage public responses or, as C. Wright Mills (1959: 8) put it, can turn 'personal troubles' into 'public issues'.

However, the efforts of the bereaved have not always engendered immediate moral and emotional understanding or response from political authorities. Rather, whether such groups are able to elicit such a response seems largely a product of whether these movements are able to identify with, communicate, and conform with conventions of the 'ideal victim' (Christie 1986; Spalek 2006). It would appear that only *certain* victims' stories gain traction in the public arena and eventually come to inform criminal justice policy. As Walklate et al. (2019) and others have explored in their analysis of victim policy and the rise of victim groups, victims' stories can play an important role in influencing public attitudes and political change. Drawing upon a case study of Rosie Batty in Australia, Walklate et al. (2019) discuss the reasons why her story in particular has become so influential in family violence policy in Australia. Rosie Batty is an advocate for victims of domestic violence who, following the murder of her 11-year-old son Luke Batty by her ex-partner, began a campaign to change public perceptions of family violence and to help develop policy responses for prevention and support. Stories, as the authors argue, gain significance depending on the way it is told, who the storyteller is, and the time and place in which it is told. If indeed the experiences of some victims are taken to be representative of others, as Garland (2001; see also Greer 2007) argues, more attention should be paid to which stories we listen to and why.

Other victims of crime, such as families of serious offenders and of those wrongfully convicted, have prompted less public and political interest. Condry (2007) reveals the moral and emotional struggles that relatives of serious offenders are confronted with following discovery of the offence and the role of self-help groups in managing the pains of stigma and shame that relatives are confronted by. As 'victims of the stigma, shock and repercussions of serious offending', families of serious offenders could be seen as 'other victims of crime' (Howarth and Rock 2000; Condry 2007: 278). By working around notions of blamelessness and responsibility, these groups offer a place of refuge and mutual support for otherwise 'stigmatised' experiences of loss. Similar examples can be found in families campaigning against the wrongful conviction of relatives under the joint enterprise law. Campaigns such as JENGbA, Joint Enterprise Not Guilty by Association, are critical vehicles for campaigning for relatives convicted under laws of Joint Enterprise: a controversial but long-standing principle in English law which allows the conviction of associates of the principal offender, or those which were present at the time of the offence, but did not participate. Families of those convicted under joint enterprise aim to address the problematic nature of such policies especially for young black and ethnic minorities.

These campaigns represent the efforts of victims of harm, loss, and wrongdoing and their struggles to publicly organise against these harms speak to the differential value placed upon victims and their stories. A 'hierarchy of victimisation' emerges in this context which places value upon certain victims' stories while disenfranchising the suffering of others (Greer 2007). However, sharing victims' stories through bereaved family activism provides the opportunity to create spaces of support and empathy for those that have suffered similar experiences. As the following section shows, the stories of bereaved family activists can provide sources of motivation, identification, and empathy at times of uncertainty.

The Story of *Mothers Against Violence*

During the 1980s and 1990s, gun and knife crime became the subject of a national public panic and a politicised debate on gangs, race, and the criminalisation of youth. As the largest city in the North West of England, Manchester was branded as the epicentre of these conflicts, with the media and politicians becoming particularly focused on the communities of Moss Side, Hulme, and Longsight. Amid increasing social exclusion of inner-city communities, the late 1990s saw marked increases in gun and knife violence in the area. In August 1999, the community was witness to a series of shootings leading to the deaths of three young men in the space of two weeks. In the following weeks, dozens of concerned mothers gathered to discuss the impact of recent events, share concerns, and agree on a way forward. *Mothers Against Violence* was established shortly after.

Since its emergence, *Mothers Against Violence* has organised marches, public events, school visits, and youth workshops across the city with the aim of promoting awareness of the effects of gun violence. Informal meetings during the early life of the organisation slowly developed into a formal constitution and the group registered as an anti-violence charity that now offers substance misuse referral services, mentoring and counselling, and support for the bereaved. The aims and objectives of *Mothers Against Violence* are, firstly, the promotion of educational and public awareness of gun and knife crime, secondly, to campaign towards the 'eradication of violence' and the relief of the 'effects of violence within the community', and, thirdly, to 'assist young people, men and women, to find meaningful training, employment or work experience' (Mothers Against Violence 2019). This year symbolises two decades of campaigning and support for the community against the effects of gun violence.

Over the past two decades, *Mothers Against Violence* has provided a space for sharing experiences across different communities, finding support in the aftermath of violence and achieving change. By harnessing their experiences of lethal violence, those involved in *Mothers Against Violence* are able to create dialogue, build trust and empathy, and bridge divides across different identities. While the purpose of bereaved family activism varied for those involved, sharing experiences of violent death and harm allows victims to share their stories as sources of motivation, empowerment, and understanding for those with similar experiences. Jane, who lost her brother to gun violence, observes the limitations of empathy from those who do not share a similar experience and the promise of bereaved family activism in the wake of this:

> I think having that sense of belonging with like—I don't want to say like-minded people—but people who have been through it really helps. Because

I think that unless that has happened to you, I don't think you can possibly understand. I think you can empathise. And that's what empathy is, being alongside somebody and being there but that feeling is like something—there's nothing to describe it when that happens to you at all. And being around those that it's happened to and seeing that they're able to move forward and carry on, is so powerful. Honestly, it's so powerful. [emphasis added]

I definitely remember feeling welcome and being part of it and feeling listened to. But I think it was the acknowledgement and even though it's been acknowledged off other people, I think being surrounded by other people who have lost y'know close family members, is so endearing and nurturing.

Jane underlines the empowering effects of sharing stories of suffering with those who have similar experiences and speaks to the importance of such stories as sources of motivation. Becoming involved in *Mothers Against Violence* allowed Jane to invest in and learn from the experiences of others. Violent death creates boundaries of understanding between people, but can perhaps be reconciled by the efforts of bereaved families towards collective defiance. James, who also lost his brother to gun violence, voiced a similar sentiment, emphasising the role of stories in harnessing pain for the purpose of instigating change within the community:

And I think that the lesson for me in this is that you can—when things like this happen to you, because they're so unpredictable, you can't plan for the murder of a relative—but what you can do is use it either for good or for either—I think some people get very angry and very bitter and can sometimes hate life...I think if you do I guess address that internal pain and channel it into something positive you can turn these things around to reach and to become something beautiful.

...because I feel I can help others who are going through this now, who are fearful of their youngsters who are involved might be in gangs. I think, yeah, it's given me a way of being able to use my pain to channel that into something positive so that I can see, I can see the impact of it and then it becomes itself the healing to the loss that I experienced in '99, in 1999 when my brother was murdered.

The emotional, social, and spiritual spaces provided by bereaved family activism allows those involved to draw strength from collective sentiment and dialogue. Gaining acknowledgement and being heard in circumstances which could be otherwise disempowering and isolating allows participants, like James, to find meaning from a 'world that has been thrown into chaos' and to gather 'knowledge that might restore control' (Rock 2004: 414). While the effects of lethal violence can be debilitating and enduring, the stories of June (see below) and James also speak to the opportunity for personal growth, transformation and reflection in the aftermath of violence. Drawing comparisons between her search for answers before *Mothers Against Violence* and her resolve after, June discusses the importance of finding purpose in the aftermath of violence:

> Why's he dead, Lord? You know what I mean—but now I can see the why him. And because of the way I think that he is in a better place and his life was for a purpose, the life that he lived, the 20 years that he lived, was for a purpose and that purpose was being fulfilled by the things that I did do you get what I'm saying?

Not all of those involved in *Mothers Against Violence* have suffered the violent death of a relative. However, those that have, communicated their sharing of experiences in terms of empowerment, change, and growth with bereaved family activism presenting new opportunities for learning different ways of coping and responding to lethal violence. Both James and Jane allude to this when drawing connections between such experiences and their efforts in *Mothers Against Violence*:

> …So, and I still do feel to this day, when I've achieved something that I've achieved it for him, as well as achieved for myself. That was the way I think I internalised things and how I dealt with things that if I could achieve anything and credit it to him then that was my way of dealing with his loss. [James]
>
> For me, it was more of a transformation in a sense, that's all I can say. It was ridiculously difficult for us all, don't get me wrong but I kind of—and I think it's the impact of being around June as well, being around other mums, we kind of got strength and I learnt a different way of dealing with things. [Jane]

Mothers Against Violence also provides an opportunity for keeping connections with lost relatives. James and Jane regain control over their stories as they become catalysts for change rather than stories that stifle and suspend action. Andrea observes the significance of sharing these stories with others and the role that they could play in encouraging solidarity and identification across communities with the same experience:

> I came through that over a period of time but then I realised that if somebody else is going through something like that—the shock, the loss of bereavement, a loved one—then to have someone there on the other end of the phone, someone you can talk to, to share your fears, and concerns with then that's where I wanted to give back. So, I was a survivor and I wanted to help others who was going through. [Andrea]

Mothers Against Violence provides an opportunity for reflection, helping people to realise new qualities and ways of thinking about their experiences. Victims' stories, it seems, can be sources for motivation and empowerment when shared in a space that encourages support, provides platforms for marginalised communities, and inspires a critical dialogue of issues. In this way, stories can become transformative for the communities in which they are heard and prompt others to act where public bodies have failed to.

Conclusion

Since the rise of the victim movement and rebalancing of criminal justice towards victim interests, victims' voices have been increasingly recognised in policy and public debate. Drawing upon a number of different examples, this chapter has sought to demonstrate the significance that stories of suffering can hold in public life and what can be learned from the experiences of bereaved families. Having considered bereaved family activism in this chapter, three lessons can be observed. Firstly, we can witness the influence the victims' movement holds in shaping criminal justice policy and driving forward policy changes, criminal investigations, and public inquiries. Doreen Lawrence is a prominent example of what such activism can achieve and her story shows how particular victims can bridge the 'public political divide' and enter the 'internal policy making world' (Rock 2004: 65). Secondly, engagement with the bereaved offers a keen understanding of how families address harms privately and/or publicly and how the latter might hinder or help the former. Violent death confronts victims with uncertainty and disruption. However, bereaved family activism presents an opportunity to reconcile these experiences and to draw strength and legitimacy from others involved. Thirdly, by paying closer attention to the stories of the bereaved we can come to a critical appreciation of the traction that different victims' stories gain in public life. More attention must be paid to which stories are given public and political sympathy and which are not.

The case study of *Mothers Against Violence* demonstrates the importance of bereaved family activism in providing spaces for support, encouraging identification, and reinforcing solidarity between those with similar experiences of harm and injustice. By harnessing their collective experiences, *Mothers Against Violence* provides a space where relatives bereaved by gun violence can find empathy from those with similar experiences and gather inspiration during times of uncertainty. The practice of sharing these experiential stories brings these personal experiences out of the private and out of the isolated. Such forms of activism can encourage victims to make sense of lethal violence, reclaim control, and gain recognition. The role of bereaved families in raising awareness of unheard harms therefore remains an important one. Victimological engagement with the efforts of bereaved families in the aftermath of violence reveals how personal experiences are able to prompt public recognition and political change.

References

Barker, V. (2007). The Politics of Pain: A Political Institutionalist Analysis of Crime Victims' Moral Protests. *Law and Society Review, 41*(3), 619–664.

Brennan, M. (2017). Closure for the 96? Sudden Death, Traumatic Grief and the New Hillsborough Inquests. In N. Thompson, G. Cox, & R. Stevenson (Eds.), *Handbook of Traumatic Loss: A Guide to Theory and Practice*. London: Routledge.

Christie, N. (1977). Conflict as Property. *British Journal of Criminology*, *17*(1), 1–15.

Christie, N. (1986). The Ideal Victim. In I. Fattah (Ed.), *From Crime Policy to Victim Policy*. London: The Macmillan Press.

Christie, N. (2010). Victim Movements at a Crossroad. *Punishment & Society*, *12*(2), 115–122.

Cohen, S. (2001). *States of Denial: Knowing About Atrocities and Suffering*. Cambridge: Polity Press.

Condry, R. (2007). *Families Shamed: The Consequences of Crime for Relatives of Serious Offenders*. Cullompton: Willan Publishing.

Cooper, V., & Whyte, D. (2018). Grenfell, Austerity, and Institutional Violence. *Sociological Research Online, 00*(0), 1–18. https://journals.sagepub.com/doi/pdf/10.1177/1360780418800066.

Duggan, M., & Heap, V. (2014). *Administrating Victimization: The Politics of Anti-Social Behaviour and Hate Crime Policy*. Basingstoke: Palgrave Macmillan.

Elias, R. (1993). *Victims Still: The Political Manipulation of Crime Victims*. London: Sage Publications.

Evans, B., & Giroux, H. (2015). *Disposable Futures: The Seduction of Violence in the Age of Spectacle*. San Francisco: City Light.

Fast, J. (2003). After Columbine: How People Mourn Sudden Death. *Social Work, 48*(4), 484–491.

Gadd, D. (2015). In the Aftermath of Violence: What Constitutes a Responsive Response? *British Journal of Criminology, 55*, 1031–1039.

Garland, D. (2001). *The Culture of Control: Crime and Social Order in Contemporary Society*. Oxford: Oxford University Press.

Goodey, J. (2005). *Victims and Victimology*. London: Pearson.

Greer, C. (2004). Crime, Media and Community: Grief and Virtual Engagement in Late Modernity. In J. Ferrell et al. (Eds.), *Cultural Criminology Unleashed*. London: GlassHouse Press.

Greer, C. (2007). News Media, Victims and Crime. In P. Davies, P. Francis, & C. Greer (Eds.), *Victims, Crime and Society*. London: Sage Publications.

Grenfell Speaks. (2019). Grenfell Speaks. Retrieved January 11, 2019, from http://www.grenfellspeaks.com/.

Grenfell United. (2019). About Grenfell United. Retrieved January 11, 2019, from https://www.grenfellunited.org/.

Hanisch, C. (1970). The Personal Is Political. In S. Firestone & A. Koedt (Eds.), *First Published in Notes from the Second Year: Women's Liberation*. New York: Radical Feminists.

Harper, C., & Treadwell, J. (2013). Counterblast: Punitive Payne, Justice Campaigns, and Popular Punitivism – Where Next for 'Public Criminology?'. *The Howard Journal of Criminal Justice, 52*(2), 216–222.

Howarth, G., & Rock, P. (2000). Aftermath and the Construction of Victimisation: "The Other Victims of Crime". *The Howard Journal of Criminal Justice, 39*(1), 58–77.

Hoyle, C. (2012). Victims, the Criminal Process, and Restorative Justice. In R. Morgan, M. Maguire, & R. Reiner (Eds.), *The Oxford Handbook of Criminology*. Oxford: Oxford University Press.

Hughson, J., & Spaaij, R. (2011). "You Are Always on Our Mind": The Hillsborough Tragedy as Cultural Trauma. *Acta Sociologica, 54*(3), 283–295.

Justice4Grenfell. (2019). Objectives. Retrieved January 11, 2019, from https://justice4grenfell.org/objectives/.

Karstedt, S. (2010). From Absence to Presence, From Silence to Voice: Victims in International and Transitional Justice Since the Nuremberg Trials. *International Review of Victimology, 17*(1), 9–30.

Lawrence, D. (2006). *And Still I Rise: Seeking justice for Stephen*. London: Faber & Faber.

Lawther, C. (2015). The Construction and Politicisation of Victimhood. In O. Lynch & J. Argomaniz (Eds.), *Victims of Terrorism: A Comparative and Interdisciplinary Study*. London: Routledge.

Macleod, G. (2018). The Grenfell Tower Atrocity. *City, 22*(4), 460–489.

McEvoy, K., & Jamieson, R. (2007). Conflict, Suffering and the Promise of Human Rights. In D. Downes et al. (Eds.), *Crime, Social Control and Human Rights: From Moral Panics to States of Denial – Essays in Honour of Stanley Cohen*. Cullompton: Willan Publishing.

McGarry, R., & Walklate, S. L. (2015). *Victims: Trauma, Testimony and Justice*. London: Routledge.

Miers, D. (1978). *Responses to Victimisation: A Comparative Study of Compensation for Criminal Violence in Great Britain and Ontari*. Abingdon: Professional Books.

Mothers Against Violence. (2019). Aims & Objectives. Retrieved March 13, 2019, from http://mavuk.org/about/what-we-do/.

O'Leary, N. (2018). Public–Private Tragedy: Stigma, Victimization and Community Identity. *International Review of Victimology, 24*(2), 165–181.

Pemberton, A. (2009). Victim Movements: From Diversified Needs to Varying Criminal Justice Agendas. *Acta Criminologica, 22*(3), 1–23.

Rentschler, C. (2011). *Second Wounds: Victims' Rights and the Media in the U.S.* London: Duke University Press.

Rock, P. (2002). On Becoming a Victim. In C. Hoyle & R. Young (Eds.), *New Visions of Crime Victims*. Oxford: Hart Publishing.

Rock, P. (2004). *Constructing Victims' Rights: The Home Office, New Labour, and Victims*. Oxford: Oxford University Press.

Scraton, P. (2016). *Hillsborough: The Truth*. Edinburgh: Mainstream Publishing Projects.

Shapland, J. (1984). Victims, the Criminal Justice System and Compensation. *The British Journal of Criminology, 24*(2), 131–149.

Shute, J. (2016). Bereaved Family Activism in Contexts of Organised Mass Violence. In S. Walklate & D. Spencer (Eds.), *Reconceptualizing Critical Victimology: Interventions and Possibilities*. Lanham, MD: Lexington Books.

Spalek, B. (2006). *Crime Victims: Theory, Policy and Practice*. Basingstoke: Palgrave Macmillan.

Stauffer, J. (2015). *Ethical Loneliness*. New York: Columbia University Press.

Tombs, S. (2017). Grenfell: Unfolding Dimensions of Harm. *Brave New Europe*. Retrieved from https://braveneweurope.com/steve-tombs-grenfell-unfolding-dimensions-of-harm.

Walklate, S. (2006). *Imagining the Victim of Crime*. Maidenhead: Open University Press.

Walklate, S., Maher, J., McCulloch, J., Fitz-Gibbon, K., & Beavis, K. (2019). Victims Stories and Victim Policy. Is there a Case for a Narrative Victimology? *Crime, Media, Culture, 15*(2), 199–215. Sage Publications, Ltd.

Wright Mills, C. (1959). *The Sociological Imagination*. Oxford: Oxford University Press.

Zedner, L. (2002). Victims. In M. Maguire, R. Morgan, & R. Reiner (Eds.), *The Oxford Handbook of Criminology*. Oxford: Oxford University Press.

6

Feminist Framings of Victim Advocacy in Criminal Justice Contexts

Michele Burman and Oona Brooks-Hay

Introduction

Gender-based violence has profound and far-reaching effects on those who directly experience it, as well as on those around them. Feelings of fear, subjection and powerlessness resulting from victimisation due to rape or domestic abuse, render many women in need of robust emotional support and practical advice, as well as a sympathetic and informed criminal justice response. UK governments have prioritised responses to gender-based violence in recent years and there has been the implementation of legislative, policy and practice reforms aimed at addressing the well-documented shortcomings of the criminal justice approach. Yet

M. Burman (✉)
Scottish Centre for Crime and Justice Research (SCCJR), School of Social and Political Sciences, University of Glasgow, Glasgow, Scotland
e-mail: Michele.Burman@glasgow.ac.uk

O. Brooks-Hay
Scottish Centre for Crime and Justice Research (SCCJR), University of Glasgow, Glasgow, Scotland
e-mail: Oona.Brooks@glasgow.ac.uk

© The Author(s) 2020
J. Tapley, P. Davies (eds.), *Victimology*,
https://doi.org/10.1007/978-3-030-42288-2_6

responses to gender-based violence are often severely inadequate (Sullivan 2012; Taylor-Dunn 2016; Kelly 2005; Bybee and Sullivan 2002), and there remain strong concerns that those who report rape and/or domestic abuse are let down by a system which fails to fully comprehend the far-reaching consequences of the complex interaction between their experiences of abuse and their encounters with the criminal justice process (Brooks and Burman 2017; Robinson 2009b). Within an adversarial context, victim-survivors find themselves in the midst, but not in control of, what can be a protracted and bewildering process, whilst managing the demands of their everyday life and a range of other issues resulting from the abuse (e.g. health, housing and personal safety).

A fundamental concern about the inadequacy of the criminal justice response is the 'secondary victimisation' experienced by victim-survivors arising as a result of the investigative, prosecutorial and court room processes that can exacerbate the primary trauma. Ample research shows that police handling of rape can re-victimise those who report it, and is often referred to as 'the second assault' (Robinson and Hudson 2011; Campbell and Raja 1999). Prosecutorial processes are beset with uncertainties and long delays in the progression of cases, with poor levels of communication about trial processes and the stage of case progression such that victim-survivors feel unprepared for what might happen in court (HM Inspectorate of Prosecution 2017). Throughout the investigation, victim-survivors have to recount the details of their experience and potentially encounter challenging questions about their conduct and lifestyle (Burman 2009; Brooks-Hay et al. 2015, 2018). Many victim-survivors are understandably reluctant to engage, and there are high levels of 'drop-out' or case attrition throughout the criminal justice process (Daly and Bouhours 2010; Lovett and Kelly 2009). For cases that do progress, conviction rates remain low (Hohl and Stanko 2015; Kelly et al. 2005).

These concerns provide both the background and the impetus for the development of advocacy services to assist and empower victim-survivors in their interactions with criminal justice, health and other agencies (Bybee and Sullivan 2002; Daly 2011). Against a background of advocacy service proliferation, however, there are important questions concerning where services are physically located and how they are delivered, along with their level of (financial, operational) autonomy. The development of advocacy services linked to or located within statutory agencies, for example, has attracted criticism on the basis that this may represent an erosion of their founding feminist ideals and a loss of independence (Nichols 2014).

In this chapter, we trace the evolution of contemporary advocacy service provision and its history of use in feminist activism, and by so doing highlight the different forms it may take. We review the available evidence on the impact of advocacy on victim-survivors of domestic abuse and of rape, in terms of their engagement with the criminal justice system but also in terms of their wider lives beyond the criminal justice experience. Using findings from research within the UK and elsewhere as a lens, we highlight the tensions that may accompany the delivery of advocacy within sites of criminal justice. We dwell in particular on the challenges of working within and across agencies with different understandings of the purpose of advocacy. Finally, we point to the risk of appropriation of purpose and potential for erosion of feminist principles, whilst highlighting the advantages of specialised forms of independent victim advocacy for achieving social justice.

The Evolution of Victim Advocacy: From Feminist Framings to Multi-Agency Partnership

First initiated as part of grassroots feminist work within women's refuges, individual victim advocacy has been used within specialist violence against women organisations since the late 1960s, and continued throughout the 1970s (Goodman and Epstein 2008). Practical and emotional support for women experiencing domestic violence was provided in refuges by women, many of whom had themselves previously been in abusive relationships (Saathoff and Stoffel 1999; Schechter 1982; Nichols 2013). Whilst feminist understandings of domestic abuse as rooted in patriarchy guided the development of early forms of victim advocacy (Nichols 2011, 2013), some differences can be discerned in principles and practice. Early feminist advocates worked towards collaborative survivor-defined practices because they held hierarchal practices to be patriarchal and oppressive to women (Rodriguez 1988; Srinivasan and Davis 1991). This perspective maintained that hierarchal interactions between advocates and survivors put abused women in a position of reduced power, mimicking the same power dynamics that are conducive to domestic abuse (Saathoff and Stoffel 1999). Survivor-defined advocacy focused on the empowerment of women by collaboratively facilitating decision-making, economic empowerment and social independence (Rodriguez 1988; Saathoff and Stoffel 1999; Srinivasan and Davis 1991). These approaches allow and encourage women to make their own decisions based on individual goals, situations, and needs with the help and support of advocates (Goodman and Epstein 2008; Nichols 2013).

With the increasing recognition of women's social and economic inequality as a structural influence on gender-based violence, women's organisations also took on more overtly political forms of advocacy to gain expanded support services and highlight the problem of domestic and sexual violence to wider public and political attention (Goodman and Epstein 2008). While much of this lobbying work has been undertaken at a local level by women's organisations, feminist activism has developed considerably at national and international levels. By contrast to individual advocacy support models then, some organisations define their advocacy primarily in terms of political activism aimed at strengthening women's rights and/or changing the social structural conditions that contribute to gender inequalities which can in turn sustain gender-based violence (Goodman and Epstein 2008; Saathoff and Stoffel 1999). For example, the feminist network Women Against Violence Europe (WAVE) describe their advocacy work as 'Influencing policy makers to promote, protect and strengthen the human rights of women and children in Europe' (Blank et al. 2014: 4). Forms of political advocacy like that conducted by WAVE are aimed at raising awareness, reforming laws and policy, and influencing decisions within social and political systems and institutions in order to facilitate change.

In the UK, until the 1990s, victim advocacy was predominantly delivered by independent women's organisations, although from this point forward, stand-alone advocacy projects and those embedded within other statutory agencies such as criminal justice and health services began to become more commonplace. Throughout the late 1990s onwards, victim advocacy providers evolved to include more organisations, notably health, social service and criminal justice agencies, with whom they work collaboratively. With the development of multi-agency working across all public sectors (see Davies, Chapter 11), there was growing acknowledgement of the benefits of partnership working. Kelly and Humphreys (2000), in their review of the advocacy work delivered by 'civilian' support workers based in a police station who followed up domestic abuse incidents, highlighted the growing recognition of the need for more integration in response to domestic abuse, operationally and strategically.

In the context of contemporary criminal justice and other agency responses to victim-survivors of gender-based violence, there are differing definitions, understandings and purposes of advocacy, each with distinctive characteristics in relation to the nature of the work undertaken, the location of the advocacy services (Brooks-Hay and Burman 2017), and whether the work is undertaken at an individual, organisational or societal level. Advocates can be located in different places: community-based support projects, police stations, hospitals, A&E departments, Sexual Assault Referral Centres (SARCs), NGOs, specialist domestic abuse courts, and local authority hubs, depending on the aims and intentions of their advocacy service (Hester and Westmarland 2005; Coy and Kelly 2011; Scottish Government 2017; Robinson 2009a). The terms 'community-based' or 'system-based' advocacy are used to differentiate between independent advocates and those employed by statutory law enforcement agencies or who work in close collaboration with them as part of a multi-agency approach (Coy and Kelly 2010; Robinson 2009a, b).

The terminology used to describe those who deliver advocacy in this context is also variable: 'victim advocacy' (Campbell 2006), 'support workers' (Home Office 2005), 'outreach workers' (Home Office 2005), 'advocates' (Bell and Goodman 2001), 'advocacy workers' (Brooks-Hay et al. 2015) 'independent domestic violence advocates' (Robinson 2003), 'independent sexual violence advocates' (Brooks-Hay and Burman 2017) and 'stewards' (Shepard 1999). Within the criminal justice context, models of advocacy providing individual support to victim-survivors describe the role of advocates as providing information and advice, making referrals, explaining options, and accompanying victim-survivors to police stations or medical examinations, and/or providing support during court and post-court processes (Allen et al. 2004; Parkinson 2010). Some years ago, Kelly and Humphreys (2000) emphasised the need for specialised and independent advocacy provision which stretches beyond the delivery of support in relation to the criminal justice process, on the basis that:

> individuals coming from positions of fear and isolation will often require the skills of an advocate to negotiate housing, legal support and benefit entitlements. It is the emphasis on rights and entitlements which distinguishes advocacy from other more familiar concepts like support.

Advocacy work can be further distinguished by its duration which can be 'short-term' and/or 'long-term' (Home Office 2005); it may involve short-term crisis intervention, designed to address immediate risk, support throughout a victim-survivor's engagement with legal and court processes, the promotion of access to justice and rights, or longer-term provision for considerable time thereafter, particularly with regard to sexual violence (Howarth et al. 2009; Robinson 2009a; Coy and Kelly 2011; Brooks-Hay et al. 2018).

In the following sections, we highlight developments in multi-agency working and advocacy provision in relation to domestic abuse and rape in the UK, before discussing the key challenges to feminist-informed advocacy provision in criminal justice contexts.

Domestic Abuse Advocacy Services

Advocacy services for those experiencing domestic abuse are now well-established across the UK. In 2001, the establishment of the Women's Safety Unit in Cardiff, was set up as a 'one stop shop' for victim-survivors of domestic abuse providing individual level advocacy support, information and assistance in relation to health and housing as well as safety planning (Robinson 2003). In the recognition that high-risk victim-survivors require a distinctive form of service provision, it was from here that the idea of a victim focused information-sharing and risk management forum to be attended by all key agencies was formed in order to facilitate an informed assessment of the risk of future harm from perpetrators to those experiencing domestic abuse and their children. The role of Multi-Agency Risk Assessment Conferences (MARAC), the first one of which was established in Cardiff, is to facilitate, monitor and evaluate effective information sharing to enable appropriate actions to be taken to increase public safety. MARACs combine relevant risk information with an assessment of a victim-survivor's needs (Robinson 2003). In recent years, the Independent Domestic Violence Advocate (IDVA) role has become increasingly synonymous with MARACs and the support of 'high risk' victims (Coy and Kelly 2010), as opposed to the original focus of supporting victim-survivors through specialist domestic abuse courts.

In Scotland, MARACs were introduced from 2005; domestic abuse advocacy services developed in tandem with the emergence of the Scottish MARACs and the first domestic abuse advocacy project, ASSIST, was set up to support the pilot specialised domestic abuse court in Glasgow. The evaluation of this court acknowledged the value of the advocacy service, and a subsequent feasibility study recommended that the court, including the advocacy service, should develop across Scotland (Reid-Howie 2007; Scottish Executive 2008).

The introduction of trained IDVAs to provide advice and support to victim-survivors deemed to be at high risk of harm and going through specialist domestic abuse courts ensured the provision of specialist and independent advocacy to those experiencing domestic abuse. The accepted definition of an IDVA service is that it:

> involves the professional provision of advice, information and support to survivors of intimate partner violence living in the community about the range, effectiveness and suitability of options to improve their safety and that of their children. This advice must be based on a thorough understanding and assessment of risk and its management, where possible as part of a multi-agency risk management strategy or MARAC process.[1]

Formalised risk assessment has developed much more in relation to domestic abuse than in other forms of gender-based violence, and safety issues are discussed in the MARAC setting. IDVAs are key players in the

MARAC fora, playing an important role in terms of crisis intervention, carrying out risk assessments and safety planning, and coordinating other services (Howarth et al. 2009; Robinson 2009a). Working within a multi-agency framework, the IDVA's role is to keep the victim-survivor's perspective central to the process (Taylor-Dunn 2016), including representing their views at MARACs (Howarth et al. 2009; Robinson 2009a, b; Coy and Kelly 2011). Their work includes the provision of longer-term solutions, which may include specific actions from the MARAC as well as sanctions available through the criminal and civil courts, housing options and other available services. IDVA safety planning continues regardless of prosecution and ongoing work aims to address longer-term safety, recognising that many victim-survivors feel less safe after the court case when bail conditions may have ended, and statutory agencies are no longer involved (Taylor-Dunn 2016; Howarth et al. 2009; Coy and Kelly 2011). Safety planning is dynamic and updated to take account of any changing circumstances of the victim-survivor and the perpetrator. Importantly, it is a process done 'with' not 'for' the victim (Campbell 2004).

IDVAs, therefore, play a multifaceted role: supporting victim-survivors going through the criminal justice process, whilst also supporting those at high levels of risk through the MARAC process. They liaise with other agencies involved in multi-agency responses to victim-survivors, and are the point of contact for agencies involved with individual women (Howarth et al. 2009; Robinson 2009a, b; Coy and Kelly 2011). They are essentially a 'one stop shop' for information and updates about what other agencies are doing. The role of advocacy workers in a coordinated multi-agency response is operational, but they also work strategically. This may include identifying and challenging poor practice where it exists (Coy and Kelly 2011: 12) and as such they play an important institutional advocacy role. As they negotiate the nexus of criminal justice/housing/social work/welfare systems, advocates are able to form a picture of what is and what is not working; they are able to highlight (and plug) gaps, overcome barriers and ultimately improve system responses and processes (Howarth et al. 2009; Robinson 2009a; Coy and Kelly 2011; Taylor-Dunn 2016). Advocates are therefore integral to a coordinated and effective multi-agency response (Howarth et al. 2009; Robinson 2009a, b; Coy and Kelly 2011).

There is a robust body of research evidence about the operation of advocacy services in relation to domestic abuse (Howarth et al. 2009; Parmar et al. 2005; Sullivan 1991; Taylor-Dunn 2016). Survivors consistently report that advocacy services have improved their safety, well-being and quality of life (Reid-Howie 2007; Coy and Kelly 2011; SafeLives 2016). Further, several studies identify positive changes across a range of outcome indicators for women engaged with IDVA or similar advocacy services. For example, by case closure, the majority of those engaging with IDVAs had experienced a cessation or near cessation of abuse, and reported significant reductions in the occurrence of all forms of abuse (Bybee and Sullivan 2002; Howarth and Robinson 2016; Sullivan 1991). Research by Robinson (2004) found that when high-risk individuals engage with an IDVA, there are clear and measurable improvements in safety, including a reduction in the escalation and severity of abuse, and a reduction or even cessation in repeat incidents of abuse. Many victim-survivors report enhanced feelings of safety and improvements in their emotional health (Hathaway et al. 2008; Howarth et al. 2009; Robinson and Tregidga 2007) and experience lower levels of depression (Allen et al. 2004; Bybee and Sullivan 2002; Sullivan and Bybee 1999). Those who accessed advocacy support reported a higher quality of life; less difficulty with obtaining community resources and social support (Allen et al. 2004; Bybee and Sullivan 2002; Sullivan and Bybee 1999); were more optimistic about their situations; and less likely to be drawn back into abusive relationships (Howarth and Robinson 2016). Taylor-Dunn's (2016) UK study also found that victim-survivors supported by IDVAs are more likely to continue with the criminal justice process.

A key indicator of success is that users of advocacy services became more confident in their knowledge of available services and legal rights and in their dealings with the criminal justice system. In keeping with feminist principles, this constitutes evidence of how advocacy in practice can equip women with awareness of their entitlements. Coy and Kelly (2011) term this 'empowerment through knowledge': providing information and options in order that women can make evidence-based decisions.

Rape and Sexual Violence Advocacy Services

The feminist movement has been instrumental in the development of activism and advocacy in relation to rape and other forms of gender-based violence (Nichols 2013). Specialist violence against women organisations such as Rape Crisis have provided information and advocacy to survivors engaging with the criminal justice system for some time as part of their broader remit in providing support to survivors. However, more formal recognition of advocacy services has been augmented via the development of Independent Sexual Violence Advocate (ISVA) roles in England and Wales and the deployment of dedicated Advocacy Workers within the Rape Crisis Scotland National Advocacy Project. Within the UK, the use of ISVAs and other advocacy roles in relation to rape has grown in recent years. ISVAs are far more prominent in England and Wales where they are located within Sexual Assault Referral Centres (SARCs) or Rape Crisis services to provide a point of contact and coordination of services for victim-survivors. It is noteworthy that dedicated support services such as Rape Crisis Centres and SARCs both provide specialist support, but operate different models of service provision and have different origins. Rape Crisis Centres have grown out of the women's movement and, since the 1970s, have operated as independent voluntary sector organisations offering services, primarily to women who have experienced rape or sexual assault. They may work with police to provide support to those going through the criminal justice system; however, they also have an autonomous role in providing support for victim-survivors who choose not to report to the police. Crucially, they have been at the forefront of raising awareness of sexual violence and influencing the public and statutory response to victim-survivors. This work is underpinned by a feminist analysis of rape and the associated belief that violence against women is a consequence of structural inequality.

Formalised sexual violence advocacy emerged alongside the development of multi-agency approaches to sexual violence. ISVAs were introduced in several areas in England and Wales in the mid-2000s following research into SARCs, which identified that victim-survivors of sexual assault wanted a 'more flexible and practical form of support' in the immediate aftermath of sexual violence, and that support, advocacy and information about the justice process were their priority requirements (Lovett et al. 2004: 74). This stemmed from mounting evidence showing the effectiveness of providing victim advocates within other settings, particularly domestic abuse (Howarth et al. 2009; Parmar et al. 2005; Robinson 2003, 2006; Sullivan 1991; Sullivan and Bybee 1999).

The first advocacy services in relation to rape and serious sexual assault in Scotland were implemented in 2013 with the piloting of the 'Support to Report' (S2R) service in Glasgow (Brooks-Hay et al. 2015). Advocacy services were extended nationally to form the Rape Crisis Scotland National Advocacy Project (NAP), operating from 15 hubs across Scotland following positive feedback from victim-survivors who were supported through the initial pilot services (Brooks-Hay et al. 2015, 2018). Like IDVAs, it is the combination of emotional support and practical assistance that is the hallmark of the sexual violence advocate role; however, the roles are not completely transferable, not least because not all rape and sexual violence occurs within intimate relationships or in domestic settings. ISVAs fill an important gap in service provision (Robinson 2009b; Daly 2011) providing support, information and advice to victim-survivors, helping them to navigate the criminal justice process from the reporting to the police stage, informing them of the importance of forensic DNA retrieval, and liaising with other relevant agencies on their behalf (Smith and Skinner 2017). Victim-survivors of rape access advocacy support in different ways and at different points within the criminal justice process, including while considering reporting to the police, following a police statement, upon hearing that a case would not be proceeding to trial, and on the lead up to court. Advocacy in response to sexual violence can begin as a crisis intervention in the immediate aftermath of an incident, but may also be focused on signposting and support for survivors of historic sexual abuse and may potentially involve a longer engagement with victim-survivors, reflecting more protracted involvement with the legal system experienced by sexual assault victim-survivors (Robinson 2009b; Brooks-Hay et al. 2015).

Part of the rationale behind advocacy services for victim-survivors of rape is that the service will reduce fear and uncertainty about the criminal justice process for victim-survivors, and encourage their participation.

A key component is outreach: advocates respond to third-party referrals, offering their service rather than waiting for the victim-survivor to self-refer. This might include offering the service repeatedly if it is declined or if there is no response at the first approach (Kelly and Humphreys 2000; Howarth et al. 2009; Robinson 2009a; Coy and Kelly 2011). Some services also accept self-referrals, but it is the proactive response to third-party referrals that is seen as a distinctive element of the role. Lovett et al. (2004) found that advocates provide information about the court process, explain what will be expected in terms of giving evidence to police and in court, how to make a victim personal statement, the implications of making a withdrawal statement, and helping to arrange and/or attend pre-court visits. Unsurprisingly, victim-survivors in this study spoke highly about receiving this type of assistance, which made them feel 'less alone' and more empowered; they felt that their ISVA was the one person who could, and did, provide them with the information that they needed about their cases—above and beyond any other practitioners with whom they had come into contact. While not always directly related to the criminal justice process, it has been found that holistic practical and emotional advocacy support for victim-survivors of sexual violence facilitates sustained engagement in the criminal justice process (Brooks-Hay and Burman 2017).

With a few exceptions (e.g. Campbell 2006; Robinson 2009b; Brooks-Hay et al. 2015, 2018), less is known about the efficacy of advocacy support in relation to rape (Daly 2011). However, from the relatively few studies that have been conducted, advocacy support is considered to be effective at reducing secondary trauma (Jordan 2002; Skinner and Taylor 2009), at reducing attrition (or drop-out) and thus increasing conviction rates (Robinson 2009b; Lovett et al. 2004; Sullivan and Bybee 1999). The presence of an advocate is considered both a valuable resource and a comfort by victim-survivors (Maier 2008: 799; Brooks-Hay and Burman 2017).

Given the vagaries and uncertainties reported by those going through the criminal justice system, the provision of accurate information about case progression is considered particularly important, as is the provision of emotional support through an intensely disempowering process.

Victims-survivors in the Scottish studies by Brooks-Hay et al. (2015; 2018) were overwhelmingly positive about the support that they had received, describing it as 'invaluable' and 'life-changing'. They described imbalances in the criminal justice system, reflecting its adversarial nature and the strong perception that it protected the interests of the accused before that of the victim. Advocacy support was, therefore, understood to improve victim-survivors' experiences by providing someone who is independent of any investigative or prosecutorial process and whose sole remit is to protect and represent the interests of the victim-survivor (Brooks-Hay and Burman 2017). The most valued features of advocacy were described as: the extensive range of criminal justice and non-criminal justice support provided; the flexibility, reliability and consistency of support; the provision of information to assist understanding of developments in both individual cases and the criminal justice system more generally; and emotional support provided within an ethos of victim-survivor-led empowerment (Brooks-Hay and Burman 2017). For some, however, improvements in experiences were hampered by the continuing difficulties within the criminal justice process, relating primarily to its adversarial nature, lengthy time scales, delays and uncertainty about proceedings (Brooks-Hay et al. 2018).

Like IDVAs, ISVAs are embedded in multi-agency networks and are also seen as providing 'institutional advocacy' contributing to improved multi-agency partnership work on sexual violence (Lovett et al. 2004). In the Scottish studies, Brooks-Hay et al. (2015; 2018) found that such services facilitated stronger professional relationships and greater exchange of information by statutory agencies which could facilitate smoother and swifter processes, leading to a more effective response. Advocacy was also seen to have improved communication, both locally and nationally, between statutory agencies and advocacy workers, with some clear examples provided of increased communication and greater familiarity between individuals breaking down professional barriers. Successful partnership working is key to the effective operation of advocacy; it facilitates smooth referrals and supports the flow of information about particular cases, which in turn can support investigation and prosecution processes and enhance the experiences of victim-survivors (Brooks-Hay et al. 2015; 2018).

Challenges of Delivering Advocacy

The growing evidence base on advocacy provision is overwhelmingly positive about the benefits it can bring, both in the provision of vital support to individual victim-survivors as they navigate what can be a complex and daunting criminal justice process, and also in relation to delivering benefits through enhancing professional working relationships and productive partnerships across sectors. There is also evidence to suggest that advocacy has a positive effect in supporting engagement with the criminal justice system (Brooks-Hay et al. 2015; 2018). However, there are a number of inter-related challenges of delivering advocacy services in a criminal justice context; namely in the form of debate about the location and independence of services, partnership working, varied understandings of the meaning and legitimacy of advocacy work, and managing demand for services.

Advocacy services delivered at a community level through specialist women's organisations, where advocacy provision is informed by feminist framings of gender-based violence, adhere most closely to the earlier iterations of survivor-led advocacy practised by those working within refuges. A key conclusion from the existing research evidence is that independence in terms of the nature of service delivery and the location of advocates in independent organisations, where victim-survivor's interests are placed at the heart of advocacy services is a major strength that enables engagement with victim-survivors in a way that statutory services have always found difficult, while also allowing them to challenge the responses of statutory services if necessary (Taylor-Dunn 2016; Cook et al. 2004; Hucklesby and Worrall 2007; Robinson 2009a).

In order for advocates to deliver quality and consistent care, they must be supported and cared for through management of caseloads, ongoing supervision and mentoring, training and, very importantly, sustainable funding (Robinson 2009a, b; Howarth et al. 2009; Coy and Kelly 2011; Brooks-Hay et al. 2015, 2018). The delivery and autonomy of advocacy services are considerably influenced by their operational locations and funding arrangements. Robinson (2009a) found that IDVAs are best embedded within community-based projects, as statutory settings could potentially compromise their (perceived or actual) independence through either a loss of identity (the 'IDVA' role being subsumed into the statutory role) and/or a change in practice (prioritising the work of the statutory partner rather than the safety of victims). Similarly, if advocates are located in a police station, for example, this may potentially act as a barrier for some women, specifically those who distrust police and fear that engaging with the service might lock them into criminal procedures with repercussions for their safety (Coy and Kelly 2011). However, regardless of physical location, research concurs that advocates must be independent of 'the system' in order to represent the best interests of victim-survivors. Their independence is critical to the success of the advocacy role and the extent to which victim-survivors and practitioners can trust them (Howarth et al. 2009; Robinson 2009a, b; Coy and Kelly 2011).

Robinson and Hudson (2011) explored the strengths and limitations of two different types of settings that provide specialist support to victim-survivors of sexual violence in the UK: SARCs and voluntary sector organizations such as Rape Crisis. Qualitative data from six case study sites and quantitative data from 35 sexual violence advocacy projects in England and Wales revealed that the type of setting affected the types of referrals received and this, in turn, shaped the services required and thus the nature of the work performed. Consequently, each type of project had different emphases in their workload with which they were particularly well equipped to handle. Each type also had its own unique challenges; for example, while there were notable benefits from delivering support in partnership models, such as SARCs, their affiliation with statutory partners was perceived by some as a disadvantage, especially for those seeking support in relation to historical sexual abuse. On the other hand, those delivering support in voluntary sector projects had to work harder to establish and maintain relationships with other agencies, but their independence was seen to be greater and this was perceived as a strength for gaining access to victim-survivors and maintaining their confidence. The researchers conclude that while there were distinct challenges and benefits associated with service provision in both settings, they should be viewed as complementary approaches.

The two main factors that can influence advocacy service independence are sources of funding and location (Robinson 2009a). Those who work from within specialist women's support organisations, on the whole, enjoy greater levels of autonomy in terms of the nature of the service delivered but are beset with grave uncertainties over the sustainability of funding. An uncertain funding landscape can create significant challenges for the planning of ongoing support for service users and unsurprisingly staff retention and stress can be an issue (See Hall, Chapter 10). Funding sources—such as through 'Big Lottery' or charitable sources—are seen to enable flexibility and independence, whilst government funding, although both needed and welcomed, is viewed as a 'necessary evil' that requires careful management, as it could not only compromise the independence of services, but also change the way they deliver advocacy, and to whom (Robinson 2009a).

Independent service provision, however, is not without its challenges. In relation to domestic abuse work, Coy and Kelly (2011: 12) argue that advocates should be viewed by criminal justice agencies as 'critical allies'. In practice, this is a difficult space for advocates to occupy. On the one hand, they have an important role in challenging inadequate policy and practices of criminal justice agencies on behalf of victim-survivors, while also maintaining smooth relations with those same 'partner' agencies.

Brooks-Hay et al. (2018) describe 'teething issues' following the launch of the Rape Crisis Scotland NAP and cited advocacy worker concerns about 'stepping on toes' and being accepted into local networks. In the early phase of the NAP, local projects encountered mixed responses from other services in terms of their receptiveness to the new service and willingness to share information or make referrals; this was primarily linked to a lack of understanding about the role and remit of the NAP and how it might interface with the work of other agencies. Moreover, some advocates also reported poor recognition of their value and qualifications (e.g. in relation to acting as a supporter in court). The fuzzy nature of advocacy in relation to definition, purpose and scale can be problematic. On the one hand, the lack of a unified definition and understanding of advocacy can present challenges for service delivery and achieving consistency of service. On the other hand, it can be argued that it allows for flexibility to meet needs as they arise. The elasticity can be discerned in the ways in which advocacy services have evolved and proliferated across the women's sector but also in the variations in advocacy provision to respond to different forms of gender-based violence. Perhaps reflecting the broad-ranging nature of advocacy, different understandings of advocacy appear to operate, including between advocates, prosecutors, police and other stakeholders (Brooks-Hay and Burman 2017). These differences are primarily related to the perceived *purpose* of advocacy in terms of whether it supports the needs of the victim-survivor or the needs of the investigative and prosecution process (though these aims are not mutually exclusive). This is likely to have implications for how the advocacy role is understood and communicated to partner agencies, and ultimately victim-survivors.

The provision of flexible and reliable advocacy support also creates particular demands on resources. Specialist women's organisations, within which independent advocacy services sit, are often severely financially constrained and many have received reductions in funding as a result of austerity measures. Against a backdrop of increasing demand, maintaining 24 hours on-call, or even 9–5 advocacy provision and managerial oversight of the service can prove extremely challenging and any additional pull on time can have a knock-on effect on other areas of the organisation's work. Moreover, demand for advocacy provision is exacerbated by the often very lengthy nature of the criminal justice process, which can be in excess of two years in some cases. While victim-survivors may not be receiving intensive advocacy support throughout all of this period, clearly, there are resourcing implications attached to providing 'end-to-end' support through such a lengthy process and advocates are often overstretched due to high demand. In some cases, this has resulted in services becoming primarily telephone based. This is disadvantageous given that victim-survivors value the close contact and proximity of advocacy support delivered by a 'known person' who has a clear and informed understanding of their individual needs (Brooks-Hay and Burman 2017). In other areas, advocacy services have had to set up waiting lists, which is problematic for such a time-sensitive service. Current levels of funding of advocacy services are not adequate, particularly in areas of high demand where case volumes are high or where there may be only one advocacy worker covering large geographical areas. As a result, services are significantly compromised leaving victim-survivors without much-needed support. It is likely that aspects of the service most valued by victim-survivors, such as flexible, reliable and consistent support, will become increasingly difficult to deliver if services continue to be overstretched and under-funded.

Conclusion: Multifaceted Advocacy Work

'Advocacy', then, ranges from representing the interests of individual victim-survivors, providing one-to-one information and advice, help with accommodation, finances, risk assessment and safety planning, linking with health services, the police or other criminal justice agencies, to negotiating on their behalf in a legal setting (criminal and/or civil), acting as their 'eyes' and 'ears', keeping them updated throughout the process, and empowering them to secure their rights in a community or wider political context (Allen et al. 2004; Brooks-Hay and Burman 2017). It can incorporate wider awareness raising through media and campaigns, as well as forms of political lobbying.

As well as providing invaluable support at an individual level, the presence of an advocate within the criminal justice process, within police stations, within examination suites and within prosecutor offices has the potential to impact on agency practices and relations. The role advocates can play in terms of 'institutional advocacy' is therefore significant. Yet there are also challenges in partnership working and in occupying the role of 'critical allies' that require close and constant consideration. Operating within a framework underpinned by feminist principles of empowerment and choice, including the decision not to report may be at odds with criminal justice imperatives. The accomplishments of advocacy can be hampered by the continuing difficulties in the criminal justice response to gender-based violence, so political advocacy is also needed. Separating individual rights and political advocacy is a false distinction; years of feminist activism has demonstrated that one cannot be advanced without the other.

Note

1. www.caada.org.uk.

References

Allen, N. E., Bybee, D. L., & Sullivan, C. M. (2004). Battered Women's Multitude of Needs. *Violence Against Women, 10*, 1015–1035.

Bell, M., & Goodman, L. (2001). Supporting Battered Women Involved with the Court System: An Evaluation of a Law School-Based Advocacy Intervention. *Violence Against Women, 7*, 1377–1404.

Blank, K., Lesur, M., & Logar, R. (2014). *Women Against Violence Europe Report 2014: Specialized Women's Support Services and New Tools for Combating Gender-Based Violence in Europe*. Vienna, Austria: WAVE Network.

Brooks-Hay, O., & Burman, M. (2017). Reporting Rape: Victim Perspectives on Advocacy Support in the Criminal Justice Process. *Criminology and Criminal Justice, 17*(2), 209–225.

Brooks-Hay, O., Burman, M., & Kyle, D. (2015). *Evaluation of Support to Report Pilot Advocacy Service: Summary Report SCCJR Briefing Paper No.1/2015*. Glasgow, UK: Scottish Centre for Crime and Justice Research.

Brooks-Hay, O., Burman, M., Bradley, L., & Kyle, D. (2018). *Evaluation of the Rape Crisis Scotland National Advocacy Project: Final Report*. SCCJR Research Report. Glasgow, UK: Scottish Centre for Crime & Justice Research.

Burman, M. (2009). Evidencing Sexual Assault: Women in the Witness Box. *Probation Journal, 56*(4), 1–20.

Bybee, D. I., & Sullivan, C. M. (2002). The Process Through Which an Advocacy Intervention Resulted in Positive Change for Battered Women Over Time. *American Journal of Community Psychology, 30*, 103–132.

Campbell, J. C. (2004). Helping Women Understand Their Risk. *Journal of Interpersonal Violence, 19*(12), 1464–1477.

Campbell, R. (2006). 'Rape Survivors' Experiences with the Legal and Medical Systems: Do Rape Victim Advocates Make a Difference? *Violence Against Women, 12*(1), 30–45.

Campbell, R., & Raja, S. (1999). Secondary Victimization of Rape Victims: Insights from Mental Health Professionals Who Treat Survivors of Violence. *Violence and Victims, 14*(3), 261–276.

Cook, D., Burton, M., Robinson, A. L., & Vallely, C. (2004). *Evaluation of Specialist Domestic Violence Courts/Fast-Track Systems*. London: Crown Prosecution Service and Department of Constitutional Affairs.

Coy, M., & Kelly. L. (2010). *Islands in the Stream: An Evaluation of Four London Independent Domestic Abuse Advocacy Schemes*. London: London Metropolitan University.

Coy, M., & Kelly, L. (2011). *Islands in the Stream: An Evaluation of Four London Independent Domestic Violence Advocacy Schemes*. London: Child and Woman Abuse Studies Unit, London Metropolitan University.

Daly, K. (2011). *Conventional and Innovative Justice Responses to Sexual Violence*. ACSSA Issues No. 12. Melbourne, VIC: Australian Centre for the Study of Sexual Assault, Australian Government: Australian Institute of Family Studies.

Daly, K., & Bouhours, B. (2010). Rape and Attrition in the Legal Process: A Comparative Analysis of Five Countries. *Crime and Justice, 39*(1), 565–650.

Goodman, L. A., & Epstein, D. (2008). *Listening to Battered Women: A Survivor-Centered Approach to Advocacy, Mental Health, and Justice*. Washington, DC: American Psychological Association.

Hathaway, J. E., Zimmer, B., Willis, G., & Silverman, J. G. (2008). Perceived Changes in Health and Safety Following Participation in a Health Care-Based Domestic Violence Program. *Journal of Midwifery & Women's Health, 53*, 547–555.

Hester, M., & Westmarland, N. (2005). *Tackling Domestic Violence: Effective Interventions and Approaches*. Home Office Research Study No. 290. London: Home Office.

HM Inspectorate of Prosecution in Scotland. (2017). Thematic Review of the Investigation and Prosecution of Sexual Crimes. Edinburgh: Scottish Government Available at https://www.gov.scot/publications/thematic-review-investigation-prosecution-sexual-crimes/

Hohl, K., & Stanko, E. (2015). Complaints of Rape and the Criminal Justice System: Fresh Evidence on the Attrition Problem in England and Wales. *European Journal of Criminology, 12*(3), 324–341.

Home Office. (2005). *Tackling Domestic Violence: Providing Advocacy and Support to Survivors from Black and Minority Ethnic Communities*. Home Office Development and Practice Report 35. London: Home Office.

Howarth, E., & Robinson, A. (2016). Responding Effectively to Women Experiencing Severe Abuse: Identifying Key Components of a British Advocacy Intervention. *Violence Against Women, 22*(1), 41–63.

Howarth, E., Stimpson, L., Barran, D., & Robinson, A. (2009). *Safety in Numbers: A Multi-site Evaluation of IDVA Services*. London: The Henry Smith Charity.

Hucklesby, A., & Worrall, J. (2007). The Voluntary Sector and Prisoners' Resettlement. In L. Hagley-Dickinson & A. Hucklesby (Eds.), *Prisoner Resettlement: Policy and Practice* (pp. 174–198). Cullompton: Willan Publishing.

Jordan J. (2002). 'Will Any Woman Do? Police, Gender and Rape Victims', *Policing: An International Journal of Police Strategies and Management, 25*(2), 314–319.

Kelly, L. (2005). Promising Practices Addressing Sexual Violence, Expert Paper Prepared for the Expert Group Meeting on Violence Against Women: Good Practices in Combating and Eliminating Violence Against Women. UN Division for the Advancement of Women in collaboration with UN Office on Drugs and Crime, 17–20 May, Vienna.

Kelly, L., & Humphreys, C. (2000). *Reducing Domestic Violence? Outreach and Advocacy Approaches.* London: Home Office.

Kelly, L., Lovett, J., & Regan, L. (2005). *A Gap or a Chasm? Attrition in Reported Rape Cases.* Home Office Research Study 293. London: Home Office.

Lovett, J., & Kelly, L. (2009). *Different Systems, Similar Outcomes? Tracking Attrition in Reported Rape Cases Across Europe.* London: CWASU.

Lovett, J., Regan, L., & Kelly, L. (2004). *Sexual Assault Referral Centres: Developing Good Practice and Maximising Potentials.* Home Office Research Study 285. London: Home Office.

Maier, S. L. (2008). "I Have Heard Horrible Stories …": Rape Victim Advocates' Perceptions of the Revictimization of Rape Victims by the Police and Medical System. *Violence Against Women, 14*(7), 786–808.

Nichols, A. J. (2011). Gendered Organizations: Challenges for Domestic Violence Victim Advocates and Feminist Advocacy. *Feminist Criminology, 6,* 111–131.

Nichols, A. (2013). Meaning-Making and Domestic Violence Victim Advocacy: An Examination of Feminist Identities, Ideologies, and Practices. *Feminist Criminology, 8*(3), 177–201.

Nichols, A. (2014). *Feminist Advocacy: Gendered Organisations in Community-Based Responses to Domestic Violence.* Plymouth: Lexington.

Parkinson, D. (2010). *Supporting Victims Through the Legal Process: The Role of Sexual Assault Service Providers.* ACSSA Wrap 8. Melbourne: Australian Institute of Family Studies.

Parmar, A., Sampson, A., & Diamond, A. (2005). *Tackling Domestic Violence: Providing Advocacy and Support to Survivors of Domestic Violence.* Home Office Development and Practice Report 3. London: Home Office.

Reid-Howie Associates. (2007). *Evaluation of the Pilot Domestic Abuse Court.* Edinburgh: Scottish Executive.

Robinson, A. (2003). *The Cardiff Women's Safety Unit: A Multi-agency Approach to Domestic Violence.* Cardiff: Cardiff University.

Robinson, A. (2004). *Domestic Violence MARACs (Multi-agency Risk Assessment Conferences) for Very High-Risk Victims in Cardiff, Wales: A Process and Outcome Evaluation.* Cardiff: Cardiff University.

Robinson, A. L. (2006). Reducing Repeat Victimisation Among High-Risk Victims of Domestic Violence: The Benefits of a Coordinated Community Response in Cardiff, Wales. *Violence Against Women, 12*(8), 761–788.

Robinson, A. (2009a). *Independent Domestic Violence Advisers: A Process Evaluation.* London: Home Office.

Robinson, A. (2009b). *Independent Sexual Violence Advisers: A Process Evaluation.* London: Home Office.

Robinson, A., & Hudson, K. (2011). Different Yet Complementary: Two Approaches to Supporting Victims of Sexual Violence in the UK. *Criminology and Criminal Justice, 11*(5), 515–533.

Robinson, A. L., & Tregidga, J. (2007). The Perception of High-Risk Victims of Domestic Violence to a Coordinated Community Response in Cardiff, Wales. *Violence Against Women, 13*, 1130–1148.

Rodriguez, N. (1988). Transcending Bureaucracy: Feminist Politics at a Shelter for Battered Women. *Gender and Society, 2*, 214–227.

Saathoff, A., & Stoffel, E. (1999). Community Based Domestic Violence Services. *Domestic Violence and Children, 9*, 97–110.

SafeLives. (2016). *A Cry for Health: Why We Must Invest in Domestic Abuse Services in Hospitals.* Bristol: SafeLives.

Schechter, S. (1982). *Women and Male Violence: The Visions and Struggles of the Battered Women's Movement.* Boston, MA: South End.

Scottish Executive. (2008). *Glasgow Domestic Abuse Court Feasibility Study Group: Report to the Scottish Executive.* Edinburgh: Scottish Executive.

Scottish Government. (2017). *National Scoping Exercise of Advocacy Services for Victims of Violence Against Women and Girls.* Blake Stevenson Limited.

Shepard, M. F. (1999). Advocacy for Battered Women: Implications for a Coordinated Community Response. In M. F. Shepard & E. L. Pence (Eds.), *Coordinating Community Responses to Domestic Violence: Lessons from Duluth and Beyond* (pp. 115–125). Thousand Oaks, CA: Sage.

Skinner, T., & Taylor, H. (2009). Being Shut Out in the Dark Young Survivors' Experiences of Reporting Rape and Sexual Assault. *Feminist Criminology, 4*(2), 130–150.

Smith, O., & Skinner, T. (2017). How Rape Myths are Used and Challenged in Rape and Sexual Assault Trials. *Social & Legal Studies, 26*(4), 441–466.

Srinivasan, M., & Davis, L. (1991). A Shelter: An Organization Like Any Other? *Affilia, 6*, 38–57.

Stanley, N., & Humphreys, C. (2014). Multi-agency Risk Assessment and Management for Children and Families Experiencing Domestic Violence *Children and Youth Services Review, 47*, 78–85.

Sullivan, C. M. (1991). The Provision of Advocacy Services to Women Leaving Abusive Partners: An Exploratory Study. *Journal of Interpersonal Violence, 6*(1), 45–54.

Sullivan, C. M. (2012). *Advocacy Services for Women with Abusive Partners: A Review of the Empirical Evidence.* Harrisburg, PA: National Resource Center on Domestic Violence. Retrieved March 16, 2020 from http://www.dvevidenceproject.org.

Sullivan, C. M., & Bybee, D. I. (1999). Reducing Violence Using Community-Based Advocacy for Women with Abusive Partners. *Journal of Consulting and Clinical Psychology, 67*(1), 43–53.

Taylor-Dunn, H. (2016). The Impact of Victim Advocacy on the Prosecution of Domestic Violence Offences: Lessons from a Realistic Evaluation. *Criminology & Criminal Justice, 16*(1), 21–39.

7

From Invisible to Conspicuous: The Rise of Victim Activism in the Politics of Justice

Nicola O'Leary and Simon Green

Introduction

It is now commonplace to start any discussion of victims of crime with reference to early, classic victimological studies that asserted the victim was the 'non-person' of criminal justice (Shapland et al. 1985). Aphorisms like this were undoubtedly correct and whilst many would argue that victims are still not afforded the respect and support they deserve, it is also the case that things have changed. Over the last 40 years, the prominence of crime victims in public life has grown significantly, and this can be seen very clearly in criminal justice legislation and policy, academic research and media attention. In this chapter, we begin by explaining this growth before focusing on the rise of victim activism and its relationship

N. O'Leary (✉)
Department of Criminology and Sociology, University of Hull, Hull, UK
e-mail: n.oleary@hull.ac.uk

S. Green
Faculty of Arts, Culture and Education, University of Hull, Hull, UK
e-mail: S.T.Green@hull.ac.uk

© The Author(s) 2020
J. Tapley, P. Davies (eds.), *Victimology*,
https://doi.org/10.1007/978-3-030-42288-2_7

to the politics of justice. To do this we shall compare the top-down political invocation of crime victims with bottom-up victim activism and explore the role of the media in shaping both perspectives. To help us achieve this we shall enlist the aid of three very different high-profile victim campaigns that we think provide excellent case studies for exploring the dynamics of how victim activism can be both extremely controversial and extremely effective at challenging the status quo. The first case study will be the campaign for justice pursued by the parents of Stephen Lawrence. The second case study is the tabloid-led campaigns for various offender registers (Megan's Law, Sarah's Law, Clare's Law). The third case study is the more recent #MeToo campaign on Twitter and its influence on public debates about sexual harassment in the workplace. These case studies will provide the real-world examples of our main argument which is that wider social, cultural and technological changes have provided a new platform in which the victim's voice has become increasingly powerful.

Victims and Culture

Over the last 40 years, there has been significant academic commentary on the growing cultural salience of the crime victim in the 'late-modern' world (Garland 2000; Green 2011; McGarry and Walklate 2015). Underpinned by the growth of victim 'sensitive' laws, policies and procedures, the symbolic resonance of crime victims has steadily ascended the political agenda. Whilst it has been argued that this growing significance exposes crime victims to forms of political manipulation (Elias 1993; Green 2007a), it also creates a platform through which victims can campaign for justice. Between political slogans and victim activism inevitably sits the media—in all its various forms—privileging some voices and issues over others. Before examining the media dynamics of victim campaigns in more detail, this chapter begins by reviewing the theoretical basis that helps explain and contextualise the growing cultural importance of crime victims.

Beginning in the late 1960s and 1970s, a growing realisation about the marginalisation of the victim within the criminal justice system emerged

(Shapland et al. 1985; Mawby and Walklate 1994). This realisation led to persistent attempts to give victims of crime a new voice in criminal justice procedures. Whether extra-legal in the form of support and services, or procedural in the form of state and offender compensation, victim impact statements, vulnerable witness provision or restorative justice, these changes began to reintroduce victims' emotions into criminal justice (Green 2011; Karstedt 2002; McGarry and Walklate 2015). Driven by a growing victims' lobby that argued justice was not being delivered for crime victims, these reforms began to shift the contours of how the criminal justice system functions. Alongside the traditional courtroom dynamics of state prosecutor versus defendant, the role of the victim has become increasingly debated. The introduction of crime victims in the criminal justice process reintroduces those directly affected by the crime and, in particular, all of their feelings and frustrations, back into a system that had been designed to exclude subjective emotion in favour of objective evidence from the delivery of justice. Loader and de Haan (2002) have pointed to a number of ways in which emotions have become more central to the delivery of justice, concluding that emotions have become 'inescapably implicated in both the "volatile and contradictory" nature of late-modern penality' (Loader and de Haan 2002: 247).

Karstedt (2002) considers the impact of these conditions on the way in which the criminal justice process functions. Whilst she acknowledges the emotional context in which crime and criminal justice has always occurred, she argues that since the early 1990s there has been a noticeable increase in the emotional content of public discourses about crime and the introduction of punishments that 'are explicitly based on—or designed to arouse—emotions' (Karstedt 2002: 301). These emotions are also increasingly evident in wider society, following high-profile crimes becoming more significant as instant outpourings are immediately captured and reproduced for a mass audience. Such emotion is itself culturally prominent as it demonstrates both authenticity and honesty in a world increasingly negotiated through a mediatised lens. These emotions then spill out beyond those directly affected into public demonstrations, victim campaigns, newspaper headlines and victim testimonies (McGarry and Walklate 2015). Think of Stephen Lawrence's parents' campaign for justice, the tabloid campaign for a sex offender's register, the 3.7 million people marching through Paris after the Charlie Hebdo attack, public displays of anger and grief following gun-related killing sprees in the USA and the #MeToo Twitter phenomenon regarding sexual harassment in the workplace. As David Garland (2001: 144) proposed:

> The victim is every victim, she could be you or related to you. This personalizing trope, repeated endlessly on television news and documentaries, represents the crime victim as the real life, 'it could-be-you' metonym for the problem of personal security. And in so doing, it shifts the debate away from the instrumental reasoning of crime control analysis towards the visceral emotions of identification and righteous indignation.

As a combination of structural, cultural and political drivers in late-modern society push the individual and the individual's feelings to the foreground, so they are correspondingly pushed to the centre of criminal justice debates and processes. In a world in which everything is doubted and in which people's lives are less and less governed by external structures and networks, the individual and the emotional become increasingly important as the unit through which authentic and legitimate decisions are made. Emotions thus become the basis of a new trust currency and emotional communication a crucial element in communicating both personal and cultural meaning and intent.

Social media provides a readily accessible and instantly shareable platform for victim activism. Perhaps the best example of this is the ongoing #MeToo phenomenon which has become global in both reach and consequence (see Sugiura and Smith, Chapter 3 in this volume). Cutting through the mediated lens of traditional print journalism and its editorial discretion, social media engines can provide an instant recourse for victims who want to either share their experiences of injustice or hold the authorities to account. Whilst arguably open to different forms of bias, prejudice and misrepresentation, there can be little doubt that #MeToo provides a powerful example of how new media can enable victim activism.

Case Study 1   #MeToo

Description: The #MeToo movement is a social media campaign against sexual harassment in the workplace. Spread virally via Twitter from October 2017, the social media campaign was brought to public attention by the Hollywood actress Alyssa Milano who encouraged people to come forward and raise awareness about the extent of the problem.

Background: The Me Too movement predates the Twitter phenomenon and has its roots in black American social activist and community organiser, Tarana Burke. However, the movement was brought to wider public and media attention in the autumn of 2017, following a scandal when well-known Hollywood producer Harvey Weinstein was accused of sexual abuse by multiple former employees and associates. Subsequently, the Twitter hashtag MeToo went viral with tens of thousands of people, including hundreds of celebrities, responding to Alyssa Milano's encouragement to share their stories of sexual harassment in the workplace. In particular, the number of Hollywood actresses sharing their experiences has kept the issue in the media spotlight ever since. In the USA alone over 200 high-profile male celebrities, politicians, media moguls, clergymen, academics, sports coaches and business leaders have had allegations made against them in what has become known as the 'Weinstein effect'. Whilst some have been charged and prosecuted, many more have been fired from jobs or stepped down from powerful positions following accusations made against them.

The Role of the Media: The growing list of high-profile public figures either making revelations of victimisation or being accused of sexual harassment fuelled a tabloid and television frenzy. However, the #MeToo viral campaign on social media is the key media phenomenon in this example of victim activism. With over 200,000 tweets by the end of the first day after Alyssa Milano's original posting and somewhere in the region of 12 million Facebook postings using the #MeToo words in the first 24 hours, the extent of disclosures about sexual harassment in the workplace was unprecedented. Equivalent hashtags in at least 18 different languages have emerged and new hashtags in related areas such as #HimToo and #ChurchToo have been launched. #MeToo is a form of grassroots victim activism demonstrating the role of social media in providing an easily shared platform for uncovering hidden forms of victimisation.

The Role of Politicians: With the exception of male politicians accused of sexual harassment in the workplace, the main contribution has been a growing debate in legislatures about whether there is a need for new laws about sexual harassment in the workplace. Some female politicians have also added their voices to #MeToo, sharing their experiences of sexual harassment and in the USA. Congresswoman Jacki Speier introduced a new Bill intended to make sexual harassment easier to report on Capitol Hill. In the UK, there were a number of allegations in Westminster against politicians by junior staff, which led to two Cabinet Ministers resigning

(continued)

(continued)

their positions in government. In December 2018, the UK Government released a new Code of Practice to Tackle Sexual Harassment at Work.

The Impact on Criminal Justice: has so far been minimal beyond a handful of very high-profile convictions for serious sexual offences in the USA (for example, Harvey Weinstein). Nevertheless, debates about the criminalisation of sexual harassment in the workplace have grown in the wake of #MeToo. Saudi Arabia and Chile have introduced sexual harassment into their criminal codes and such developments have been the subject of debate in the Netherlands and Estonia. Given that #MeToo is still an ongoing phenomenon, how far this criminalisation trend will grow is not yet known.

The Impact on Society: Given the number of celebrity accusations, the global reach and availability of the #MeToo Twitter phenomenon, the issue of sexual harassment in the workplace has ignited debate across the globe. For example, in France the actress and feminist Catherine Deneuve and 99 other prominent French women denounced #MeToo as a 'puritanical ...wave of purification' arguing that whilst rape is a crime, trying to seduce someone is not. And in the USA, criticism has been levelled against #MeToo for ignoring women of colour, whilst others have argued the movement overemphasises and sensationalises high-profile allegations at the expense of challenging institutional and cultural norms. And in a YouGov survey in the USA it seems the American public have become more sceptical of sexual harassment allegations in what The Economist reported as 'mansblaming'. The impact on society is therefore profound in terms of public debate about acceptable sexual behaviour, celebrity scandals, dating norms and cultural values.

Key Academic Sources:

#MeToo Has Done What the Law Could Not (Professor Catherine A. Mackinnon in the New York Times (Op-Ed 4th February 2018).

Angela Onwuachi-Willig, What About #UsToo?: The Invisibility of Race in the #MeToo Movement, 128 *YALE L.J.F.* 105 (2018), https://www.yalelaw-journal.org/forum/what-about-ustoo.

Tenzer, Leslie Y. Garfield, #MeToo, Statutory Rape Laws and the Persistence of Gender Stereotypes (February 8, 2018). Available at SSRN: https://ssrn.com/abstract=3120348 or https://doi.org/10.2139/ssrn.3120348

Key Media Sources:

#metoo (Twitter)

MeTooRising (interactive Google map)

Vox list of #MeToo allegations

Key Legislative and Policy Sources:

Violence against women: an EU-wide survey. (2014). European Union agency for Fundamental rights

H.R.4396 MeToo Congress Act (introduced 15/11/2017 by Congresswoman Jackie Speier

UK Government Announces New Code of Practice to Tackle Sexual Harassment at Work (Press release 18/12/2018))

Victims and Politics: The Politicisation of Victims

A key dimension to victim activism is how it interfaces with political institutions. Green (2007b) has argued that restorative justice can be understood in the context of the political manipulation of crime victims. This argument draws upon a wider critique of new right transatlantic politics (Elias 1993) that invokes the victims of crime to introduce retributive sentencing policies that are driven by a condemnatory explanation of crime rooted in moral decline and individual responsibility (Green 2015). This argument can underplay victim activism and the role the media play in either reifying or challenging the political and cultural status quo. Here we refine the political manipulation argument, but first a brief review of victims and politics.

Electoral Manipulation: In the USA, Elias (1993) claimed that victims are still largely marginalised in the criminal justice system. The basis of his claim lies in a range of different criticisms including poorly enforced legislation and schemes at both the state and federal levels. Elias (1993) argues that although it would seem obvious that victims should be the beneficiaries of victim-centred reform, it is those in political power who have really been the winners. In the USA, Elias (1993) points to the Reagan and Bush administrations' support for the victims of crime and argues that their policies have in fact bolstered the status quo, reinforcing orthodox conceptions of criminal victimisation and diverting attention away from the arenas in which the majority of victimisation occurs: the lower-class minorities. Instead, politically 'safe' victims have been targeted, notably children and the elderly.

> The movement may have been co-opted not only by being diffused, but also by being "used" for reforms that may have little to do with victims. Yet it allows victims to be manipulated to enhance political legitimacy, government police powers, and an apparent agenda to further civil rights erosion, a symbolic use of politics to convert liberal rhetoric into thin air or conservative ends. (Elias 1993: 48)

Whilst this argument is specific to the USA, parallel concerns have also been raised in the UK, particularly in relation to the Victim's Charter (Mawby and Walklate 1994), the forerunner to the Victim's Code and the focus on the 'ideal victim'. In this sense, Williams (1999) makes a very similar point to Elias (1993), suggesting that the real beneficiaries of victim reforms have been the politicians who have used such changes to appear tough on crime.

Ideological Manipulation: Another explanation for the growth of victim-centred justice can be attributed to a shift in the prevailing ideological vogue. This shift can be described as a move from welfarism to neoliberalism, or the decline of the redistributive ethos and a shift from social or structural explanations to individualised notions of personal responsibility (Young and Matthews 2003; Green 2015). Mawby and Walklate (1994) suggest that since the late 1970s, the tensions within state welfare capitalism have become increasingly more evident and unworkable. To rectify this tension the state has shifted the language of welfare from 'universal' to 'selective' benefits accessed when applied for and according to certain conditions. Victim-centred justice can therefore also be understood as a form of ideological manipulation as it makes judgements about both what a victim is, and what types of victims can access 'justice'.

Thus, the shift towards rebalancing criminal justice in favour of the victim can be understood as ideologically motivated. Usually couched in emotional appeals to justice and fairness, victimisation is separated from wider structural inequalities, leaving intact both a notion of the 'ideal victim' (Christie 1977) and a presumption of individual responsibility as the primary cause for criminality and the harm it inflicts on others (O'Malley 2001; Sullivan 2003). Socio-economic and structural inequalities are therefore often backgrounded in explanations of victimisation leaving an ideologically motivated gap in understanding patterns of victimisation (Green 2007a).

Governmental Manipulation: Garland (1996; 2001) explores the underlying tensions that exist within criminal justice and points to strategies of 'responsibilisation' which seek to devolve some of the state's responsibility for crime control to other sectors. This implies a different type of manipulation, where the aim is not direct political gain, but a subtle shift in focus that fulfils a wider governmental strategy designed to paper over the cracks of a spiralling crime rate it struggles to control. This presents an alternative motive behind the increasing adoption of victim-centred policies that has little to do with the needs of victims and everything to do with how governments exercise power. Although this may go some way to help explain why practices such as victim impact statements and restorative justice have grown in stature, it does not necessarily mean these processes do not also have substantial benefits to the victims of crime. However, in a similar fashion to the concerns raised by Elias (1993), it does cast doubt over whether the needs of victims are actually being pursued, or whether they simply form part of an expedient tool designed to benefit the state's need to appear to be doing something about crime.

All three of these types of manipulation provide useful ways of understanding how crime victims underpin the role of individual agency in shaping victim campaigns and reform. Wider structural forces play an important part in understanding why the victims of crime play an increasingly more significant role in public life and the criminal justice system, but they tell us little about how victims drive change from the bottom up and almost nothing about the role of traditional and new media in channelling victim activism. We shall now spend some time addressing this. Drawing on two further case study examples, we explore how victim activism has played a central role in changing attitudes and laws about victimisation and justice.

Case Study 2: Justice for Stephen Lawrence

A prime example of victim activism is Doreen and Neville Lawrence's campaign for justice for their murdered son Stephen. Their sustained campaign exemplifies how a combination of victim tenacity, combined with print media headlines and pressure on politicians, can be a powerful force for victim and criminal justice reform.

Case Study 2   Justice for Stephen Lawrence

Description: Stephen Lawrence was an 18-year-old black man who was stabbed to death whilst waiting for a bus in Eltham in south-east London on the 22nd April 1993. He was at the bus stop with his friend Duwayne Brooks who witnessed five or six white men attack Stephen. Duwayne and Stephen ran away and it was only then that Duwayne realised his friend was injured. Stephen collapsed and bled to death by the roadside a short while later.

Background: A police investigation was launched and several prime suspects were identified and interviewed. 12 months after Stephen's murder the Crown Prosecution Service stated that they did not have sufficient evidence for murder charges. In reaction to this outcome, Stephen's parents—Doreen and Neville Lawrence—took the unusual step of launching a private prosecution against five suspects. In 1996, the charges were dropped against two of the suspects for lack of evidence and the remaining three were acquitted of murder at the trial due to the judge ruling that Duwayne Brooks' identification evidence was unreliable. For the next 15 years, Stephen's murder went unsolved until 2011–2012, when two of the suspects were retried and convicted for the murder of Stephen Lawrence. This was only possible due to an unprecedented series of events that included a damning indictment of the Metropolitan Police; changes to the law, and a relentless campaign by Doreen and Neville Lawrence who continued to struggle for justice for their murdered son.

The Role of the Media: The immediate aftermath of Stephen's murder, attracted comparatively little media attention. However, this began to change after a trip to the UK by South African President, Nelson Mandela, who made a public statement that 'black lives are cheap' in relation to Stephen's murder. But the real game changer came in February 1997, when the *Daily Mail* cleared its front page to print pictures of the five suspects under the headline 'Murderers'. This controversial headline helped set the scene for Jack Straw, the Home Secretary in a newly elected Labour Government to launch the Macpherson inquiry. The *Daily Mail* journalist, Stephen Wright continued to write about the Lawrence case and was awarded a Special Campaign Award in 2012 for his work on this case.

The Role of Politicians: Doreen and Neville Lawrence's battle for justice kept the pressure on the politicians and the newly elected Labour Government initiated a full independent inquiry into the death of Stephen Lawrence. Sir William Macpherson led the inquiry, the findings of which were published in his report in 1999. A series of poor practices, assumptions and decisions made by the Metropolitan Police were highlighted. Institutional racism was a key factor in these mistakes and the consequence was a failure to bring Stephen's killers to justice. The Macpherson report

(continued)

(continued)

defined institutional racism as the 'procedures, operations and culture of public or private institutions—reinforcing individual prejudices and being reinforced by them in turn'.

The Impact on Criminal Justice: The Macpherson report contained 70 recommendations to address institutional racism. The impact of the Macpherson report reverberated across the media and within the Metropolitan Police and had a profound effect on how racism and other hate crimes would come to be understood, and responded to, by the criminal justice system. In particular, a racist incident was to be defined as encompassing any incident perceived as racist by the victim or any other person. Other recommendations were aimed at improving police investigations, ethnic and cultural representation within the police and stronger disciplinary consequences for racist words or acts by police staff.

The Impact on Law: Following the Macpherson report, the government produced the 'Justice for All' white paper in 2002 which aimed at 'rebalancing' the criminal justice system in favour of the victim. The murder of Stephen Lawrence and the subsequent police investigation was one of the main drivers of this document that eventually culminated in the Criminal Justice Act 2003. Both the white paper and Act were intended to help restore public confidence in criminal justice and saw a raft of new victim-centred reforms; the most significant of which was the removal of the double jeopardy rule for serious offences when new evidence emerges. The double jeopardy rule meant that no one could be tried for the same offence if they had been acquitted. Its removal meant that two of the acquitted defendants for Stephen Lawrence's murder could be retried and after new forensic techniques provided fresh evidence, both were convicted for murder in 2012.

The Impact on Society: The murder of Stephen Lawrence came at a time when several high-profile miscarriages of justice were brought to light. Several involved people were convicted of IRA terrorist attacks. New DNA forensic tests combined with evidence of unsafe confessions due to oppressive policing practices led to a number of convictions being quashed. Taken alongside the abject failure of the police to hold anyone to account for Stephen's murder, confidence in the British criminal justice system was significantly shaken. The outcome was a political, legal and social shift towards victim rights. Furthermore, the concept of institutional racism was introduced into British culture and hate crimes into the British law in the Crime and Disorder Act 1998. In 2013, Stephen's mother, Doreen Lawrence, was elevated to the House of Lords as Baroness Lawrence of Clarendon.

(continued)

(continued)

Key Academic Sources:
Greer, C. (2016) News Media, Victims and Crime. In P. Davies. P. Francis and C. Greer (Eds.) *Victims, Crime and Society: An introduction* (2nd Ed.) London: Sage (pp. 48–65).
Rowe, M. (Ed.) (2007) *Policing Beyond Macpherson.* London: Routledge.
Souhami, A. (2014) Institutional racism and police reform: An empirical critique. *Policing and Society,* 24(1): 1–21.

Key Media Sources:
BBC News Timeline of Stephen Lawrence story
Daily Mail Front Page (February 14th 1997)
Stephen Lawrence Charitable Trust

Key Legislative and Policy sources:
The Macpherson Report (The Stephen Lawrence Inquiry: Report of an inquiry by Sir William MacPherson of Cluny, Cm 4262-I, February 1999)
Justice for All White Paper (Cm 5563, July 2002)
Criminal Justice Act 2003

Victim Hierarchies and the Media

One of the many conceptual, practical and political problems associated with the notions of 'victim' and 'victimhood' is the determination of who can legitimately claim victim status and as such this remains a matter of debate which is influenced to a large extent by social divisions including class, ethnicity, sexuality and gender. This reflects how criminal victimisation is a process. How victimhood is defined and constructed is publicly framed by the news media. Research evidence consistently affirms that it is victims of violent and fatal interpersonal crimes who receive the greatest media attention (Marsh 1991; Reiner et al. 2000). However, even within this consideration, it is abundantly clear that news constructions of criminal victimisation and victims are highly selective and atypical, focusing on particular types of victims, suffering particular types of victimization (Gekoski et al. 2012; Greer and Reiner 2012). As such, a critical understanding of news media constructions of crime victims is vital. The place of victims has taken on unprecedented significance in media and criminal justice discourses, in the development of crime policy and in the popular cultural imagination (Maguire and Pointing 1988; Rock 2004).

Few crimes generate high-profile emotionally charged news coverage and public outcry as much as the abduction of a child (Critcher 2011). Along with the very old, children are viewed as the most vulnerable members of society, and the least able to resist victimisation, harm and abuse. A child who has been abducted is readily accorded the status of 'ideal victim' (Christie 1986). Yet even within this group, perceived as vulnerable and innocent, only a minority of such cases are deemed worthy of sustained and extensive news media coverage. Disproportionate attention is given to children, but within this group priority is often given to those who are young, white, pretty and female. The social construction of such 'ideal' victims in this way indicates the power of the media and their tendency to sympathise with some (innocent) victims while blaming others (Jewkes 2015). Assumptions based on this stereotypical image of the 'ideal victim' helps to generate criteria by which those in the media assess the 'newsworthiness' of specific crime stories. This 'hierarchy of victimisation' (Greer 2017) is also reflected and reinforced within crime news reporting of high-profile victim cases. This 'pecking order' illuminates the differential status of particular types and categories of crime victim in media and is reflected in official discourses. 'Ideal victims' (e.g. some child abduction or murder victims) are at the top of the hierarchy, whilst some are perceived as undeserving/illegitimate victims (e.g. victims with offending histories or those deemed in some way culpable for their situation, drunk when victimised) are near the bottom, often passing unnoticed in the wider social sphere (Smolej 2010).

Our third case study focuses on the abduction and murder of Sarah Payne in 2000. During the second half of the 1990s, the UK witnessed a

Case Study 3   Campaigning for 'Sarah's Law'

Description: Sarah Payne was eight years old when she was murdered on 1 July 2000. Sarah had been playing 'hide and seek' with her three siblings in a field near her grandparents' home at Kingston Gorse, West Sussex. Having dipped through a gap in the hedge, leading to a country lane back to her grandparents' house, Sarah was abducted by convicted child sex offender Roy Whiting. Sarah's disappearance was noticed by her brother almost immediately and a search, initially led by her family and later by the police

(continued)

(continued)

was swiftly undertaken. Following a police hunt involving 1300 officers, Sarah's unclothed dead body was found by a farm worker 16 days later. She had been left in the woods at the side of a road (near Pulborough, West Sussex), about 15 miles away from where she disappeared.

Background: Roy Whiting was found guilty of the abduction and murder of Sarah Payne and was sentenced to life in prison at Lewes Crown Court in December 2001 in what became one of Britain's most high-profile child murder cases. After Whiting was convicted, jurors were told that he had a relevant previous conviction. Some five years earlier, he had abducted and indecently assaulted a nine-year-old girl. Whiting was placed on the sex offenders register and jailed for four years for this crime, but was freed after 30 months. Revelations of his history of child abuse prompted a nationwide debate about paedophiles and the justice system.

The Role of the Media: In the days following Sarah's disappearance, press coverage was unrelenting, as newspapers variously sympathised with the Payne family plight, pontificated upon what could have happened to Sarah and reported the search in significant detail. Within days the *News of the World* newspaper, led by editor Rebekah Wade and supported by Sarah Payne's parents, launched a campaign calling for the introduction of 'Sarah's Law', a UK version of Megan's Law. As part of that campaign, later in July 2000, the newspaper also launched a 'naming and shaming' campaign, publishing the names, photographs and general locations of a number of people it said were convicted paedophiles. This led to a spate of vigilante attacks, in some cases on innocent members of the public who happened to have the same name as those named by the *News of the World*. The campaign was suspended in August 2000. However, the campaign for legal change continued.

The Role of Politicians: The Home Secretary at the time, Jack Straw, initially opposed the campaign but then changed his mind saying it should be 'urgently considered'. Straw favoured leaving control of any disclosure of information to police, probation and other relevant agencies. It was not until June 2007 that Home Secretary, John Reid, introduced a package of measures branded as 'Sarah's Law proposals'. In 2009, Jack Straw, now Minister for Justice, was to feature prominently again, this time as a key player in the appointment of Sara Payne (Sarah's mother) as Britain's first Victims' Champion; a new 'independent public voice' for victims of and witnesses to crime.

The Impact on Criminal Justice: The murder of Sarah Payne was not only a call for greater child safety protections, but also it was indicative of a failure of law and order. In particular, it was a symbol of governmental failure to respond to an agenda set by the print press. There is undoubtedly a

(continued)

(continued)

greater reverence and centrality for victims in modern society, with victimhood at the centre of criminal justice debates and victims' names harnessed to criminal justice initiatives. The terminology of Sarah's Law became readily accessible and was used in the media in place of the legislative terminology (Jones and Newburn 2013). In the victim-centred, modern criminal justice system, this is not an unusual phenomenon. As other case studies in this chapter show, The Stephen Lawrence Inquiry and the Damilola Taylor Murder Investigation Review Report have firmly embedded these names in the social and legal realm. The overall impact on criminal justice was a refocusing of the system towards victims' rights.

The Impact on the Law: In the months following the murder of Sarah Payne, the government ruled out calls for public access to the sexual offender database, but later did embark upon a review of the management of sexual offenders in the community (see Home Office 2007). During the course of this review, another high-profile murder involving children occurred. In August 2002, in Soham, Cambridgeshire, 10-year-old girls, Holly Wells and Jessica Chapman, were murdered by school caretaker, Ian Huntley. The later well-publicised revelations that Huntley had previously been investigated for numerous sexual offences (including offences against children) saw public moral outrage intensify and a continued push from certain sections of the media for a 'Sarah's Law'.

- In 2012 legislation was eventually introduced by way of the Child Sex Offender Disclosure Scheme, colloquially known as 'Sarah's Law'.
- This was implemented as Section 140 of the *Criminal Justice and Immigration Act 2008*, which inserted a new section 327A and 327B into the *Criminal Justice Act 2003*.
- This is a community notification scheme that allows parents, guardians and carers (later extended to all members of the public) to ask the police if someone who might have contact with their children has a criminal record for child sex offences. Police will reveal details confidentially if they think it's in the child's interests.

The Impact on Society: During the 1990s, the social concern around reports of stranger danger and increasing frequency of media stories of sexual offences against children resulted in what might be termed 'moral panic' level. By 2000, and following the murder of Sarah Payne, press coverage of paedophilia had reached unprecedented levels. This resulted in popular punitive rhetoric on crime and victimisation more generally, but fears particularly crystallised around the cardinal news values of children, (sexual) violence and the predatory offender. This in turn fuelled the debates

(continued)

(continued)

around 'risk and dangerousness', 'punishment and rehabilitation' and 'surveillance and control' (Silverman and Wilson 2002). The enduring nature of such debates intensify considerably when seen through the lens of the next high-profile case, where the construction of the 'ideal' victim garners public attention and media exposure alongside increased political and social significance.

Key Academic Sources:

Ashenden, S. (2002) 'Policing Perversion: The Contemporary Governance of Paedophilia', *Cultural Values,* 6: 1–2, 197–222.

Savage, S.P. and Charman, S. (2010) 'Public protectionism and 'Sarah's Law: exerting pressure through single issue campaigns', in M. Nash and A. Williams (eds.) *Handbook of Public Protection,* Cullompton: Willan.

Jones, T. and Newburn, T. (2013) 'Policy convergence, politics and comparative penal reform: sex offender notification schemes in the USA and UK', *Punishment and Society,* 15(5): 439–67.

Key Media Sources:

BBC News Timeline of Sarah Payne story
Sara Payne becomes Victims Champion
http://news.bbc.co.uk/1/hi/uk/7850785.stm
Naming and shaming campaign
http://news.bbc.co.uk/1/hi/uk/1709708.stm

Key Legislative and Policy sources:

Lipscombe, S. (2012) Sarah's Law: the child sex offender disclosure scheme
    http://www.legislation.gov.uk/ukpga/2003/42/pdfs/ukpga_20030042_en.
pdf (Sex Offences Act 2003)
    https://www.legislation.gov.uk/ukpga/1998/37/contents   (Crime   and
Disorder Act 1998 – Sections 2–4)

Payne, S. (2009) Redefining Justice: Addressing the individual needs of victims' and witnesses http://library.college.police.uk/docs/moj/sara-payne-redefining-justice.pdf

confluence of events which heightened public awareness of cases involving child sexual abuse in residential care homes and care settings. 1996 was also the year in which 'Megan's Law' was created in the USA, following the rape and murder two years earlier of seven-year-old Megan Kanka by a twice-convicted sex offender who lived in the same street in New Jersey. These cases, and the subsequent media coverage, all tapped in to escalating public anxieties and concerns. With the introduction of community notification legislation in the USA—Megan's Law—lobbyists in England and Wales were given a powerful new focal point for their campaigns.

Many high-profile victim cases invoke feelings (often fear, uncertainty, anger) amongst public consumers of crime news. Empathetic following of these stories is activated and encouraged by journalists and editors who are well versed in giving the public what it wants (Jewkes 2015). Those who manage to acquire or are granted 'ideal victim' status may attract substantial levels of media attention, international public empathy and mourning, and may even drive significant change to social and criminal justice policy and practice (as seen with the case studies in this chapter). However, the attribution of legitimate or ideal victim status and related levels of media interest (or otherwise) are often influenced by demographic characteristics. Class or more accurately notions of respectability and gender are often the defining features of the cases featuring 'ideal victims', where the media interest is automatic and certain. Ethnicity is also central. In contrast to the 'ideal victim' status awarded in some of the cases described above, in the *immediate* aftermath of the crime, the parents of Stephen Lawrence faced a distinct lack of media interest in their son's murder. Thus, the legitimate status for Stephen was not automatic; media interest and the battle for legitimate victim status had to be fought and won.

Symbolic and Agentic Victims

Although paths to victim status are varied, cases such as that of Sarah Payne and Stephen Lawrence generate intense mediatised debate and often, public anger. In such circumstances, and faced with a barrage of critical media coverage and moral outrage, the agencies and authorities publicly implicated are pressured to respond. Indeed, in both the cases of Sarah Payne and Stephen Lawrence, we can identify how the intense media coverage was sustained in part by the evidence of serious institutional failings, where the courts and the police were variously implicated.

The role of news media is central here to generating, sustaining and shaping public debate.

In each of the case studies in this chapter, the media played a central role in publicly defining cases, inscribing the victims' images in the popular imagination, generating and focusing collective moral outrage and, critically, keeping the stories at the forefront of the political and popular consciousness, in some cases long after the criminal investigation had concluded. Pivotal to this, and other significant signal crimes (Innes 2014), is the victim's agentic and symbolic power. Here we refer to an agent as one who acts (e.g. Sara Payne or Doreen Lawrence), rather than one who is acted upon. In such cases, these actions resonate beyond the individual and become symbolic and representative of wider issues and debates on public safety, social and criminal justice and on occasion, the nature of society itself (O'Leary 2016). Mediatised campaigns launched in the victim's name, whether trying to change policy or introduce new legislation, are likely to command high levels of public support (Chancer 2005). The appointment of Sara Payne (Sarah's mother) as Victims' Champion in 2009 is a case in point. This appointment signalled the deep significance of Sara Payne as a *person* and as a *role holder* for effective campaigning. Much of the power of the Sarah's Law campaign related to the agency, potency and symbolism of the image of Sara Payne herself as a grieving mother fighting for justice. In matters of criminal justice, champions are increasingly heralded as 'experts' and often thus regarded as conduits of knowledge (Rojek 2001).

Media as a Platform for Victim's Voice

The strategies explored in this chapter so far are heralded as progressive and the media's potential for supporting and facilitating victim agency in such cases can often be understated (O'Leary 2018). For example, The *News of the World* and more latterly *The Sun*'s use of Sara Payne as a figure head and a 'crime-fighter' (Harper and Treadwell 2013: 216) is an emotional strategy for effecting changes in matters of crime and justice. Having a campaigning 'champion' representing and personifying the direct effects of crime gives the position context and a perception of validity. For some victims of crime caught in the media maelstrom, their campaign for justice or path to recovery can be aided by utilising the powerful platform that the media provides to give them a voice. Interest from the media also provides comfort for others. Some victims (and witnesses) are reassured and encouraged from media interest in them. Talking to the media, telling their story, can help them to feel that they are doing something to help with the criminal investigation or campaign for change (Mulley 2001). In addition, it is clear that popular news interest in victims more broadly has given voice to new positive forms of political engagement. More people consume the news today than at any time previously, and there is an undoubted valuable investigative tradition in tabloid journalism which continues to play an important role, not least in uncovering miscarriages of justice, police or political corruption and holding politicians and others in authority to account.

There is, however, a cautionary tale to the heightened and emotionally charged media interest in crime victims. In 2007, *News of the World* royal editor Clive Goodman and private investigator Glenn Mulcaire were convicted of illegal interception of phone messages. Evidence existed that this practice extended beyond these individuals. In July 2011, it was revealed that *News of the World* reporters had hacked the voicemail of murder victim Milly Dowler. In 2002, 13-year-old Millie Dowler had disappeared on her way home from school in Walton on Thames, Surrey. She was later found to have been abducted and murdered by Levi Bellfield (found guilty in 2011). Millie Dowler's murder played a significant role in the *News of the World* phone-hacking scandal. In 2011, media reported that *News of the World* reporters had accessed Dowler's voicemail after she was reported missing. These revelations of phone hacking by journalists represented a nadir in the history of the popular press. Public outcry and legal repercussions resulted in the closure of the 168-year-old newspaper in 2011. At the same time, Prime Minister David Cameron announced a wide-ranging public inquiry into press standards, practices and ethics, chaired by Lord Justice Leveson (see Leveson 2012).

However, the overall common denominator with both of the positions above is the increased interest around crime victims in the media as one of the most significant changes in media representations of crime and control since the Second World War (Reiner et al. 2000). Here, the cases of Sarah Payne, Stephen Lawrence and the #MeToo movement exemplify the complex interconnections between crime news reporting, victimisation and public reaction to the processes by which particular high-profile crimes are selected, produced and consumed. Yet the victims' voices that find resonance in the media represent only a small fraction of those who experience criminal victimisation and harm (Peelo 2006). The media and particularly newspapers express emotions surrounding major events and 'mega cases' of homicide (Soothill et al. 2002), which can bring to the surface social divisions and tensions that are difficult for a society to manage. 'Mega' media stories on homicide are unusual cases which particularly offend society; some are *repeatedly* reported, transforming them into a point of reference which can help us to interpret later killings (ibid.: 420). As Peelo (2006: 160) describes:

> Mega cases are often framed to appear most supportive of those immediately hurt by killing. Yet, this alignment is really a point of entry to a social commentary by which newspapers and their readers can restore a sense of control by confirming a viewpoint of society and its ills, and neutralize anguish by objectifying victims of homicide who have become, therein, public property.

It is still the case that many victims of crime remain marginalized or ignored in official and mediated representations. Examples spanning the last 30 years illustrate this in action. The summer of 2002 saw international media attention and the biggest manhunt ever conducted in Britain for the Soham school girls, Holly Wells and Jessica Chapman. In 1996 two boys of similar age, Patrick Warren and David Spencer, went missing from their homes. Their disappearance, however, failed to register much interest outside some local press. Similarly, shortly after 13-year-old Millie Dowler went missing in 2002, the body of another teenage girl was recovered from a disused quarry near Tilbury Docks. Amid much speculation, the body was identified as that of 14-year-old Hannah Williams. Whilst the hunt for Millie continued to dominate, Hannah only received a few sentences on the inside pages (Greer 2017). Hannah was working class, raised by a single mother on low income and had run away before. Similarly, David and Patrick were working-class boys, lived on a rough West Midlands council estate and had been in trouble at school. For every Holly and Jessica and every Millie, there are many more victims, such as Hannah, Patrick and David, whose voices and stories are denied 'ideal' or 'deserving 'status.

The attribution or otherwise of legitimate or ideal victim status and related level of media interest is clearly influenced in some cases by demographic characteristics. However, it is not simply the case that race, gender or class or any other social division holds an absolute defining influence over media interest in crime victims, this of course can change from case to case and reporting of criminal victimisation is a culturally dynamic and fluid activity. Indeed, our case studies here demonstrate that it is often a combination of context of the crime, a sense of injustice, political will and personal tragedy that shapes the level of attention and media exposure. It is a crucial endeavour, therefore, to not forget those marginalised victims or those who are stereotyped as less 'legitimate' victims, who feel the pains of victimisation most acutely, but whose voices are stifled rather than amplified in news media discourses and should, therefore, continue to be a central concern for criminological and victimological research.

Conclusion

Sometimes, victims are made the focus of political and media agendas. They are used for political advantage and for selling newspapers. But at other times, victims can hold politicians and the media to account through their own activism and agency. What cannot be doubted is that the cultural significance of the victim has grown over the last 30–40 years and this has led to many changes in criminal justice policy, the law and society more generally. Furthermore, social media technologies have provided new forums in which victims can make their voices heard or have them misappropriated. Our goal has been to demonstrate that political and media engagement with victims is two-way traffic: both top-down and bottom-up. At their best, the media have supported some of the most influential 'bottom-up' victim campaigns that have held governments and criminal justice agencies to account. And at their worst, they have exacerbated suffering and misrepresented the needs of crime victims. Throughout our discussion we have sought to demonstrate, by drawing upon high-profile case studies, some of the complexities through which politics, the media and victim activism generate change.

Victim-driven activism can drive changes in public attitudes, criminal justice policy and the law. Activism driven by the energies of coping with loss; the changing face of political influence; the growth of new social media platforms and the rise of single-issue, media-driven interest movements should not be underestimated. All demonstrate the increasing power and potency of justice campaigns and the cultural significance of crime victims. Our conclusion is that whilst these irresistible forces bring with them the potential for social division and political misrepresentation, they also provide crime victims, and indeed all of us, with a genuine opportunity for moral debate and democratic engagement.

Acknowledgement We would like to thank the EU COST Action (CA18121) that funds the research network we both participate in called Cultures of Victimology: Understanding Processes of Victimization Across Europe. And we are very grateful to the British Academy and Leverhulme Trust (SG161060) who funded our project: 'Giving voice' to Victims: a strengths-based investigation into victim identities' and the research participants on this project whose insights helped shape the ideas in this chapter. And thanks also to Professor Suzan van der Aa at the University of Maastricht for her contribution to a joint paper with Dr Simon Green at the European Society of Criminology annual conference in Sarajevo (2018) entitled: 'Sexual Harassment in the Workplace: A Victimological Analysis of the #MeToo Campaign'.

References

Chancer, L. (2005). *High-Profile Crimes: When Legal Cases Become Social Causes.* Chicago, IL: University of Chicago Press.

Christie, N. (1977). Conflicts as Property. *British Journal of Criminology, 17*(1), 1–15.

Christie, N. (1986). The Ideal Victim. In E. A. Fattah (Ed.), *From Crime Policy to Victim Policy: Reorienting the Justice System.* Basingstoke: Macmillan.

Critcher, C. (2011). For a Political Economy of Moral Panics. *Crime, Media, Culture, 7*(3), 259–275.

Elias, R. (1993). *Victims Still: The Political Manipulation of Crime Victims.* London: Sage.

Garland, D. (1996). The Limits of the Sovereign State: Strategies of Crime Control in Contemporary Society. *British Journal of Criminology, 36*(4), 445–471.

Garland, D. (2000). The Culture of High Crime Societies: Some Preconditions of Recent 'Law and Order' Policies. *British Journal of Criminology, 40*(3), 347–375.

Garland, D. (2001). *The Culture of Control.* Oxford: Oxford University Press.

Gekoski, A., Gray, J., & Adler, J. (2012). What Makes a Homicide Newsworthy? *British Journal of Criminology, 52*(6), 1212–1232.

Green, S. (2007a). Crime, Victimisation and Vulnerability. In S. Walklate (Ed.), *Handbook of Victims and Victimology.* Cullompton: Willan.

Green, S. (2007b). Restorative Justice and the Victims' Movement. In G. Johnstone & D. Van Ness (Eds.), *A Handbook of Restorative Justice.* Collumpton: Willan.

Green, S. (2011). Vengeance and Furies: Existential Dilemmas in Penal Decision-Making. In R. Lippens & J. Hardie-Bick (Eds.), *Crime, Governance and Existential Predicaments.* Basingstoke: Palgrave Macmillan.

Green, S. (2015). *Crime, Community and Morality.* London: Routledge.

Greer, C. (2017). News Media, Victims and Crime. In P. Davies, P. Francis, & C. Greer (Eds.), *Victims, Crime and Society.* London: Sage.

Greer, C., & Reiner, R. (2012). Media Made Criminality: The Representation of Crime in the Mass Media. In M. Maguire, R. Morgan, & R. Reiner (Eds.), *The Oxford Handbook of Criminology* (3rd ed.). Oxford: OUP.

Harper, C., & Treadwell, J. (2013). Counterblast: Punitive Payne, Justice Campaigns, and Popular Punitivism – Where Next for 'Public Criminology'? *The Howard Journal of Criminal Justice, 52*(2), 216–222.

Home Office. (2007). *Review of the Protection of Children from Sex Offenders.* London: Home Office.

Innes, M. (2014). *Signal Crime: Social Reactions to Crime, Disorder and Control.* Oxford: OUP.

Jewkes, Y. (2015). *Media and Crime* (3rd ed.). London: Sage.

Jones, T., & Newburn, T. (2013). Policy Convergence, Politics and Comparative Penal Reform: Sex Offender Notification Schemes in the USA and UK. *Punishment and Society, 15*(5), 439–467.

Karstedt, S. (2002). Emotions and Criminal Justice. *Theoretical Criminology, 6*(3), 299–317.

Loader, I., & de Haan, W. (2002). On Emotions of Crime, Punishment and Social Control. *Theoretical Criminology, 6*(3), 243–253.

Leveson Inquiry. (2012). Report into the Culture, Practice and Ethics of the Press. Retrieved from http://www.official-documents.gov.uk/documents/hc1213/hc07/0780/0780.asp.

Maguire, M., & Pointing, J. (Eds.). (1988). *Victims of Crime: A New Deal?* Milton Keynes: OUP.

Marsh, H. L. (1991). A Comparative Analysis of Crime Coverage in Newspapers in the United States and Other Countries from 1960–1989: A Review of the Literature. *Journal of Criminal Justice, 19*(1), 60–80.

Mawby, R. I., & Walklate, S. (1994). *Critical Victimology*. London: Sage.

McGarry, R., & Walklate, S. (2015). *Victims: Trauma, Testimony and Justice*. London: Routledge.

Mulley, K. (2001). Victimized by the Media. *Criminal Justice Matters, 43*, 30–31.

O'Leary, N. (2016). 'Ethics and Methods in Victim Research' and 'Notoriety and Victims'. In K. Corteen et al. (Eds.), *Companion to Crime, Harm and Victimisation*. Bristol: Policy Press.

O'Leary, N. (2018). Public-Private Tragedy: Stigma, Victimisation and Community Identity. *International Review of Victimology, 24*(2), 165–181.

O'Malley, P. (2001). Policing Crime Risks in the Neo-liberal Era. In K. Stenson & R. R. Sullivan (Eds.), *Crime, Risk and Justice: The Politics of Crime Control in Liberal Democracies*. Collumpton: Willan.

Peelo, M. (2006). Framing Homicide Narratives in Newspapers: Mediated Witness and the Construction of Virtual Victimhood. *Crime, Media, Culture: An International Journal, 2*(2), 159–175.

Reiner, R., Livingstone, S., & Allen, J. (2000). Casino Culture: Media and Crime in a Winner-Loser Society. In K. Stenson & D. Cowell (Eds.), *Crime, Risk and Justice*. Collumpton: Willan.

Rock, P. (2004). *Constructing Victims' Rights: The Home Office, New Labour and Victims*. Oxford: OUP.

Rojek, C. (2001). *Celebrity*. London: Reaktion books.

Shapland, J., Willmore, J., & Duff, P. (1985). *Victims of Crime in the Criminal Justice System*. Aldershot: Gower.

Silverman, J., & Wilson, D. (2002). *Innocence Betrayed: Paedophilia, the Media, and Society*. Cambridge: Polity.

Smolej, M. (2010). Constructing Ideal Victims? Violence Narratives in Finnish Crime-Appeal Programming. *Crime Media Culture, 6*(1), 69–85.

Soothill, K., Francis, B., Ackerley, E., & Fligelstone, R. (2002). *Murder and Serious Sexual Assault: What Criminal Histories Can Reveal About Future Serious Offending*. Police Research Series Paper 144. London: Home Office.

Sullivan, R. R. (2003). The Schizophrenic State: Neo-liberal Criminal Justice. In K. Stenson & R. R. Sullivan (Eds.), *Crime, Risk and Justice: The Politics of Crime Control in Liberal Democracies*. Cullompton: Willan.

Williams, B. (1999). *Working with Victims of Crime: Policies, Politics and Practice*. London: Jessica Kingsley.

Young, J., & Matthews, R. (2003). New Labour, Crime Control and Social Exclusion. In R. Matthews & J. Young (Eds.), *The New Politics of Crime and Punishment*. Collompton: Willan.

8

Disablist Hate Crime: A Scar on the Conscience of the Criminal Justice System?

Jemma Tyson

Introduction

There is no universal definition of hate crime, with terminology, and therefore policies and legislation, varying significantly from jurisdiction to jurisdiction. The diverging context of hate crime is perhaps most evident in the numbers of these offences that are recorded around the world, as published by the Organisation for Security and Cooperation in Europe (OSCE 2018). For example, in 2017 Greece recorded 128 hate crimes, Denmark recorded 446 and the US recorded 8437. However, despite having a much smaller population than the US, the UK recorded 95,552 hate crimes and has consistently recorded more than any other country year on year. In relation to disablist hate crimes more specifically, of the 57 participating states reporting to the OSCE, only 11 states recorded

J. Tyson (✉)

Institute of Criminal Justice Studies, Faculty of Humanities and Social Sciences University of Portsmouth, Portsmouth, UK
e-mail: jemma.tyson@port.ac.uk

© The Author(s) 2020
J. Tapley, P. Davies (eds.), *Victimology*,
https://doi.org/10.1007/978-3-030-42288-2_8

data on crimes against people with disabilities. The US recorded just 128 disablist hate crimes compared to 7226 recorded in the UK.

This significant difference between jurisdictions does not suggest that the UK is more hostile than other countries nor that the risk of victimisation is significantly higher. Instead, it can be argued that these statistics, which should be treated with considerable caution, suggest identification and recording practices, and possibly even trust and confidence amongst victims and communities, are stronger in the UK than elsewhere. The policies and practices currently in place are the result of a number of events and campaigns that have occurred over the last 25 years, not least the tragic murder of Stephen Lawrence in 1993. This case, and the subsequent inquiry, were the catalyst for change in how hate crime is defined and reported, allowing for the victim, or any other person, to define their victimisation as a hate crime, without facing the prospect of being overruled by the police. This also served to draw attention to the victimisation of other communities subject to hate crimes motivated by prejudices and hostility beyond race. This tragedy is now widely recognised as being one of the most significant events in the history of the criminal justice system within the UK (Giannasi 2015).

The primary focus for academics and politicians within England and Wales has historically been on racially motivated hate crimes, amplified since the EU referendum, but this chapter will concentrate specifically on disablist hate crime. Whilst this is not to ignore the existence of intersections between class-race-age-gender and other characteristics, there are unique dimensions associated with disablist hate crime that are worthy of particular attention.

To start, this chapter will explore the meaning of the term disablist hate crime and then explore the nature and extent of this problem. The impact of such victimisation on individuals and wider communities will also be discussed, highlighting the challenges faced in recognising this type of victimisation. The complexities surrounding disablist hate crime and the significance of criminal justice responses will then be explored. Finally, the role of identity politics in shaping responses to disablist hate crime will be considered, in addition to highlighting a perceived hierarchy within hate crime, and exploring drivers for change within this field.

What Is Disablist Hate Crime?

The term *disability* is an umbrella term for a number of *impairments* (see Vik Finkelstein 2001 and Oliver 1996 for more discussion on this). For criminal justice practitioners, disability is often understood with reference to the definition set in Section 6 of the Equality Act 2010. This definition refers to physical or mental impairments that have a substantial and long-term effect on an individual. The definition is broad and thus brings unique challenges for those responding to disablist hate crime victimisation.

There is no hate crime legislation per se in England and Wales, but there is a shared working definition of hate crime and hate incidents used by criminal justice agencies outlined by the College of Policing (2014: 4) as:

> any crime or incident where the perpetrator's hostility or prejudice against an identifiable group of people is a factor in determining who is victimised.

As agreed at the Association of Chief Police Officers (now the National Police Chiefs' Council) conference in 2007 (Giannasi 2015: 109), disablist hate crime can be understood as:

> any criminal offence which is perceived, by the victim or any other person, to be motivated by a hostility or prejudice based on a person's disability or perceived disability.

The Criminal Justice Act 2003 contains provisions aimed at addressing offences motivated and aggravated by hostility on the basis of disability. Section 146 affords an increased tariff on offences which:

a) at the time of committing the offence, or immediately before or after doing so, the offender demonstrated towards the victim of the offence hostility based on…

  ii. a disability (or presumed disability) of the victim, or

b) that the offence is motivated (wholly or partly)-…

   ii. by hostility towards persons who have a disability or particular disability.

Civil law also provides some protection against discrimination towards people with disabilities. The Equality Act 2010 aims to tackle discrimination and 'prohibit victimisation in certain circumstances'. This Act brings together nine pieces of legislation, including the Disability Discrimination Act 1995, the Race Relations Act 1976 and the Equality Act 2006. It strengthens the protection from discrimination for people with disabilities by including disability as one of the protected characteristics (Section 6), bringing disability to an equal standing alongside race and religion. Whilst the aforementioned legislation provides some protection from discriminatory behaviours, they do not create a specific criminal offence of disablist aggravated offences. This is to be contrasted with racist and religiously aggravated offences and the legislation provided by the Crime and Disorder Act 1998.

Many interpretations of disability are framed according to the social model of disability. This model influences the perspective adopted in this chapter. Social model theorists argue that it is the way society isolates and excludes those with impairments from full participation in society that creates a disability, rather than being caused by the impairment itself (Abberley 1996; Finkelstein 2001; Oliver 1996; Porter 2015). Whilst reiterating the notion of marginalisation discussed in other models (such as the medical model), this model places an emphasis on social processes and social policies to promote participation and empowerment for those with disabilities (Porter 2015: 21). The term *disablist hate crime* is therefore used throughout this chapter, rather than *disability hate crime*. The latter is problematic as other forms of hate crime are referred to by the type of prejudice that causes them, such as *racist* and *homophobic*. However, *disability* is often used rather than *disablist* (Mason-Bish 2013: 21). This therefore places an emphasis on the disability of the victim rather than the motivating prejudice of the offender; positioning blame on the victim, presenting their disabilities as 'the problem' and denying them a victim status. Combined with the victimisation itself, this can not only alter the perceptions that people with disabilities have of themselves but also how people will perceive individuals with disabilities. *Disablist* hate crime, on the other hand, positions the problem within the motivating prejudice.

The Rise of Disablist Hate Crime as a Political and Social Issue

Examples of early forms of discrimination and hate-motivated behaviour can be evidenced throughout history, from the hostile treatment of people with disabilities in Ancient Greece to the genocide of various groups during the Holocaust (see Hall (2013) for an extensive discussion on this). The Middle Ages also saw people with disabilities as the subjects of superstition and persecution, with disability closely associated with evil and witchcraft, and widely considered a divine judgement for wrong-doing (Barnes 2010; Haffter 1968). In 1834, the Poor Law Reform Act demonstrated further hostile attitudes towards disability, with the need for welfare and support recognised but yet seen as inherently less desirable than paid work and the principle of less eligibility crept in (Harris and Roulstone 2001: 8). Here one can see a mirroring of Aristotle's views; 'A condition of unfit for hard work is…undesirable' (350/1992: 442), clearly displaying negative connotations of disability. This gave premise for the rise of the eugenics movement during the Second World War and focus on improving the human race through sterilisation and extermination, culminating in the murder of nearly 100,000 people with disabilities by the Nazi regime (Barnes 2010; Wolfensberger 1980).

Within the UK, the disability rights movement really took hold in the 1960s with the work of disabled activists, alongside a backdrop of other social movements that challenged the post-war consensus, such as the civil rights movement, feminist and LGBT activism. Hunt's (1966) edited collection, 'Stigma: The Experience of Disability', challenged the perceptions of the 'suffering' of individuals with disabilities and highlighted the dominance of able-bodied norms forced upon others. In 1972, the Union of the Physically Impaired Against Segregation (UPIAS) was founded by Hunt and other disability campaigners, such as Vik Finkelstein and Maggie Davis. The Union redefined disability as a 'restriction of activity caused by contemporary social organisation which takes no or little account of people with physical impairments' (UPIAS 1976: 3–4), enabling the emergence of the social model of disability. In 1970, a key step forward for equality was evidenced with the introduction of the Chronically Sick and Disabled Person's Act, which focused on improving environmental access for people with disabilities. This Act recognised the need for comprehensive services to support the chronically sick and disabled and their individual needs. The effectiveness of this legislation is debateable, but the movement for anti-discrimination laws had clearly begun in the decade of the 1970s. By the 1980s, despite the reluctance of the Conservative Thatcher government to recognise discrimination against people with disabilities (Barnes 2010), after 14 attempts the Disability Discrimination Act was eventually passed in 1995.

However, it was not until the late 1990s that the term we now understand and recognise as *hate crime* was really established within political and scholarly debate. The murder of Stephen Lawrence in April 1993, and more specifically the public inquiry that followed in 1999, was arguably the catalyst for the development of current policy and legislation to tackle hate crime. Racist murders, and racist violence more widely, were not uncommon at that time, with a number of similar incidents taking place prior to April 1993, but the impact of Stephen's murder was, however, exceptional. The failings of the Metropolitan Police Service and wider criminal justice system were criticised by Lord Macpherson's inquiry findings published in 1999. The inquiry was commissioned by the then Home Secretary, Jack Straw MP, in response to the campaign for justice by Stephen's parents, Neville and Doreen Lawrence.

The inquiry, which identified multiple failings and produced the finding of *institutional racism*, ultimately served to place hate crime on the political agenda. However, it was the unrelenting campaigning for change by the Lawrence family, notably Stephen's parents, that drove the significant changes in criminal justice policy and practice that were to follow (see O'Leary and Green, Chapter 7). Their efforts and those of the activists and lobbyists that followed ultimately allowed for:

- the profile of hate crimes motivated by other factors, such as religion, gender, sexual orientation and of course disability, to be raised
- the ability for the victim, or any other person, to define their victimisation as a hate crime, without needing to evidence or justify this when reporting to the police
- the integration of the use of independent advisory groups into mainstream policing.

The move to perception-based recording, allowing the victim or any other person to perceive a crime as a hate crime and requiring the police to record it as such, represented an important shift in how we understand hate crime. This further opened the doors for other forms of targeted victimisation, beyond race, to be given political, social and academic focus. In many ways, the Lawrence family gave a voice to those who had previously not been heard by those in positions of power.

Evidence of this in recent times can be seen with the creation and ongoing existence of various non-governmental and charitable organisations, with a collective aim of raising the profile of disablist hate crime, providing supporting to victims and communities and scrutinising criminal justice agencies in their handling of such cases. Examples of such organisations are:

- Dimensions—founded in 1976, Dimensions supports individuals with learning disabilities to have more choice and control of their lives.
- Disability Rights UK—founded in 2012 following the merge of several disability charities, with the majority of members and trustees being people with disabilities. The organisations campaigns to strengthen and protect the rights of people with disabilities.
- The Foundation for People with Learning Disabilities—founded in 1999 and part of the Mental Health Foundation. It works to influence government and local authority policies and services on the rights of people with learning disabilities.
- Stop Hate UK—founded in 1995 as a service for victims of racial harassment, as a response to the murder of Stephen Lawrence. It relaunched in 2007 to reflect a wider remit to support victims and challenge all forms of hate crime and they now have a specific helpline for victims of learning disablist hate crime.

Drivers for Change

Often referred to as disability's 'Lawrence' moment is the tragic case of Fiona Pilkington and Francecca Hardwick. In 2007, Fiona drove herself and her disabled daughter, Francecca, to a lay-by near their home and set fire to the car with them inside, killing them both. The inquest that followed in 2009 found that there were failings in police procedures and the recognition of repeat victimisation, and that the deaths were due to the stress surrounding their ongoing victimisation by local youths. It was found that Fiona had made 33 calls to the police between 1997 and 2007, yet there was no link made between the targeted anti-social behaviour and the vulnerability of the family (IPCC 2011: 24) nor were the disabilities of Francecca, and her brother Anthony, taken into consideration by the police as motivating factors for their victimisation.

In response to the deaths of Fiona Pilkington and Francecca Hardwick, and wider concerns about violence and hostility towards people with disabilities throughout Britain, two inquiries conducted by the Equality and Human Rights Commission (EHRC) are further drivers for change. Building on the findings of an earlier report in 2009, the first of these two reports, published in 2011, was named 'Hidden in Plain Sight'—a pertinent title for the 18-month report into disability related harassment which highlighted 'systemic failures by organisations in preventing disability-related harassment and in tackling it effectively' (EHRC 2011: 5). This inquiry examined ten cases of severe victimisation against people with disabilities, all of whom were targeted because of their disabilities yet none were identified as disablist hate crimes. Similar failings across the cases were identified within the police forces and partner agencies involved. Seven core recommendations were made with a further 79 detailed recommendations, not just for criminal justice agencies but for government, social housing, public transport operators, healthcare providers and schools, to name just a few. These reflect the concerns of campaigners in the 1960s regarding broad social inequalities.

In 2012, the EHRC published their follow-up report to the 2011 inquiry, named 'Out in the Open'. This report concluded that many of the recommendations made previously still needed to be actioned and achieved, and whilst disablist hate crime may be *out in the open*, there was still much to be resolved.

The Nature and Extent of Disablist Hate Crime

As with the concept of disability, disablist hate crime is also a complex concept. It is important to highlight here, particularly to those who are not familiar with this literature and discourse, that there is an absence of *hate* in the definitions provided above. The terminology used instead places an emphasis on *hostility* and *prejudice*, two terms that are themselves convoluted. As Jacobs and Potter (1998) argue, all individuals have prejudices and the more we search for them, the more we will find. The inclusion of hostility and prejudice in the definitions is therefore significant and crucial in understanding the nature and extent of hate crime. The thresholds for demonstrating hostility and prejudice are much lower than those of *hate*, meaning a lesser degree of animosity needs to be demonstrated in order to fulfil the legislation that hate crime reflects. Consequently, this not only widens the boundaries of disablist hate crime to lower level offending, but it also allows for the inclusion of non-crime incidents to be recorded as disablist hate incidents. With the latter, whilst the behaviour committed is not a criminal offence, the disablist motivation is still evidenced. It is important that hate incidents are monitored as they draw attention to lower level incidents, which have a disproportionate impact on the victim and wider communities and are often the precursors to more serious crimes.

It is perhaps not surprising that the distinction between anti-social behaviour and disablist hate crime is often blurred (Hayden and Nardone 2012). Section 2 of the Anti-social Behaviour, Crime and Disorder Act 2014 defines anti-social behaviour as:

a) conduct that has caused, or is likely to cause, harassment, alarm or distress to any person,
b) conduct capable of causing nuisance or annoyance to a person in relation to that person's occupation of residential premises, or
c) conduct capable of causing housing-related nuisance or annoyance to any person.

As can be seen with this definition, no *crime* needs to be committed, but the negative *impact* on the victim(s) is what differentiates behaviour from anti-social behaviour. As stressed earlier when discussing the definition of hate crime, the use of ambiguous and loose terminology is present—for example, 'harassment', 'alarm' or 'distress', 'nuisance' or 'annoyance'—and similarity confusing is the everyday definition of hostility (discussed later on in the chapter).

The Nature of Disablist Hate Crime

The nature of disablist hate crime differs from other hate crimes, particularly with the notion of 'mate crime' (a term that arguably creates the same problem as disability hate crime) and the move away from a perceived 'stranger danger'. Common examples of behaviours associated with disablist hate crimes are:

- physical and verbal abuse
- threat and intimidation
- inhibiting day-to-day activities, such as knowingly moving items out of reach
- deception, such as charging a person with disabilities for 'house sitting'
- cuckooing—where young or vulnerable persons are exploited 'to achieve the storage and/or supply of drugs, movement of cash proceeds and to secure the use of dwellings' (National Crime Agency 2017: 2)

Whilst some of these may not be considered to be criminal, they can have a negative impact on the targeted individual, with clear demonstrations of hostility. The following examples help to demonstrate the wide scale of behaviour associated with disablist hate crime:

- Steven Hoskin was a 38-year-old man with learning disabilities whose murder was the culmination of ongoing abuse. Prior to his death in July 2006, he had been tortured, suffering various injuries inflicted upon him by a group of perpetrators and was forced to make a false confession that he was a paedophile. Despite previous increased contact with police and health services, this did not trigger any safeguarding referral.

- David Askew, another individual with learning disabilities, reported 88 incidents to the police between 2004 and 2010, with only one incident recorded as a disablist hate crime. The onus was also placed on David's family to reduce his victimisation, with the presumption made by police that he would not be a very good witness (EHRC 2011). David died of a heart attack at his home in March 2010, minutes after local youths had reportedly thrown a wheelie bin around and tampered with his mother's mobility scooter.
- In 2011, a BBC Panorama programme exposed the widespread physical and psychological abuse against people with learning disabilities by staff at Winterbourne View, a residential care home. Despite a senior nurse previously reporting concerns to the management and the Care Quality Commission, this was not followed up. Eleven members of staff were convicted of neglect and abuse and the home was shut down, alongside two others.

To further distinguish disablist hate crime from other forms of hate crime, perpetrators of the former often have the opportunity to exert control over the victim, particularly when they are relatives, friends or carers and do so in order to stop the exposure of their behaviour (Tyson and Hall 2015: 81). In addition, some individuals with disabilities are unaware that they are or have been victims of disablist hate crime. Sin et al. (2009: vii) argue that the victimisation is often accepted as being part of everyday life, with the understanding that everyone else has the same experiences. As Brookes (2013: 91) recalls in his account of the daily hostility he has experienced, individuals underestimate how often they are targeted. Some individuals, particularly those with learning disabilities, may also not understand the processes involved in reporting and prosecuting incidences of disablist hate crime, hindering their access to justice.

Conceptualising Disablist Hate Crime as a Process

Within his work on racism, Ben Bowling (1993: 238) argues that racism, and by analogy disablist hate crime, is a *process*, rather than a *static event*:

> process implies an analysis which is dynamic, includes the social relationships between all the actors involved in the process; can capture the continuity across physical violence, threat, intimidation; can capture the dynamic of repeated or systematic victimization; incorporates historical context; and takes account of the social relationships which inform definitions of appropriate and inappropriate behaviour.

Similarly, Hollomotz (2013) has identified a continuum of violence specifically pertaining to disability. This continuum highlights the fact that boundaries between daily exclusions, derogatory treatment and violence are not distinct. This can create difficulties in distinguishing between behaviours that are common intrusions and incidences of hate crime.

Collectively, this interpretation of disablist hate crime as both a process and a continuum places an importance on the development of the sustained prejudiced views, rather than on a specific event where such prejudice is demonstrated. When applying this approach to disablist hate crime, one can perhaps better understand the impact and context surrounding the daily, repeated victimisation that individuals with disabilities often experience. The ongoing nature of this process and the impact of such victimisation becomes a part of lived reality. The very nature of criminal law, however, suggests that the criminal justice system must respond to incidents, which places it at odds with the processual nature of the offending behaviour within disablist hate crimes.

Walklate (2004) also challenges the conceptualisation of victimisation, more generally, as a one-off event and instead argues that victimisation is a highly complex process comprising of three elements. The primary victimisation is where the interaction between the offender and the victim occurs during the commission of an offence. This is followed by the victim's reaction to this, perhaps involving any formal response. The final element relates to further interactions between the victim and the offender and secondary victimisation may occur if this has a negative impact on the victim. She argues that all three elements should be acknowledged in order to understand the full impact of any victimisation.

The difficulties outlined above can mean that disablist hate crime is not discovered until it is too late and the extent of these offences, and the subsequent victimisation, is not fully known or appreciated. A brief analysis of available statistics on disablist hate crime can help to illustrate this. In 2017/2018, 7226 disablist hate crimes were recorded by police in England and Wales (HM Government 2018: 12). However, the combined 2015/2016 to 2017/2018 Crime Survey of England and Wales data estimates that there were 52,000 disablist hate crimes per year (HM Government 2018: 27). Whilst the number of disablist hate crimes recorded to the police has increased from the previous year (from 5558), this is still far from the amount reported in the victimisation survey.

Impacts of Victimisation

Impact on the Individual

A growing volume of literature demonstrates that hate crimes have a disproportionate impact on the victim (College of Policing 2014; Corcoran and Smith 2016; Hollomotz 2013; Stone 2015). Iganski's (2001) influential text, aptly titled 'Hate Crimes Hurt More', represents one of the earliest accounts of this acute impact. He claims that there are two types of injury received by a victim of hate crime. First, a *psychic injury* that refers to the emotional and psychological impact hate crimes have. Second, the *in terrorem* effect. This is the message sent to members of the group the victim is associated with (in this case those with disabilities), meaning the harm inflicted on the individual victim is accompanied by the harm inflicted on the victim's cultural group, and potentially other minority groups, through a fear of victimisation (Perry 2015). When applying both of these injuries to victims of disablist hate crime, combined with the unique additional challenges faced by these victims (as discussed below), it is reasonable to argue that *disablist* hate crimes hurt most.

Victims of disablist hate crime have often been advised to employ avoidance strategies to reduce their victimisation and not put themselves in risky situations (Sin et al. 2009: vi), such as walking a different way home, not going out at particular times and carrying a personal alarm. However, this places a primary responsibility on the victim to change their behaviour, rather than dealing with the disablist attitudes of the offender. This is very similar to the position of those impacted by *disability hate crime*. The impact of victimisation on the lives of the victims is thus exacerbated. Combined with the exceptional issues surrounding the familiarity of the perpetrators, the lack of confidence in police responses and the existing perceptions towards individuals with disabilities, disablist hate crime can cause an already ostracised group to experience further discrimination.

Impact on Access to Justice

As mentioned above, perpetrators are often individuals known to the victim and this personal intrusion can cause victims to fear harm or reprisals if they report such behaviour (Joint Committee on Human Rights 2008; Saxton et al. 2001). This is akin to the challenges faced by domestic abuse victims, as Saxton et al. (2001) explored. In addition, there is also the fear of not knowing what will happen once information is reported to the police and this is a particular issue for those with learning disabilities (Sin 2015).

The reluctance to report is compounded by low levels of trust and confidence in the police response to such victimisation. A joint inspection by HMCPSI, HMIC and HMI Probation (2013) criticised the police for missing opportunities to engage, communicate and build bridges with people with disabilities, in turn causing these individuals to feel marginalised by the police, in addition to the primary victimisation. Research by Williams et al. (2008) found barriers to reporting largely revolve around a lack of confidence in the ability of the police to resolve the harassment and victimisation. This is supported by Sin et al. (2009). Barriers also include the attitudes of others towards people with disabilities. The imprecise use of language has been mentioned earlier and interpretations of 'disability' tend to focus on what people cannot do, rather than what they can do. There is often a perception that people with learning disabilities are unreliable witnesses with an inability to give evidence

(Sin 2013), but such views tend not to be as prevalent with other forms of hate crime. People with disabilities are often also described as easy targets and 'vulnerable' by society (Roulstone and Sadique 2013), promoting a social care response or protection measures, rather than a criminal justice response (Chakraborti and Garland 2012; Perry 2008).

It has been widely reported that people with disabilities fear they will not be believed and/or taken seriously by the police or other agencies (HMCPSI, HMIC and HMI Probation 2013; Sin 2013; Sharp 2001; Sin et al. 2009). Whilst this is also true for victims of other crime types, this is more acute for those of disablist hate crime. Previous experiences of engaging with the police are an important determinate in the levels of confidence afforded to police. This is an important factor across the hate crime arena as hate crime victims are more likely to be affected by their victimisation and less satisfied with the police response, than victims of crime overall. For example, 52% of hate crime victims were very or fairly satisfied with the handling of the incident, a figure much lower than the 73% satisfaction levels from victims of crime overall (Corcoran and Smith 2016: 21). The cases of Fiona Pilkington and Francecca Hardwick, David Askew and Steven Hoskin are all examples of failed criminal justice responses, each made numerous reports to police with negative results (EHRC 2011). This also reflects some of the difficulties that police have in correctly identifying disablist hate crime and the victims (Trickett and Hamilton 2016). Combined with the social marginalisation experienced by people with disabilities, this denied access to justice can severely impede the life opportunities available to these individuals.

Complexities Within the Criminal Justice System

In 2008, former Director of Public Prosecutions (DPP), Sir Ken MacDonald QC claimed that:

> [Disablist hate crime] ... is a scar on the conscience of the criminal justice system. And all bodies and all institutions involved in the delivery of justice... share the responsibility.

Here, the responsibility to respond effectively to disablist hate crime and deliver justice to victims is shared by all agencies working within the criminal justice system, not just the police. There is therefore a need to understand the unique challenges that disablist hate crime presents for those delivering justice (or attempting to); challenges that are not present with other hate crime victims. Some of the issues raised by MacDonald's statement have already been mentioned, but the 'vulnerability versus hostility' debate is of particular importance here. Roulstone and Morgan (2009) argues that whilst there are some individuals who may be vulnerable in certain circumstances due to the severity of their impairment, it would be erroneous to apply this term to all individuals with a disability. Although not unique to disability, when the notion of vulnerability is used to exclude incidents of victimisation from the hate crime arena, this has harmful consequences. As with the term *disability*, *vulnerability* is also a term with negative connotations, suggesting a weakness of the individual and is often applied to an oppressed group by a powerful majority (Roulstone and Sadique 2013). The victimisation of individuals with disabilities tends to be associated with their vulnerable situation. This dominant view places responsibility on the victim's behaviour rather than the offender's motivation, putting their victim status in jeopardy. As Das (2007: 63) states, 'To be vulnerable is not the same as to be a victim'. The associations and connotations of the term vulnerability raise doubt as to whether a hostility towards the disability, or perceived disability, motivates the offending behaviour or whether the victim was seen as an 'easy target'.

The Crown Prosecution Service (2016) policy on hate crime states that hostility can be understood to mean *unfriendliness, ill-will, spite* and *dislike*, amongst other terms. Although one can argue that choosing to target an individual with a disability because they are perceived to be an easy target is a demonstration of ill-will, this is difficult to prove in court. So, whilst there is recognition of disablist hostility within the Criminal Justice Act 2003, the application of the *vulnerable* label to people with disabilities, combined with the avoidance strategies mentioned previously, are denying the identity politics of disability. Combined with the variations in legislative provisions, this only fuels the perception of a hate crime hierarchy, where a greater focus is placed on race hate crimes than those of a disablist nature (Chakraborti and Garland 2012; Mason-Bish 2013; Roulstone and Sadique 2013).

At the time of writing, the most recent assessment of criminal justice provision in response to disablist hate crime can be found in the HMICFRS and HMCPSI inspection report (2018). The findings acknowledged that whilst improvements have been made within some aspects of casework, police and prosecutors are still not sufficiently considering the needs of victims, particularly in relation to the provision of reasonable adjustments when giving evidence.

Identity Politics and Campaigning

As outlined in the discussion so far, the development of current policy and legislation surrounding hate crime has largely been the result of campaigning and advocacy in the wake of tragic cases. The very inclusion of the five centrally monitored strands of hate crime—race, religion, sexual orientation, disability and gender identity—in England and Wales is testament to the endeavours of such victim and campaign groups (Jacobs and Potter 1998; Mason-Bish 2010). This has taken place within the wider politicisation of victims more generally.

In the context of the US, Jacobs and Potter (1998) argue in their seminal text that anti-hate crime movements are influenced by the emphasis society places on identity politics, not by 'epidemics of unprecedented bigotry'. They explain identity politics to mean:

> politics whereby individuals relate to one another as members of competing groups based on characteristics like race, gender, religion, and sexual orientation. According to the logic of identity politics, it is strategically advantageous to be recognized as disadvantaged and victimised. The greater a group's victimization, the stronger its moral claim on the larger society. (Jacobs and Potter 1998: 5)

In other words, Jacob and Potter's position is that hate crime has emerged within political agendas due to certain groups achieving recognition of their plight. In relation to England and Wales, Hall (2005: 54) has argued that:

the legislative widening of the net beyond the original provisions for race contained within the Crime and Disorder Act is [due to] a complex combination of 'identity politics' and the need to respond to widespread concerns resulting from national…events.

The formal recognition of disablist hate crime is therefore a product of increased concern relating to issues surrounding the extent, nature and impact of such victimisation. Often driven by *cause celebres*, there has been notable success in bringing the problem of disablist hate crime to the attention of those with the power and authority to address it. There are, however, a number of complex issues in this process, which this chapter will now explore.

Identity Politics and the Challenges in Achieving Justice for Victims of Disablist Hate Crime

With many groups trying to get their voices heard, minority groups are often unwilling to report their achievements as there is a fear of being removed from the political agenda should they be deemed to 'no longer need' the support and attention. Furthermore, there is also the danger of being too eager in collaboration with governments, as this runs the risk of governments taking over the agendas and people with disabilities losing control of their agenda (Barnes and Oliver 1995). There is therefore a complex balance between being detached enough from government in order to maintain independence, but close enough to exert influence.

The very recognition of disablist hate crime as a centrally monitored strand of hate crime can be deemed a success. This requires all forces within England and Wales to record such offences and in doing so, helps to place disablist hate crime within policy and strategic agendas of policing. The rates of successful use of s146 of the Criminal Justice Act, however, remain low. In 2017/2018, 754 disablist hate crime referrals were made to the CPS from police, a decrease of 234 from the previous year. The number of completed prosecutions was 752, with 24.8% of successfully completed prosecutions resulting in an announced and recorded sentence uplift. Whilst the number of completed prosecutions has dropped by 257 from 2016/2017 (which had the highest number of completed prosecutions to date), the percentage resulting in a sentence uplift has increased by 9.3% from the previous year. A sentence uplift refers to the increase in punishment administered upon evidence of targeted hostility against a protected characteristic. The small percentage of cases that receive a sentence uplift is however still a cause for concern and indicative of the difficulties and complexities in achieving such a result. Furthermore, with a significant attrition rate between the reports to the Crime Survey of England and Wales and the successful prosecutions with an uplift, the necessity for campaigning and raising the profile of the disablist hate crime within this field is still very much present.

The monitoring and prosecution of such cases does however reaffirm the message that disablist hate crime is unacceptable. Cultural constructions of such victimisations also begin to shift with a wider recognition of this as a problem. In addition, within the 2014 College of Policing guidance on hate crime disablist hate crime is the first of the five strands to be discussed over 12.5 pages (longer than the sections on the other four strands). Perhaps most significantly, the document spends a considerable amount of time explaining the nature of disablist hate crimes and unpicking some of the common misconceptions associated with the identification of this type of offence. Following Jacobs and Potter's work, the identity politics surrounding disablist hate crime has therefore contributed to the recognition of the victimisation experienced by this minority group.

The summary provided above is, however, perhaps a reductionist and simplistic overview and several problems remain. Firstly, Hall (2013) argues that the way in which hate crime is officially defined and conceptualised (through identity politics) determines the volume and nature of such recorded incidents. With a huge disparity between police recording of racist and disablist hate crimes (the former at 71,251 and the latter at 7226 (HM Government 2018), this would suggest that the conceptualisation and definition of racist compared to disablist hate are different, yet a hostility towards a particular characteristic underlies both types of hate crime. As discussed previously, there is no offence of disablist hate crime, but legislation does establish racially and religiously aggravated offences. Such an approach demonstrates a hierarchy of hate crime (see earlier discussion) and, in turn, a hierarchy of hate crime victimisation whereby greater focus is placed upon racist offences than those motivated by disablist hostility and prejudice (see Mason-Bish (2010), Roulstone and Sadique (2013) and Tyson et al. (2015) for further discussions on this). The strength of identity politics in relation to other groups therefore appears to be stronger than that in relation to disability. The emphasis placed on hate victimisation appears unequal between victim groups. So whilst disablist hate crime has been recognised, this lags behind the developments in other areas.

There is a perceived tension between groups who are campaigning and lobbying to raise the profile and understanding of disablist hate crime, primarily surrounding the level of funding afforded to groups. Mason-Bish's (2010) research found tension between social movement activists and large-scale campaign groups. Whilst they strive for the same goal, the larger charities (often run by non-disabled people) tend to receive much larger funding than the smaller groups, which people with disabilities run. Such frustration was also highlighted by Anne Novis MBE (2013), when reflecting upon her experiences as an individual with a disability and as a campaigner. She argues that although larger charitable organisations have had significant influences on policy, it is these 'non-disabled people's organisations who are…listened to by governments rather than our own DPOs' [disabled people organisations] (Novis 2013: 122). Charities that do not solely have people with disabilities running the organisation arguably do not have a mandate to speak on their behalf. Therefore, particular types of campaigners and lobbyists have arguably influenced the process by which disablist hate crime has been recognised by governments and authorities. It is important to recognise the wider context of austerity here. Morgan (2002: 32) argued that the competition for funding and resources resulted in groups that have a less organised campaign base being 'frozen out'. With recent cuts in public spending and funds for charitable organisations, this competition is therefore now more acute than ever before. This has further enhanced the difficulties that smaller, more local organisations face in maintaining their work, compared to the larger, national organisations which are not run by people with disabilities.

As previously discussed, *disability* is itself an umbrella term for a variety of disabilities, with examples of disablist hate crimes in the EHRCs reports involving people with learning and physical disabilities. As above, it is perhaps more helpful to recognise 'difference'. Several disability groups appear to be competing within this arena to have their own victimisation heard and addressed. For example, there are numerous organisations that focus solely on raising the profile of victimisation experienced by people with learning disabilities, for people with autism or for people with physical disabilities. Within these sub-groups, there are a variety of charities and non-governmental organisations that are increasingly pitted against one another competing for funding and to be the leading organisation. Those specifically supporting learning disability victims would seem to be lagging behind those pioneering the case for those with a physical disability. Identity politics are therefore not only between the various hate crime strands but also within them. Racial groups are pitted against each other for recognition. The profile of racist hate crime as a whole (perhaps due to the social and historical context surrounding race), sees significant recognition of the plight of racist hate crime.

Disablist victimisation may never attain the same profile as racially or religiously aggravated victimisation, but it is important that the efforts of those who have campaigned for the recognition of this are acknowledged. Much of this chapter has focused on identity politics. Such politics are a response to a relatively recent recognition of a problem surrounding the targeted victimisation of individuals with disabilities and such activism has undoubtedly raised the profile of this type of victimisation.

Policy and Practice

In 2009, the first cross-government Hate Crime Action Plan was published by the Labour government, ten years after the Macpherson report into Stephen Lawrence's murder. Aside from the legislation already in place to respond to hate crime, this marked the start of an important train of publications by governments. The then Home Secretary, Alan Johnson, stated in the foreword to the first action plan that it was:

a reminder to us of where we have come from, what we have learned, what
we have achieved and how much further we have to go. (HM
Government 2009: 3)

The key purpose of this report was to set out the strategic actions the
Labour government would take to tackle hate crime and to help assist
local partners in how they respond to this problem. The report made
reference to disablist (or in this case disability) hate crime 127 times. In
2012, the Coalition government of the Conservatives and Liberal
Democrats published their strategic Action Plan with 38 references to
disablist hate crime. The 2016 Action Plan of the Conservative government made only 30 references to such crime. These Action Plan reports
are an important marker in developments. They signify the national and
political agenda on hate crime. However, the trend within the publications suggests a visible, decreased focus on disablist hate crime. The
Action Plans guide national policing strategies for hate crime, which in
turn impact on local strategies. The shrinking profile represents a worrying decline in the attention afforded to disablist hate crime and suggests
the campaigning and lobbying that surrounds this topic is becoming less
impactive, or that other crimes have taken priority.

At the time of writing this chapter, the context that surrounds hate
crime is unprecedented and like nothing we have seen before. Following
the results of the EU referendum in June 2016 and the four terror attacks
in England between March and June 2017, hate crime received a renewed
focus from politicians, the media and criminal justice professionals. Due
to the terrorism-related nature of these events, this renewed focus is
mainly directed towards racial and religious hate crimes, rather than all
five centrally monitored strands. This is also reflected in the decline of
disability-related action points within the Hate Crime Action Plan. At
the National Police Chiefs' Councils hate crime conference in Manchester
in 2017, the National Police lead on hate crime, ACC Mark Hamilton,
expressed concerns that disablist hate crime was taking a back seat and
the previous work to raise the profile of disablist hate crime, by organisations such as the CPS, was being undone. Attention from politicians and
the media has been deflected, reinforcing a hate crime hierarchy.

Summary and Next Steps

The Macpherson Report in 1999 recommended the use of Independent Advisory Groups (IAGs) within policing. This group of community members would provide an impartial perspective and advice on policing through monitoring, observing and participating in police activity. A good practice example of this is the IAG to the Cross-Government Hate Crime Programme established in 2007. This IAG advises government on matters of policy and practice. Disability is represented amongst the membership of the IAG, with a number of individuals with disabilities involved in this group and the programme more widely. Such a process allows for direct pressure to be exerted on government, through this advisory group. The use of IAGs is also now common practice for all police forces (as recommended by the College of Policing). The independent groups provide an opportunity for community members to voice their opinions on matters within their local communities. In this sense, campaigners for disability rights are now able to exert influence from the inside rather than simply from the outside, as has generally been the case in the past. As such, these individuals have an important role to play in seeking to shape official responses to disablist hate crime in the future.

In 2014, the Law Commission published their review of existing legislation relating to hate offences and recommended that stirring up offences which stir up hatred should not be extended to include disability nor gender identity. Whilst the Commission recognised the desire to equally apply legislation to all monitored strands, it recommended a full-scale review of an enhanced sentencing system due to concerns over the effectiveness of current aggravated offences. This recommendation was belatedly acted upon by government, with the Law Commission finally invited to begin this review in late 2018. This lengthy delay in responding inevitably gives the impression that disablist hate crime, and perhaps hate crime more generally, is not a priority for the government.

This chapter has reviewed the monumental challenges faced by activists, campaign groups, lobbyist and individuals with disabilities themselves to secure positive change and sustained attention. Whilst the UK is leading the way in recording and responding to disablist hate crime, this has been a difficult road, and will no doubt continue to be so. Whilst there has been some success in raising the profile of disablist hate crime and incidents, with this type of victimisation deemed worthy of inclusion in hate crime policy, the specific needs of individuals with disabilities remain unmet. The biggest challenge is to maintain the movement that started in the 1960s, and became reinvigorated following the Stephen Lawrence Inquiry. Although raising awareness alone will not be enough to prevent future victimisation, this will, at the very least, push disablist hate crime into more conversations at national and local levels, thereby keeping the disability agenda firmly on the table. Maybe then, disablist hate crime can become less of a scar on the conscience of the criminal justice system.

References

Abberley, P. (1996). Work, Utopia and Impairment. In L. Barton (Ed.), *Disability and Society* (pp. 61–79). London: Longman.

Aristotle. (1992). *The Politics* (T. A. Sinclair, Trans.). London: Penguin. (Original work published 350BC).

Barnes, C. (2010). A Brief History of Discrimination and Disabled People. In L. J. Davies (Ed.), *The Disability Studies Reader* (pp. 20–32). New York: Routledge.

Barnes, C., & Oliver, M. (1995). Disability Rights: Rhetoric and Reality in the UK. *Disability and Society, 10*(1), 111–116.

Bowling, B. (1993). *Violent Racism: Victimisation, Policing and Social Context.* Oxford: Oxford University Press.

Brookes, M. (2013). A Different Reality. In A. Roulstone & H. Mason-Bish (Eds.), *Disability, Hate Crime and Violence* (pp. 90–97). London: Routledge.

Chakraborti, N., & Garland, J. (2012). Reconceptualizing Hate Crime Victimisation Through the Lens of Vulnerability and Difference. *Theoretical Criminology, 16*(4), 499–514.

College of Policing. (2014). *Hate Crime Operational Guidance.* Coventry: College of Policing Limited.

Corcoran, H., & Smith, K. (2016). *Hate Crime, England and Wales 2015/16.* London: Home Office.

Crown Prosecution Service. (2016). *Disability Hate Crime – CPS Action Plan.* Retrieved from https://www.cps.gov.uk/publications/docs/disability_hate_crime_action_plan_ 2014.pdf.

Das, V. (2007). *Life and Words: Violence and the Descent into the Ordinary.* Berkeley, CA: University of California Press.

Equality and Human Rights Commission (EHRC). (2011). *Hidden in Plain Sight: Inquiry into Disability Related Harassment.* Retrieved from http://www.equalityhumanrights.com/uploaded_files/disabilityfi/ehrc_hidden_in_plain_sight_3.pdf.

Finkelstein, V. (2001). The Social Model of Disability Repossessed. Retrieved from http://disability-studies.leeds.ac.uk/files/library /finkelstein-soc-mod-repossessed.pdf.

Giannasi, P. (2015). Hate Crime in the United Kingdom. In N. Hall, A. Corb, P. Giannasi, & J. G. D. Grieve (Eds.), *The Routledge International Handbook on Hate Crime* (pp. 105–116). Oxon: Routledge.

Haffter, C. (1968). The Changeling: History and Psychodynamics of Attitudes to Handicapped Children in European Folklore. *Journal of the History of Behavioural Studies, 4*(1), 55–61.

Hall, N. (2005). *Hate Crime.* Devon: Willan Publishing.

Hall, N. (2013). *Hate Crime* (2nd ed.). Oxon: Routledge.

Harris, J., & Roulstone, A. (2001). *Disability, Policy and Professional Practice.* London: Sage Publications.

Hayden, C., & Nardone, A. (2012). Moving in to Social Housing and the Dynamics of Difference. "Neighbours from Hell" with Nothing to Lose. *Internet Journal of Criminology.*

HM Government. (2009). *Hate Crime – The Cross-Government Action Plan.* Retrieved from http://www.niacro.co.uk/sites/default/files/publications/Hate%20Crime%20-The%20Cross-Government%20Action%20Plan-%20Home%20Office-Sep%202009.pdf.

HM Government. (2018). *Hate Crime, England and Wales, 2017/18.* London: Home Office.

HMCPSI, HMIC, and HMI Probation. (2013). *Living in a Different World: Joint Review of Disability Hate Crime.* Retrieved from the HMIC Website: http://www.hmic.gov.uk/media/a-joint-review-of-disability-hate-crime-living-in-a-different-world-20130321.pdf.

HMICFRS and HMCPSI. (2018). *Joint Inspection of the Handling of Cases Involving Disability Hate Crime.* Retrieved from the HMICFRS Website: https://www.justiceinspectorates.gov.uk/cjji/wp-content/uploads/sites/2/2018/10/CJJI_DHC_thm_Oct18._rpt.pdf.

Hollomotz, A. (2013). Disability and the Continuum of Violence. In A. Roulstone & H. Mason-Bish (Eds.), *Disability, Hate Crime and Violence* (pp. 52–63). London: Routledge.

Hunt, P. (1966). *Stigma: The Experience of Disability*. London: Geoffrey Chapman.

Iganski, P. (2001). Hate Crimes Hurt More. *American Behavioural Scientist, 45*(4), 626–638.

IPCC. (2011). *IPCC Report into the Contact Between Fiona Pilkington and Leicestershire Constabulary 2004–2007: Independent Investigation Final Report*. Retrieved from http://www.ipcc.gov.uk/en/Pages/inv_reports_central_region.aspx.

Jacobs, J. B., & Potter, K. (1998). *Hate Crimes: Criminal Law and Identity Politics*. New York: Oxford University Press.

Joint Committee on Human Rights. (2008). *A Life Like Any Other? Human Rights If Adults with Learning Disabilities*. HL Paper 40-I HC 73-I. London: House of Lords, House of Commons Joint Committee on Human Rights.

Mason-Bish, H. (2010). Future Challenges for Hate Crime Policy: Lessons from the Past. In N. Chakraborti (Ed.), *Hate Crime: Concepts, Policy, Future Directions* (pp. 58–77). Devon: Willan Publishing.

Mason-Bish, H. (2013). Conceptual Issues in the Construction of Disability Hate Crime. In A. Roulstone & H. Mason-Bish (Eds.), *Disability, Hate Crime and Violence* (pp. 11–24). London: Routledge.

Morgan, J. (2002). US Hate Crime Legislation: A Legal Model to Avoid in Australia. *Journal of Sociology, 38*(1), 25–48.

National Crime Agency. (2017). *County Lines Violence, Exploitation and Drug Supply 2017 National Briefing Report*. Retrieved from http://www.nationalcrimeagency.gov.uk/publications/832-county-lines-violence-exploitation-and-drug-supply-2017/file.

Novis, A. (2013). Disability Hate Crime: A Campaign Perspective. In A. Roulstone & H. Mason-Bish (Eds.), *Disability, Hate Crime and Violence* (pp. 118–125). London: Routledge.

Oliver, M. (1996). *Understanding Disability: From Theory to Practice*. Basingstoke: Palgrave.

OSCE. (2018). *Bias Against Other Groups – People with Disabilities*. Retrieved from http://hatecrime.osce.org/what-hate-crime/bias-against-other-groups-%E2%80%93-people-disabilities.

Perry, J. (2008). The 'Perils' of an Identity Politics Approach to the Legal Recognition of Harm. *Liverpool Law Review, 29*(1), 19–36. https://doi.org/10.1177/1362480612439432.

Perry, B. (2015). Exploring the Community Impacts of Hate Crime. In N. Hall, A. Corb, P. Giannasi, & J. G. D. Grieve (Eds.), *The Routledge International Handbook on Hate Crime* (pp. 47–58). Oxon: Routledge.

Porter, J. (2015). *Understanding and Responding to the Experience of Disability*. London: Routledge.

Roulstone, A., & Morgan, H. (2009). Neo-liberal Individualism or Taking Control? Are We All Speaking the Same Language on Modernising Adult Social Care? *Social Policy and Society, 8*(3), 333–345.

Roulstone, A., & Sadique, K. (2013). Vulnerable to Misinterpretation: Disabled People, 'Vulnerability' and the Fight for Legal Recognition. In A. Roulstone & H. Mason-Bish (Eds.), *Disability, Hate Crime and Violence* (pp. 25–39). Oxon: Routledge.

Saxton, M., Curry, M. A., Powers, L. E., Maley, S., Eckels, K., & Gross, J. (2001). Bring My Scooter So I Can Leave You: A Study of Disabled Women Handling Abuse by Personal Assistance Providers. *Violence Against Women, 7*(4), 393–417.

Sharp, H. (2001). Steps Towards Justice for People with Learning Disabilities as Victims of Crime: The Important Role of the Police. *British Journal of Learning Disabilities, 29*(1), 88–92.

Sin, C. H. (2013). Making Disablist Hate Crime Visible. In A. Roulstone & H. Mason-Bish (Eds.), *Disability, Hate Crime and Violence* (pp. 147–165). Oxon: Routledge.

Sin, C. H. (2015). Hate Crime Against People with Disabilities. In N. Hall, A. Corb, P. Giannasi, & J. G. D. Grieve (Eds.), *The Routledge International Handbook on Hate Crime* (pp. 193–206). Oxon: Routledge.

Sin, C. H., Hedges, A., Cook, C., Mguni, N., & Comber, N. (2009). *Disabled People's Experiences of Targeted Violence and Hostility*. Research Report 21. London: Office for Public Management.

Stone, K. (2015). Absent Presence. In R. Shah & P. Giannasi (Eds.), *Tackling Discrimination and Disability Hate Crime* (pp. 116–122). London: Jessica Kingsley Publishers.

Trickett, L., & Hamilton, P. (2016). *Hate Crime Training of Police Officers in Nottingham: A Critical Review*. Retrieved from http://irep.ntu.ac.uk/id/eprint/28089/7/5642Trickett.pdf.

Tyson, J., & Hall, N. (2015). Perpetrators of Disability Hate Crime. In R. Shah & P. Giannasi (Eds.), *Tackling Discrimination and Disability Hate Crime* (pp. 69–87). London: Jessica Kingsley Publishers.

Tyson, J., Giannasi, P., & Hall, N. (2015). Johnny Come Lately? The International and Domestic Policy Context of Disability Hate Crime. In R. Shah & P. Giannasi (Eds.), *Tackling Discrimination and Disability Hate Crime* (pp. 20–35). London: Jessica Kingsley Publishers.

UPIAS. (1976). *Fundamental Principles of Disability*. London: Union of the Physically Impaired Against Segregation.

Walklate, S. (2004). *Gender, Crime and Criminal Justice* (2nd Ed). Cullompton: Willan Publishing.

Williams, B., Copestake, P., Eversley, J., & Strafford, B. (2008). *Experiences and Expectations of Disabled People*. London: Office for Disability Issues.

Wolfensberger, W. (1980). The Extermination of Handicapped People in World War II. *American Journal on Mental Deficiency, 19*(1), 1–7.

9

Politics, Policies and Professional Cultures: Creating Space for a Victim Perspective in the Crown Prosecution Service

Jacki Tapley

Introduction

Earlier chapters in this book have explored the diverse and complex factors that have contributed to the politicisation of crime victims. This has included the fundamental role of individuals and groups impacted by victimisation, either directly or indirectly, in raising awareness of their experiences and campaigning for reforms when criminal justice responses have been found to fall short of what should reasonably be expected. This chapter examines the impact of the subsequent development of reforms aimed at improving victims' experiences of the criminal justice system as a consequence of 'academic' and 'humanist' victimology working together. It explores the powerful influence of this alliance upon professional practices, whilst recognising that the introduction of policies

J. Tapley (✉)

Institute of Criminal Justice Studies, Faculty of Humanities and Social Sciences, University of Portsmouth, Portsmouth, UK
e-mail: jacki.tapley@port.ac.uk

© The Author(s) 2020
J. Tapley, P. Davies (eds.), *Victimology*,
https://doi.org/10.1007/978-3-030-42288-2_9

and legislation alone is not the panacea for ensuring the entitlements of victims and witnesses are enforced. The combination of activism, theory and research demonstrates what Goodey (2005: 94) proposed can be achieved when the different 'camps' within victimology work together, in that 'research can inform activism and policy development, and, in turn, activism and policy shape research.' The necessity for this cyclical and reflective oscillation between stakeholders to be continuous is demonstrated by research that provides consistent and substantial evidence that organisational and cultural barriers remain, preventing policies from being delivered as intended, thereby exposing an implementation gap that reflects negatively upon professional practices and the experiences of victims (Wedlock and Tapley 2016; HMICFRS 2017; HMICFRS and HMCPSI 2019).

Whilst the police are often considered to be the primary agents or gatekeepers of the criminal justice system by the public and many victims of crime, this chapter focuses on the lesser known and publicly understood role of the Crown Prosecution Service (CPS). The latter because it is the decision-making and actions of the CPS that are pivotal in victims' ability to gain access to justice (Tapley 2003; Kirchengast 2016). Created as an independent prosecuting authority on behalf of the state, this chapter examines the profound shift in the professional culture of the CPS imposed by a political reform agenda determined to 'rebalance the criminal justice system in favour of victims' (Home Office 2002: 2), regardless of how justified or controversial such a rebalancing of the criminal justice system is perceived to be (Jackson 2003). As observed by Kirchengast (2016: 104):

> boundaries which once separated the victim from substantive participation in adversarial systems of justice are now being eroded and dismantled in favour of rights and powers that can be enforced against the state or the accused, albeit in an unconventional, fragmented and at times controversial way.

In the context of this shifting criminal justice landscape, this chapter examines the evolving legal culture of the CPS necessitated by the introduction of victim participatory reforms. In particular, it considers whether the CPS's expanding responsibilities to engage directly with victims and witnesses, whilst maintaining its role as an independent prosecuting authority, threatens to compromise the integrity of the service, given the escalating political and public pressure and increasing scrutiny it faces to improve performance. Or, whether by adopting a more transparent and accountable approach through actively engaging with the communities it serves, it can both improve prosecutorial decision making within the adversarial framework and strengthen public confidence. These ideas link with those made by Erez, Liang and Laster in Chapter 13 of this volume, where they seek to identify a model of justice and the criteria required to create a criminal justice process that can be inclusive of victims' rights without undermining the 'time-honoured protections of the accused.'

The ability of the CPS to achieve this balance remains the focus of critical debates that have existed since its inception (Macdonald 2008). Striking a reasonable and fair balance is compounded further by an increasing emphasis on implementing political strategies to accommodate victims and tackle violence against women and girls in particular (Home Office 2010, 2016; CPS 2012). To understand better the challenges now being faced by the CPS, the chapter will start by considering its historical origins and then go on to examine the impact of reforms aimed at accommodating a victim perspective upon the role and professional culture of the CPS. In addition to exploring the relevant literature and research, this chapter is further informed by reflections from the author's own experience as an Independent Facilitator for a CPS Scrutiny Panel and sitting on a local Victim and Witness Working Group. This has provided privileged access to confidential information and a crucial insight to the importance of collaborative partnership working between agencies. It would not be ethical or methodologically appropriate to go into specifics (as the information has not been gathered systematically for the purposes of research), but the role and work of the author is highlighted for the purpose of transparency. The chapter will then conclude by considering the role of independent victim advocates, as proposed by others (see Wiper and Lewis, Chapter 2) and supported by the Victims' Commissioner (2019a), and whether the development of a wider victim advocacy model would assist the CPS to operate as an independent prosecuting authority, whilst fulfilling its responsibilities towards victims, without damaging the integrity of the adversarial process.

The Creation of an Independent Prosecuting Authority

The origins of the CPS are to be found in the Report of the Royal Commission on Criminal Procedure published in 1981. The Report concluded 'that it was undesirable for the police to continue both to investigate and to prosecute crime,' thereby requiring a major change in the prosecution process (cited by Glidewell 1998: 1). As a result, the Crown Prosecution Service was established in 1986 as an independent prosecuting authority under the auspices of a Director of Public Prosecutions (DPP) and governed by The Code for Crown Prosecutors (hereafter referred to as the Code). Since its inception, the Code has undergone a number of revisions, but at its most basic it outlines the principles that prosecutors must follow when deciding whether or not to prosecute criminal cases being investigated by the police and other investigative organisations in England and Wales. The Code states that prosecutors must be fair, objective and independent and, to assist in this process, prosecuting decisions are made by applying two code tests: the 'evidential test' and the 'public interest test.' This is to ensure that prosecutors are satisfied that there is sufficient evidence to provide a realistic prospect of conviction and that prosecuting is in the public interest (CPS 1994, 2018).

As an independent prosecuting authority, it was originally envisaged that the new service would have no direct or personal contact with witnesses and would be under no duty to make contact with victims, witnesses or others after disposal of the case. These principles were outlined in the Policy and Information Division Circular (13/1988) accompanying the first Home Office Circular (Home Office 20/1988) directly relating to victims of crime:

> The Home Office Circular does not alter the role of the CPS in dealing with witnesses or victims. Although there will be contact between the CPS and the police concerning the progress of cases, it is the task of the police, not the CPS, to keep witnesses, including victims, informed of the progress and result of the case (including discontinuance).

The circular makes clear that the police continue to be in the best position to advise victims of witness attendance and inform them of the progress and outcomes of cases. It also states that whilst it is part of the CPS's role 'to have in mind the interests of victims or their relatives and, in appropriate cases, to take reasonable steps to ensure that the police are in contact with them to keep them informed … the CPS has no responsibility itself to keep victims informed.' The circular goes on to reiterate that even in the case of a fatality, the same principles apply, although in cases where it has been decided not to proceed, 'on request by a relative of the victim brief reasons for the action taken by the CPS should be given … [but] it should be restricted to the broad facts upon which the decision was taken' (Policy and Information Division Circular, 13/1988).

The circular clearly depicts the role of the CPS as a remote and distant prosecuting authority, with no obligation to have any contact with victims and witnesses, but instead to 'take reasonable steps to ensure that the police' relay the decisions made on its behalf (ibid.). This has provided the CPS with not only a high level of independence and autonomy but has also rendered the discretionary judgements made regarding prosecutorial decisions, immune to review and unaccountable. As observed by Flynn (2016: 567), the process has lacked any transparency as to how such decisions have been reached, to the point that it distances the CPS from explaining their decisions to those they effect the most and instead has left this job to the police. In fact, despite the wording of the Code, very little consideration has been given to the victims or victims' families when making these decisions (Cretney et al. 1994), which Erez et al. (2014: 172) argue is a consequence of an adversarial process, whereby the pursuit of professional ends and institutional priorities conflict with the needs and interests of victims. Whilst the Code (1994: 11) reiterates that the CPS acts in the public interest, not in the interests of just one individual [the victim], it does state that Crown Prosecutors must 'always think carefully about the interests of the victim.' However, as part of a longitudinal study following the experiences of victims of violent crime, Tapley (2003: 194) found that apart from the victim's original witness statement, there was no other mechanism available for prosecutors to even know or be aware of victims' interests, as at this time they had no direct contact with them. In fact, the research found very little evidence of prosecutors demonstrating any concern for victims, with the exception of a single, quite revolutionary Chief Crown Prosecutor who was very supportive of initiatives to improve the experiences of victims and who helped the author as a researcher to gain access to victims of violent crime through the Local Trials Issues Group when the local police constabulary had initially refused to do so (Tapley 2003: 39).

Although the introduction of the Victim's Charter initiatives (Home Office 1990, 1996) outlined the responsibilities of the criminal justice agencies towards victims and witnesses, including the responsibilities of the CPS, it continued to remain the responsibility of the police to notify victims of the decisions made by the CPS, including whether to change or drop (discontinue) a charge. Indeed, the CPS published its own policy, 'A statement on the treatment of victims and witnesses by the CPS,' and whilst acknowledging its responsibilities outlined in the Victim's Charter, it reiterated its key role as an independent prosecution authority:

> The CPS does not act directly on behalf of individual victims or represent them in court in criminal proceedings because it has to take decisions reflecting the overall public interest rather than the particular interests of any one person. Nevertheless, the interests of the victim are very important when we make decisions. (CPS 1994: 1)

Acknowledging the difficulties involved with police relaying information to victims based on decisions made by the CPS, the Royal Commission of Justice (1994) recommended that where appropriate, the CPS should pass on information to the victims and witnesses directly rather than through the police. This heralded the beginning of a significant cultural shift in CPS professional practice and its relationship with victims and prosecution witnesses. This was further strengthened via the Home Office Circular (55/1998) *Keeping Victims Informed of Developments in their Case*. This Circular instruction signalled a substantial transformation in criminal justice policy introduced by a New Labour government, committed to modernising the criminal justice system as part of its 1997 election manifesto. The same manifesto placing at the centre of its reforms a promise to 'put victims at the heart of the criminal justice system' (Home Office 2002; Jackson 2003).

Despite amendments to guidance, none of which were statutory, research continued to reveal a legal culture resistant to engaging with victims and witnesses and a culture which actively constrained its own ability to fulfil its responsibilities (Cretney and Davis 1997; Tapley 2003: 197). This was also contrary to earlier changes that had already been made to the Bar Code of Conduct in 1995, giving barristers considerably wider discretion to talk to witnesses and placing a responsibility on them 'to ensure that those facing unfamiliar court procedures are put at as much ease as possible, especially if the witness is nervous or vulnerable, or the victim of crime' (CPS 1995: 2, cited by Tapley 2003: 199). This advice was finalised in a Guidance Letter to Chief Crown Prosecutors (CPS 06.11.1996, cited by Tapley 2003: 200), which, among the principle changes affecting criminal practitioners, confirmed that:

> There is no longer any rule preventing a barrister from having contact with any witness and barristers are now free to introduce themselves to witnesses and to explain or answer questions about court procedures, especially the procedure for giving evidence ... but, it remains inappropriate in contested criminal cases for barristers to discuss with witnesses the substance of their evidence, or the evidence of others, save in wholly exceptional circumstances.

This position was further reiterated in a letter from the Attorney General, Peter Goldsmith, to the Chairman of the Bar Council, Jonathan Hirst QC, concerning his misgivings about 'signs of reluctance on the part of practitioners to have contact with witnesses, even for the very proper purposes covered by the recent changes by the bar to its professional rules,' as had been detected by the Chief Inspector of the CPS, Stephen Wooler (CPS, 14.08.2000b, cited by Tapley 2003: 200). Therefore, despite changes in CPS guidance from the highest authorities clarifying their responsibilities to have contact with victims and witnesses, research found evidence of counsels' reluctance to have 'proper, direct contact with witnesses' (*ibis*). Tapley (2003: 190) found several examples of this in her study when victims who were required to give evidence in court tried to gain information from the CPS. One prosecutor indicated that resources were the issue, as none had been provided to undertake victim contact work, but he also appeared unaware of the guidance, stating 'the lines are blurred as to whose responsibility it is ... our remit is to deal with cases fairly and firmly with the aim of getting a conviction.' However, he did accept his reliance upon them: 'we rely on these people so it is in our best interest to keep them on board' (Tapley 2003: 190). This quote not only demonstrates the apparent reluctance to speak to victims, referred to by Stephen Wooler above, but also acknowledges the need to keep victims engaged as their participation is crucial to the success of the CPS. Another CPS prosecutor, when asked to contact a victim of historic sexual abuse who was distressed because the date of the trial had been further delayed, explained that 'the relationship with witnesses is fraught with difficulties as we cannot be seen to be rehearsing witnesses.' However, he did acknowledge that prosecuting barristers could now talk to witnesses and, although there was little he could do about the changes to trial dates, he agreed to contact the victim and make 'reassuring noises' (Tapley 2003: 190).

These examples demonstrate a reluctance by prosecutors to have direct contact with victims, despite guidance being in place that requires them to do so. The research revealed the existence of a parallel discourse, with the agenda dominated by professional discourse, whilst actively excluding the victim. Erez et al. refer to this in Chapter 13, with their observation that victims' entitlements are often incompatible with professional routines and practices, hence their reluctance to engage with victims. Thereby, whilst the role of the CPS is pivotal in determining the progress of the case, a bureaucratic response to victims appeared to be the order of the day rather than tangible improvements in their treatment. As a consequence, victims were left to seek information out for themselves, essentially bridging the gap, provided they were confident and able to do so. However, for many, this was not possible and instead their confidence and willingness to engage in the criminal justice process declined. Tapley (2003: 265) found that by distancing the victim from the CPS decision-making process, victims continued to be viewed as merely a source of information to assist the prosecution in gaining a successful conviction, rather than as a crucial participant. As observed by Lord Justice Auld (2001) in his review of the criminal courts, the system pursues this goal without due consideration for the rights and protection of the victim (cited by Tapley, ibid.) and the author contends that it is this emphasis within legal culture, the courts and the criminal process that blocks attempts to integrate a victim perspective and contributes to the implementation failure of reforms. In particular, evidence from research indicates that the fear, anxiety and vulnerability felt by victims waiting to be witnesses is vastly underestimated by all professionals within the system, but most notably prosecution solicitors and barristers, compounded by a failure to acknowledge that a lack of information regarding decisions made in their case can lead to victims disengaging with the whole of the criminal justice process (Jordan 2015; Wedlock and Tapley 2016; Rossetti et al. 2017).

Overcoming Resistance and Implementing Reform

Whilst the impact of reforms has been gradual, the shift in perspective over the last three decades from an offender to a victim-focussed criminal justice system has undoubtedly impacted upon the professional culture of the CPS. Whilst the police, as frontline responders, have always had contact with victims of crime (of notably varying standards), for the CPS, set up as an independent prosecuting authority, the shift has presented a number of challenges which require a quite remarkable change in legal mind-set. Since it was first established in 1986, the CPS has encountered several tests from other public bodies and advocacy groups, including powerful opposition from the police, whose prosecutorial role it usurped, to suspicion from legal professions and political allies, who feared that an independent state prosecution authority may threaten their own interests (Macdonald 2008: 10). In the face of such adversity, the CPS has experienced a troubled background and found itself placed at the centre of debates over the rights of victims and offenders. In just over a decade into its existence, it was accused of becoming 'excessively bureaucratic and failing to meet the aspirations of its own staff and the public' (*The Times* 1998: 4). Amidst such criticisms, the CPS was made subject to a number of reviews as part of New Labour's wider plans to modernise the criminal justice system (Jackson 2003). Addressing the needs of victims and witnesses was becoming increasingly politicised (Garland 2000) and improving public confidence was routinely recognised as a central objective to achieving this, as demonstrated in the *Criminal Justice System's Strategic Plan 1999–2002* (Home Office 1999: 1): 'The criminal justice system stands or falls on whether it jointly meets what people can reasonably expect of it—victims, witnesses, jurors and the wider public—whose confidence and trust need to be earned, and interests respected,' and later by Tony Blair (Office of Criminal Justice Reform 2004: 5, cited by Tapley 2005a: 249):

> We start with one overriding principle—that the law-abiding citizen must be at the heart of our criminal justice system. For too long, that was far from the case. The system seemed to think only about the rights of the accused. The interests of victims appeared to be an afterthought, if considered at all. This whole programme amounts to a modernising and rebalancing of the entire criminal justice system in favour of victims and the community.

The political rhetoric was informed by an extraordinary increase in criminological research on victims of crime since the mid-1980s, fuelled by the findings from the 1982 British Crime Survey, the first national victimisation survey which exposed far higher incidents of victimisation than previously indicated by police recorded crime (Zedner 2002). In particular, the data revealed that the criminal justice system needed to do more to deal effectively with crime and to assist those most affected by it, resulting in New Labour's programme of victim-centred reforms (Tapley 2003: 263).

Published in 1997, the Narey report focused on reducing delays in the courts, highlighting the tensions that existed between the police and CPS as contributing to this, with one agency frequently blaming the other. As a consequence, and as indicated above, victims and witnesses often suffered as a result, with neither agency (police or CPS) providing sufficient information about the process, explanations for decisions made or the subsequent outcomes. Following further recommendations by Glidewell's (1998) *Review of the Crown Prosecution Service*, and amidst concerns that 'a national prosecution service could become too centralised and bureaucratic' (ibid.: 3), the 13 existing CPS areas were further divided into 42, to coincide with the number of police forces, and police and CPS staff were co-located in a single integrated unit (Criminal Justice Units) to expedite case progression. The final part of the Glidewell report focused on the role of the CPS in relation to victims and witnesses and its obligations arising from the Victims Charter (Home Office 1996). Of particular significance was the recommendation that the CPS should take over responsibilities from the police to provide victims with information about decisions made by the CPS, including 'where desired' to provide an explanation to complainants/victims. This led to the introduction of a new policy 'CPS Direct Communication with Victims' (CPS 2001), supported by a CPS/ACPO national framework for the development of local protocols to inform victims of decisions not to prosecute, to discontinue or to substantially alter a charge. In addition, Her Majesty's Crown Prosecution Service Inspectorate (HMCPSI) was established by the CPS Inspectorate Act 2000, creating an independent statutory body tasked with inspecting CPS practices, although it holds no regulatory powers. As a consequence, whilst HMCPSI's recommendations are not enforceable, they do go to the relevant ministers and the reports are published. Such reports, including joint thematic reports undertaken with HMICFRS (Her Majesty's Inspectorate of Constabulary and Fire and Rescue Services), frequently examine the ability of the police and CPS to fulfil their responsibilities to victims and witnesses and, whilst undoubtedly improvements have been made during the last three decades, concerns remain that many reforms are still not being implemented as intended (Criminal Justice Joint Inspectorate 2015; CPS 2015; HMCPSI 2016a).

The introduction of victim-centred reforms exposes the often complex and uneasy relationship in an adversarial criminal justice process between the CPS, victims and prosecution witnesses, as evidenced above. Whilst retaining its function as an independent prosecuting authority, acting fairly and independently, the CPS is now required to communicate directly with victims and witnesses to ensure they are provided with relevant and timely information relating to their case prior to, during and after the trial. The CPS is also required to ensure the needs of vulnerable and intimidated victims, and witnesses are identified and their enhanced entitlements under the Victim's Code of Practice provided (Ministry of Justice 2015). These developments allude to the ambiguity often associated with introducing victim participatory reforms into adversarial legal systems (Erez et al. 2014). In England and Wales, the role entrusted to the CPS is to determine on an evidential and public interest basis whether a person should be prosecuted and go forward for a judgement before the courts (House of Commons Justice Select Committee 2009). Whilst as an independent prosecuting authority the CPS Prosecutor's Code requires prosecutors to retain that independence when making decisions, the victim-centred reforms require prosecutors to increasingly engage with victims and victims' families to take into account their concerns when making those decisions, thereby raising concerns which may influence the independence of their decision making. Equally, there have been concerns that prosecutors may exert influence when consulting with victims to ensure that a swifter conclusion is achieved, for example, the common practice of accepting a lesser charge to secure a guilty plea (plea-bargaining), which whilst securing a successful prosecution may not necessarily be in the best interests of the victim (Fenwick 1997a; Cretney and Davis 1997; Tapley 2003).

This reveals the inherent tension that in an adversarial process the CPS cannot act as a representative of the victim. Although the defendant has the right to be represented by legal counsel and has opportunities to receive advice and discuss the case well in advance of a trial, many victims are surprised to find that there is no one statutory agency within the criminal justice system responsible for them, tasked to act in their best interests (House of Commons Justice Select Committee 2009). Mindful of their status as independent prosecutors, some CPS professionals remain wary of 'coaching' witnesses and may use this to retain some distance from engaging with victims and witnesses. However, guidelines revisiting the role of prosecutors before and at court were published in 2015 following a consultation, and further revised in 2018. The aim of the guidance is to set out clearly what it describes as the 'core part' of the prosecutors' role, to ensure witnesses are able to give their best evidence and to address concerns that some prosecutors may be uncertain about what they are allowed to say to witnesses: 'This guidance makes it clear what is expected and permissible and explains the difference between assisting a witness to be better able to deal with the rigors of giving evidence (which is permitted) and witness coaching (which is not permitted)' (CPS 2018: 2). If followed, these guidelines should help to reduce a prosecutor's concerns that they may be seen to be 'coaching' a witness and reduce the apprehension some witnesses may feel about giving evidence by providing them with information about what to expect when attending court.

Further reforms have created and extended specialist prosecutor roles to focus on specific offences and improve case management where particularly vulnerable and intimidated witnesses are involved, including rape and sexual violence, stalking and harassment, and domestic abuse. This has been in response to political strategies aimed at tackling violence against women and girls (VAWG), resulting in the implementation of specialist domestic violence courts (Cook et al. 2004), the introduction in 2013 of Rape and Serious Sexual Offence (RASSO) Units in each CPS area (HMCPSI 2016b), a joint action plan to improve police and CPS responses to rape (CPS and Metropolitan Police 2015) and the implementation of Victim Liaison Units in 2014 to undertake direct communication with victims and witnesses (HMCPSI 2018). Whilst these reforms have compelled the CPS to review its responsibilities towards victims and witnesses, it essentially remains an independent prosecution authority, and whilst significant changes in professional culture have been achieved, debates about the role of victims in an adversarial justice system and the challenges this presents for the CPS remain the focus of controversial and often high-profile debates (House of Commons Justice Committee 2009, 2018).

Creating Space for a Victim Perspective

The introduction of victim-centred reforms has given rise to ongoing concerns regarding the possible consequences of increased consideration and involvement of victims in the criminal justice process. In particular, concerns that introduce reforms to increase victim participation would impact negatively on the rights of the defendant (Ashworth 1993; Elias

1986; Erez and Rogers 1999; Fattah 2000). However, as argued by Erez et al. in Chapter 13 of this book, whilst some progress has been made, many of the reforms introduced have not yet fully realised their intended objectives. Instead, arguments supporting greater victim participation often focus on the need to encompass procedural justice ideals rather than demanding specific legislative rights. Central to the concept of procedural justice is the perception of fair treatment within legal processes which impacts on peoples' perceptions of legitimacy and compliance (Laxminarayan 2015). Evidence suggests that the quality of the interaction and the services that victims receive is often more important than the final outcome of their case (Elliott et al. 2014; Wedlock and Tapley 2016).

Research consistently indicates that what victims want is accurate and timely information, validation of the harm suffered, an opportunity to voice their concerns, the ability to regain some sense of control, and access to a criminal justice process without suffering secondary victimisation by the process itself (Wedlock and Tapley 2016: 16; Iliadis and Flynn 2018). Fenwick (1997b) argued that the provision of information, particularly at the stages prior to conviction, remains relatively non-threatening to the existing model of criminal justice, there being no direct conflict with issues of due process and the rights of the defendant. In fact, when balanced with the likely benefits that giving victims information may bring, including increasing their confidence, satisfaction and likelihood of remaining engaged with the process, it may be considered a fairly inexpensive way of improving the efficiency of the criminal justice system. However, research continues to find that the greatest frustration experienced by victims of crime is the failure of criminal justice agencies to consistently provide timely and accurate information about the criminal justice process, the progress of their case, access to their entitlements and information about the support services available to assist them (Wedlock and Tapley 2016). Since 2015, the majority of services are now commissioned locally by the Police and Crime Commissioners (PCCs); therefore, information about local support services ought to be disseminated locally by the PCCs. However, the introduction of different models of victim care across the 42 PCCs means that the services provided are not necessarily consistent across all areas and remain a postcode lottery for many victims (Wedlock and Tapley 2016; Simmonds 2018). In Chapter 10, Matthew Hall critically examines the new commissioning model and the shift in the development and delivery of support services from an activist-led endeavour to one that is now primarily market-driven.

Other victim-centred reforms include the gradual introduction of special measures since 1999, to assist victims and witnesses to give their best evidence (Hall 2007; Plotnikoff and Woolfson 2015). The catalyst for the introduction of special measures was the publication of the *Speaking Up for Justice* report (Home Office 1998b) which made 78 recommendations to improve the treatment of vulnerable and intimidated witnesses and to enable them to give their best evidence in criminal proceedings (Burton et al. 2006). Victim Personal Statements were introduced in England and Wales in 2001 as part of the Victim's Charters initiatives and to provide victims with a way to express and voice what the effects of the crime were (Roberts and Erez 2010; Booth et al. 2018). However, a number of reviews undertaken by the Victim Commissioner for England and Wales indicate that the VPS is not being implemented as intended. Evidence from research shows that few victims report being offered an opportunity to make a VPS by police, and of those who had made a VPS, many did not feel their statement had been taken into account as part of the criminal justice process (Victim Commissioner 2019b).

To improve communication with victims required to attend court as a witness, Witness Care Units (WCUs) were introduced in 2005 as part of the wider *No Witness, No Justice* project (Criminal Justice System 2004, cited by Tapley 2005b: 33). This was a joint initiative involving ACPO, CPS, Home Office and the Prime Minister's Office of Public Sector Reform. Five pilot areas were set up to offer a more 'customer focussed' service to victims and witnesses with the aim of reducing the rate of ineffective and cracked trials (caused mainly by defendants or witnesses not attending) and to increase victim and witness satisfaction (Tapley 2005b: 33). The WCUs were originally a joint police and CPS enterprise, staffed by both police and CPS staff and housed in the co-located Criminal Justice Departments. However, the impact of austerity measures from 2008 resulted in the reversal of the Glidewell (1998) recommendations and the 42 CPS areas were restructured to form 14 regional areas, each led by a Chief Crown Prosecutor. As a result, the majority of WCUs remain in police buildings and are police staffed. Reforms imposed by an austerity agenda and significant cuts to both police and CPS budgets have meant the disbandment of co-location with partners, the centralisation of CPS offices within a wider region and the additional challenge for CPS regional areas to work with up to three different police forces within their area. Initial and out-of-hours charging advice is also given by CPS Direct, which is a 'virtual' 15th area headed by a Chief Crown Prosecutor (CPS 2019a). To receive a charging decision, police officers can call a single national number to be connected to a duty solicitor or they can submit and receive charging decisions digitally. The impact of austerity measures has been to remove the CPS from local areas and police forces and locate them in more distant centralised hubs, contrary to the Glidewell (1998) recommendations.

A further attempt to incorporate a victim perspective within the traditional parameters of an adversarial criminal process and increased participatory rights has been the introduction of the Victims' Right to Review (VRR). This initiative aimed to address the lack of transparency surrounding prosecutorial decision making. Introduced in England and Wales in 2013, the VRR enables victims to request a review of a prosecutor's decision not to proceed with charges, to discontinue a case, to offer no evidence or to leave all charges in the proceedings to 'lie on file' (CPS 2016). As observed by Iliadis and Flynn (2018: 556), 'a key benefit is the VRR's capacity to provide a mechanism for victims to pursue and challenge what were once finite prosecutorial decisions, theoretically creating greater accountability in the decisions being made, and simultaneously offering victims a sense of control.' Whilst research has identified some positive outcomes of introducing VRRs, including the reversal of some decisions, Iliadis and Flynn (2018: 566) concluded that the absence of data regarding pre-charge decision-making, a perceived lack of independence in the review process itself and victims not being made aware of the VRR meant that it 'may unfortunately attract similar criticisms applied to many victim-focused law reforms … whereby the reform has more "symbolic value than actual effect in practice"' (Stubbs 2003, cited by Iliadis and Flynn 2018: 566).

Responding to Public and Political Pressures: A Threat to the Integrity of Independence?

There is no doubt that attempts to improve the accountability and transparency of prosecutorial decision-making can be seen as part of the effort to respond to victims' procedural justice needs (Iliadis and Flynn 2018: 557). If a prosecutor is aware that their decision making may be subject to closer scrutiny, the need for greater clarity when explaining the reasons for the decision made has the potential to lead to improvements in the quality of those decisions. This is perhaps especially important when the CPS is considering changing or dropping a charge during proceedings at court, whereby prosecutors are advised to consult with the victim (CPS 2018). However, scrutiny of this nature opens up cause for concern about the independence of the CPS and the impartiality of its decision making, especially at a time when the service is under political and public pressure to increase prosecutions and convictions. This has been particularly evident in cases relating to rape and sexual offences, where the CPS has faced criticisms at either extreme. Following the introduction of reforms, the Director of Public Prosecutions (DPP) at the time—Alison Saunders—was accused of bias in favour of victims (McCann 2018) and heavily criticised by a House of Commons Justice Committee report (2018), which held her responsible for the collapse of rape trials as a result of disclosure failings. These criticisms emerge against a background of persistent and prevalent concerns regarding high attrition rates in cases of rape and sexual assault over the last two decades (Harris and Grace 1999). Despite the introduction of a range of reforms and an increase in reporting, data from the CPS (2019b) *Violence Against Women and Girls Report* indicates that, compared to 2017–18, pre-charge decisions completed by the CPS fell by 14.9%, from 6012 to 5114. The proportion of pre-charge decisions that led to a charge fell from 46.9% to 34.4%. Completed prosecutions fell by 32.8%, from 4517 to 3034, and convictions fell by 26.9%, from 2635 to 1925. The proportion of cases where the police did not respond to CPS requests for additional evidence or reasonable lines of enquiry within three months increased from 21.7% to 28.6%, and the overall conviction rate increased from 58.3% to 63.4%, although this differs between CPS regional areas.

The reduction in prosecutions has led to fierce criticism of the CPS. The service has been accused by victim advocates of effectively 'decriminalising rape' and of adopting a 'more risk averse approach' to rape cases by taking a proportion of 'weak cases' out of the system (*The Guardian* 2019). At the time of writing, the Centre for Women's Justice launched a judicial review challenge against the CPS, alleging that the service has changed the way it makes prosecutorial decisions as far back as 2016. They argue that 'The test should be a realistic prospect of conviction … not second-guessing what the jury will decide. What we are supposed to do is to look at all the evidence objectively' (Radio 4, BBC 2019, cited by *The Guardian* 2019). In response, Max Hill (DPP in 2019) agreed that the fall in charging rates is concerning and announced an independent review by HMCPSI to place charging decisions under greater scrutiny, stating 'I have every confidence in the work of our dedicated prosecutors, but it is important that the public has confidence too' (Davies 2019).

The seriousness of sexual offences, the impact on victims and the potential consequences for defendants understandably creates deeply impassioned, emotive and controversial debates. The complex factors relating to the investigation and prosecution of sexual offences have been widely reported in the media, and women's groups have continued to challenge the common myths and stereotypes still attributed to victims of rape. 'Ideal victim' status and 'real rape' gold standards continue to be held as yardsticks against which all rape victims and all rape cases are measured (Bows 2018). See also Erez et al., Chapter 13 of this book for their observations of a set of persistent myths that continue to underscore attitudes towards victims. The investigation and prosecution of sexual violence and rape cases has seen the introduction of specialist police investigation officers, specialist RASSO units to make charge and prosecution decisions, and to advocate in trials, and the introduction of specialist support services, for example, SARCs (Sexual Assault Referral Centres) and Independent Sexual Violence Advocates (ISVAs) (Lovett et al. 2004). Whilst such victim-centred reforms have led to an increased awareness of the difficulties in dealing with cases of rape and sexual assault, and whilst significant improvements have been made in criminal justice responses to victims of rape, the publication of VAWG data (CPS

2019b) demonstrates that a number of significant factors and processes remain that continue to act as a barrier to achieving successful prosecutions.

Despite the introduction of a range of victim-centred reforms, research highlights that there still remains a lack of consistency within and between criminal justice agencies resulting in a postcode lottery for victims (Erez et al. 2014; Wedlock and Tapley 2016). The causes of such inconsistencies include a lack of training and resources, the attitude and influence of key senior staff in specific teams, the wider culture of the agency, and a clear understanding of the purposes and intentions of some policies and legislation. The above, all of which may impact on CPS prosecutors and the subsequent decisions they make, raises legitimate concerns regarding their attempts to implement these reforms and whether they may act to impede the CPS in its role as a truly independent prosecutor. It could be contended that increasing political and public pressure to improve performance, measured by prosecution and conviction rates, threatens to compromise the integrity and independence of CPS decision making.

As outlined above, the CPS is required to apply two tests when making prosecutorial decisions—the *evidential test* and the *public interest* test. To improve decisions in any case, including sexual violence, sufficient and robust evidence is required, supported by the testament and engagement of the victim. This requires the police and the CPS to work together to ensure greater clarity around the collection of evidence and pre-charging advice, the CPS to decide on the final charges laid and any subsequent changes to those charges, and the implementation of policies to support the victim. Another factor that may improve consistency in prosecutorial decision making is improving the confidence of prosecutors in the decisions they make by reducing the influence of public and political pressures reported widely in the media. One way of achieving this is through more direct engagement with the actual people and communities they serve. This can provide the CPS with an opportunity to provide greater clarity around its role and to promote an increased understanding among stakeholders as to what processes need to be followed and what is required to achieve successful prosecutions. The next section examines some of the attempts made by the CPS to engage with stakeholders in their local communities.

Improving Public Confidence Through Community Engagement

To encourage and develop greater transparency, the CPS embarked upon a community engagement strategy under the auspices of the DPP Ken Macdonald, who warned in his annual report that 'the interests of justice are not served by ignoring the interests of victims and witnesses' and outlined a number of initiatives aimed at:

- Strengthening the prosecution process to bring offenders to justice
- Championing justice and the rights of victims
- Inspiring the confidence of the communities it serves
- Driving change and delivery in the criminal justice system
- Being renowned for fairness, excellent career opportunities, and the commitment and skills of all our people. (CPS Vision 2008: 6)

The report outlined a number of initiatives aimed at improving community engagement (CPS 2008). At CPS area level, this included the introduction of area-based Hate Crime Scrutiny Panels and Community Involvement Panels, and at national level, a Community Accountability Forum. The purpose of local Hate Crime Scrutiny Panels is to consider CPS performance on the handling of hate crime cases by scrutinising finalised cases and acting on the learning from the scrutiny process (CPS 2008). The panel consists of an Independent Facilitator, who selects the cases to be scrutinised, a senior CPS prosecutor to lead the panel through the case, police officers from the CPS area, a court representative, and lay members who represent groups within the community, including community leaders, victim advocacy groups, and third-sector support services. Panel members are given time before the panel starts to read through the files and then they are taken through the case by the CPS prosecutor, scrutinising the decisions made, including pre-charge advice, the charges laid and any subsequent changes to the charge, and the final outcome. This includes a review of the support given to victims and whether victims were provided with their entitlements under the Victim's Code of Practice (Ministry of Justice 2015).

The author acted as the Independent Facilitator for one local Hate Crime Panel from 2008 to 2013. Following the restructuring of CPS areas from 42 to 14 regional areas and the introduction of the CPS VAWG strategy, the local area CPS decided to create a VAWG Scrutiny Panel in 2013. I relinquished my role on the Hate Crime Scrutiny Panel and took up the role as Independent Facilitator for the VAWG Scrutiny Panel. The panel sits three times a year and its members include representatives from a range of local support services working with victims of domestic abuse, sexual violence and rape, stalking and harassment, and police officers from the three forces that come under the local CPS regional area. Members also include a representative from the courts, a retired magistrate and for a brief time a representative from one of the local Police and Crime Commissioner's (PCC's) office. Attendance may vary, but on average, the panel consists of approximately 14 members. Whilst there has been no strategic review of the Scrutiny Panels to date, I believe the key strength of the VAWG Scrutiny Panel is the willingness of the local Chief Crown Prosecutor (who regularly attends), and the senior prosecutor who guides the panel through the cases, to discuss openly and transparently the decisions made and to discuss whether they were the correct decisions in the circumstances. Having police officers present enables them to provide some background of the case and their role in the investigation, the collection of evidence and engagement with the victim. The support services provide a victim perspective and can provide further information if they supported the victim. This enables a holistic view of the case and provides an opportunity to identify good practice and where further improvements are required. This information is fed back to the relevant individuals and agencies so good practice is shared. In cases where it is agreed the wrong prosecutorial decision was made, this will be raised with the prosecutor and the lessons taken forward.

An essential part of the work of the Scrutiny Panel is the learning gained and how this is fed back into the agencies concerned and to the communities affected. As an Independent Facilitator, I have observed how the Scrutiny Panel acts as a mechanism to create a shared understanding between the different agencies and to develop an appreciation of their different roles and perspectives. I have also witnessed the improved understanding that lay panel members now have of the role of the police and the CPS and the rules and processes their work is governed by. However, whilst this has increased their confidence in the professionals and agencies involved, it has not always necessarily increased their confidence in criminal justice processes and the decisions made in the courts by juries and the judiciary, in particular, sentencing decisions. As observed by Erez et al. in Chapter 13, there is a cost to transparency as it sometimes reveals processes that may remain better unseen. Despite this, as an Independent Facilitator, I believe the success of the VAWG Scrutiny Panel and the continued commitment of Panel members is due to the actions taken as a result of the panel's findings to improve professional practices and the experiences of victims and witnesses. The willingness of the CPS and the police to be transparent and to have their decisions scrutinised and challenged has built trust with community partners and contributed to improvements in professional practice.

A further example of a local initiative to improve community engagement is the introduction of CPS Community Conversations. The aim of these events is to improve public confidence in the work of the CPS and the criminal justice system. In June 2019, the first one held in a CPS area in the South of England focussed on issues effecting Black, Asian and Minority Ethnic (BAME) communities. Senior community leaders were invited to meet with CPS prosecutors to discuss local issues and ask questions on behalf of their communities, in order to develop a closer relationship with the CPS. A second CPS Community Conversation in the same area took place in December 2019 and focused on domestic abuse, stalking and sexual violence. The event was extremely well attended, with representatives from local support services, medical professionals, the office of the PCC, and other stakeholders, who were given an opportunity to ask questions of senior and specialist CPS prosecutors and police to discuss local concerns and issues. As CPS conversations are a very new initiative, no formal evaluation has yet been undertaken, but the aim is to improve dialogue between community leaders, local groups and the CPS and police, to increase understanding and build public confidence. One further example of the CPS working in partnership with other criminal justice agencies and services is the development of local Stalking Clinics, whereby specialist independent stalking advocates assist in assessing risk and referring high-risk cases to a multi-agency Stalking Clinic to ensure victims are provided with support, advice and safety planning and to ensure their concerns are heard throughout the process. A Joint Inspectorate report (HMIC and HMCPSI 2017: 50) found that the introduction of Stalking Clinics provided evidence of effective commissioning and joint working, resulting in the use of specialist services for victims of harassment and stalking.

The literature reviewed above provides evidence of what victims want and how their participation and satisfaction within an adversarial framework can be improved. It has also acknowledged how the police and the CPS have developed policies, training and practices to improve their work with victims and witnesses, but that evidence remains of an implementation gap, caused by reforms not being implemented as intended. This creates a barrier between victims and criminal justice professionals, and this chapter now examines how the implementation gap could be bridged by the introduction of professional victim advocates.

The Victim Advocate

Tapley (2003, cited by Tapley 2005b: 29) concluded 'that the redefinition of victims as consumers has resulted in victims being denied the status of "active citizens" with rights, and has instead rendered them as "passive consumers" of criminal justice services.' In particular, Tapley (ibid.) argued that a 'lack of sufficient information and effective communication with victims demonstrated the need for information to be provided by one single point of contact' (See also Tapley et al. 2014). Since this time, the concept of victim advocacy remains relatively new and currently exists in a variety of different formats. In particular, the role of victim advocate has been introduced for victims of specific crimes, for example, Independent Domestic Violence Advocates (IDVAs) and Independent Sexual Violence Advocates (ISVAs). To gain a better understanding of the victim advocacy interventions that currently exist, the Victim Commissioner (2019a) has published a Rapid Evidence Assessment (RAE) that examines the evidence of victim advocacy models in England and Wales and similar jurisdictions. This follows on from an earlier REA published by the Victims' Commissioner exploring 'what works' to effectively support victims of crime (Wedlock and Tapley 2016). This review established that there are four key principles that underpin effective support: information and communication; procedural justice; multi-agency working and the professionalisation of victims' services, and proposed that these principles could potentially be met and fulfilled by an independent victims' advocate. The REA focusing on victim advocates has been described as an extension of the earlier report, 'as it to some extent tests the underlying question raised in the earlier REA's conclusion regarding whether advocates provide effective support to victims' (Victim's Commissioner 2019a: 2).

The report found that the strengths of an advocacy model provide a personable, non-judgemental approach, which enables a flexible response to fit in with the individual needs of the victim. It also demonstrates the importance of the quality of the contact: 'Contact that is frequent, proactive and consistent over time, has been reported by a range of studies as features that victims, stakeholders and advocates all regard as beneficial' (ibid.: 8). In addition to the practical and emotional support, which helps victims to make more informed choices, the role of the advocate extends beyond victims to include the decisions made by other professionals (ibid.: 8) and can contribute to improved justice outcomes for some victims (ibid.: 11). In particular, the report reveals how the advocates' role can influence how victims interact with the criminal justice process and can assist in developing victims' confidence to participate. Hester and Lilley (2018, cited by Victim's Commissioner 2019a: 15) found that at certain stages, the support needs of the victim can become more intense, particularly at the beginning (following the offence) and the time leading up to the trial, when the CPS has responsibilities to communicate with victims.

Coy and Kelly's (2011, ibid.: 15) research found that the victim advocate's knowledge of the system was important for 'cutting through the bureaucracy' and simplifying the 'jargon' for service users [victims]. The depth and breadth of knowledge held by advocates was acknowledged as central to their role, 'as advocates utilise this capability to conduct what Robinson and Payton (2016: 268) term 'institutional advocacy' (ibid.: 18), which refers to advocates serving 'as a champion for victim rights, both in individual cases and with the potential to challenge local policy and practice more generally' (ibid.: 18). In particular, the report highlights how 'institutional advocacy' can be used to challenge victim-blaming attitudes through meetings, training and collaboration. The development of CPS Scrutiny Panels and CPS Conversations, as discussed above, can also be considered as facilitating institutional advocacy, by involving support services and drawing upon the expertise of victim advocates from the relevant communities when scrutinising finalised cases. Whilst the report highlights that the advocate role also raises some issues, including ensuring their independence, the importance of where they are located and avoiding any overlapping of the advocates' role with criminal justice specialist roles, the literature concludes that the key role of advocates is to 'complement and enhance the role and responsibilities of other agencies towards victims, and should not be viewed as a tool for replacing them' (ibid.: 18). The report also notes that the ability of the advocates to deliver their services was dependent upon and constrained by the responses from other agencies, which at times was 'slow, inadequate or simply not forthcoming' (ibid.: 21).

Whilst acknowledging some of the challenges, the report concludes that victim advocate models can assist in addressing the four key themes identified in working effectively with and supporting victims through the criminal justice process and their recovery (Wedlock and Tapley 2016). In particular, the report highlights the role of advocates as 'connectors' (ibid.: 23), where advocates are able to build collaborative relationships with other professionals and agencies, facilitating the exchange of information, promoting the interests of victims and helping them to access services. In summary, the role of the victim advocate could assist criminal justice professionals to navigate the ambiguities created by adversarial legal rules and the introduction of victim-centred reforms. In particular, the role of the victim advocate could reduce the conflict prosecutors may feel when communicating with victims, without discharging their responsibilities for them. By facilitating the exchange of information, victim advocates can contribute to improving victim confidence, encourage their engagement with the criminal justice process and contribute to better outcomes.

An Independent but More Outwardly Focussed CPS

The CPS has undoubtedly shifted from being a distant and remote prosecuting authority reluctant to engage with victims and witnesses to a prosecution service not only compelled to communicate with victims and witnesses but also more willing to listen to their concerns. This is shown by the gradual shift in sentiment reflected in the statements made by those who have held the post of Director of Public Prosecutors during the last two decades. From Keir Starmer (2009) describing the role of a prosecution service for the twenty-first century as one that helps 'to secure both the interests of the community, especially victims of crime, and the rights of defendants in criminal justice' to Alison Saunders (2015) as DPP reiterating her support for victim-centred reforms: 'I'm proud to lead an organisation that is committed to delivering justice for victims and witnesses and I'm determined that during my time as DPP we will improve the service we give to these vital participants in the justice process … the service we provide to victims and witnesses must be central to everything we do.'

It is perhaps disappointing that the attempts made by Alison Saunders as DPP to improve the CPS response to victims were overshadowed by system failures that were evident before her tenure began and continue under her successor, Max Hill. To assist the CPS in retaining its position as an independent prosecuting authority, whilst fulfilling its responsibilities to victims without compromising its integrity, the CPS needs to collaborate with both criminal justice and community partners, endeavouring to achieve transparency in the decisions it makes. This chapter has identified and examined two ways in which this can be achieved. The first is by engaging with local communities and responding to the challenges they raise, as this can promote clarity and assurance in their own decision making by explaining them, whilst increasing the confidence of the communities they serve. The second is by developing and extending further the role of the victim advocate to provide a single point of contact for victims. This will ensure that the interests of victims are represented independently, without compromising the independence of the CPS. As highlighted by Hall in Chapter 10, some of the PCCs are developing models that provide an increasingly collaborative approach and are developing victim advocacy roles. More specifically, Hall observes how PCCs themselves are assuming a greater advocacy role for victims on the national stage and whilst having PCCs as victims' allies may be viewed positively, Hall warns we need to remain vigilant to their underlying political agendas, given they are elected officials. As observed above, whilst the implementation of policies has been inconsistent, the one thing that has remained steadfast is the political rhetoric promising to *put victims at the heart of the criminal justice system*, a mantra now widely adopted by the PCCs. Although a victim's law remains a political aspiration outlined in election manifestos, the conservative government has only succeeded in publishing a cross-government *Victims Strategy* (HM Government 2018: 19). This has promised to review the role of victim supporters and advocates as part of its wider review of the Victims' Code, but progress has been slow and it remains to be seen whether political rhetoric can be realised and the experiences of victims improved through the implementation of carefully considered and well-resourced reforms. It is essential and wise to remember that a fair and inclusive criminal justice system relies upon the interests of victims, defendants and offenders being equally represented, and that as citizens, our rights are best upheld by the balance favouring neither party, but by ensuring that the rights of each are fairly adhered to. Whilst some progress has been made, there is still some way to go before the aspiration of victims' rights can be fully realised.

References

Ashworth, A. (1993). Victim Impact Statements and Sentencing. *Criminal Law Review, 40*, 498–509.

Association of Chief Police Officers. (2002). *The Search for the Truth*. ACPO Media Initiative, London (10.01.2002).

Booth, T., Bosma, A., & Lens, K. (2018). Accommodating the Expressive Function of Victim Impact Statements: The Scope for Victims' Voices in Dutch Courtrooms. *British Journal of Criminology, 58*, 1480–1498.

Bows, H. (2018). The "Ideal" Rape Victim and the Elderly Woman: A Contradiction in Terms? In M. Duggan (Ed.), *Revisiting the 'Ideal Victim': Developments in Critical Victimology*. Bristol: Policy Press, University of Bristol.

Burton, M., Evans, R., & Sanders, A. (2006). *Are Special Measures for Vulnerable and Intimidated Witnesses Working?* Home Office On-Line Report No. 01/06. London: Home Office.

Cook, D., Burton, M., Robinson, A., & Vallely, C. (2004). *Evaluation of Specialist Domestic Violence Courts/Fast Track Systems*. Cardiff and Leicester: University of Cardiff and University of Leicester.

Coy, M., & Kelly, L. (2011). Islands in the Stream: An Evaluation of Four London Independent Domestic Violence Advocacy Services. Final Report [Online]. Retrieved November 2018, from https://www.trustforlondon.org.uk/publications/islands-stream-evaluation-independent-domesticviolence-advocacy-scheme/.

Cretney, A., & Davis, G. (1997). Prosecuting Domestic Assault: Victims Failing Courts, or Courts Failing Victims? *The Howard Journal, 36*(2), 146–157.

Cretney, A., Davis, G., Clarkson, C., & Shepherd, J. (1994). Criminalizing Assault: The Failure of the 'Offence Against Society' Model. *British Journal of Criminology, 34*(1), 15–29.

Criminal Justice Joint Inspectorate. (2015). *Witness for the Prosecution: Identifying Victim and Witness Vulnerability in Criminal Case Files*. London: HMIC.

Crown Prosecution Service. (1994). *The Code for Crown Prosecutors*. London: HMSO.

Crown Prosecution Service. (2001). CPS Direct Communication with Victims – CPS/ACPO National Framework for Local Protocols. Retrieved from https://www.cps.gov.uk/publication/cps-direct-communication-victims-cpsacpo-national-framework-local-protocols.

Crown Prosecution Service. (2008). *The CPS Annual Report and Resource Accounts 2007/08*. London: HMSO.

Crown Prosecution Service. (2012). Violence Against Women and Girls. Retrieved September 23, 2019, from https://webarchive.nationalarchives.gov.uk/20121210191444/http://www.cps.gov.uk/publications/equality/vaw/index.html.

Crown Prosecution Service. (2015). *Victim and Witness Satisfaction Survey*. London: NatCen Social Research and IFF Research.

Crown Prosecution Service. (2016). Victim's Right to Review Scheme. Retrieved October 30, 2019, from https://www.cps.gov.uk/legal-guidance/victims-right-review-scheme.

Crown Prosecution Service. (2018). Speaking to Witnesses at Court. Retrieved October 30, 2019, from https://www.cps.gov.uk/legal-guidance/speaking-witnesses-court.

Crown Prosecution Service. (2019a). CPS Areas and CPS Direct. Retrieved October 21, 2019, from https://www.cps.gov.uk/cps-areas-and-cps-direct.

Crown Prosecution Service. (2019b). Violence Against Women and Girls Report CPS: London. Retrieved September 30, 2019, from https://www.cps.gov.uk/sites/default/files/documents/publications/cps-vawg-report-2019.pdf.

Crown Prosecution Service and Metropolitan Police. (2015). *Joint CPS and Police Action Plan on Rape*. Retrieved October 21, 2019, from https://www.cps.gov.uk/sites/default/files/documents/publications/rape_action_plan_april_2015.pdf.

Davies, G. (2019). Rape Convictions at Record Low, as CPS Launches Review to Examine 'Myths and Stereotypes' About Sexual Violence'. *The Telegraph*. Retrieved September 12, 2019, from https://www.telegraph.co.uk/news/2019/09/12/rape-convictions-record-low-cps-launches-review-examine-myths/.

Elias, R. (1986). *The Politics of Victimisation*. Oxford: Oxford University Press.

Elliott, I., Thomas, S., & Ogloff, J. (2014). Procedural Justice in Victim-Police Interactions and Victims' Recovery from Victimisation Experiences. *Policing & Society, 24*(5), 588–601.

Erez, E., & Rogers, L. (1999). Victim Impact Statements and Sentencing Outcomes and Processes: The Perspectives of Legal Professionals. *British Journal of Criminology, 39*(2), 216–239.

Erez, E., Globokar, J. L., & Ibarra, P. R. (2014). Outsiders Inside: Victim Management in an Era of Participatory Reforms. *International Review of Victimology, 20*(1), 169–188.

Fattah, E. A. (2000). Victimology: Past, Present and Future. *Criminologie, 33*(1), 17–46.

Fenwick, H. (1997a). Charge Bargaining and Sentence Discount: The Victim's Perspective. *International Review of Victimology, 5*(1), 23–36.

Fenwick, H. (1997b). Procedural "Rights" of Victims of Crime: Public or Private Ordering of the Criminal Justice Process? *The Modern Law Review, 60*(3), 317–333.

Flynn, A. (2016). Plea-negotiations, Prosecutors and Discretion: An Argument for Legal Reform. *Australian and New Zealand Journal of Criminology, 49*, 564–582.

Fohring, H., & Hall, M. (2018). Supporting Victims of Crime in England and Wales: Local Commissioning Meeting Local Needs? *International Review of Victimology, 24*(2), 219–237.

Garland, D. (2000). The Culture of High Crime Societies. *The British Journal of Criminology, 40*(3), 347–375. https://doi.org/10.1093/bjc/40.3.347.

Glidewell, I. (1998). *The Review of the Crown Prosecution Service: A Report.* CMND. 3960. London: HMSO.

Goodey, J. (2005). *Victims and Victimology: Research, policy and Practice.* Harlow: Pearson Education Limited.

Hall, M. (2007). The Use and Abuse of Special Measures: Giving Victims the Choice? *Journal of Scandinavian Studies in Criminology and Crime Prevention, 8*(S1), 33–53. https://doi.org/10.1080/14043850701686139.

Harris, J., & Grace, S. (1999). *A Question of Evidence? Investigating and prosecuting Rape in the 1990's.* Home Office Research Study 196. London: HMSO.

Hester, M., & Lilley, S.-J. (2018). More Than Support to Court: Rape Victims and Specialist Sexual Violence Services. *International Review of Victimology, 24*(3), 313–328.

HM Crown Prosecution Service Inspectorate (HMCPSI). (2016a). *Communicating with Victims.* London: HMSO.

HM Crown Prosecution Service Inspectorate. (2016b). *Thematic Review of the CPS Rape and Serious Sexual Offences Units.* London: HMSO.

HM Crown Prosecution Service Inspectorate. (2017). *Living in Fear – The Police and CPS Response to Harassment and Stalking.* London: HMCPSI.

HM Crown Prosecution Service Inspectorate. (2018). *Victim Liaison Units: Letters Sent to the Public by the CPS.* London: HMCPSI.

HM Government. (2018). *Victims Strategy.* Cm 9700. London: HMSO.

HM Inspectorate of Constabulary and Fire and Rescue Services (HMICFRS) and HMCPSI. (2017). *Living in Fear – The Police and CPS Response to Harassment and Stalking.* London: HMICRFS & HMCPSI.

HM Inspectorate of Constabulary and Fire and Rescue Services (HMICFRS) and HMCPSI. (2019). *The Poor Relation. The Police and CPS Response to Crimes Against Older People.* London: HMICRFS & HMCPSI.

Home Office. (1988). *Victims of Crime.* Circular Instruction 20/1988. London: HMSO.

Home Office. (1990). *Victim's Charter: A Statement of the Rights of Victims.* London: HMSO.

Home Office. (1996). *Victim's Charter: A Statement of Service Standards for Victims of Crime*. London: HMSO.

Home Office. (1998a). *Keeping Victims Informed of Developments in their Case*. Circular Instruction 55/1998. London: HMSO.

Home Office. (1998b). *Speaking Up for Justice*. Report. London: HMSO.

Home Office. (1999). *Criminal Justice System Strategic Plan 1999–2002*. London: Home Office.

Home Office. (2002). *Justice For All*. Cm5563. London: HMSO.

Home Office. (2010). *Call to End Violence Against Women and Girls*. London: Home Office. Retrieved October 20, 2019, from www.gov.uk/government/publications.

Home Office. (2016). *Violence Against Women and Girls National Statement of Expectations*. Retrieved October 26, 2019, from www.gov.uk/government/publications.

House of Commons Justice Committee. (2009). *The Crown Prosecution Service: Gatekeeper of the Criminal Justice System*. Ninth Report of Session 2008–09. HC 186. London: HMSO.

House of Commons Justice Committee. (2018). *Disclosure of Evidence in Criminal Cases*. Eleventh Report of Session 2017–19. HC 859. London: House of Commons.

Howarth, E., & Robinson, A. (2016). Responding Effectively to Women Experiencing Severe Abuse: Identifying Key Components of a British Advocacy Intervention. *Violence Against Women, 22*(1), 41–63.

Iliadis, M., & Flynn, A. (2018). Providing a Check on Prosecutorial Decision-Making: An Analysis of the Victim's Right to Review Reform. *British Journal of Criminology, 58*(3), 550–568. https://doi.org/10.1093/bjc/azx036.

Jackson, J. D. (2003). Justice for All: Putting Victims at the Heart of Criminal Justice? *Journal of Law and Society, 30*(2), 309–326.

Jordan, J. (2015). Justice for Rape Victims? The Spirit May Sound Willing, But the Flesh Remains Weak. In D. Wilson & S. Ross (Eds.), *Crime, Victims and Policy*. London: Palgrave.

Kirchengast, T. (2016). 'Victims' Rights and the Right to Review: A Corollary of the Victim's Pre-Trial Rights to Justice. *International Journal for Crime, Justice and Social Democracy, 5*(4), 103–115. https://doi.org/10.5204/ijcjsd.v5i4.295.

Laxminarayan, M. (2015). Enhancing Trust in the Legal System Through Victims' Rights Mechanisms. *International Review of Victimology, 21*(3), 273–286.

Lovett, J., Regan, L., & Kelly, L. (2004). *Sexual Assault Referral Centres: Developing Good Practice and Maximising Potentials*. Home Office Research Study 285. London: Home Office.

Macdonald, K. (2008). Building a Modern Prosecuting Authority. *International Review of Law Computers & Technology, 22*(1–2), 7–16.

McCann, K. (2018). Frontrunner to Replace Alison Saunders as DPP Could Overturn Rape Policy. *The Telegraph*. Retrieved April 2, 2018, from https://www.telegraph.co.uk/news/2018/04/02/frontrunner-replace-alison-saunders-previously-attacked-police/.

Ministry of Justice. (2015). *Code of Practice for Victims of Crime*. London: HMSO.

Narey. (1997). *Review of Delay in Criminal Justice System*. Retrieved from www.homeoffice.gov.uk/cpd/pvu/crimerev.htm.

Plotnikoff, J., & Woolfson, R. (2015). *Intermediaries in the Criminal Justice System: Improving Communication for Vulnerable Witnesses and Defendants*. Bristol, UK; Chicago, IL: Bristol University Press. https://doi.org/10.2307/j.ctt1t89326.

Roberts, J. V., & Erez, E. (2010). Communication at Sentencing: The Expressive Function of Victim Impact Statements. In A. Bottoms & J. V. Roberts (Eds.), *Hearing the Victim: Adversarial Justice, Crime Victims and the STATE*. Cullompton: Willan Publishing.

Rossetti, P., Mayes, A., & Moroz, A. (2017). *Victim of the System*. London: Victim Support.

Saunders, A. (2015). *The CPS Annual Report and Resource Accounts 2014/15*. CPS. London: HMSO.

Simmonds, L. (2018). The Impact of Local Commissioning on Victim Services in England and Wales: An Empirical Study. *International Review of Victimology*, 1–19. https://doi.org/10.1177/0269758018787938.

Starmer, K. (2009). *CPS Speech—A prosecution service for the 21st century*. London: Crown Prosecution Service. Accessed February 4, 2009, from http://www.cps.gov.uk/news/nationalnews/prosecuting_service_for_the_21st_century.

Tapley, J. (2003). *From 'Good Citizen' to 'Deserving Client': The Relationship Between Victims of Violent Crime and the State Using Citizenship as the Conceptualising Tool*. Unpublished PhD Thesis, University of Southampton.

Tapley, J. (2005a). Improving Confidence in Criminal Justice: Achieving Community Justice for Victims and Witnesses. In J. Winstone & F. Pakes (Eds.), *Community Justice: Issues for Probation and Criminal Justice*. Cullompton: Willan Publishing.

Tapley, J. (2005b). Public Confidence Costs – Criminal Justice from a Victim's Perspective. *British Journal of Community Justice, 3*(2), 25–37.

Tapley, J., Stark, A., Watkins, M., & Peneva, B. (2014). *A Strategic Assessment of Support Services for Victims of Crime in the South East.* Portsmouth: University of Portsmouth.

The Guardian. (2019, September 12). Rape Prosecutions in England and Wales at Lowest Level in a Decade. Retrieved from https://www.theguardian.com/law/2019/sep/12/prosecutions-in-england-and-wales-at-lowest-level-in-a-decade.

The Law Gazette. (2019). Retrieved from https://www.lawgazette.co.uk/news/coalition-prepares-to-sue-dpp-over-rape-prosecution-numbers/5101425.article.

The Times. (1998). Too Tied Up in Red Tape to Prosecute. London: *The Times,* March 6, 1998, p. 1.

Victim Commissioner. (2019a). *Victim Advocates: A Rapid Evidence Assessment.* London: Victim's Commissioner for England and Wales.

Victim Commissioner. (2019b). *Analysis of the Offer and Take-Up of Victim Personal Statements 2018 to 2019.* London: Victim's Commissioner for England and Wales.

Wedlock, E., & Tapley, J. (2016). *What Works in Supporting Victims of Crime: A Rapid Evidence Assessment.* London: Victims' Commissioner. Ministry of Justice.

Zedner, L. (2002). Victims. In M. Maguire, R. Morgan, & R. Reiner (Eds.), *The Oxford Handbook of Criminology* (3rd ed.). Oxford: Oxford University Press.

10

Police and Crime Commissioners and Victim Service Commissioning: From Activism to Marketisation?

Matthew Hall

Introduction

This chapter builds on previous study undertaken by the author in 2016 which reviewed the England and Wales Police and Crime Commissioners' (PCCs) early approaches to their service commissioning role (Hall 2018). Building on that study, this chapter offers a comparison between the UK's new approach to commissioning and the means by which public (and other) monies for victim services are distributed in the rest of the EU. The chapter also focuses specifically on the commissioning process itself in order to test more fully the assertion made by Hall (2018) and others (Mawby 2016) that PCCs are not in a position to adequately assess 'local' need. Conclusions will be drawn as to the overall impact of local commissioning and how this reform has established PCCs as a central aspect of the victim reform agenda in England and Wales. In particular, it will argue that these developments represent a significant watershed in

M. Hall (✉)
Lincoln Law School, University of Lincoln, Lincoln, UK
e-mail: mhall@lincoln.ac.uk

© The Author(s) 2020
J. Tapley, P. Davies (eds.), *Victimology*,
https://doi.org/10.1007/978-3-030-42288-2_10

the long-running transportation of victim services from being activist-driven to market-driven.

The year 2012 saw significant changes to the way police forces in England and Wales are managed. For the first time, Police and Crime Commissioners (PCCs) were elected and became responsible for policing in their local areas. Responsibility for the commissioning of victims' services was introduced in 2014 for some early adopters and 2015 nationally. Effectively, this heralded the end of the national charity Victim Support's near-monopoly on state-funded victim support service provision.[1] This chapter outlines the recent history of support for victims of crime in England and Wales and uses this 2014 watershed moment to reflect on this break with more traditional activist-driven support services. It considers and critically reflects on the governance arrangements that now exist to support those affected by different types of victimisation and examines the evidence for how the system of local commissioning has worked and developed in the three to four years since it was rolled out.

In pursuing the agenda outlined above, a comprehensive review of information and reports published by all PCCs (and regional Mayors) has been carried out.[2] The chapter also draws on relevant government policy documents and the (relatively small pool of) academic literature on the issue. The chapter is further informed by reflections from the author's own experience of sitting on the Lincolnshire PCC's Victims' Commissioning Group, which was constituted as a means of informing and facilitating commissioning decisions in that area.[3]

Background to Victim Services in the UK and the EU

In November 2015, the coming into force of the EU's Directive establishing minimum standards on the rights, support and protection of victims of crime[4] heralded the start of a new chapter for the development of victim policy across the continent. Whilst by this point in the development of what has been termed the 'victims' movement' (Goodey 2005), many EU countries had made marked strides in addressing the needs of victims and supporting them at various points within and (although often to a lesser extent, see Hall 2017) beyond the criminal justice process, the pace of change varied greatly between countries.

Indeed, this was a movement characterised as much by division as by unity. Pointing and Maguire (1988) discuss how the 'victims' movement' in the US and later the UK was driven by a host of 'strange bedfellows' concerned with different aspects of victimisation ranging from feminists[5] and the European women's movement to mental health practitioners and survivors of Nazi concentration camps (see Young 1997). As such, developments like the EU Directive, whilst a significant step forward at the legal and political level, inevitably also presented for some victims' groups a marginalisation of their own theoretical and activist approach to the victims' question, most notably the feminist grass roots component, or what Williams (1999) called the 'hidden wing' of the victim's movement. Indeed, even so restricted, reports on the implementation of the EU's previous 2001 Council Framework Decision about this issue had been extremely mixed (Hall 2017), and thus the Directive was seen by many as a chance to solidify the gains victims had made whilst ensuring consistency of approach.

Planning and implementation for the major changes heralded by the 2015 Directive in Europe combined with a turn to more centre-right political and economic thinking in the UK. Whilst public funding for the national victim assistance charity Victim Support had remained at the heart of government strategy for supporting victims throughout the period of the previous Labour governments (1997–2010), the Coalition was from an early stage far more concerned with expanding the *local* commissioning of such services. Of course, in making this observation, we must be aware that such broad generalisations are always oversimplistic. In fact, the original funding model for Victim Support had been implemented by the pre-1997 Conservative government (see Rock 1990), and indeed the diffusion of victims of crime from being the concern of this one 'national' support organisation to the heavier reliance on local actors was a process well underway under Labour, pre-2010. Indeed, this was not so much a development as an acknowledgement that local charities had always in practice been largely responsible for supporting specific kinds of victims of domestic violence and rape (for example), in which Victim Support had no expertise and had been doing so with very limited funding. Hence, from 2003, Local Criminal Justice Boards (LCJBs) had been given overall responsibility for meeting targets relating to supporting victims and for achieving metrics such as low court waiting times for witnesses.

Criticisms have been made that by passing responsibility to local agencies for the support of victims, successive governments have effectively absolved themselves of a responsibility which should lie with the state (see Pointing and Maguire 1988). This is perhaps reflected by the eclectic nature of the 'victim minister' position which has existed in some form since 2010, but which Duggan and Heap (2014) label an often-opaque position with little clear focus. This notwithstanding, the Coalition government certainly brought with it a more direct mandate to open victim services up to unbridled market forces as the principle means of *cost-effectively* achieving the requirements of the Directive (see Ministry of Justice 2013). This impetus would develop into a full-fledged system of local commissioning of victim services under the direction of newly created Police and Crime Commissioners.

Delivering Support Entitlements to Victims Under the Directive

In order to ensure the UK's policy on victims was consistent with the Directive, the government implemented updates to its national Code of Practice for Victims of Crime (Ministry of Justice 2015) (hereafter 'the Victims' Code'), once in 2013 and then again in 2015. In particular, these changes extended the Code to cover victims of *all* offences, as opposed to limiting this to victims of 'recordable' (i.e. generally more serious) crimes. The amended Code also now employs a definition of victims which includes family members. A separate chapter was created focusing on the support entitlements of child victims and, going somewhat beyond the letter of the Directive, the Code also sets out certain service entitlements to businesses which become criminally victimised.

In terms of supporting victims specifically, Article 8 of the Directive enshrines victims' right 'to access victim support services', which are here described in the following terms:

> Member States shall ensure that victims, in accordance with their needs, have access to confidential victim support services, free of charge, acting in the interests of the victims before, during and for an appropriate time after criminal proceedings (Art.8(1))

Article 9 proceeds to list the services which support organisations must provide, including: information, advice and support relevant to the rights of victims, including accessing national compensation schemes for criminal injuries, and on their role in criminal proceedings including preparation for attendance at the trial; information about or direct referral to any relevant specialist support services in place; emotional and, where available, psychological support; advice relating to financial and practical issues arising from the crime; unless otherwise provided by other public or private services, advice relating to the risk and prevention of secondary and repeat victimisation, of intimidation and of retaliation.

In many respects, the UK was already compliant with these requirements for victims of recordable offences, at least on paper if not universally in practice. Where it was not, relatively minor additions to the Code of Practice were implemented. The more significant change would in fact come in the manner of delivery of such services. Indications of this change began with the publication by the 2010 Coalition government's green paper, *Breaking the Cycle*, in December 2010 (Ministry of Justice 2010). Here the government expressed a commitment to placing more of the 'responsibility' for supporting victims onto offenders themselves. This was to be achieved through requiring offenders to pay reparations to their specific victims as well as to contribute to the funding of victim services through an extension of a victim surcharge, increasing the amount paid on the receipt of fines and, controversially, also applying the surcharge in cases where defendants received a conditional discharge. Having laid this groundwork, in January 2012, the government ran a major public consultation *Getting It Right for Victims and Witnesses* (Ministry of Justice 2012a). Key to the plans set out here was the announcement of 'a new commissioning framework for victim services' (p. 19) which would 'provide clarity about the outcomes for victims, and ensure that there is a practical and agreed mechanism for measuring performance' (ibid.).

In a parallel development in criminal justice policy, the Coalition government had introduced provisions for local, elected Police and Crime Commissioners through the Police Reform and Social Responsibility Act 2011. Ostensibly, this new role would bring greater democratic accountability to policing by replacing the previously unelected Police Authorities across England and Wales. The Act had not itself listed victim issues or services specifically as being within the remit of the new position,[6] with such a role only being allocated to PCCs after this had been proposed in the *Getting It Right* consultation. Ultimately then, the two policy areas came together, and the proposals taken forward were to make regional Police and Crime Commissioners responsible for the allocation of public funds to support and run service provisions for victims at a local level. Justifications for this approach were essentially put as a matter of efficiency. The argument was that victims' needs varied from region to region and that PCCs would be best placed to establish what their communities needed. The government's commitment to this position is reflected by the fact that it proceeded with the plan despite most respondents to the *Getting It Right* consultation being against it (Ministry of Justice 2012b). As such, national-level commissioning would be reserved only for a few more specialised services such as the Homicide Service and the in-court Witness Service. This would ultimately mean that 'the vast majority of services will be commissioned locally' (p. 21).

The first Police and Crime Commissioners were elected in November 2012 with a term of three-and-a-half years. By the second round of PCC elections in 2016, the addition of service commissioning to this role meant that many more candidates drew on familiar political rhetoric of 'putting victims at the heart of criminal justice' system in their campaigns. In this second round of elections, the candidates were far more frequently affiliated with specific political parties—a move which Duggan and Heap (2014) predicted would raise questions about the politicisation of victims as vote-winners. As per the policy set out in *Getting It Right*, PCCs were given the option to take responsibility for commissioning the majority of support services for victims from October 2014, and this became a requirement from April 2015. The Ministry of Justice issued a guidelines document—the 'Victim Services Commissioning Framework' (Ministry of Justice 2013)—to prepare PCCs and other local actors for this role. The document is telling, in that it sets out in clear tones the demarcation of responsibilities as the Ministry of Justice saw them. Thus, 'the majority of emotional and practical support services for victims of crime will be commissioned locally by Police and Crime Commissioners' (p. 5). Whereas 'at a national level the Ministry of Justice will commission a witness service, a homicide service, support for victims of human trafficking, support for victims of rape through rape support centres, some victims' national telephone help-lines and some other support for victims of domestic and sexual violence' (ibid.). In the intervening period, there has in fact been little movement on the national development of most of these 'reserved services', perhaps hinting once against that certain aspects of the victim's movement continue to be side-lined under the new system.

I have previously written more extensively on the theoretical implications of the 2014 shift to local commissioning of victim services (Hall 2018) and thus will not go into these aspects in great detail here. Suffice to say, this was a major change in direction from that followed by the Labour governments, not least for the national charity Victim Support which effectively lost not only its 'preferred supplier' status but also in doing so, arguably, its traditional 'seat at the table' of policy development which it had built on since the 1980s. This is somewhat ironic given that in many ways in order to achieve this status, Victim Support had been compelled to give up its more activist credentials in favour of working more closely with successive governments (Rock 1990), a move which had contributed to the ostracisation of more politically charged victim groups. Indeed, perhaps the most profound impact of this change came in the November 2014 bidding round, in which Victim Support lost its contract to run the Witness Service in all criminal courts. The organisation had campaigned for this service since close to its inception (see Rock 2004; Hall 2009) and had run the scheme with government funding in all Crown Court centres since 1996, extending to all magistrates' courts in 1999. The contract was instead awarded to the Citizen's Advice Bureau despite the latter's lack of proven track record in supporting victims or in specialist work in the courtroom context.

Other commentators too have emphasised the significance of the shift, Mawby (2016) characterising this as an 'end to an era' leaving Victim Support in a 'precarious position'. Both Simmonds (2016) and Mawby (2016) predicted that the reality of the local Commissioning Framework would be that smaller, more activist-inspired, agencies would now be required to bid for more complex contracts, an involved and time-consuming process which they would not always have the infrastructure or expertise to support. That said, having spent years 'in the wilderness', it is certainly true that smaller charities had in fact developed sophisticated and indeed tenacious approaches to gaining funding, whilst at the same time preserving their ability to actively criticise the functioning of the criminal justice system vis-a-vis victims in practice (as opposed to on paper) (see Tapley et al. 2014).

In March 2016, the Commissioner for Victims and Witnesses commissioned a 'rapid evidence assessment' of 'what works in supporting victims of crime' (Wedlock and Tapley 2016). The report from this exercise reflected a tone of quiet optimism about the new system of local commissioning which, in the authors' words, provides 'an opportunity to develop a consistent, coherent and sustainable approach to the provision of high-quality services, accessible to all victims of crime who need and require them' (p. 7). That said, the report also hints at the difficulties of injecting a more marketised ethos into the victim support structure, reflecting the view of Tapley et al. (2014: 7):

> In times of austerity, increasing competition for funding has created tensions and distrust between agencies, which can actively discourage information sharing and partnership working. This has resulted in the duplication of services in some areas, whereas in other areas services remain patchy and inconsistent.

The report puts strong emphasis on the need for victims of crime to have access to a single point of contact for their support needs, which it notes has been rolled out by many PCCs in the early years of the new model. This cements an impression that has persisted since *Getting It Right* that the previous 'good neighbour' model of support favoured by Victim Support for most of its history has given way to a 'victim care unit' approach (Hall 2018), albeit one heavily reliant on the work of small charities to pick up the ensuing slack. This approach emphasises giving information to victims about the progress of their cases (which as surveys have always indicated victims want [see Shapland and Hall 2007]) as opposed to emotional support. A significant question to be asked here is not only how this local commissioning system has operated in practice, but also whether commissioning has facilitated more or less funding to the previously marginalised groups who have remained activists and willing to criticise the criminal justice system, an issue to be addressed below.

Local Commissioning of Victim Services by PCCs: Organisation, Needs Assessments and Outcomes

The commissioning cycle envisaged by the government has been variously described and adapted by different PCCs in variations of 'understand, plan, do, and review' (Office of the Police and Crime Commissioner for Devon and Cornwall & the Isles of Scilly 2014: 4). The emphasis is on assessing local need and delivering tailored services to local victims, filling gaps wherever they exist. It is also an outcomes-based approach designed to shift focus away from 'counting' the number of victims that are 'supported' and on to the practical outcomes of that provision. 'Outcomes' are described in the Commissioning Framework document as 'the changes, benefits, learning or other effects that happen as a result of services and activities provided by an organisation which result in a sustainable change in user behaviour, condition and/or satisfaction' (Ministry of Justice 2013: 21). For the purposes of assessing how this Framework is now working in practice the following discussion distinguishes between three key themes: the practical structures put in place by PCCs to facilitate this work; how the local needs of victims are assessed in different areas in accordance with the above principles and how 'outcomes' so far have been conceptualised and demonstrated. This section will also comment on some of the wider roles and positions PCCs appear to be adopting in the national conversation on victims of crime and the impact upon the smaller charities and activist groups previously sidelined by the government in favour of Victim Support.

Organisation of the Commissioning Process

Structurally, many PCCs have responded to victim service commissioning by establishing dedicated working groups of various descriptions and compositions, following the lead of some Local Criminal Justice Boards before them. Thus, the PCCs for Surrey and Sussex, having come together to form a joint strategic partnership on criminal justice, have established 'separate Victim and Witness Groups with the prime focus for Sussex being to secure an "outcomes measurement" framework and for Surrey to learn from victim feedback provided through the PCC's Victims Champion' (Tippen 2017: 2). The Victim Champion mentioned here is Surrey's Assistant Police and Crime Commissioner, to whom this issue has been delegated. The West Mercia PCC has a 'coordinating Victims Board' and Lincolnshire has a 'Victims' Commissioning Group to bring together senior local stakeholders from Lincolnshire Police and county council [to] coordinate the commissioning of services for victims, as well as oversee performance' (Office of the Police and Crime Commissioner for Lincolnshire 2018: 8). The PCC of North Yorkshire, it is noted on her web pages, 'devolves her responsibility for commissioning and managing these services to the Joint Corporate Commissioning and Partnership department' (Office of the Police and Crime Commissioner for North Yorkshire 2018). In Staffordshire, the PCC has pledged to:

> Continue to work with criminal justice and other partners to develop and enhance the services provided for victims and witnesses across Staffordshire and Stoke-on-Trent. A multi-agency strategic Victim and Witness Commissioning and Development Board will be established before the end of the 2017/18 financial year to make sure that there is a coherent multi-agency approach to provide support. (Office of the Police and Crime Commissioner for Staffordshire 2016: 22)

The exact composition of these boards is variable between areas but, for the most part, they appear to be inter-agency groups comprising of local 'stakeholders' mainly representing different parts of the criminal justice system (police, CPS, probation). One interesting case is that of the West Midlands PCC, who consulted more specifically on how the area's

'Victims Commission' should be constituted. Four models for the Commission were proposed, briefly described as: a geographically representational model; a thematically based model; a Local Policing and Crime Boards-based model and a victim and service provider model (Office of the Police and Crime Commissioner for West Midlands 2014). In particular, Option 4 envisioned a greater role for local victim service providers themselves within the Commission. Ultimately, the West Midlands opted for the 'thematic model' whereby 'The Victims Commission will be made up of representatives from the victim support community on a thematic basis such as domestic violence, sexual violence and hate crime' (Office of the Police and Crime Commissioner for West Midlands 2015: 8). Nevertheless, the inclusivity of this approach (at least on paper) may represent a considerable opening up of a sector which, as has been noted above, was until recently marginalising the voices of many smaller activist groups in favour of Victim Support. The most common pattern across areas, however, seems to be that victim service providers do not have direct representation on such boards, but rather are asked to feed in to its decision-making at various points through events, conferences and seminars to which service providers are selectively invited.

One might derive from the above evidence a counterpoint to the initial fears that government was effectively creating a discordant of local marketplace with local organisations competing doggedly for limited funds. The overarching impression is rather that many PPCs appear to have galvanised communities of such organisations to work together both through their relevant victim boards and local events. Indeed, in the case of Cheshire, the PCC has begun publishing a regular newsletter for all victim service providers, with a drive to create a collegiate atmosphere between local activist groups and other organisations (Office of the Police, Crime and Victims' Commissioner for Cheshire 2016: 6).

One notable development since the first rollout of the victims Commissioning Framework appears to be increasing cooperation *between* PCC areas on the victim issue as well as other aspects of their work. Thus, the PCCs from Avon and Somerset, Wiltshire, Gloucestershire, Devon and Cornwall & the Isles of Scilly and Dorset meet regularly for a Joint Regional Police and Crime Commissioners Meeting, which has produced joint and collaborative approaches to the provision of victim services between these regions (see Office of the Police and Crime Commissioner for Devon and Cornwall & the Isles of Scilly 2018). In another example, the East Midland Policing Academic Collaboration brings together police, academics and the PCCs from Derbyshire, Leicestershire, Lincolnshire, Northamptonshire and Nottinghamshire. The collaboration between Sussex and Surrey on criminal justice matters has also been noted and the Association of Police and Crime Commissioners (APCC) has its own dedicated victims' group.

Such regional cooperation and organisation is a positive step, given the difficulties previously noted in identifying distinct local needs within individual PCC regions. Indeed, this may hint that the police force area is not the most efficient or appropriate level of commissioning. This leads us to the key question of how, in keeping with the Commissioning Framework, PCCs have sought to ascertain what the local needs of victims are in order to commission appropriately *tailored* services. We turn to this issue below.

Assessment of Local Victim Needs by PCCs

As noted above, PCCs are required to undertake comprehensive needs assessments of crime victims in their area in order to ensure that the commissioning of relevant services is evidence-based (Ministry of Justice 2013). Such localised assessment is key to the premise of the system that individual areas will indeed have *specific* sets of needs that are better and more cost-effectively met by a tailored programme/suite of support services. Herein of course lies a potential stumbling block given the known difficulties in successfully identifying the needs of victims, or indeed the full impact of crime upon them, which in the shorter term may not be clear even to the victims themselves. Shapland and Hall (2007: 179) commented in this respect that:

> It has been known for some time that it is extremely difficult to predict which individual victim will suffer which effects to what extent...This is why victim support and assistance schemes have been designed on a uni-

versalistic basis, offered to all victims of crime proactively through outreach means, or through widely advertised hot-lines, with referrals of those then found to be affected in particular ways to more specialist services for particular victims.

Pertinent here is the connection drawn by these authors between the previously adopted 'generic' approach to supporting victims in England and Wales and the difficulties in establishing more specific, individualistic, needs. For his part, Mawby (2016: 215) strongly disputes the assertion that PCCs are in any position to identify those victims with the greatest need, arguing:

> The…assumption that those most in need of support can be identified through the seriousness of the crime (measured by offence type), revictimisation, and social and personal circumstances is only weakly supported by research.

Under the Code of Practice for Victims of Crime, Police and Crime Commissioners have a duty to consult with victims in setting the policing priorities in their area, ensuring victims' needs are identified and met. In a previous review focusing on the means by which Police and Crime Commissioners have purported to gain insight into the genuine local needs of victims, it was noted that, for the most part, this was often attempted through small-scale local crime surveys, the methodological integrity of which were difficult to judge (Hall 2018). By 2018, it appears that more PCCs have published specific reports on the commissioning process (for victims and other commissioning roles, as noted above) and, from these, information concerning the gathering of data about victims in the local area is in some cases much more transparent. Generally, however, this material also reveals ongoing and often considerable variation in the methods by which PCCs have approached this process. So, for example, in both Devon and Cornwall & the Isles of Scilly and in Northumbria, there is evidence of major research projects being commissioned for the purpose of measuring local needs (see Tapley 2016: 10).

As noted above, in practice, Police and Crime Commissioners have organised consultation events to hear from multiple service providers, including restorative justice operators. The PCC of Thames Valley (perhaps somewhat tellingly) refers to these activities as 'market engagement events.' Sometimes the events have been open to the public and have also in places been attended by national figures in the victim's movement. For example, Gwent PCC's 'victim focused delivery event' on the delivery of victim services is described in the following terms:

> The seminar was attended by over 70 delegates that included statutory and voluntary sector partners as well as members of the public that had participated in the Victim's Voice workshops that had taken place earlier in the year. Guest speakers for the day included Baroness Newlove, Victim's Commissioner for England and Wales, Gwent Police ACC Lorraine Bottomley, Mandy Wilmot, Victim Support Divisional Manager for Wales, and the former Police and Crime Commissioner, Ian Johnston QPM. (Office of the Police and Crime Commissioner for Gwent 2018)

In most areas it nonetheless remains unclear to exactly what extent the Office of the PCC has engaged with victims or indeed victim activist groups directly, although many PCC offices in their plans and reports do mention having conducted online and offline surveys, getting 'feedback from victims' or being in the process of preparing to do so. Hence, the PCC of Surrey's Commissioning Strategy notes that:

> Over the past 4 years, the APCC [Assistant Police and Crime Commissioner] has met and heard from hundreds of victims—from adults whose houses have been burgled to children affected by domestic abuse and victims of rape and sexual abuse. Listening to their experiences tells us we cannot succeed without our partners. Services across statutory agencies and the voluntary sector all affect how a person is able to cope with the immediate impact of crime and recover as far as possible from the harm they have experienced. (Office of the Police and Crime Commissioner for Surrey 2016: 4)

Northamptonshire too has documented multiple surveys with victims, as set out in its 2017 Victims of Crime Consultation Report:

> In May 2013 the Police and Crime Commissioner for Northamptonshire launched a consultation with victims of crime to understand their experi-

ence of the criminal justice system and the agencies that support them. As a result of this consultation, the Victims' Voice report was published and 'Voice', the victim and witness service for Northamptonshire, was created. As part of the recommissioning process in January 2017, a shorter consultation was undertaken to directly inform the process and development for future victim and witness services. A total of 238 people responded to an online survey which was promoted through Facebook and Twitter and sent directly to community groups. Twenty-eight stated they were witnesses while 200 stated they were victims (10 people did not state). Of those, 72 were victims who had been supported by Voice and 123 were victims who had not. Alongside the survey, face-to-face discussions were held with nine victims who had received support from Voice and were willing to share their experiences. (Office of the Police and Crime Commissioner for Surrey 2016: 4)

Some PCCs have gone beyond this to commission much more detailed reports on victim services and the needs of victims in their areas, albeit the sources of data for such reports do tend to vary quite widely. In Bedfordshire, for example, such a report (Office of the Police and Crime Commissioner for Bedfordshire 2015) was produced in August 2015. The report is detailed, running to some 99 pages, and covers a great deal of information including referrals to local support agencies, victim satisfaction with various aspects of the criminal justice system, reporting rates and impacts of crime. Notably, most of these data are drawn from existing sources: including national census data and the Crime Survey for England and Wales. This is combined with local police data as well as qualitative interviews carried out with criminal justice agency representatives. Whilst all of this has clearly produced some very localised information, a telling issue is the apparent lack of direct victim involvement. Hence, under 'victim input' the report (ibid.: 15) reads as follows:

With more time, a specific timetable of focus groups and interviews with victims would have been possible. However, within the constraints of the project, views of victims were gathered in a variety of ways:

- Agencies were asked to approach victims that had already indicated that they were willing to provide feedback—and request short written summaries of their experiences. Whilst this of course is self-selecting and has a bias, it did provide honest and useful comment.

- Some victims agreed to 1-1 meetings with the consultant

This seems to suggest a rather ad hoc, small-scale exercise in terms of the number of victims directly consulted for these purposes. The report also notes an intention to sit in on Victim Support-run focus groups with victims which were ultimately unable to proceed within the designated timeframe. Other areas that have produced dedicated and substantial victim impact reports include Surrey, North Wales and Warwick. In Northamptonshire, the PCC commissioned the Institute for Public Safety, Crime and Justice to produce a more general 'victim experience' report, released in May 2016. This report is based on "2,491 surveys…conducted with victims" (Office of the Police and Crime Commissioner for Northamptonshire 2016: 28). The report goes on to note how such independently commissioned research directly fed into the service delivery model adopted in the area and has 'ultimately recommended a new delivery model that includes local communities helping to enable victims to recover from crime' (p. 32). As noted previously, PCCs in both Devon and Cornwall and the Isles of Scilly (Tapley 2016) and in Northumbria can be distinguished by their direct engagement with academic experts in their attempts to generate robust information on victims in their areas.

Assessing the Outcomes of Local Commissioning

Armed with such information as can be gleaned from the sources discussed in the last subsection, most PCCs are at the time of writing in the process of completing their second or third round of victim service commissioning. This allows us not only to examine what PCCs, broadly speaking, have done with the money they have been allocated for this purpose but also to see how they quantify and assess the outcomes, as required by the Commissioning Framework (Ministry of Justice 2013). It also affords us clues as to what has become of Williams' (1999) more hidden wing of the victim's movement under this process now that Victim Support has lost its preferential (a-political) status. The former question is made easier to answer by the fact that the reporting of such budgetary information is mandatory (as opposed to the precise nature of their consultations or evidence-base, which is not). Thus, clear breakdowns are available in PCCs' annual reports. Cambridgeshire PCC's version of such a report is reproduced (minimally adapted) here as an example of one that is particularly clear and substantively quite typical:

As I have previously argued (Hall 2018), generally speaking, most areas (approximately 70% of PCCs) have initiated a 'case managed' approach to supporting the majority of victims through centralised 'one-stop' Victim Care Units, rather than subscribing to the 'good neighbour' model previously used by Victim Support whereby volunteers visit victims in their homes (Simmonds 2013). From Table 10.1, we see

Table 10.1 Victim Services Awards 2017/19 (Cambridgeshire)

Service provision	Provider	Funding £
Safeguarding the Vulnerable		
Victim and Witness Hub Proactively contacts all victims of crime by letter or phone (depending on need)—offers telephone-based emotional support, onward referral and supportive signposting or face-to-face support from in-house Community Volunteers. Receives all self-referrals for support.	Cambridgeshire Constabulary	446,000
Specialist Victim Care Co-ordinator— Migrant Victims of Exploitation	Cambridgeshire Constabulary	33,445
Specialist Victim Care Co-ordinator—Young Victims of Crime	Family Action	32,670
Practical Support for Young Victims of Crime	Embrace—Child Victims of Crime	2000
Multi Agency Restorative Justice Hub Receives all enquiries and referrals from victims and other agencies about RJ. Co-ordinates all RJ interventions.	Cambridgeshire Constabulary	52,750
Victim Pathfinders—Mental Health Nurses Provide expertise, support and a referral capability for victims with suspected mental health issues identifying and co-ordinating pathways into treatment.	Cambridgeshire & Peterborough Foundation Trust	75,000
Home Security for Elderly Victims of Burglary Target hardening work to reduce repeat victimisation	Shrievalty Trust	50,000

(continued)

Table 10.1 (continued)

Service provision	Provider	Funding £
Young Person Independent Domestic Violence Advisor Support and advocacy for young victims of intimate partner domestic violence (part of wider partnership)	Cambridgeshire County Council	40,000
Specialist Support Services—Countywide Sexual Violence Service Funding contribution for end-to-end support service to include: telephone helpline, triage and assessment, emotional support, group work and counselling provision. This also includes independent sexual violence advisers and children and young persons' independent sexual violence advisers' provision.	Cambridge & Peterborough Rape Crisis Partnership	213,000 (378,000)
Independent Sexual Violence Advocate One off mid-year funding award to provide additional capacity to respond to increase in reporting of sexual violence	Cambridge & Peterborough Rape Crisis Partnership	7434
Counselling Service for Young Victims of Sexual Violence and Domestic Abuse SARC-based match-funded post to provide emotional support for young victims of sexual violence and domestic abuse.	Embrace—Child Victims of Crime	11,000
Specialist Independent Domestic Violence Advisor—Stalking and Harassment Pilot post to provide specialist support and guidance to victims of stalking and harassment	Cambridgeshire County Council (part of wider DA services model)	5500
Development of Operation Encompass Support to develop capacity to inform schools when one of their pupils has been involved in a domestic abuse incident to ensure appropriate support can be offered.	Multi Agency Safeguarding Hub	2500
Development of Communication and Awareness Channels • Single web portal • Sexual violence support literature • Commissioning support	Chameleon Studios Brookhill Design Studio	14,795
Total allocated spends		986,094

Adapted from Office of the Police and Crime Commissioner for Cambridgeshire 2018

Cambridge's version of this 'Victims Hub' providing generic victim services through the police and receiving by far the largest share of funding. There follows a list of more specialist commissioned services, which have been deemed proportionally cost-efficient based on an assessment of local needs. In terms of its content, this list is fairly typical, with specialist organisations providing support for victims of domestic violence, sexual violence and for young people. The charities listed here range from medium to large, which again seems fairly typical. The organisations funded also appear to fall much more in the less activist wing of the victim's movement, with many appearing to have become very adept at 'chasing' large pots of money.

Focus on the elderly and migrant victims in the Cambridgeshire commissioning framework is less typical and may be an indication that PCCs are indeed beginning to develop more nuanced understandings of local needs in their areas. On this point, I previously argued (Hall 2018) that in many cases the findings reported by PCCs from local needs assessments were very similar to the results of more general investigations into victim needs at the national level. Thus, it was not clear that it had been possible to truly assess victims' local needs in the way envisioned by the Commissioning Framework or even that such distinctly localised issues exist in all areas. What many of the first round of PCC reports *did* indicate is that the needs of victims often varied not by geographical area, but by individual: the implication being that victims' needs assessments must first and foremost be conducted at the individual level.

Whilst the observations made in the previous paragraph still broadly hold true, a fresh assessment suggests, as in Cambridgeshire, that progress does appear to have been made in the sense that more specific types of victimisation are now being considered by different PCCs. In one example, the Lancashire PCC reports that Lancashire's Victim Services (LVCs) were able to provide comprehensive support to two victims of the Tunisia shootings in 2015 who live in the county (Office of the Police and Crime Commissioner for Lancashire 2016). In another example, Staffordshire PCC's Police and Crime Plan specifically identified business-related crime as being a particular problem for that area (Office of the Police and Crime Commissioner for Staffordshire 2016).

Reports from different areas also indicate PCCs' appreciation for the need to robustly assess the outcomes of the commissioning exercise for victims, themselves. In particular, many PCCs have developed an approach which focuses less on raw quantitative figures which measure the number of victims referred or 'assisted'. Thus, the Surrey and Sussex PCC criminal justice partnership note not only the importance of gaining direct victim feedback on commissioned services but also that of taking what he calls a 'whole person approach' which looks at the overall needs of individuals and their families (Tippen 2017: 3).

That said, it is notable that whilst the emphasis of the Commissioning System was on moving away from uninformative 'service figures', many PCCs do still draw heavily on these, and indeed on the raw figures of money invested (as in Table 1), as evidence of the 'success' of such commissioning. Thus, the section on 'Supporting Victims' in Leicestershire's PCCs 2016/17 annual report begins by citing statistics from its Victim First Service, indicating the service has achieved an 'average of 889.5 referrals a month (an increase of 8% compared to 2015/16)' (Police and Crime Commissioner for Leicestershire 2016: 10). Similarly, the Warwick local Victims and Witnesses Charter draws heavily on referral rates to the charity Victim Support as evidence of the success of its measures. Although a number of PCCs do buttress this with reference to victim satisfaction surveys, the variability of the approaches to assessment across all the PCC areas makes it very difficult to conclusively assess the real-world impact of the commissioning process as a whole on victims of crime in England and Wales.

Wider Profile of PCCs on the Victim's Agenda

As noted previously, different PCCs have appeared to view the victims commissioning brief as having different levels of centrality within their overall role. In some cases, there is a sense of arms-length delegation to the relevant 'victims board'. In other cases, however, certain PCCs have built a substantial platform around the victim issue specifically, encroaching at the national level with regard to the treatment and the rights of victims of crime. Thus, the Dorset PCC has called for the institution of 'victim lawyers':

I will lobby Government to sponsor a pilot Victims' Lawyer Scheme in Dorset, similar to the model used in parts of Europe. The Victims' Lawyer would represent victims at all stages of a prosecution, rather than the current system where a victim is only formally recognised by the court upon the conviction of another individual. (Police and Crime Commissioner for Dorset 2016: 13)

The notion of victims having their own lawyers has long been debated in victimological circles but remains somewhat radical, at least in the adversarial criminal justice model adopted in the UK. As such, this pledge points to a far wider advocacy of victim issues by some PCCs. For his part, the Lincolnshire PCC has taken the lead of the PCC Association's Victims Group, with a national remit. In Northumbria, a previous PCC, former Solicitor-General Dame Vera Baird, has been a long-term and outspoken advocate for victims of crime. It has been noted that the Staffordshire PCC has taken a lead on local business crime issues and is seeking to make this a national priority, doing so in a report which also discusses the national expansion of special measures for vulnerable and intimidated witnesses giving evidence (Office of the Police and Crime Commissioner for Staffordshire 2016).

In sum, it can be appreciated that for some PCCs, the victims' brief has truly bedded in to the point where they are seeking to exert influence on the national level. This is important as it cements the impression of the PCC role as now being central to the development of victim policy in England and Wales, rather than being restricted to the local tailoring of victim services. Of course, given that the PCCs are politicians we might remain wary of early concerns that awarding them this role might render victims political pawns (Duggan and Heap 2014), a criticism that has been made of victim reform in multiple countries for at least 30 years (Rock 2004).

Discussion

In 2016, the national Victims Commissioner, Baroness Newlove, reported that the Police and Crime Commissioners had developed 'innovative ways of commissioning and managing local services for victims'

(Commissioner for Victims and Witnesses 2016: 4). At this point, however, the commissioning role of the PCCs had had less time to bed in and evidence of its more prolonged effectiveness was unclear.[7] When I first examined this system in 2016, I noted a number of concerns including an apparent lack of systematic engagement with victims directly in many PCC areas in forming their commissioning strategy (Hall 2018). It was not clear whether PCCs were in a position to identify genuine local need (if indeed such *distinct* need existed), and the victim service role sometimes appeared to have assumed a marginal position within the much broader remit of many of the Commissioners. There was also lingering concern that the organisations best placed to support victims of crime did not have the time or expertise to competitively seek tenders in the local commissioning system, with even Victim Support failing to win the contract to continue running the Witness Service, having campaigned and later operated this service since its inception (see Rock 2004; Hall 2009).

Over three years later, and with a new Victims Commissioner, there is evidence that the situation has moved on and indeed in some places for the better. Certainly, a fresh review of publicly available materials indicates that more PCCs are now seeing victims and victim service commissioning as core aspects of their roles. Compared to 2016, more prominence is generally given to victims on PCC websites, and there is more transparency and publication of dedicated policies, commissioning goals, reports and analyses of victims' local needs. Furthermore, there are real potential benefits to be had from some PCCs assuming a greater advocacy role for victims on the national stage. Indeed, it is striking how in many ways this role has quickly assumed a central position in the wider victims' debate, alongside the national Victims Commissioner (see Hall 2017), London creating its own Victim Commissioner in 2017.

The above notwithstanding, the robustness of a lot of the information on which PCCs base their commissioning decision is still somewhat questionable. In many areas, such data remain grounded in ad hoc consultations and knowledge exchange events or else drawn from rather small-scale and often non-representative surveys. As noted above, only a handful of PCCs have taken the step of commissioning professional external researchers to undertake their needs analysis or indeed their outcomes analysis. In the latter case, for all the talk of outcomes-based approaches, many of the annual reports produced by PCCs still fall back on familiar generic metrics which essentially count the number of victims served without assessing the impact on those victims.

In identifying genuinely 'local issues' which require a tailored commissioning of services, there is some indication in the dataset that PCCs are beginning to uncover such localised problems or aspects of problems: elder abuse, business crime, impacts of terrorism and child sexual exploitation being key examples. Nevertheless, much of what the needs assessments derive from the sources discussed above are still broadly in line with most of the existing literature in the area on victims' needs (see Shapland and Hall 2007) and with national-level studies (Freeman 2013). As such, the case that local commissioning can and will reveal the intricacies of specific local need is not fully borne out by the evidence. That said, the degree of local activity, development and understanding being generated around victim issues may well have reached the point where we are arguably in a better state of overall qualitative knowledge than we were under previous government strategies of commissioning the large-scale Witness and Victims Experience Survey (see Commissioner for Victims and Witnesses in England & Wales 2011), and before that, court-based Vulnerable and Intimated Witnesses Surveys (Hamlyn et al. 2004). Of course, whilst the *quantity* of the data may have increased, the *quality* in terms of its systematic methodology (and therefore its comparability between areas) has almost certainly decreased under local commissioning arrangements.

More positively, it is notable that, contrary to some predictions, there has not been a great deal of public evidence to suggest a large number of local victim service providers are being forced out of the new 'market' that has been created by the Commissioning Framework as a result of lacking time or expertise to compete for commissioned money. More often, there is a sense of collective engagement with the commissioning exercise drawing links between such organisations, the PCC's office and/ or newly commissioned Victim Care Units as hubs for collaborative activities. Of course, this observation needs to be tested further by speaking to victim service organisations themselves and certainly much more research on how local commissioning has impacted positively or negatively 'on the ground' from the service providers' perspectives is called for. In this regard, we must recognise that it is in the interests of PCCs to present a 'united front' and to emphasise the services that have been *funded* rather than those which have not, no PCC having published data on this latter issue. Certainly there have been local services that have closed in different areas due to funding being withdrawn and still in areas previously described as the 'hidden wing', impacting on victims of rape and domestic abuse (see Williams 1999). With a lot of the main commissioning contracts going to larger charities, there remains a concern that smaller more activist-inspired groups still remain marginalised under the new arrangements despite the opportunities implied by the end of Victim Support's previous monopoly.

Perhaps most significantly, further research is required to answer the major underlying question of whether, even with positive aspects considered, the developing model of local victim service commissioning is in fact achieving what it promised: that is, supporting more victims, more cost-effectively and in a way that meets their actual needs. Such conclusive evidence that the new model has worked to these ends over and above the more generic, national approach still favoured by most other European jurisdictions is still not forthcoming.

Conclusions

In sum, the findings of this review are, if anything, more optimistic than previous discussions on the experiment, that is, local commissioning of victim services in England and Wales. Many PCCs have indeed found creative ways to gather data on victims' needs in their local area and are commissioning services in accordance with the best data they have. Overall, the degree of discussion and debate going on around the issue of victim services up and down the country is almost certainly greater than it was when the issue was largely dealt with at a national level. The commissioning framework has also opened opportunities (or potential opportunities) for the so-called hidden wing of the victim's movement to further its work, especially in the area of sexual violence. That said, we have seen evidence that on the whole larger charities still tend to dominate this new 'marketplace' of supply for victim services, and thus we are far from a return to the more activist-based support base for victims of crime seen before the rise of Victim Support as a national 'preferred supplier'. This is significant because in such circumstances, the ability of such organisations to challenge the government and criticise the criminal justice system, and indeed the PCCs themselves, on victim policies remains curtailed. In addition, we also still lack hard figures to prove the economic effectiveness of this system, the quality of the services available or their genuine impact on victims. We also know very little about the service providers who might have lost out as a result of local commissioning. There is also the lingering question of the politicisation of victims. PCCs being (by definition) politicians, the line between using this role as a platform to advocate on behalf of victims of crime at the regional or national level, and exploiting them for political gain, is often a grey one.

Notes

1. The reform was not extended to Scotland, whilst in Northern Ireland roles broadly comparable to those of a PCC are carried out by the Northern Ireland Policing Board.
2. As a minimum all PCCs are required to publish a Police and Crime Plan to cover their entire tenure in the role as well as annual reports on the progress of that plan.
3. Broad reflections only will be included here as information from the Group is confidential and was not gathered systematically or originally for the purposes of research. It would therefore be neither methodologically sound nor ethically acceptable to go into specifics. The point is raised largely for the purpose of transparency.
4. Directive 2012/29/EU of the European Parliament and of the Council of 25 October 2012 establishing minimum standards on the rights, support and protection of victims of crime and replacing Council Framework Decision 2001/220/JHA.
5. The role of second wave feminism is emphasised by Kearon and Godfrey (2007).

6. Except in relation to adding victims of crime as a group to be consulted on local policing issues though an amendment of the Police Act 1996 (s.14 of the 2011 legislation).
7. Subsequently Newlove visited all PCC offices up and down the country to review provisions first hand.

References

Commissioner for Victims and Witnesses in England & Wales. (2011). *Victims' Views of Court and Sentencing Qualitative research with WAVES victims*. London: Office of the Commissioner for Victims and Witnesses in England & Wales.

Commissioner for Victims and Witnesses. (2016). *Commissioner for Victims and Witnesses: Annual Report for 2015–16*. London: Office of the Commissioner for Victims and Witnesses.

Duggan, M., & Heap, V. (2014). *Administrating Victimization: The Politics of Anti-Social Behaviour and Hate Crime Policy*. London: Palgrave.

Freeman, L. (2013). *Support for Victims: Findings from the Crime Survey for England and Wales*. London: Ministry of Justice.

Goodey, J. (2005). *Victims and Victimology: Research, Policy and Practice*. Edinburgh: Pearson.

Hall, M. (2009). *Victims of Crime: Policy and Practice in Criminal Justice*. Cullompton: Willan.

Hall, M. (2017). *Victims of Crime: Constructions, Governance and Policy*. London: Palgrave.

Hall, M. (2018). Supporting Victims of Crime in England and Wales: Local Commissioning Meeting Local Needs? *International Review of Victimology, 24*(2), 219–237.

Hamlyn, B., Phelps, A., Turtle, J., & Sattar, G. (2004). *Are Special Measures Working? Evidence from Surveys of Vulnerable and Intimidated Witnesses*. Home Office Research Study 283. London: Home Office.

Kearon, T., & Godfrey, B. (2007). Setting the Scene: a Question of History. In S. Walklate (Ed.), *Handbook of Victims and Victimology* (pp.17–36). Cullompton: Willan Publishing.

Mawby, R. (2016). Victim Support in England and Wales: The End of an Era? *International Review of Victimology, 22*(3), 203–221.

Ministry of Justice. (2010). *Breaking the Cycle: Effective Punishment, Rehabilitation and Sentencing of Offenders*. London: Ministry of Justice.

Ministry of Justice. (2012a). *Getting It Right for Victims and Witnesses*. Consultation Paper CP3/201. London: Ministry of Justice.

Ministry of Justice. (2012b). *Getting It Right for Victims and Witnesses: The Government Response*. London: Ministry of Justice.

Ministry of Justice. (2013). *Victims' Services Commissioning Framework*. London: Ministry of Justice.

Ministry of Justice. (2015). *Code of Practice for Victims of Crime*. London: Ministry of Justice.

Office of the Police and Crime Commissioner for Bedfordshire. (2015). *Bedfordshire Victim Needs Assessment*. Bedford: Office of the Police and Crime Commissioner for Bedfordshire.

Office of the Police and Crime Commissioner for Cambridgeshire. (2018). *Victim Services Awards 2017/18*. Cambridge: Office of the Police and Crime Commissioner for Cambridgeshire.

Office of the Police and Crime Commissioner for Devon and Cornwall & the Isles of Scilly. (2014). *Needs Assessment for Victim Services*. Exeter: Office of the Police and Crime Commissioner for Devon and Cornwall & the Isles of Scilly.

Office of the Police and Crime Commissioner for Devon and Cornwall & the Isles of Scilly. (2018). *Regional Collaboration* [Online]. Retrieved July 13, 2018, from http://www.devonandcornwall-pcc.gov.uk/meetings-and-events/other meetings/regional-pccs/.

Office of the Police, Crime and Victims' Commissioner for Durham. (2016). *Delivering Change for Victims and Witnesses: From Policy to Reality*. Durham: Office of the Police, Crime and Victims' Commissioner for Durham.

Office of the Police and Crime Commissioner for Gwent. (2018). *Victims* [Online]. Retrieved July 13, 2018, from http://www.gwent.pcc.police.uk/engagement/victims/.

Office of the Police and Crime Commissioner for Lancashire. (2016). *Annual Report 2015/16*. Preston: Office of the Police and Crime Commissioner for Lancashire.

Office of the Police and Crime Commissioner for Lincolnshire. (2018). *Annual Report 2017–18*. Lincoln: Office of the Police and Crime Commissioner for Lincolnshire.

Office of the Police and Crime Commissioner for Northamptonshire. (2016). *Victim Experience Annual Report*. Northampton: Office of the Police and Crime Commissioner for Northamptonshire.

Office of the Police and Crime Commissioner for North Yorkshire. (2018). *PCC Funding* [Online]. Retrieved July 13, 2018, from https://www.northyorkshire-pcc.gov.uk/police-oversight/finances/grants/.

Office of the Police and Crime Commissioner for Staffordshire. (2016). *Safer, Fairer, United Communities for Staffordshire 2016–2020*. Stoke-on-Trent: Office of the Police and Crime Commissioner for Staffordshire.

Office of the Police and Crime Commissioner for Surrey. (2016). *Commissioning Strategy 2016–2020*. Guildford: Office of the Police and Crime Commissioner for Surrey.

Office of the Police and Crime Commissioner for West Midlands. (2014). *Victim Services Strategy 2014–2016: From Local to National Commissioning*. Birmingham: Office of the Police and Crime Commissioner for West Midlands.

Office of the Police and Crime Commissioner for West Midlands. (2015). *National to Local Commissioning*. Birmingham: Office of the Police and Crime Commissioner for West Midlands.

Pointing, J., & Maguire, M. (1988). Introduction: The Rediscovery of the Crime Victim. In M. Maguire & J. Pointing (Eds.), *Victims of Crime: A New Deal?* (pp. 1–13). Milton Keynes: Open University Press.

Police and Crime Commissioner for Leicestershire. (2016). *Annual Report 2016/2017*. Leicester: Police and Crime Commissioner for Leicestershire.

Rock, P. (1990). *Helping Victims of Crime: The Home Office and the Rise of Victim Support in England and Wales*. Oxford: Oxford University Press.

Rock, P. (2004). *Constructing Victims' Rights: The Home Office, New Labour and Victims*. Oxford: Clarendon Press.

Shapland, J., & Hall, M. (2007). What Do We Know About the Effect of Crime on Victims? *International Review of Victimology, 14*(2), 175–217.

Simmonds, L. (2013). Lost in Transition? The Changing Face of Victim Support. *International Review of Victimology, 19*(2), 201–217.

Simmonds, L. (2016). The Potential Impact of Local Commissioning on Victim Services in England and Wales. *International Review of Victimology, 22*(3), 223–237.

Tapley, J. (2016). *An Evaluation of the Devon and Cornwall & The Isles of Scilly Victim Care Model*. Exeter: Office of the Police and Crime Commissioner for Devon and Cornwall & The Isles of Scilly.

Tapley, J., Stark, A., Watkins, M., & Peneva, B. (2014). *A Strategic Assessment of Support Services for Victims of Crime in the South East.* Portsmouth: University of Portsmouth.

Tippen, B. (2017). *Surrey and Sussex Criminal Justice Partnerships Delivery Plan – Updated May 2017.* Guildford: Office of the Police and Crime Commissioner for Surrey.

Wedlock, E., & Tapley, J. (2016). *What Works in Supporting Victims of Crime: A Rapid Evidence Assessment.* London: Office of the Commissioner for Victims and Witnesses.

Williams, B. (1999). *Working with Victims of Crime: Policies, Politics and Practice.* London: J. Kingsley.

Young, M. (1997). Victim Rights and Services: A Modern Saga. In R. Davis, A. Lurigio, & W. Skogan (Eds.), *Victims of Crime* (2nd ed., pp. 194–210). Thousand Oaks, CA: Sage Publications.

11

Partnerships and Activism: Community Safety, Multi-agency Partnerships and Safeguarding Victims

Pamela Davies

Introduction

In the last two decades of the twentieth century, a shift took place in the field of crime prevention, policing and justice, such that there is increased preoccupation with security (Johnston and Shearing 2003) at individual, local, national and global levels. The marked shift saw the primary function of policing become more forward looking. Until the 1970s, policing had become focused on responding to crime with the prevention function reduced to deterrence. Since this decade, there has been a greater focus on security and ways of predicting and reducing risk with a move to evidence-based policing (EBP). Broader modernisation of the criminal justice system and a range of reforms and legislation, diminished faith in offender rehabilitation and widespread belief that the welfarist approach to crime reduction was not working saw an increasingly punitive

P. Davies (✉)

Department of Social Sciences, Northumbria University, Newcastle upon Tyne, UK

e-mail: pamela.davies@northumbria.ac.uk

© The Author(s) 2020

J. Tapley, P. Davies (eds.), *Victimology*,

https://doi.org/10.1007/978-3-030-42288-2_11

neo-classical approach creeping across England and Wales, such that emerging trends in the governance of criminal justice are now complex. Some of the more recent developments are further explored below, but currently the approach to tacking perpetrators and safeguarding victims has been impacted by the 2011, Reform and Responsibility Act, which prefaced the election of Police and Crime Commissioners (PCCs) (and the Mayor's Office for Policing in the Metropolitan Police Authority in London) and saw PCCs becoming responsible for ensuring the maintenance of the police force and that the service is efficient and effective. PCCs also publish Police and Crime Plans, which set out local police and crime objectives. This reform has also established PCCs as a central aspect of the victim reform agenda in England and Wales and, as Matthew Hall argues in Chapter 10 of this volume, these developments represent a significant watershed in the long-running transportation of victim services from being activist-driven to market-driven. Processes of managerialism and ever-greater government influence and centralisation see national management of criminal justice institutions at the same time as increased marketization sees the growing profile of the private sector and voluntary organisations playing a significant role in supervision of offenders in the community and in supporting victims of crime. Amidst these complex developments around the governance of criminal justice and the shift towards plural policing, partnership approaches and multi-agency collaborations remain the touchstone for community safety and security.

This chapter focuses on multi-agency partnerships as a means of exploring the ways in which activism manifests in safeguarding victims. A range of supportive provisions and victim assistance schemes can now be identified in most jurisdictions across the world, all of which have differing relationships to their respective criminal justice systems. Some victim services are at arm's length or fully independent of the government, some are provided under statute, others by voluntary groups and charities. Several have been pioneered through the efforts of feminist activism. This chapter engages in a critical review of twenty-first-century pluralised multi-agency approaches to tackling crime, preventing harm, responsibilising perpetrators and supporting victims. It will explore the strategies and politics that have seen an increasing emphasis upon prevention and individual responsibility on both victims and offenders. The chapter reflects on these developments and the conundrums and dilemmas this poses for victim safety and safeguarding. It does so through a focus on multi-agency partnerships to tackle crime, disorder and harm at local levels and by drawing on a case study example: tackling serial perpetrators of domestic abuse through Multi-agency Tasking and Co-ordination (MATAC) and the subsequent Domestic Abuse Whole Systems Approach (DAWSA), both pioneered in the North East of England, the UK. Though the examples drawn on emerge from local and regional approaches, the issues raised in this chapter are in no sense parochial. Violence against women and girls (VAWG) is recognised as a global issue. The discussion offers insight into what this means in terms of community safety agendas: whose safety and security is prioritised? Why are multi-agency approaches continuing to proliferate? In particular, the chapter will consider what these developments appear to mean in terms of partnerships, activism, crime prevention, community safety and safeguarding victims. It will demonstrate altered relationships and shifting politics between how members of third-sector organisations work in partnership with the police and other statutory agencies whilst remaining critical and engaged in campaigning for further reforms.

Background Context: Crime Prevention, Community Safety and Multi-agency Partnerships

In twenty-first-century England and Wales, as noted above, there has been marked shift in the nature of policing from that which dominated much of the previous century. There is now a greater focus on security and ways of predicting and reducing risk. The rational choice and routine activity orthodoxy and community crime prevention initiatives of the latter quarter of the twentieth century paved the way for the birth of community safety, in the early 1980s. The concept and practice of community crime prevention and multi-agency partnership approaches to combatting crime and disorder have become the new tradition in preventing crime and safeguarding and protecting from harm and criminal victimisation. The concept of community safety is now over 30 years old, and during this period, the position of the victim in matters of safety and criminal justice has become increasingly foregrounded. All of these developments were in the context of emerging evidence that the criminal justice system and police were ineffective in reducing crime, diminished faith in offender rehabilitation and weakened state and welfare provision and a socio-political climate where new-right politics was flourishing (van Ginneken 2017). By the mid-1980s, the Five Towns Initiative (1986) had expanded and the Safer Cities Programme was launched in 1988, two years before the Morgan Report (1991) was published recommending the replacement of the concept of crime prevention with community safety. By 1998, the New Labour government paved the way for the creation of Community Safety Partnerships via the 1998 Crime and Disorder Act. Police and local authorities, in partnership with probation and health authorities gave impetus to multi-agency collaboration.

Whilst the above provides a very brief background context to crime, prevention, community safety and multi-agency partnerships, taking into account the political climate in which developments took place, it is important to capture the extent to which these developments were exclusive to particular types of safety and security threat concerns and to particular sources of such threats.

Community Safety: For Who and from What?

In the context of tackling domestic abuse, the story of statutory partnership working to tackle such offending and reduce victimisation has been slow and is not yet won. Part of the reason for this goes to the heart of the limitations of the community safety agenda. One of the key criticisms about multi-agency working to tackle crime and disorder and of community safety partnerships are the questions about whose safety is prioritised and safety from what?

Though community safety has the potential to embrace a wide range of anti-social experiences in its remit, the paradigm that unfolded emphasised the partiality of the dominant community safety project (Davies 2008). The image of community assumed by the mainstream community safety industry was, for a long time, at odds with a gendered approach to understanding and responding to crime, offending, social harm and criminal victimisation. The 'broken windows' thesis of Wilson and Kelling (1982) (Walklate and Evans 1999) took hold in the 1980s and early 1990s. The windows smashed and boarded up in their thesis, however, are those broken by incivilities caused from the outside and not from within. Whilst feminist campaigning on violence against women was vociferous in this period, the zero-tolerance approach that unfolded did little to seriously challenge the dominant ethos of community safety, which prioritises making public places safe whilst marginalising the safety concerns behind closed doors. As Walklate (2018) has observed much more recently, so much remains to be done in terms of understanding the precarious existence of women who live with violence, and gendered thinking still needs to inform our community safety agendas.

The voice of reason embedded within the rational, progressive, modern and objective rational choice theoretic, which underpinned the dominant community safety agenda, is an abstracted form of reason, a masculinist, and instrumental/economic choice form of rationality (Davies 2011). Such a model provides only a partial understanding of what social (economic) life is really about especially for women who are coercively controlled and who are constantly in fear of being raped (Brownmiller 1975) and who suffer repeatedly and silently from men's physical violence in their own homes. Others writing in this volume (O'Leary and Green in Chapter 7) observe how emotions have been stripped from our criminal justice processes. Rational choice reduces emotions and they are especially constricted with respect to crimes which are intimate and of a sexual nature (Hayward 2007).

Following other feminist-inspired commentators on the community safety agenda, I have argued for a more refined approach to community safety in which violence and abuse that emerges from within households is accounted for and responded to (Davies 2008). Using the example of domestic violence as a crime involving intimate insiders (Crawford 2007), I have drawn attention to the artificial division between the public and private realm in relation to community safety where a pane of glass literally represents the cut-off between public and domestic disorder. This line of arguments suggests that community safety approaches generally and responses to violence and abuse specifically are often removed from the everyday, usually highly local and frequently familial existence in which they are embedded. They are too far removed and abstracted from the (albeit often dysfunctional and malignant) micro communities which they seek to change for the safer. The conclusions of such arguments support recommendations for a more proactive, relevant and closer to home policy response following Walklate and Evans (1999). Such policy would have a greater emphasis on families and sets of personal relationships, on local social dynamics, formal and informal networks in communities in order to restore the local equilibrium. Close ties, the local and 'quite small units' (Walklate and Evans 1999: 138) need to matter. These 'quite small units' include family living arrangements, intimate and personal, formal and informal relationships and ties, working and professional relationships. Very, very local areas and small units possess harm-reducing skills, which are capable of producing successful and effective outcomes to conflict and for restoring equilibrium at the same time as they are also capable of wreaking havoc, destroying trust and producing conflict.

Thus, in 2008, I concluded that 'Operationalising community safety at the very local levels requires a much more grass roots understanding of how windows can be broken from within and not always from without' (Davies 2008: 220). By engaging more effectively with 'knowledge holders' at very local levels, a more inclusive crime prevention and community safety paradigm might be more successful in tackling serial perpetrators of domestic abuse. As noted above, feminist activism has made inroads to the community safety agenda in the 1980s and 1990s by raising awareness of abuse and the unsafety of women in the home. As I will now outline, the story of multi-agency working to tackle domestic abuse has remained work in progress.

Multi-agency Working and Domestic Abuse

Partnership approaches were identified early in the new era of community safety as a way of tackling domestic abuse (Barton and Valero-Silva 2012). Since the mid-to-late 1980s, there has been increasing reliance on such partnerships to prevent abuse and protect from it. Prior to this, single agency responses were typical and there was very little information sharing, particularly between statutory and voluntary agencies. Domestic violence forums proliferated in the 1990s inspired by the 'Duluth approach' in Minnesota, USA. During this decade, government leadership on domestic abuse saw national action plans emerge. By the turn of the twenty-first century, prompted by a combination of Home Office guidance and legislative requirements to form partnerships to tackle crime and disorder, information sharing in England and Wales became more routinised (Westmarland 2012).

Though a tradition of partnership approaches to tackling inter-personal violence and abuse are well established in England and Wales, they have tended to operate largely within the confines of a traditional criminal justice paradigm, which seeks to hold perpetrators to account through legal sanctions and mandated rehabilitation solutions. We shall return to this question of criminal justice solutions later in the chapter. First, we pause to consider the nature and extent of activist-driven service provision.

Activist-Driven and Research Underpinned Service Provision and Policy Development

As noted above, feminist campaigning on violence against women slowly impacted on the policing of domestic violence abuse in the early 1990s. The first Home Office Circular on victims (in general) and policing was published in 1990. It took another ten years for the second to be published in 2000 with little other policy documentation featuring violence against women and girls until the 2000s. Activist-driven developments have played a significant part in securing services for victims of inter-personal violence. However, as also noted above, this sits alongside the emergence of market-driven victim services.

Broadly understood, activism concerns taking collective action in order to bring about change. Goddard et al. (2014) outline three types of grassroots counter movements and social justice organisations in the US, each of these aim to raise consciousness and fight for justice system reform: *activist social justice organisations* where advocacy and organising work is at the core of what they do, *programme and service delivery social justice organisations* centring on consciousness raising of systemic injustices and deprivations and third, *advocacy and policymaking organisations* which often serve as umbrella organisations helping organise and coordinate protests and bring the voices and viewpoints of grassroots organisations directly to the offices of lawmakers. Goddard et al. (2014: 85) point out that the social justice organisations that fall within this typology nevertheless fall within a continuum:

> on the one end are more liberal-oriented organisations that works within formal government channels; and on the other end are more radical organisations that are openly critical of the government and working towards community sovereignty.

Historical examples of collective social action include violent and non-violent strategies to effect change, and these can include raising public consciousness and awareness of specific issues, lobbying either for or against such issues, and a variety of other pressure group activities including demonstrations, marches, protests and petitions. Examples of feminist activism are many and varied, and in the context of raising the profile of women as victims/survivors, national feminist activism has undoubtedly played a key part in effecting change. The great hostility faced by feminist influenced activists of the 1960s and 1970s nevertheless saw the salience of gender in understanding all matters connected to crime, victimisation and justice gather momentum.

As noted in Chapter 2 of this volume, it was the 1960s and 1970s in the UK and the US that saw the emergence of the modern movements against violence against women as part of the wider women's liberation movement. Whilst a variety of new and different feminist perspectives can now be identified, each prioritising different political strategies, there are some common features across feminist positions regarding violence against women and girls. The most obvious of these is that they ask *the woman question* and this means effecting change through doing criminological and victimological research, *for* rather than *on* women (Smith and Wincup 2000). Feminist strands of scholarship, activism and research have exposed 'domestic secrets' (Heidensohn and Gelsthorpe 2007), and in the 1970s, the enormity of the problem of what was then called 'wife battering' began to emerge. Since the 1980s, this activist-inspired scholarship has all exposed the domestic sphere as a key site for the violence and sexual abuse experienced by women and children (see Brownmiller 1975; Dobash and Dobash 1979, 1998; Hanmer and Maynard 1987; Hanmer and Saunders 1984; Kelly 1988; Kelly and Radford 1987; Stanko 1988, 1990). These knowledges, 'get behind the mere appearance of things' (Mawby and Walklate 1994: 19) and at the events that 'go on behind closed doors' that we do not 'see' (Walklate 2007: 49) and as such have been key to furthering a more inclusive crime prevention and community safety strategy. Such knowledge challenges the domain assumptions that have always informed the law and order agenda and those that more recently have shaped the community safety agenda. They problematise gender stereotypical strategies and policies whereby only some qualify as suitable targets for community safety interventions. Indoor sites for criminal victimisation have been overlooked, as have the risks of serious violence and abuse, particularly to those women and children who spend much of their time at home with those they know and often trust the most.

The impetus of the wider women's liberation movement impacted on the increased centrality of the victim within the criminal justice system in the latter part of the twentieth century. Feminist influences on the victim movement drew particular attention to the under-reporting and poor recording of domestic abuse and violence against women as well as the cultural constraints that conceived domestic abuse as 'rubbish' police work, not real crime, not real policing and thus produced the poor policing response. The victims' movement corresponded with, and blurred with, the 'second-wave' feminist movement. The latter raised awareness of the victimisation of women in the home and of women's experiences of sexual violence and campaigned for such violence with all of its attendant emotional and psychological impacts to be recognised by the criminal justice system and society more widely (Davies 2011). Similar movements gathered pace elsewhere in the world. Over the last 40–50 years, women and children suffering serious, multiple, repeat and serial forms of violence and abuse from men within the familial and intimate context—now termed domestic abuse—is recognised as a wider violence against women and girls' problem (VAWG) and a global issue. As Sebba (2001: 36) notes, lobbying by feminists and organisations devoted to victim assistance was:

> instrumental in the intensive barrage of victim-related legislation and policy reform which were instigated in the 1980s and 1990s … and included the granting of procedural rights to victims in the course of the trial process (and subsequent proceedings), victim-oriented sentencing dispositions such as restitution, the introduction of state compensation boards and victim assistance programmes.

Safeguarding from Violence and Abuse Since the Turn of the Century

Since the 1990s, the politicisation of crime victims in Western liberal societies has fuelled a rhetoric espousing that victims of crime should be at 'the heart of the criminal justice system'. Pressure for change has involved activism around campaigning for victims' rights as well as procedural justice. This can be as seen in the various iterations of the Victims Charter since 1990 (Home Office 1990) through, to the introduction of and revisions to, the Code of Practice for Victims of Crime (Ministry of Justice 2015). Indeed, some progress had been made from the late 1990s to early 2000s. Co-location of criminal justice agencies has emerged in some jurisdictions and joint-working has proliferated in some areas, but this progress has been negatively impacted/undone by subsequent austerity measures (Davies and Biddle 2017). Policies applied by the 2010–2015 Coalition government, and continued under the Conservative administration, have changed the way victim support is managed. Featherstone et al. (2012: 177) call this a period of 'austerity localism' which—in the context of domestic abuse, where it interfaces with women's safety—is problematic (Vacchelli 2015). Collaboration between statutory agencies and local women's networks have been compromised and local feminist-inspired women's groups perceive they have lost out, resulting in the further marginalisation of domestic abuse victims (Buser 2013; Clayton et al. 2016; Vacchelli 2015; Westwood 2011). From 2014 to 2015, provision of services for many victims have rested with Police and Crime Commissioners, who are also responsible for establishing local policing priorities. The current national strategy 2016–2020 (Home Office 2016) promotes a co-ordinated response, within which regional and local initiatives have proliferated.

There has been significant economic and political change in the period since multi-agency working became the dominant approach to tackling domestic abuse, which have influenced partnership working in many areas of social policy and have affected local agenda-setting and commissioning. At the same time, significant victim-focused policy reform has occurred. Whilst significant attention is now paid to the problem of VAWG, the so-called 'criminal justice response' remains stubbornly ineffective in terms of tackling the problem. There is a plethora of civil and criminal justice options in the criminal justice toolkit for tackling domestic abuse yet, despite such commitments, too many women become victims. An estimated 1.2 million in England and Wales experience such abuse in the year ending March 2017 (ONS 2018a) and, on average, two women are killed each week by a current or former partner (ONS 2018b). Legislative changes to the definition of domestic abuse in England and Wales followed two decades of policy reform directed towards an integrated strategy to tackle VAWG (HMIC 2014, 2015). There are many criminal and civil intervention options, some of which see prospective victims provided with information about their partner's previous violent behaviour, advocating preventive ideologies. For example, legally enforceable short-term protective measures include Protection Notices (DVPNs) and Protection Orders (DVPOs), introduced via the Crime & Security Act (2010). DVPOs resemble the 'barring orders' operating elsewhere in Europe: the Austrian Protection against Domestic Violence Act 1996 and the German Protection from Violence Act 2002 (Bessant 2015). Additionally, the Domestic Violence Disclosure Scheme 2014 (DVDS or Clare's Law) (see Chapter 7 in this volume) provides a framework for members of the public to ask about a person's history of domestic abuse or intimate partner violence. The latter are part of a recent shift occurring internationally, of further legislation and campaigns targeting primary prevention at men (Cismaru and Lavack 2011). Additionally, significant recent change affecting the 'policing' of domestic abuse across many countries is the widespread recognition that domestic abuse is an issue of power and control.

Power and (Coercive) Control

Intimate partner violence, whether between heterosexual or same sex couples (Donovan and Barnes 2017), is widely understood as a pattern of behaviour that can be physical, emotional, economic and sexual in nature. In the UK, it is now recognised that the dynamics of domestic abuse are connected to the concept of coercive control, which captures both the psychological and physical aspects and on-going nature of the behaviour and the extent to which the actions of the perpetrator control the victim through isolation, intimidation, degradation and micro-regulation of everyday life (HMIC 2015).

Walklate et al. (2017) note that the implementation of this offence in England and Wales has so far been patchy, and based on their gendered analysis of coercive control, they conclude that more law will not improve responses to intimate partner violence. Others are also wary of the wholesale adoption of coercive control as an approach that seeks to explain variations in domestic violence (Walby and Towers 2018). In Brisbane, Australia, Douglas (2017) reports legal engagement can be an opportunity to extend an intimate partner's coercive control. Coining the phrase 'legal systems abuse', Douglas (2017) cites survivors' comments as evidence of how the legal system continues to be harnessed by perpetrators as a tool to extend coercive control beyond separation.

The question of what to do about violence against women has long been a concern of UK governmental policy and VAWG is recognised as a global issue. It has been on the agenda of the United Nations for over 20 years, and in 2016, member-states of the World Health Organisation adopted a plan of action to tackle it. Broader international obligations derive from human rights protections enforceable through the European Court of Human Rights. Other international provisions include the 2011 Council of Europe Convention on preventing and combating violence against women and domestic violence (the 'Istanbul Convention').

Article 16 relates to treatment programmes for perpetrators, and the Convention requires signatories to provide legislative or other measures to support prevention together with specialist support for victims. Thus, feminist activism has developed and impacted considerably at local, national and international levels.

Despite considerable reforms to provide a more effective response to victims of domestic abuse, the dominant criminal justice paradigm (recourse to legislative interventions paying particular attention to the role of the police) has been centre stage. This approach remains inadequate in respect of safeguarding women and tackling perpetrators. The challenge to effect change remains in the lap of a broader range of local stakeholders.

Recent Developments: Tackling Serial Perpetrators of Domestic Abuse and Safeguarding Victims

Multi-agency Tasking and Co-ordination (MATAC)

Developed in a northern police region of the UK, MATAC is the shorthand name for a new type of collaborative partnership to tackle serial perpetrators of domestic abuse. MATAC is an intelligence-led approach to targeting the most harmful and serial domestic abuse perpetrators. The multi-agency process ensures that the relevant agencies are involved in the effective management of perpetrators. The partner agencies are key stakeholders who all have a shared aim to protect from domestic abuse, reduce such victimisation and prevent from further harm whilst responsibilising the perpetrator. Representatives from a range of agencies (including local government, third sector, health, criminal justice and housing), have a common investment to share information and determine actions to manage perpetrators. MATAC was launched as a new approach to tackling perpetrators of domestic abuse and was rolled out when training on the new coercive control legislation was being delivered in a north of England police area. The overall aim is to prevent further domestic abuse-related offending. The objectives are to improve victim's safety; criminal justice system outcomes; offender behaviour and partnership engagement. The operationalisation of the MATAC is now detailed in the MATAC Handbook, but the kernel of the innovation remains a multi-agency collaborative partnership. Evaluations of the MATAC found positive outcomes. However, for the purposes of this chapter, it is the tensions that emerged during the course of the evaluation, particularly those linked to feminist framed advocacy service stakeholder organisations and representatives, that are of interest. The arguments in this chapter are similar to those articulated in Chapter 2 of this volume, where the focus is specifically on feminist framings of victim advocacy and the tensions that accompany the delivery of advocacy within sites of criminal justice.

As noted above, though the evaluation showed positive outcomes, tensions surfaced within this holistic strategy designed to *prevent* violence and *protect* from it. The theory of change underpinning the MATAC approach seeks to tackle serial domestic abuse perpetrators at the same time as working to protect victims and prevent future victimisation. Recently, there has been a marked shift towards the targeting of perpetrators. Holding perpetrators to account and efforts to reduce re-offending are now part of a comprehensive strategy (Devaney 2014; Donovan and Hester 2014; Featherstone and Fraser 2012). This orthodoxy suggests that a co-ordinated and holistic response is most likely to be effective (Dobash et al. 2000; Gondolf 2002; Kelly and Westmarland 2015; Rajagopalan et al. 2008; Rivett 2010). However, there are nuanced ideological differences and political sensitivities regarding *what* should be done and *how* it should be done. As noted earlier, different feminist perspectives have subtly distinct allegiances to the concepts of male domination, sexual inequality, gender hierarchies, dominance and power arrangements. Our research encountered perceived concerns about victim safety, alongside the heightened focus on perpetrators, and this is a manifestation of the nuanced ideological approaches to tackling domestic abuse by those who are generally wedded to a feminist-influenced theory of change.

The contentious issues and anxieties that emerged in relation to this holistic strategy coalesced around victim safeguarding, safety and risk and the idea of 'responsibilising' serial perpetrators. The question of whether or not concerns about victims' safety and risk are well founded is a very pertinent one. The imbalance of power in abusive relationships is the crux of the problem. Stakeholders are all too aware that at the points of intervention, there are escalated risks to victims' safety. Seemingly dissenting views about the capacity of MATAC to prevent and protect are healthy reminders of how highly volatile, threatening and risky domestic situations can be and how women, who are separated from their violent partners, are at risk of post-separation fatal violence. The undercurrents of concern that emerged during the evaluation are rooted in real anxieties and reflect the complex feelings, emotions and frustrations felt by those affected by, and those concerned with improving the way we tackle, domestic abuse. Cautionary voices in the form of healthy scepticism from a minority of different partners in the MATAC provide a constant reminder of the subtle and coercive forms that domestic abuse can take. Friction between practitioners who work with perpetrators and those who work with victims is a positive friction. The tensions around these issues ensure all multi-agency partners and stakeholders are aware of the safeguarding protections surrounding victims and the importance of safety planning.

The roll-out and operationalisation of MATAC raised tensions common in multi-agency partnerships. The safety of victims is paramount and the central aim of a domestic violence reduction strategy. The *prevent* strand of such a strategy is operationalised alongside the support and service provision or *protect* strand. The former and the latter are designed to do two things simultaneously—tackle perpetrators and support victims. This 'holistic' strategy can present challenges for multi-agency approaches to domestic abuse, and this was evident in the MATAC partnership. The policing of domestic abuse and strategies designed to tackle and prevent continue to rely on multi-agency partnerships in local communities. Long-standing tensions are inherent in such partnerships working to tackle VAWG. The MATAC is an innovative way to tackle serial domestic abuse perpetrators at the same time as working to protect victims, and this process inevitably produces a complex mix of feelings and emotions from perpetrators, victims and stakeholders. Tensions are evident within MATAC, notably from members whose organisational and/

or personal priority is ideologically and historically more clearly wedded to prioritising energy and funding towards only one aspect of this overall strategy.

The MATAC process is now part of core police business—see below—and thus it is important that the MATAC meetings are a multi-agency workplace for professional reflection, information sharing and genuine collaboration. A focus on perpetrators has traditionally not been 'everyone's business' (HMIC 2014), and as partners grasp the importance of recognising mutual interests, tensions between key partner agencies is likely to subside. The tensions identified by the evaluation team illustrate the long-standing inherent conflicts in multi-agency partnership working generally including the need for continuous information sharing and communication. This is especially keenly felt in the context of multi-agency working to tackle serial perpetrators of domestic abuse and safeguarding of victims (Davies 2018). In the context of the MATAC, which has a heightened focus on perpetrators, the underlying politics of community safety surfaced very readily in the heightened and intensified politicised climate of austerity localism (Davies and Biddle 2017). These tensions serve as healthy reminders of the divergent paradigms, ideologies, politics and working cultures at stake in multi-agency partnerships (Davies 2018).

Domestic Abuse Whole Systems Approach (DAWSA)

The integrated whole systems approach aims to bring about transformative change across key services dealing with domestic abuse. This includes the family courts and criminal justice system. Six police forces across the North East of England (Northumbria, Cleveland, Durham, North Yorkshire, West Yorkshire and Humberside) have come together to provide services across policing, partner agencies and third-sector support agencies to provide better protection to victims and their families and to bring perpetrators to justice. The joint aim is:

> To transform domestic abuse services with a strategic and integrated approach, giving police and partner agencies the ability to truly deliver lasting change and provide a template for all forces and partnerships to deliver

on, for the benefit of domestic abuse victims and their children. http://www.dawsa.org.uk/about/

The co-ordinated approach seeks to provide effective working within the criminal justice system, partnership work with civil and family courts and multi-agency support and offender management. The approach is developed out of an identified need to plug current gaps in services and is designed to join up disjointed and silo working practices between partners, which hamper the ability of partnerships to effectively respond to domestic abuse. Pioneered by Northumbria Police over a period of three years (2016–2019), the project addresses three main elements:

1. Effective working within the criminal justice system
2. Partnership work with civil and family courts
3. Multi-agency victim support and offender management

The third component in the whole systems approach is especially focussed on tackling domestic abuse. It recognises that support for victims is provided whilst also addressing the root causes of perpetrator behaviour, particularly those who cause the highest levels of harm and engage in serial patterns of abusive behaviour. The approach builds on previous innovative approaches and embraces the MATAC, which seek to ensure multi-agency approaches address both victim safety and perpetrator management.

From Activist and Research Underpinned Safety Agendas to a Mixed Economy of New (Institutionalised) Activism

So, where are the current divers for change coming from? What is the current state of play as regards partnerships, activism and safeguarding? The overview of safeguarding from violence and abuse well into the twenty-first century illustrates what amounts to a new mixed economy of collaboration and partnership working to safeguarding victims of domestic abuse. It is clear that there remains a solid and enduring commitment to, and reliance on, multi-agency working to tackle such abuse. However, the importance and spirit of multi-agency working in the context of violence against women sees continued priority given to criminal justice responses. The examples noted above—MATAC and the Whole Systems Approach (DAWSA)—illustrate that where there are shared visions to reduce domestic abuse via tackling serial perpetrators, protecting and supporting victims and preventing future victimisation, new partnerships appear less wedded to the criminal justice paradigm and more committed to a holistic approach where tackling domestic abuse is increasingly everyone's business (HMIC 2015). Preventing victimisation from domestic abuse, safeguarding victims and responsibilising perpetrators is becoming embedded and normal at the local level.

The spur to recent developments around the policing of domestic abuse is a complex mix of political—including diverse feminist-influenced—drivers pushing for change. There are different feminist framings of victim advocacy in criminal justice contexts (well illustrated in Chapter 6 of this volume). The MATAC—a non-statutory partnership—features stakeholders whose allegiance to activism is wedded to particular social justice organisations. The core underpinning activist values of these stakeholders might vary on a continuum (Goddard et al. 2014). At one end, there are the more liberal-oriented partners who are comfortable working with formal criminal justice organisations and existing legal frameworks. At the other end, there are partners committed to a more radical approach where they are openly critical of state agencies and those who abide by these institutional practices. The healthy mix of scepticism evident in partnership working means that collaboration is hard work. Stakeholders from charities and statutory bodies must find a way of working such that they become 'critical allies'. The MATAC is a non-statutory partnership that provides the platform for this alliance to take shape. It operates effectively in spite of the austere local socio-economic and political context.

The earlier part of this chapter has outlined the various ways in which the community safety agenda has been variously advanced by a conflation of research, activism and policy developments. Several writers have marshalled these ideas together to develop an agenda for change as regards tackling violence against women. In the early 1980s, a series of 'short and simple' books entitled 'What is to be done about' were published by Penguin in several countries. The books dealt with the central social and political issues of the day in an effort to offer a political agenda for the 1980s. As Walklate (2018) reminds us, as part of that series, Elizabeth Wilson, in *What is to be Done About Violence Against Women* (1983), advocated a whole systems approach. It is now approaching 40 years since the publication of this larger social context agenda for tackling violence against women in the 1980s. The DAWSA approach outlined above has just (in 2019) been embedded across six police forces with additional limited involvement from two other force areas in the UK. The speed of change in revolutionising how violence against women is addressed has been staggeringly slow with little shift in behaviour and more continuity with the past than discontinuity. In this new mixed economy of collaboration and partnership for safeguarding victims of domestic abuse, there are promising examples of collaboration and, indeed, whole systems approaches.

As a final observation, I turn to the fate of Victim Support. Commentators have opined that, in the 1980s, Victim Support, became 'institutionalised'. This charity had been a pioneering and radical service provider with roots in an activist-driven movement with a critical edge. As its source of funding became increasingly tied to government, it became less of an 'at arm's length' service provider and increasingly beholden to the Home Office. In 2002, the Home Office stated explicitly that Victim Support should provide 'value for money' (National Audit Office 2002) and the rationing of services become a key feature of service provision for victims of crime. I draw attention to this particular trajectory because there are similarities evident between this pathway and that of the pathway of multi-agency approaches to tackling domestic abuse. The assimilation and incorporation of different feminist voices within the established multi-agency approach to tackling domestic abuse is, at one level, a success story. However, as with the trajectory of Victim Support, there are now concerns that the larger players (SafeLives) are taking over at the expense of smaller local activist and innovative groups. Those winning the tenders to provide support may be pressurised to succumb to operate according to professional codes and institutional practices. The healthily critical and often dissenting feminist-inspired voices are in danger of becoming voices from the inside, the stubborn, often seen as difficult, once independent partner having compromised their independence by becoming contained within the collaborative partnership. Does this signify a loss or trade-off whereby the 'at arm's length' activist has become the hamstrung activist from within? At worst inertia, at best slow change rather than revolutionary activism, perhaps now characterises partnership approaches to tackling domestic abuse and safeguarding victims.

References

Barton, H., & Valero-Silva, N. (2012). Policing in Partnership. *Public Sector Management, 26*(7), 543–553.

Bessant, C. (2015). Protecting Victims of Domestic Violence – Have We Got the Balance Right? *The Journal of Criminal Law, 79*(2), 102–121.

Brownmiller, S. (1975). *Against Our Will: Men, Women and Rape.* London: Secker and Warburg.

Buser, M. (2013). Tracing the Democratic Narrative: Big Society, Localism and Civic Engagement. *Local Government Studies, 39*(1), 3–21.

Cismaru, M., & Lavack, A. M. (2011). Campaigns Targeting Perpetrators of Intimate Partner Violence. *Trauma, Violence and Abuse, 12*(4), 183–197.

Clayton, J., Donovan, C., & Marchant, J. (2016). Distancing and Limited Resourcefulness: Third Sector Service Provision Under Austerity Localism in the North East of England. *Urban Studies, 53*(4), 723–740.

Crawford, A. (2007). Crime Prevention and Community Safety. In M. Maguire, R. Morgan, & R. Reiner (Eds.), *The Oxford Handbook of Criminology* (4th ed.). Oxford: Oxford University Press.

Davies, P. (2008). Looking Out a Broken Old Window: Community Safety, Gendered Crimes and Victimisations. *Crime Prevention and Community Safety: An International Journal, 10*(4), 207–225.

Davies, P. (2011). Post-Emotional Man and a Community Safety with Feeling. *Crime Prevention and Community Safety: An International Journal, 13*(1), 34–52.

Davies, P. (2018). Tackling Domestic Abuse Locally: Paradigms, Ideologies and the Political Tensions of Multi-agency Working. *Journal of Gender-Based Violence, 2*(3), 429–446.

Davies, P., & Biddle, P. (2017). Implementing a Perpetrator Focused Partnership Approach to Tackling Domestic Abuse: The Opportunities and Challenges of Criminal Justice Localism. *Criminology & Criminal Justice, 18*(4), 468–487.

DAWSA. Retrieved from http://www.dawsa.org.uk/about/.

Devaney, J. (2014). Male Perpetrators of Domestic Abuse: How Should We Hold Them to Account? *The Political Quarterly, 85*(4), 480–486.

Dobash, R., & Dobash, R. (1979). *Violence Against Wives: A Case Against the Patriarchy*. New York: Free Press.

Dobash, R., & Dobash, R. (1998). *Rethinking Violence Against Women*. SAGE Series on Violence Against Women; Vol. 9. Thousand Oaks, CA: Sage.

Dobash, R. E., Dobash, R. P., Cavanagh, K., & Lewis, R. (2000). *Changing Violent Men*. London: Sage.

Donovan, C., & Barnes, R. (2017). Domestic Violence and Abuse in Lesbian, Gay, Bisexual and/or Transgender (LGB and/or T) Relationships. *Sexualities*. https://doi.org/10.1177/1363460716681491.

Donovan, C., & Hester, M. (2014). *Domestic Violence and Sexuality*. Bristol: Policy Press.

Douglas, H. (2017). Legal Systems Abuse and Coercive Control. *Criminology & Criminal Justice, 18*(1), 84–99.

Featherstone, B., & Fraser, C. (2012). Working with Fathers around Domestic Violence. *Child Abuse Review, 21*, 255–263.

Featherstone, D., Ince, A., Mackinnon, D., Strauss, K., & Cumbers, L. (2012). Progressive Localism and the Construction of Political Alternatives. *Transactions, 37*(2), 177–182.

Goddard, T., Myers, R. R., & Robison, K. J. (2014). Potential Partnerships: Progressive Criminology, Grassroots Organizations and Social Justice. *International Journal for Crime, Justice and Social Democracy, 4*(4), 76–90.

Gondolf, E. W. (2002). *Batterer Intervention Systems*. Thousand Oaks, CA: Sage.

Hanmer, J., & Maynard, M. (1987). *Women, Violence and Social Control. Explorations in Sociology*. British Sociological Association Conference Volume Series. London: Palgrave Macmillan.

Hanmer, J., & Saunders, S. (1984). *Well-founded Fear: A Community Study of Violence to Women*. London: Hutchinson.

Hayward, K. (2007). Situational Crime Prevention and Its Discontents: Rational Choice Theory Versus the 'Culture of Now'. *Social Policy & Administration, 41*(3), 232–250.

Heidensohn, F., & Gelsthorpe, L. (2007). Gender and Crime. In M. Maguire, R. Morgan, & R. Reiner (Eds.), *The Oxford Handbook of Criminology* (4th ed.). Oxford: Oxford Press.

HMIC. (2014). *Everyone's Business. Improving the Response to Domestic Abuse.* London: HMIC.

HMIC. (2015). *Increasingly Everyone's Business. A Progress Report on Improving the Response to Domestic Abuse.* London: HMIC.

Home Office. (1990). *The Victims Charter: A Statement of Rights for Victims of Crime.* London: Home Office.

Home Office. (2016). *Ending Violence Against Women and Girls Strategy, 2016–2020.* London: HM Government.

Johnston, L., & Shearing, C. (2003). *Governing Security: Explorations in Policing and Justice.* Abingdon: Routledge.

Kelly, L. (1988). *Surviving Sexual Violence.* Cambridge: Polity Press.

Kelly, L., & Radford, J. (1987). The Problem of Men: Feminist Perspectives on Sexual Violence. In P. Scraton (Ed.), *Law, Order and the Authoritarian State.* Milton Keynes: Open University Press.

Kelly, L., & Westmarland, N. (2015). *Domestic Violence Perpetrator Programmes: Steps Towards Change. Project Mirabal Final Report.* London: London Metropolitan University and Durham University.

Mawby, R. I., & Walklate, S. L. (1994). *Critical Victimology.* London: Sage.

Ministry of Justice. (2015). *Code of Practice for Victims of Crime.* London: Ministry of Justice.

National Audit Office. (2002). *Helping Victims and Witnesses: The Work of Victim Support.* Report by the Comptroller and Auditor General, House of Commons Session1212, 2001–2002: 23rd October 2002, London: The Stationery Office.

Office for National Statistics. (2018a). *Domestic Abuse: Findings from the Crime Survey for England and Wales: Year Ending March 2017.* Published Online: ONS.

Office for National Statistics. (2018b). *Homicide in England and Wales: Year Ending March 2017.* Published Online: ONS.

Rajagopalan, V., Price, P., & Donaghy, P. (2008). An Evaluation of the East London DVIP.

Rivett, M. (2010). Working with Violent Male Carers (Fathers and Step Fathers). In B. Featherstone et al. (Eds.), *Gender and Child Welfare in Society.* John Wiley & Sons.

Sebba, L. (2001). On the Relationship Between Criminological Research and Policy: The Case of Crime Victims. *Criminology & Criminal Justice, 1*(1), 27–58.

Smith, C., & Wincup, E. (2000). Breaking in: Researching Criminal Justice Institutions for Women. In R. King & E. Wincup (Eds.), *Doing Research on Crime and Justice*. Oxford: Oxford University Press.

Stanko, E. A. (1988). Hidden Violence Against Women. In M. Maguire & J. Pointing (Eds.), *Victims of Crime: A New Deal?* Milton Keynes: Open University Press.

Stanko, E. (1990). *Everyday Violence: How Women and Men Experience Sexual and Physical Danger*. London: Pandora.

Vacchelli, E. (2015). *Project Muse. Localism and Austerity: A Gender Perspective*. Lawrence and Wishart.

Van Ginneken, E. (2017). Community Safety and Crime Prevention. In P. Davies, J. Harding, & G. Mair (Eds.), *An Introduction to Criminal Justice* (pp. 189–207). London: Sage.

Walby, S., & Towers, J. (2018). Untangling the Concepts of Coercive Control: Theorizing Domestic Violet Crime. *Criminology & Criminal Justice, 18*(1), 7–28.

Walklate, S. L. (2007). Men, Victims and Crime. In P. Davies, P. Francis, & C. Greer (Eds.), *Victims, Crime and Society*. London: Sage.

Walklate, S. (2018). Reflections on Community Safety: The Ongoing Precarity of Women's Lives. *Crime Prevention and Community Safety, 20*(4), 284–295. https://doi.org/10.1057/s41300-018-0050-y.

Walklate, S. L., & Evans, K. (1999). *Zero Tolerance or Community Tolerance? Managing Crime in High Crime Areas*. Aldershot: Ashgate.

Walklate, S. L., Fitz-Gibbon, K., & McCulloch, J. (2017). Is More Law the Answer? *Seeking Justice for Victims of Intimate Partner Violence Through the Reform of Legal Categories. Criminology and Criminal Justice*, 1–17. https://doi.org/10.1177/1748895817728561.

Westmarland, N. (2012). Co-ordinating Responses to Domestic Violence. In J. M. Brown & S. L. Walklate (Eds.), *Handbook on Sexual Violence* (pp. 287–307). London: Routledge.

Westwood, A. (2011). Localism, Social Capital and the 'Big Society'. *Local Economy, 26*(8), 690–701.

Wilson, E. (1983). *What Is to Be Done About Violence Against Women?* Harmondsworth: Penguin.

Wilson, J. Q., & Kelling, G. L. (1982). Broken Windows: Police and Neighbourhood Safety. *Atlantic Monthly, 249*, 29–38.

12

Environmental Victims and Climate Change Activists

Valeria Vegh Weis and Rob White

Introduction

There are powerful examples of victims of historical and ongoing direct harms gathering forces to fight for justice and reparations: from native peoples in Canada and Australia demanding redress for harms suffered since colonial times (Cunneen and Tauri 2016; Jung 2009) to current movements against gender-based violence or racialized police brutality such as #MeToo and #BlackLivesMatter. Overcoming individual agony and organising resistance is extremely difficult in cases such as these.

Yet even more challenges appear when struggling against, allegedly, more abstract and indirect harms such as climate change.[1] Ultimately, we are all affected by environmental harms, and particularly by climate

V. Vegh Weis (✉)
Buenos Aires University, Buenos Aires, Argentina

Quilmes National University, Bernal, Argentina

R. White
School of Social Sciences, University of Tasmania, Hobart, TAS, Australia
e-mail: r.d.white@utas.edu.au

© The Author(s) 2020
J. Tapley, P. Davies (eds.), *Victimology*,
https://doi.org/10.1007/978-3-030-42288-2_12

change (Hall 2014; Watts 2018). Moreover, our own humane existence is under threat (White 2019; Sanchez-Bayo and Wyckhuys 2019). However, the impact of climate change is more diffuse, immaterial and abstract than crimes, such as murder or rape, and this peculiarity is what might make commitment to resistance even more challenging than usual.

This chapter provides a discussion of the intersection of environmental activism and victimisation. In doing so, it addresses aspects of the struggle against green harms[2] in general and climate change in particular, identifying the different actors involved, namely environmental social movements[3] and victims as activists. The chapter particularly examines the student movements for climate justice, as a case study of the evolvement from victims-to-be to activists in the here-and-now.

Notably, this analysis is based on a radical victimology perspective that includes consideration of questions of power and interests, and, as part of this, it explicitly deals with matters of social and ecological justice. Drawing from sources such as critical victimology (Mawby and Walklate 1994; Walklate 2018), cultural criminology (Brisman and South 2013; Mythen and McGowan 2018) and southern criminology (Santos 2014; Carrington et al. 2016), we likewise emphasise the importance of wider definitions of 'crime' and 'victim' than those usually conveyed in conventional criminology. For example, the notion of social harm allows for understanding environmental disastrous actions within the framework of 'crimes of the powerful' as, 'hyperbolic or not, the potential harm and victimization from environmental crimes to the earth's ecosystems may ultimately dwarf the combined harm and victimization from all the other crimes of the powerful' (Barak 2015: 2). A critical framework not only expands the restricted notion of victimhood but also sheds light on its selective nature. For instance, certain sections of the population are more likely than others to be affected by environmental hazards and to have difficulties in accessing good-quality water or air (McClanahan 2014). It is thus possible to refer to 'environmental selectivity' to expose that race, ethnicity, gender, class and religious membership play a relevant role in conditioning who are more likely to become environmental victims[4] (see also, Vegh Weis 2017a).

Environmental Victims

An environmental victim is a person who suffered or is still suffering directly from some kind of environmental calamity or disaster.

From the point of view of environmental activism and advocacy, the fact that environmental victims frequently consist of those drawn from the ranks of the poor, the disadvantaged and minority groups have significant ramifications. For example, many such victims fit into the category of 'socially expendable victims' (Fattah 2010). That is, no one really cares what happens to these specific individuals and groups, since they are already devalued in wider community terms. As Engel and Martin (2006: 479) put it: 'If victims are perceived as degraded in some sense, then it does not seem so unfair when bad things happen to them'.

Overall, we find that victims of green harms are in an extremely difficult position. First, they are still traversed by harm much the same as victims of more traditional crimes experience. Applicable to their case is the fact that the term 'victim' is a word that 'evokes strong images of submissiveness, pain, loss of control and defeat…Victims are riddled with taboos' (Rock 2007: 41).

Second, as mentioned above, the ones most affected by green harms are 'socially expendable'. Preconceptions based upon race or income adds further fuel to the debasement associated with victimisation processes. Following this lead, reacting against perpetrators of environmental harm (which, typically, includes powerful forces and organisations) often means first throwing off the chains of servitude and under-privilege that, in turn, undermine confidence and tactical wherewithal. As U.S. Congress member Ocasio Cortez (2019) states:

This is not an elitist issue, this is a quality of life issue.…

You want to tell people that their concern and their desire for clean air and clean water is elitist? Tell that to the kids of the South Bronx who are suffering from the highest rates of childhood asthma in the country. Tell that to the families in Flint, whose kids have their blood ascending in lead levels; their brains are damaged for the rest of their lives. Call them elitist. People are dying… This is serious.

Third, on top of these challenges, environmental victims have to confront immaterial, abstract and diffuse harms, such as climate change, that are not as clear and palpable as traditional or ordinary crimes. Moreover, specific groups who experience harm may not always describe or see the issues in strictly environmental terms. This may be related to lack of awareness of the environmental harm, alternative explanations for the calamity (e.g., an act of God) and socio-economic pressures to 'accept' environmental risk in return for economic reward (Julian 2004). Waldman (2007), for instance, describes a local community in South Africa that saw the contamination effects of asbestos as 'natural'. This was due to a combination of religious beliefs (that stressed a passive stance to the world around them) and the fact that often harms that are imperceptible to the senses only exist as a problem if they are constituted as such in public discourse (and in particular, the public discourse of the village community). Even worse, some productive activities are paradoxically seen as economically beneficial for local development, making its criminogenic character hardly identifiable (Vegh Weis 2017a: 2015).

Overall, the path from victims to activists seems to involve enormous challenges, including becoming aware of the harms they are suffering from, dismantling victimhood as a passive status, organising themselves, and demonstrating to the public why should they be regarded as victims and why is it worth the fight.

Victims as Activists

Considering the challenges and other obstacles noted above, it is hardly surprising that not all environmental victims turn to activism (in a mirror position to that not all activists have been directly subject to victimisation themselves).

In addition, those victims who do become active are not uniform in how they do so. Just as environmental victimisation differs concretely in its manifestation, so too victim responses vary greatly. Detailed analysis of specific events, over time, reveals stages in victims' struggle for justice, involving both spontaneous and organised actions, usually centred around justice and/or on relief. In broad terms, different events, in different countries, give rise to responses that vary from the passive to the confrontational and from those involving collaborative activities aimed at redress to those based upon violence (Williams 1996). For example, there is frequently a discrepancy between victims who seek immediate redress for harms and wrongs done to them and those who see a strategic benefit in politicising issues beyond their immediate location or circumstances (White 2010). How victims mobilise is thus, like environmental social movements, quite variable. There are differences again in tactics and strategies, as well as in perceptions of interest and with regard to over-arching ideological frameworks.

The effectiveness of specific struggles, such as those related to events in Bhopal, India, or the Cape region in South Africa, can also be analysed in terms of who defines the issues, who fights for or against the issues, who owns the struggle and how the struggle is shaped and carried out by local and international participants (Sarangi 1996; Waldman 2007; Engel and Martin 2006); Stretesky and Knight 2013). Examination of victim responses needs to take into account not only the type and extent of net-working and coalition-building, but also the lack of participation and the marginalisation of some victim groups within a wider victim movement (Waldman 2007).

Perversely, the transformation of victims (or survivors) into activists may be accompanied by a change in their social status. In particular, those who strive for justice—precisely because of victimisation—can sometimes find themselves represented as 'troublemakers' and/or arrested by the state for 'breaking the law' in pursuit of environmental justice. It is usually socially more acceptable to be a 'crying victim' rather than an 'empowered one'. Victims can thus be stigmatised, or even criminalised, insofar as they step outside the boundaries of what is deemed to be 'acceptable' victimhood. As we can acknowledge by now, the criminal justice system is not aimed at treating victims equitably and fairly. Rather victimhood and victim status have been historically traversed by selective patterns based on race, class, ethnicity, gender, age and, particularly, by the threat that they represent to those in power (Vegh Weis 2017a).

Environmental Social Movements

Environmental activists are frequently motivated by the need to protect that which otherwise would not be protected and to speak for the voiceless. The key focus of environmental social movements, therefore, is on the threats and harms pertaining to 'nature', variously defined. Non-human environmental entities, for example, include rivers, mountains, birds, flowers, forests and so on.

The focus of contestation varies (see Table 12.1). Generally speaking, struggles occur in relation to specific entities that include humans, specific ecosystems and/or animals and/or plants. From a victim perspective, an eco-justice perspective frames victimhood in terms of the particular subject or object that is harmed (White 2013).

Table 12.1 Environmental social movements

Environmental justice	Ecological justice	Species justice
	Theories and Approaches	
Universal	Biocentric	Animal welfare
Particularistic	Ecocentric	Animal rights
	Case Studies	
Love Canal, USA	Toxic chemicals	Whales
Bophal, India	Climate change	Live export of sheep
	Measuring Harm & Value	
Environmental racism	Threats to biodiversity	Speciesism
Who is victimised and why	Which landscapes protected	Which species protected
Universal victimisation	Which landscapes destroyed	Which species harvested or destroyed as pests
	Specific Social Movements	
Toxic Action Network	Earth First	Greenpeace
Environmental Justice movement	Sierra Club	Sea Shepherd
	Critiques & Contradictions	
Socially inclusive only of specific victims	Prioritises places over people	Animals over humans and environments

- *Environment justice*—**the victim is humans**
- Environmental rights are seen as an extension of human or social rights so as to enhance the quality of human life, now and into the future
- *Ecological justice*—**the victim is specific environments**
- Human beings are merely one component of complex ecosystems that should be preserved for their own sake
- *Species justice*—**the victim is animals and plants**

- Animals have an intrinsic right to not suffer abuse and plants should be protected, degradation of habitat threatens biodiversity loss

Environmental social movements tend to focus on specific categories or types of victims. This can lead to tensions between and within environmental social movements (White 2013). For example, animal welfare activists may agree to the instrumental use of non-human animals—for instance, as food for humans—but object to their poor treatment. Animal rights activists, on the other hand, may have a more absolutist position that argues for the prohibition of any kind of instrumental use of non-human animals. Activists pursuing the goals of environmental justice, oriented towards improving the environmental amenity of human communities, may find themselves opposed to or critical of those whose main focus is on preserving the nesting homes of endangered birds or conserving particular forested areas. Value judgements are constantly being made in regards where people put their time, energy and resources as activists and which 'victims' they prioritise for their actions.

The difference within and between environmental social movements can also reflect differences in tactical and strategic approaches to social change. There is a continuum of contestation upon which groups range. This is not static. For example, Greenpeace or the WWF can, on the one hand, engage in what appears to be 'conservative' activities (e.g., consultations with and accepting donations from large corporations) while, on the other, participating in mass protest rallies around specific issues. Other groups are more clearly aligned with radicalism, both ideologically (e.g., transform not simply reform the system) and politically (e.g., using illegal measures as well as legal, as in the case of breaking into laboratories in order to release captured non-human animals).

A related issue is how NGOs from 'outside' (i.e., the metropoles of the Global North) impact upon the status and livelihoods of those in other parts of the world (i.e., those who actually live in the Global South). Duffy (2010) recounts how in a number of cases transnational NGO action has translated into the criminalisation of local residents and alienation from their own lands and natural resources. There is a 'dark side' to conservation that is based upon cultural ignorance and that can, in its own right, create more harm than good and lead to both human misery and unsustainable ecological solutions.

Spectrum Politics[5]

For both environmental victims and environmental social movements, key spectrum politics questions include the composition of the resistance forces and the specific tactics and strategies to be employed as part of the resistance.

Engagement in transformation around environmental issues will require collaborations across the political spectrum (Stilwell 2018). Such 'spectrum politics', however, has to be constructed on a clear conceptual and organisational basis. Working in conjunction with others does not mean identifying with their sectional interests; rather, it is about joining forces strategically in order to progress specific demands and courses of action.

In regards climate change agitation, for example, climate change criminology involves and supports public engagement and social interventions that challenge the status quo by focusing on climate justice for humans and non-human environmental entities (White 2018). Climate justice is a perspective that values nature and all aspects of the environment (ecocentrism) and that wishes to prevent and/or prosecute serious and unsustainable transgressions against humans, ecosystems and non-human environmental entities (such as rivers, mountains, birds, kangaroos and plants). Two key concepts are central to the efforts of climate change agitators: the democratisation of mitigation and adaptation strategies in support of those that are premised upon universal human and ecological interests and the idea that there are multiple sites of intervention, including working in and against the state. Joining up diverse social forces (e.g., farmers, Indigenous people, students, environmentalists) in support of climate justice goals and objectives is not only acceptable but also essential, as are rallies, protests and active social media use that provide opposition to hegemonic policies and institutions.

Cross-class alliances and collaborations also make entirely good sense in the context of the fight for universal human interests. Certain events or scenarios generate dangers, risks and threats that reach beyond any single class or group. Nuclear war is one. Another is climate change. While the continued deterioration of the planetary environment is best explained through class analysis of capitalist power and interests, specific fractions of capital and particular wealthy individuals and business people can and do see the perils of continuing along the present economic trajectory. It is in their interests as humans and as members of the wider Earth community to join in the fight against the forces propelling us further and further into global warming. This makes them potential allies in our struggles.

Spectrum politics thus needs to be multi-pronged. This simultaneously means keeping the focus on the main game—eco-justice ideals—rather than competing with and/or attacking fellow travellers whose activism we may not entirely agree with. To put it differently, there may be different theories of social change that include bold declarations about the need to overthrow capitalism and revolutionary action outside the mainstream corridors of power, to an emphasis on more gradual and conciliatory gestures such as changing consumption habits and working within existing forums such as the United Nations. Yet, these varied tactics and strategic orientations all have their place in the wider struggle. It is the totality of activism that matters. There may be tiered boundaries and flanks—some on the outside of the conventional, some on the inside, and some who traverse the outside-inside divide—but it is the overall weight of engagement and resistance and challenge that ultimately counts.

While tactics might differ, the important thing is to agree on common objectives, regardless of disagreements as to how to attain these. The more specific the objectives, the more scope there is to build communities of practice around particular initiatives. Consider, for instance, the key demands (abridged) of the Climate Justice Network (Global Campaign to Demand Climate Justice 2018): (1) Fight for the transformation of energy systems; (2) Fight for food sovereignty, for peoples' rights to sufficient, healthy and appropriate food and sustainable food systems; (3) Fight for peoples' rights to sufficient, affordable, clean, quality water; (4) Fight for just transitions for all workers beginning with those in the dirty and harmful energy industries; (5) Fight for people's safety and security of homes and livelihoods from climate disasters; (6) Fight for the social, political, economic, cultural and reproductive rights and empowerment of all our people and communities; (7) Fight for mobilisation and delivery of climate finance by all states; (8) Fight for reparations for climate debt owed by those most responsible for climate change; (9) Fight for an end to deception and false solutions in mitigation and adaptation; (10) Fight for an end to policies, decisions and measures by governments, elites, institutions and corporations (domestic, regional and global) that increase the vulnerabilities of people and planet to impacts of climate change; (11) Fight to stop the commodification and financialisation of nature and nature's functions; (12) Fight for an international climate agreement that is rooted in science, equity and justice.

The first demand actually translates nicely into movements away from centralised energy systems to de-centralised systems that are also community-run for community benefit. Solar power at the local level is one example of such initiatives. More generally, each demand also carries with it the potential to make things better.

Standing up and speaking out, especially when the protagonists are rich, powerful and dogmatic, is always going to be hard and this includes for those involved in resisting ecocide (the degradation, destruction and/or destroying of a given territory's, or planetary-level, ecosystem due to anthropocentric causes, such as carbon emissions and deforestation). All these struggles require considerable courage and strong commitment. Politics is about necessity and choice, winning and losing, timing and opportunity. For activism today, it is notable, and hope-inspiring, that the political landscape is seemingly capable of rapid shifts in political sentiment.

Present Activism of Future Victims

Prevention is not the most widespread or favoured approach in many criminal justice systems around the world, even though the intent to intervene before it is too late makes good sense. However, students for climate justice are teaching all of us a lesson. The movement was inspired by a solo protester Greta Thunberg, then 15, taking action in Sweden in August 2018 (Taylor et al. 2019). Months later, on March 15, 2019, at her initiative, over 1 million students joined a strike that included more than 2,000 protests in 125 countries (Glenza 2019). Today, up to 70,000 schoolchildren each week hold protests in 270 towns and cities worldwide (Glenza 2019).

In the United Kingdom alone, the 2019 strike gathered more than 10,000 students from at least 60 towns and cities; three protesters of 16, 17 and 19 years old were arrested. In the United States, Alexandria Villasenor, one of the strike organisers, was a victim of 2019 wildfires in California herself (Milman 2019). She helped create Youth Climate Strike US, which follows the steps of the European school walkouts movement for climate change (see https://www.youthclimatestrikeus. org/). In Australia, students are demanding concrete action to stop Adani (a proposed coal mine in Queensland which would be the largest ever) to deter and prevent coal and gas developments and to invest in and rely upon alternative energy sources by 2030.

Students are aware that informed decision-making around climate change requires close consideration of explanations for our changing weather. They make it clear that climate change demands action on behalf of precaution, based upon heightened concerns about the intergenerational consequences of decisions being made (or not made) now. Moreover, students raise their voices in regard to the vested interests holding tight to the levers of political-economic power and to the fact that decisions about air, water, land and energy are too precious and important to be left solely in the hands of powerful elites in government and companies.

Students are demanding that democracy should be expanded beyond a small handful of politicians who seemingly do not know what they are doing. They see civil disobedience (including ignoring school attendance regulations) as a legitimate path to expose politicians' negligence in the face of urgent existential issues.

The response by contrarians and conservative forces was swift. Carbon emission apologists described and targeted students in particularly negative ways. It was alleged that students either do not 'know their own mind' (they are too young to 'really understand') or they are being 'manipulated' by climate justice activists (students are been duped into believing in climate change and engaging in climate action).

Concerning the first argument ('too young to engage in politics'), young people's status as citizens—and, thus, their legal entitlements such as an adult wage, access to unemployment benefits or income support, and/or right to purchase alcohol and vote—are, indeed, ambiguous, as reflected in widely differing definitions of youth by age across and within countries (White et al. 2017; Tarricone and Di Santi 2019). As indicated in Table 12.2, a central theme in many of the debates, commentaries and portrayals of youth in politics is, indeed, the notion of knowing their own mind. In practice, this manifests itself in varying ways, but the suspicion that young people are not competent to do it for themselves surfaces time and again, whether this be in relation to their role in youth forums or in regards to the age at which people ought to be allowed to vote.

The reality is that age provides a poor framework for defining youth, and the parameters of 'youth' tend to be defined pragmatically according to purpose. In other words, youth itself is fundamentally constructed in the interplay between state and age. Mizen (2004) describes the way in which state categorisations of rights and responsibilities establish the

Table 12.2 Dimensions of youth political engagement

Activism as either/or	Apathy/activism, passive/active, social identity, not being able to make up their mind
Activism outside of approved forums	Disapproval, being duped, not knowing their own mind
Activism inside of approved forums	Someone else's agenda, socialisation, not knowing their own mind
Voting and the age of responsibility	Being/becoming, distinct age markers, being competent enough to make up their mind

Source: White (2007)

substance of youth as a universal demarcation based on age. There is, thus, a material foundation to the proposition that age matters, based upon age-related laws, rules and regulations promulgated by the state. To exemplify, US Democrat Senator Dianne Feinstein discouraged a group of students who approached her to debate climate change legislation, telling them that they did not have the right to vote and they would better wait until having enough age to run for the Senate themselves (Milman 2019).

While such regulations are a barrier to the recognition of young people's citizenship, institutional attitudes to children and young people might be even a more serious impediment. Adult-centric agendas tend to silence children's and young people's expressions of citizenship and make them invisible (Vromen 2003). Young people's civic participation and acts of citizenship tend to occur in places that matter to them (neighborhoods, families and schools) rather than at the national level of formal politics (Wyn et al. 2012; Harris et al. 2010). There are many different degrees and ways in which young people can participate in the places and organisations that matter to them. When they do activate, however, there is frequently a right-wing backlash.

Concerning the second argument ('manipulated youth'), some commercial media has characterised the anti-climate change students struggle in particularly conspiratorial ways (see Box 12.1). To exemplify, *The Daily Telegraph* (18.02.19) published in Sydney, Australia, issued a front-page headline that said: 'Pupils Used As Climate Pawns: Activists secretly incite demo'. The rest of the paper is peppered with feature articles, editorial comment and cartoon sketches that collectively deride the student strikes and attempt to undermine their legitimacy.

Box 12.1   Right-Wing Newspaper Criticisms of Student Activism

The Daily Telegraph, February 18, 2019-02-22

Front Page Headline

'Pupils Used As Climate Pawns: Activists secretly incite demo'

Front Page Article

'Taxpayer-funded eco-warriors are coaching children to skip school next month, giving them detailed instructions on how to play truant, make posters and organise "marshals" for a climate change protest marsh.

(continued)

Box 12.1 (continued)

The well-resourced campaign even provides "phone scripts" and "text message scripts" for children to convert their friends to the cause and tells them to fill out form letters to their principals for the March 15 school strike.

Despite claims that the walkout is being "initiated" and "led" by volunteer students, *The Daily Telegraph* has uncovered extensive links between the hardline, partly tax-payer funded Australian Youth Climate Coalition and websites providing logistics for the truant day'.

A two-page spread [pp. 4–5] then elaborates on these claims.

The editorial on p. 20 is headed 'Taxes fund the climate kiddies'. It begins: 'Australian mining companies, the employees of mining companies and businesses associated with mining equipment, supplies and transport all pay a great amount of tax.

And then they find those taxes being used against them.

As *The Daily Telegraph* reports, taxpayer-funded anti-mining activists are coaching children to skip school again next month as part of a concerted campaign to erode mining interests in our country.

The campaign is particularly aimed at destroying the coal industry. Coal happens to be Australia's primary export, last year generating about $66 billion in export revenue'.

The editorial cartoon on p. 21 features two green-clad children holding placards that respectively say 'Weel neva git 2 see th grate barrier refe' and 'caus we wont bee able to reed th direcshuns'.

Such criticisms and distortions have had little effect on the future victims of global warming. Overall, students worldwide seem to be unapologetically aware of the severe consequences of climate change and they are organising themselves to confront government officials to take a stand. It is our task to analyse their resistance in order to shed light into possible paths to help us all to transition from victimhood to activism against green harms.

Conclusion

The path from victimhood to activism is a tough one and there are no one-fits-all solutions. Each country, social group and situation evolve in a very particular manner that cannot be predicted. However, the students' movement does leave some lessons to be learned.

From an activist perspective, the movement shows that bottom-up strategies built upon the involvement of those living and working at the grassroots appears as the best way to tackle top-down harms. Victims' voices are powerful and integral to social change movements, while their involvement might also represent a useful way to channel their own anger and grief into meaningful outlets that hold out the promise of change.

From an academic perspective, the movement encourages us to follow up different case studies such as this one in order to learn 'what works', 'what does not work' and 'what sometimes works' in different circumstances, while to also study corporate and state responses to activism—learn what most disturbs, annoys and unsettles the powers that be (their pain is our blueprint).

The students' movement exposes existing obstacles within environmental activism. Essentially, their experience shows that in order to sustain the movement and enhance its impact, building up social environmental movements and engaging in spectrum politics may be desirable further steps to confront backlashes. Challenging environmental crimes as well as pursuing a transformative justice towards ecological sustainability might be more feasible if victims themselves have the potential to overcome the help industry and assume a collective, proactive and leading role, in coalition with key actors and with civil society, but independently from power holders (Vegh Weis 2017b).

To do so, it is important to target the public and not only politicians—the former will lead, the latter will, eventually, follow. Moreover, besides broad claims against capitalism or climate changes, victims should be aware that larger numbers of people will engage if strategic goals that have practical effect are enlisted. This means that demands need to be concrete and specific. Moreover, it is important to articulate key principles that prioritise certain values over others, for example, clean water over carbon extraction. Also, the media should be used cleverly, and images and messages ought to be striking and simple.

Furthermore, environmental activism needs to engage with many different players at the local, regional and international levels. Resisting ecocide and environmental victimisation requires the marshalling of as many countervailing forces as possible so that 'speaking truth to power' translates into concrete institutional change (White 2018).

Overall, this chapter has examined different actors involved in the struggle against environmental harms (White and Heckenberger 2014), with the case of students for climate justice as a key example. Broadly based on radical victimology and climate change criminology, this chapter constitutes an intent to, on the one hand, develop further theoretical links between victimology and green criminology[6] and, on the other, enhance the dialogue between theory and practice in order to stop planet-wide environmental harms such as global warming. With respect to climate change, we are all, sooner than later, implicated in environmental victimhood when it comes to harms on this scale. Hence, there is urgent need for environmental activism. Our lives depend on it.

Notes

1. *Climate change*: the interrelated effects of global warming (the rapid rising of the Earth's temperature over a relatively short period of time) that manifest in changing sea levels through to temperature change affecting local environments (for example, leading to the death of coral due to temperature rises in sea water).

2. *Green harms*: also referred to as eco-crimes or environmental harms, these include legal as well as illegal environmental harms insofar as it acknowledges that some of the most ecologically harmful and destructive practices (such as clearfelling of old growth forests) may be entirely legal.

3. *Environmental social movements*: groups comprised primarily of volunteers who join together to fight for specific political goals relating to the environment, such as preserving forests, stopping big mining operations and protecting endangered wildlife.

4. *Environmental victims*: humans and non-human environmental entities (such as rivers and elephants) that are adversely affected by acts or omissions that negatively modify their natural state and/or environment (such as polluted air or water) or that directly harm them (as in the illegal killing of non-human animals).

5. *Spectrum politics*: a perspective that argues for active collaboration across diverse political divides (such as conservative and liberal; working class and middle class; farmer and environmentalist) in pursuit of the greater good, due to the existential threat posed by climate change.

6. *Green criminology*: the study by criminologists of environmental harms (that may incorporate wider definitions of crime than are provided by strictly legal definitions), environmental laws, and environmental regulation and crime prevention.

References

Barak, G. (Ed.). (2015). *The Routledge International Handbook of the Crimes of the Powerful*. Abingdon, Oxon: Routledge.

Brisman, A., & South, N. (2013). Resource Wealth, Power, Crime, and Conflict. In R. Walters, D. Solomon Westerhuis, & T. Wyatt (Eds.), *Emerging Issues in Green Criminology. Exploring Power, Justice and Harm* (pp. 57–71). Palgrave Macmillan.

Carrington, K., Hogg, R., & Sozzo, M. (2016). Southern Criminology. *British Journal of Criminology, 56*(1), 1–20.

Cunneen, C., & Tauri, J. (2016). *Indigenous Criminology*. Bristol: Policy Press.

Duffy, R. (2010). *Nature Crime: How We're Getting Conservation Wrong*. New Haven: Yale University Press.

Engel, S., & Martin, B. (2006). Union Carbide and James Hardie: Lessons in Politics and Power. *Global Society, 20*(4), 475–490.

Fattah, E. (2010). The Evolution of a Young, Promising Discipline: Sixty Years of Victimology, a Retrospective and Prospective Look. In S. Shoham, P. Knepper, & M. Kett (Eds.), *International Handbook of Victimology*. Boca Raton, FL: CRC Press.

Glenza, J. (2019, March 15). Climate Strikes Held Around the World – As It Happened. *The Guardian*.

Hall, M. (2014). Environmental Harm and Environmental Victims: Scoping Out a "Green Victimology". *International Review of Victimology, 20*(1), 129–143.

Harris, A., Wyn, J., & Younes, S. (2010). Beyond Apathetic or Activist Youth: "Ordinary" Young People and Contemporary Forms of Participation. *Young, 18*(1), 9–32.

Julian, R. (2004). Inequality, Social Differences and Environmental Resources. In R. White (Ed.), *Controversies in Environmental Sociology*. Melbourne: Cambridge University Press.

Jung, C. (2009). 'Transitional Justice for Indigenous People in a Non-transitional Society' International Center for Transitional Justice, October 2009.

Mawby, R. I., & Walklate, S. (1994). *Critical Victimology: International Perspectives Account*, pp. 15–17.

McClanahan, B. (2014). Green and Grey: Water Justice, Criminalization, and Resistance. *Critical Criminology, 22*, 403–418.

Milman, O. (2019, March 12). 'We Won't Stop Striking': The New York 13 Year-Old Taking a Stand Over Climate Change. *The Guardian*.

Mizen, P. (2004). *The Changing State of Youth*. New York: Palgrave.

Mythen, G., & McGowan, W. (2018). Cultural Victimology Revisited. Synergies of Risk, Fear, and Resilience. In S. Walklate (Ed.), *Handbook of Victims and Victimology* (pp. 364–378). London: Routledge.

Ocasio Cortez, A. (2019, March 26). Intervention in Congress. Retrieved from https://twitter.com/i/status/1110700996282343424.

Rock, P. (2007). Theoretical Perspectives on Victimisation. In S. Walklate (Ed.), *Handbook of Victims and Victimology*. Devon: Willan Publishing.

Sanchez-Bayo, F., & Wyckhuys, K. A. G. (2019). Worldwide Decline of the Entomofauna: A Review of Its Drivers. *Biological Conservation, 232*, 8–27.

Santos, B. D. S. (2014). *Epistemologies of the South: Justice Against Epistemicide*. Boulder: Paradigm Publishers.

Sarangi, S. (1996). The Movement in Bhopal & Its Lessons. *Social Justice, 23*(4), 100–108.

Stilwell, M. (2018). Climate Justice: International Civil Society Perspectives. Presentation at the Imagining a Different Future, Climate Justice Conference, Hobart, Tasmania, 9 February 2018.

Stretesky, P., & Knight, O. (2013). The Uneven Geography of Environmental Enforcement INGOs. In R. Walters, D. Solomon Westerhuis, & T. Wyatt (Eds.), *Emerging Issues in Green Criminology. Exploring Power, Justice and Harm* (pp. 173–196). Palgrave Macmillan.

Tarricone, M., & Di Santi, M. (2019, January 10). Edad de imputabilidad en la Argentina: ¿qué es y cuál es la situación actual de los adolescentes?. *Chequeado*.

Taylor, M., Laville, S., Walker, A., Noor, P., & Henley, J. (2019, February 15). School Pupils Call for Radical Climate Action in UK-Wide Strike. *The Guardian*.

Vegh Weis, V. (2017a). *Marxism and Criminology. A History of Criminal Selectivity*. Boston: Brill. Republished by Haymarket Book (2018).

Vegh Weis, V. (2017b). The Relevance of Victims' Organizations in Transitional Justice Processes. The Case of Grandmothers of Plaza de Mayo in Argentina. *Intercultural Human Rights Law Review*.

Vromen, A. (2003). People Try to Put Us Down … Participatory Citizenship of Generation X. *Australian Journal of Political Science, 38*(1), 79–99.

Waldman, L. (2007). When Social Movements Bypass the Poor: Asbestos Pollution, International Litigation and Griqua Cultural Identity. *Journal of Southern African Studies, 33*(3), 577–600.

Walklate, S. (2018). Conclusion: An Agenda for a (Critical) Victimology. In S. Walklate (Ed.), *Handbook of Victims and Victimology* (pp. 379–384). London: Routledge.

Watts, J. (2018, October 8). We Have 12 Years to Limit Climate Change Catastrophe, Warns UN. *The Guardian*.

White, R. (2007). Paradoxes of Youth Participation: Political Activism and Youth Disenchantment. In L. Saha, M. Print, & K. Edwards (Eds.), *Youth and Political Participation*. Rotterdam: Sense Publishers.

White, R. (2010). Environmental Victims and Resistance to State Crime Through Transnational Activism. *Social Justice, 36*(3), 46–60.

White, R. (2013). *Environmental Harm: An Eco-Justice Perspective*. Bristol: Policy.

White, R. (2018). *Climate Change Criminology*. Bristol: Bristol University Press.

White, R. (2019). Resisting Ecocide: Engaging in the Politics of the Future. In E. Currie & W. DeKeseredey (Eds.), *Progressive Justice in an Age of Repression: Strategies for Challenging the Rise of the Right*. New York: Routledge.

White, R., & Heckenberger, D. (2014). *Green Criminology*. London; New York: Routledge.

White, R., Wyn, J., & Robards, B. (2017). *Youth and Society*. Melbourne: Oxford University Press.

Williams, C. (1996). An Environmental Victimology. *Social Justice, 23*(4), 16–40.

Wyn, J., Lantz, S., & Harris, A. (2012). Beyond the "Transitions" Metaphor: Family Relations and Young People in Late Modernity. *Journal of Sociology, 48*(1), 1–20.

13

From Cinderella to Consumer: How Crime Victims Can Go to the Ball

Edna Erez, Jize Jiang, and Kathy Laster

Introduction

Historically, as Schafer noted in his seminal 1960 publication, crime victims were the 'Cinderellas' of the criminal justice system (Schafer 1960: 8). One of the most dramatic shifts in adversarial criminal justice since that time has been the transformation of the role of victims (Garland 2001: 11).

Authors' names appear alphabetically; all contributed equally to the chapter. Eliezer Solomon provided valuable research assistance. Ryan Kornhauser undertook additional research and provided insightful comments and suggestions as well as editing support. Parts of the chapter were presented at the 2015 American Society of Criminology meeting in San Francisco, and at the 2017 Ono Law School Biannual Conference in Israel.

E. Erez (✉)
Department of Criminology, Law, and Justice, University of Illinois at Chicago, Chicago, IL, USA
e-mail: eerez@uic.edu

J. Jiang
School of Law, Shanghai University of Finance and Economics, Shanghai, China
e-mail: jiang.jize@mail.shufe.edu.cn

© The Author(s) 2020
J. Tapley, P. Davies (eds.), *Victimology*,
https://doi.org/10.1007/978-3-030-42288-2_13

Decades of victim advocacy through the victim rights movement has led to major reforms to afford victims a greater role in criminal proceedings and better meet their needs (Roberts 2009).

In the US, as well as internationally, victims have been accorded rights aimed at integrating them into criminal justice proceedings.[1] Victims' charters of various kinds underscore the provision of tailored information resources and victim support services, such as counseling, and an obligation to treat victims with dignity and respect (O'Hara 2005; Zweig and Yahner 2013). Many jurisdictions have legislative provisions requiring that victims be notified about various stages in the proceedings against an offender (Hall 2010). Nearly all have mandated opportunities for victim input into sentencing through various forms of Victim Impact Statements (VIS) (Cassell and Erez 2011), including written documents or the opportunity for the victim to address the sentencing judge directly (referred to as the victim right of allocution). In some jurisdictions, victims also have the right to be heard at parole hearings (for an overview see Erez and Roberts 2013). These diverse victim participatory reforms acknowledge, at long last, victim rights and agency.

Victim rights charters, for instance, are common in Australia. Almost all states and territories have enshrined a charter or declaration in legislation. Broadly, these legislative statements set out how victims of crime should be treated by people and agencies such as police and courts. For example, the Victorian *Victims Charter Act 2006*, the first of its kind in Australia, lists 12 principles which govern the response to victims of crime by investigatory agencies, prosecuting agencies, and victims' service agencies. These principles include that victims should be treated respectfully, informed about their rights and the progress of the investigation, protected from unnecessary contact with the accused, and given the opportunity to make a VIS.

Despite expanded victim rights and greater victim involvement in the criminal justice system, such reforms have failed to fully realize the desired outcome of victim inclusion. The attempt to graft victim rights onto the adversarial system remains controversial and challenging. Legislative fiat

K. Laster
Sir Zelman Cowen Centre, Victoria University, Melbourne, VIC, Australia
e-mail: Kathy.Laster@vu.edu.au

alone cannot move legal culture from its historic exclusion of victims to their inclusion. Despite the grand legislative efforts over recent times, many victims continue to remain frustrated and dissatisfied with their experience and treatment (Erez et al. 2014).

In this chapter, we propose a reconceptualization of the role of victims in the criminal justice system to redress the shortcomings of current victim inclusion regimes. Conceptualising victims as 'consumers', would, we suggest, help to realize the spirit of victim reforms. At the very least, in the Digital Age, adopting a 'customer service' approach to victim participation could overcome the ambivalence towards victims and the confusion about their role.

The chapter is divided into two parts. Part 1 outlines why victim reforms, while positive in many respects, have not fully realized their intended objectives. We begin by spotlighting the strong hold that adversarial theory and practice continue to exert on current criminal justice culture and processes. We argue that victim participatory rights have not displaced traditional criminal justice approaches which, for both ideological and pragmatic reasons, have enduringly excluded victims. Legal culture has also accorded a new master status to victimhood which overshadows the diversity and individuality of victims and their varying needs and preferences. We highlight how unsupportable myths about victims continue to influence attitudes to them throughout the criminal justice system.

In Part 2, we make the case for reconceptualising victims as 'consumers' of criminal justice services. We suggest this serves as a better framework for realizing victim participatory reforms. We begin by outlining the criteria that an effective framework for victim inclusion would need to fulfill. We then review some of the alternative models proposed to better meet the needs of victims in the light of these criteria and argue that they still miss the mark. We discuss how previous attempts to conceptualize victims as consumers have been met with justified criticism for, in fact, failing to advance the interests of victims as intended. However, we contend that the contemporary status accorded to consumers in the Digital Age affords opportunities to address these past difficulties.

Drawing on the history of the consumer rights movement, we demonstrate how victims could benefit from the success of contemporary consumer advocacy and power. We go on to consider practical applications of the reconceptualization of victim as consumer, including 'victim satisfaction surveys', 'user centered design' and customer focus, to systematically gather data to improve the quality of service and enhance accountability. We use the medical context as a case study of how a more profound change is possible even in conservative systems.

In the conclusion, we explore a more radical implication of the reconceptualization of victims as consumers. We posit that, potentially, the consumer framework, where victims become the proxy for the community, could have a transformative effect on the crisis of trust in contemporary criminal justice system.

Part 1: The Limits of Victim Participation Reforms

Unquestionably, victim rights legislation has been a positive and empowering force for many victims. While still lacking full standing as parties to proceedings, victims in adversarial systems now have the opportunity to be consulted, informed, and provide input into proceedings more than ever before.

Participation in the criminal justice process has gone a considerable way to recognizing victims' needs and agency (Erez et al. 2014). Generally, it has restored victims' dignity and increased their sense of control (e.g. Erez and Tontodonato 1992). Attendance at court proceedings provides many victims with symbolic validation. A violator being referred to as 'the accused' or appearing in prison garb or handcuffs, for example, graphically highlights that their victimization is being dealt with seriously (Erez et al. 2011). The opportunity to prepare a VIS, knowing that their account of their experience will form part of the court record, has been a significant form of validation for many victims (Roberts 2009).

At the same time, victim participation rights represent a radical departure from adversarial theory and practice. Victim integration reforms over the last four decades attempted, often in an abrupt and ad hoc manner, to graft a host of victim rights on to a system which, by design and express ideology, had denied victims standing and deliberately excluded them from proceedings. It is therefore not surprising that victim rights, 'added on' to a tightly honed adversarial legal structure, remain problematic. Although some victim rights advocates view the new privileges and powers of the victim as evidence of progress toward the goal of full participation in the criminal process, for many in the criminal justice system, victim rights still present a major threat to the core values of the adversarial model (Erez 1994, 1999; Erez and Roberts 2013).

The Adversarial Challenge: One Step Forward, Two Steps Back

Historical accounts of the evolution of the modern criminal justice system document how victims were progressively banished from legal proceedings (e.g. Kirchengast 2006: 127–158). This development is celebrated as leading to the elimination of blood feuds and vigilantism. Court-based trials replaced 'trial by battle' or 'trial by ordeal' (Kirchengast 2010), and shifted the onus of prosecuting offenders from victims and their community to state-based police and prosecution services (Corns 2000; Fenwick 1997).

Critics, though, contend that the triumph of adversarial justice allowed the state to progressively 'steal' conflicts from the protagonists, including victims (Christie 1977). In adversarial theory, crime is conceptualized as harm perpetrated against the state rather than an individual. The modern criminal trial is now a (verbal) battle between two presumed equal adversaries—the state and the defendant—presided over by an impartial adjudicator—the judge. The prosecutor, as the authorized representative of the state, is required to bring the offender to justice, standing in the stead of the individual victim. At best, victims, as non-parties to proceedings, were confined to testifying at trial as witnesses (van Dijk 1988; Fenwick 1997). They were only permitted to answer questions put to them by the prosecution and the defense during examination and cross-examination, where incivility and hostility have become 'normal', common occurrences (O'Connor 2003: 226).

Victim rights legislation of the late twentieth century were designed to go some way to redress this historical shift from this victim- to- state-centric model and provide victims with various welfare and participatory rights. But an 'add victims and stir' approach did very little to challenge the foundations of adversarial proceedings. 'We are', as Duff explains

(1988: 147–148), 'endeavouring to use a social institution which has developed to fulfil one particular role for other purposes'. In criminal courts, deeply steeped in adversarial ideology and practice, 'business as usual' has prevailed.

The scale of the reforms also raised victims' expectations. Service delivery often does not keep pace with political rhetoric and the promises made to victims about meaningful reforms (Tapley 2005). And with greater opportunity to observe the routines, behaviors, and responses of what has been dubbed the 'courtroom workgroup' (the judge, prosecutor, and defense attorney (Eisenstein and Jacob 1977) victims now see for themselves the limits and failures of the system, including how legal professionals arrive at their decisions. As Otto von Bismarck reminded us over a century ago, laws—and, we would add, legal decision-making—are like sausages, 'it is better not to see them being made' (cited by Pear 2010).

For many victims, exposure to the 'law' as practiced in adversarial proceedings has been disappointing, even distressing. For instance, victims have a hard time accepting considerations such as 'convictability' (Frohmann 1991) in decisions about filing charges or prosecutors' interest in negotiating a plea that minimizes the offender's blameworthiness. Victim rights are also often incompatible with institutional demands and professional routines and practices. Legal practitioners and court staff resent and resist the 'extra work' as well as the additional players they suddenly have to accommodate. In many jurisdictions (notable American exceptions being states that have passed or adopted California's Marsy's Law: California, Illinois, Arizona, and North Dakota), there are neither sanctions nor remedies for noncompliance with, or violations of, even expressly stated victim rights (see also, in relation to the UK experience, Fenwick 1997; Jackson 2003). Implementation thus remains entirely dependent on the variable goodwill of key court actors.

Not all legal personnel can, or are willing to, mollify, placate, or attend to victims' wishes. For instance, participants with an ambiguous status such as victim advocates, staff of NGOs, and victim service agencies have described being threatened with charges of practicing law without a license for explaining mundane terms such as joint accounts to victims or being reprimanded by judges for explaining legal terminology to victims during court hearings (Globokar and Erez 2019). These kinds of incidents are indicative of failures to live up to the aspirations of victim inclusion. In the busy 'wholesaler' legal environment inhabited by professional insiders (Laster 2018), practitioners forget themselves and, at times, demonstrate a lack of sensitivity to victims. Many victims report being traumatized by legal professionals' indiscretions before, during, and after proceedings (Erez et al. 2014), such as the prosecutor and defense attorney exchanging hugs and vacation experiences in Hawaii in front of the parents of a murdered child as they waited for the trial to commence. Prosecutors are often patronizing, in one instance telling a victim that, since she is not a lawyer, she would not be able to understand the basis of a plea bargain. Victims were perturbed that judges rolled their eyes in response to a party's argument, and even apparently falling asleep during hearings (Erez et al. 2014).

Participatory reforms come at some cost and risk for victims and court professionals alike. For practical and ideological reasons, there are clear tensions in the effective implementation of victim inclusion reforms on the ground. These reforms did little to disrupt the values, prejudices and misconceptions of key actors about victims and victim status. Below, we discuss some of the contributing factors to the less than smooth adoption of hard-won victim participatory rights.

Victim as Master Status

Once victims were recognized as significant players in the criminal justice system, victimhood quickly assumed a new 'master status', a sociological concept that marks the essence of a person's social identity.

Once uttered, the term conjures up various stereotypes associated with a person of 'this kind'. As with other types of 'master status', key players in the justice system, the media, and legal scholarship tend to view victims as a homogenous and static group, rather than as diverse, dynamic, and multifaceted individuals. This is notwithstanding consistent research findings showing that victims defy the casual categorization or typecasting which is so prevalent. Victims, in short, experience crime differently and individually (Erez and Rogers 1999; Fletcher 1999; Greer 2017).

Studies confirm the diversity of victims in every respect including how they react, what they want from the law, how they view their victimization and the offender, and the response they expect to their victimization (Regehr and Alaggia 2006; Vanfraechem et al. 2014; Wemmers and Cyr 2004). Even victims of 'like' crimes, such as women who have experienced violence through sexual assault or domestic abuse, evince a variety of views, wishes, interests, and approaches to their offenders and their punishment (Herman 2005).

Our own ethnographic interviews with victims found that they do not feel listened to and that the court and other key players make often inaccurate assumptions about their needs and motivations and seek to control victims' emotions (Erez et al. 2011). In interviews we conducted in one jurisdiction, a mother of a murder victim painfully recalled being told to refrain from displays of emotion in the courtroom:

> 'I was told by the prosecutors that I was to walk in there and that I was to perform, basically. I was not to cry, I was supposed to keep my cool and they needed for me to be on my best behavior—that was their famous words. Can you imagine how hard that is … you're told that you cannot cry when you have a … murderer in the room looking at you, all these jurors, and now you're supposed to portray yourself as the cold-hearted mom who can just sit there and talk?'

For victims, their experiences, shaped largely by the conduct of lawyers, judges and others that operate within the legal system, are often just as, if not more, important than the outcome of the proceedings (Erez et al. 2014; Van Camp and Wemmers 2013). And yet, their overarching master status as the homogenous 'victim' seems to dominate criminal justice actors' responses to them (see also Hall, Chapter 10 in this volume).

To some extent, the failure to individualize responses is a feature of all bureaucratic systems, especially those with major resourcing constraints where the tyranny of numbers demands speedy disposal. Individualized approaches are sacrificed in the interests of efficiency or 'to keep things moving' (e.g. Sudnow 1965; Feeley 1979). While some agencies have specialist staff to deal with victims directly, efforts to integrate victims into the process inevitably pose an added strain on an already overloaded system. Interactions tend to be formulaic and minimalist (Kirchengast 2016). Victims find themselves 'processed'—much like defendants.

Underlying the less than accommodating attitudes to the needs of victims as individuals are the persistent (even if empirically unsupportable) myths about victims including the overarching fear that victim inclusion is a threat to the fair administration of justice, often invoked as a concern for possible infringement of defendant rights (Ashworth 1993).

Lingering Victim Myths

Despite decades of empirical research to the contrary, there are three persistent sets of myths underscoring attitudes to victims. First, victims are often assumed to be driven by punitive or vengeful motives (Herman 2005; Erez 1999). Second, there is the lingering suspicion that victims are at least partly to blame for the situation in which they find themselves and so are undeserving. Finally, victims are perceived to be 'emotional'— anathema to a legal system which prides itself on objective, 'rational' and impartial decision making (Bandes 1996).

Myth 1: Victims Are Vengeful and Punitive

The image of the victim as a person who seeks revenge—the myth of the vengeful victim—is commonly found in legal scholarship (Ashworth 1993; Fletcher 1999). It remains embodied in the attitudes of professionals who interact with victims (Erez et al. 2014) and underlies the sometimes fierce opposition from some legal practitioners to victim input into proceedings (e.g. Erez 1990, 1994), especially in the form of VIS, the nature, content, and impact of which remain controversial.

This image persists, notwithstanding that it been discredited by research on victims of diverse crimes and in all legal systems studied (Doak and O'Mahony 2006), at least in the context of adversarial national legal systems (cf. international criminal justice fora). It has been consistently shown that victims most commonly seek validation rather than retribution; they also wish to be accorded dignity, respect, and recognition, rather than to lobby for harsher punishment of their offenders (Van Camp and Wemmers 2013).

In the scores of VIS that we have read, victims request, at most, that judges merely apply the sanction meted out by the law (see also Erez and Rogers 1999). Victims maintain that they want fair, commensurate punishment—just deserts (e.g. Starkweather 1992; Erez 1999). In other cases, particularly if the perpetrator is a family member, they ask for treatment and services for their violator (Herman 2005).

Some criminal justice actors have a political bias against victim participatory reforms because these are seen to be associated with 'law and order' agendas including harsher penalties. The 'culture of crime control' that has emerged in late modernity (Garland 2001) has made victims part of its rhetoric and rationale, but it is simplistic to see victims themselves as the vanguard of what are much broader social forces.[2] As we well know, correlation is not causation. Indeed, surveys of public attitudes toward punishment confirm that victims' wishes for commensurate punishment generally reflect those of the general public; the two do not differ in their preferred type or degree of harshness in sentencing (see Roberts et al. 2007). Victims' views and preferences are closer to prevailing public sentiments than those of legal professionals. The latter, in their efforts to dispose of cases efficiently, can become insensitive to human suffering in the routine processing of cases (Davis et al. 1984). For instance, they often agree to drop charges or negotiate pleas that are more likely to result in what the wider community perceives to be overly lenient sentences.

Myth 2: Victims Are Blameworthy

There are hardly any so-called 'ideal victims' (Christie 1986), but that does not make victims responsible for their victimization. Victims do not bring their victimization upon themselves. The most pernicious and prevalent of these assumptions is that women who are victims of domestic abuse are 'asking for it' and are to blame because they do not leave or if they return to their abuser (Loseke and Cahill 1984; Erez and King 2000). Myths about rape and victim precipitation and provocation are likewise widespread and stubbornly problematic, resistant to victims' attempts at denial (Lonsway and Fitzgerald 1994).

Although criminological research has documented a substantial overlap between victims and offenders (Delong and Reichert 2019), the overwhelming majority of persons who are victimized do not become victims because of any criminal involvement (although this may be true for many offenders, see Delong and Reichert 2019).[3] Furthermore, when victims do not report victimization, or report it with significant delay, it is not because they are responsible for their misfortune, but often due to shame, fear of retaliation, or because they do not think the incident is important enough or will receive an adequate response from police (Kidd and Chayet 1984; Ullman 2010; U.S. Department of Justice 2012).

Myth 3: Victims Are Emotional

There is no denying that crime causes harm, pain and anguish to victims. And there is a natural human need to express such sentiments and have them heard and formally validated.

Underlying legal fears about emotional display is the risk that victims' emotions will inject subjectivity into the trial process, which, according to legal ideology, is meant to remain 'objective' (Erez and Rogers 1999). The criminal justice system has its own rules for emotion display (Schuster and Propen 2011). Indeed, a goodly proportion of the law of evidence is concerned with the sifting of impressions, opinions and emotions from the 'facts' that alone should determine jury decisions about guilt or innocence. Lawyers themselves are schooled that as professionals they do not 'think', 'feel' or 'believe' but rather only 'submit' or 'argue' before a court. Even judges, it is feared, might be influenced by displays of emotion, which could then skew a sentence and thus lead to sentencing disparity (Erez 1999; Roberts 2009).

'Emotions', however, are not the same as 'emotionality', and having feelings is not tantamount to allowing irrationality to reign (Bandes 1996). There is scope for victims to display their emotions, and have those emotions validated, in a legal environment, without necessarily threatening the rules-based objectivity of the legal process.

In sum, despite the evidence, and the efforts to render court culture more receptive and accommodating towards victim participation, adversarial traditions as well as 'business as usual' imperatives continue to shape responses to victims and victim participation reform. So pervasive are these prejudices that whatever the dictates of a new legislative regime might be, the cultural default position is to be suspicious of victims and their involvement in proceedings (Laster and Erez 2000). If victim participation measures are to be effective, we need to move beyond just formal reforms and create a victim-responsive culture across the criminal justice system. In Part 2 below, we consider how this might be achieved.

Part 2: Reconceptualizing the Victim as Consumer

The limitations of the adversarial system and victims' role in such criminal justice systems are well documented (Boateng and Abess 2017). Advocates of defendants and victims endlessly argue about tilting the balance of rights between each side through ad hoc procedural reforms. Here we make a case for reviving the model, or metaphor, of 'victim as consumer' of criminal justice services as a better framework for realizing victim participatory reforms. But what criteria should a victim-friendly new scheme meet?

Criteria for a New Victim Paradigm

The overarching challenge for a victim-friendly justice system is to reconceptualize the rights and role of victims without undermining the time-honored protections accorded to accused persons. Beyond this core requirement, there are five criteria that any workable victim integration approach would need to satisfy. These are:

1. *Practicality*: the new approach should be 'doable'. Criminal justice processes are already time-consuming, cumbersome and complex both for the professional workgroups including judges, legal practitioners and

court staff, as well as for offenders and victims. Simplicity and ease of administration and compliance are therefore critical.

2. Comprehensibility/Marketability: the new approach needs to be readily understood by criminal justice personnel, victims and defendants, as well as the wider public. The purpose, mode, and impact of any new process need to be self-evident and fit with the lived experience of victims and other key actors. It needs to be easily marketable, to dislodge the deep prejudices and myths prevalent in professional and public discourse about victims.

3. Affordability: the criminal justice system is already bursting at the seams with the volume of cases it is required to resolve with shrinking public resources (Laster and Kornhauser 2017). This reality is unlikely to change. New measures should therefore minimize any extra time and cost burden on the state, if they are to be viable.

4. Testability: the effectiveness of any new approach needs to be able to be measured. The experiences of victims both individually and collectively need to be evaluated to assess whether the new model/intervention is an improvement on previous efforts to accommodate victims' needs and interests. The approach needs to be capable of generating and capturing data not only for evaluation but also to serve as the basis for continuous improvement in the system's responsiveness to victims.

5. Accountability: the new model should hold the whole of the criminal justice system to account for its treatment and responsiveness to victims. Individual demonstrations of empathy and goodwill towards victims need to be generalized and standardized with criminal justice personnel held to account for any breaches or failings. Through this open approach, the public can engage with, understand, and clearly support reforms which politicians are then obliged to follow.

A number of alternative approaches to overcome some of the limitations of the adversarial system for all parties, including victims, have emerged in the last few decades. Each has its own set of advantages and disadvantages but have not, to date, reshaped the underlying attitudes to victims.

Alternative Models of Victim-Friendly Criminal Justice

Some legal scholars, conscious of the limits of adversarial approaches, have advocated for a 'victim model of criminal justice' (Beloof 1999) to complement the two main approaches of 'crime control' and 'due process' (Packer 1964). The 'third model', it is suggested, would embody important victim participation rights in criminal proceedings including fairness and respect for the dignity of victims (Beloof 1999). This third model is a variant of the 'add on' approach but with a shift in the orientation of court proceedings toward victim rights. This approach is likely to be ineffective for much the same reasons as all previous efforts to recalibrate the balance of rights between victims and defendants.

Other scholars have gone further, proposing a system of 'Parallel Justice' for victims which mirrors the rights accorded to offenders (see Herman 2010). In the United States, for example, a movement to enact a constitutional amendment to provide victims with legal standing is gaining momentum with its first victory in California, thorough the passage of Marsy's Law (Richardson 2013). Other states, including Illinois, Montana, and South Dakota followed, and efforts are currently being made to pass similar laws elsewhere.

Another variant of this approach is procedural justice, which contends that principles of respect, voice, transparency, and neutrality of decision makers will increase satisfaction and cooperation of litigants, or citizens in general, with authorities (Tyler 2003).

The major problem each of these approaches face is that they add yet another layer to what is already a highly complex system. They also reinforce the bifurcation between offenders' and victims' rights. Neither model addresses the critical issue of how to change the hearts and minds of key actors in the system about victim participation.

A relatively recent influential school of thought though has directly addressed attitudinal shift. The broad church of Therapeutic Jurisprudence (TJ) has reinvigorated traditional courts by reframing the thinking of key court actors to recognize the 'therapeutic' dimensions of court adjudication (Wexler 1993). The philosophy of TJ initially sought to transform the interactions between court officers and criminal offenders. The approach directly led to the development of specialist 'therapeutic' courts to deal with particular kinds of intractable offending behavior such as drug addiction and mental illness (Winick and Wexler 2001). Envisioning law as an instrument of healing and rehabilitation, TJ has been particularly attentive to the emotional well-being of all parties caught up in the system, including victims. For victims, TJ holds the promise of ameliorating secondary victimization at all levels and stages of the criminal justice process (Winick 2011).

A key strength of the TJ model is that it is conservative: working from within the system to reshape the attitudes of traditional court actors. Applied in ordinary court hearings, TJ approaches require minimal additional resources beyond better education and training of practitioners and judicial officers in basic therapeutic principles. The professional development is designed to improve court personnel's understanding of social interaction and the impact of behavior on the parties and the problems that regularly come before the courts. For judges in particular, TJ has provided a new philosophical raison d'etre beyond merely the 'processing' of an ever-increasing array of difficult cases (King et al. 2009; Spencer 2017).

However, TJ's 'insider' status is simultaneously its weakness. It is a judge or professional-centric approach; the individual judicial officer is allowed to be the self-defined arbiter of what is 'therapeutic' in a given instance for individual offenders and others, including victims. TJ may lead to greater empathy for victims and so improve individual victims' experience of proceedings (Erez et al. 2011), but TJ does not make judicial officers, court processes, or the system itself any more accountable for the treatment of victims individually or as a class. It bypasses a critical requirement of victim participation—active, evidence-based, systematic engagement of victims as a matter of right rather than of discretion.

The most radical response to the shortcomings of the adversarial system has been to side-step courts altogether. Arising from the critique of the failure of the formal adversarial adjudication process and its limited rehabilitative outcomes for offenders (Daly 2017), John Braithwaite's theory of 'Re-Integrative Shaming' (Braithwaite 1989) has seen the development of various alternative 'restorative justice' fora (Strang and Braithwaite 2001). These settings are designed to provide a structured, respectful meeting between victims and their offenders in the presence of supporters, facilitated by a trained mediator (McCold 2006). For some offenders and victims, these settings are a major improvement on formal court adjudication.

Although we still lack a large body of high-quality, methodologically rigorous research into the effect of restorative justice (RJ) practices on recidivism, indications to date are, on the whole, generally positive (Wilson et al. 2017). At the very least, RJ interventions perform just as well as 'traditional' court processes in terms of reducing re-offending (Piggott and Wood 2019).

Perhaps more importantly for present purposes, the evidence suggests positive victim participant outcomes. In their meta-analysis of evaluations of juvenile justice RJ programs, Wilson et al. (2017: 35) reported that victims had improved perceptions of fairness, greater satisfaction, improved attitudes toward the offender, were more likely to feel that the outcome was just, and felt their opinions and views were considered and the offender held to account.

A recent evaluation of the restorative justice conferencing program in the Australian Capital Territory, for example, found between 98% and 99% of victims who participated in the process felt it was fair and they were treated with respect, and 96% would recommend participation to others (Broadhurst et al. 2018).

Critics of RJ, however, contend that as a system, it is costly and offers little beyond that already available via existing diversionary schemes (Morris 2002). Empirically, despite the apparent rapprochement between offenders and victims during the mediation session itself, recidivism rates are hardly better than for traditional court determinations (Daly 2017). For victim rights advocates, the major concern is that RJ fora place victims in an invidious position because, directly or indirectly, they are pressured into confronting their offenders and, in some instances, 'forgiving' them (Peterson Armour and Umbreit 2006). At the very least, victims' advocates contend that restorative justice is unsuitable for particular kinds of relationships and/or to more serious types of offending (Hudson 2002).

The criteria for success outlined above suggest that a sweeping (and resource-intensive) refashioning of the formal criminal justice system probably will not work. To be effective, change, in the first instance, needs to be conceptual. How do we change hearts and minds about victims and their status in our criminal justice system? Below we outline our own arguments in support of conceptual change (see Chapter 14 in this volume for a different conceptualization that has similarities to RJ).

Reimagining Victims as Consumers of the Justice System

We argue that construing victims as 'consumers of the justice system' provides an alternative, theoretical, and practical framework which avoids casting victims as the problematic 'third wheel' in the adversarial dyad of the State vs. the Offender. It clarifies their role by providing a direct connection between the public and the courts.

The concept 'victims as consumers' is a metaphor, but powerful nonetheless. As Lakoff and Johnson (1980) so cogently established, metaphor is integral, rather than peripheral to language and abstract thought. Metaphors determine how we perceive and experience the world. Just as the image of victims as Cinderellas served as the initial catalyst for fundamental changes to the position of victims, so a reframing of victims as 'consumers of the justice system' provides a way of burying unhelpful stereotypes about victims. It should also resolve the ambivalence and confusion about victims' role in criminal justice proceedings.

The metaphor also provides a way to bypass the perennial competition in the balancing of rights between victims and offenders.

To be sure, we have been here before. In one sense, construing victims as 'consumers' of the criminal justice system and its associated services is not new. Victims (and even at one time 'prisoners') have been envisioned as consumers since the 1980s (Goodey 2005: 131). Williams (1999a) describes, for example, the UK's 1996 Victim's Charter—a 'statement of service standards for victims of crime'—as being framed in terms of consumer rights.

At the time, the construction of victims as consumers failed to empower victims and meet their needs. Nor were the victim rights that this construction promised to afford ever fully realized.

Central to this failure was the treatment of the victim-consumer as a 'passive' or 'mere' consumer of criminal justice services, and denied victims the status of 'active citizens' with enforceable and substantive rights (Tapley 2005; Williams 1999b). Victims were treated as consumers of services, 'with very little recourse to justice should these services fail' to meet expectations (Goodey 2005: 131). Writing about the construction of citizens as consumers of public services more generally, Ryan (2001: 107) argues that:

> a central problem associated with the language of citizen as consumer is that it implies a passive role for citizens rather than a participatory engagement. Consumers have less responsibility in decision-making and implementation processes than do citizens.

Viewing victim services as part of a market, consumer-based economy also imported notions of purchasing power and access to knowledge, serving to only advantage the least marginalized victims (Goodey 2005: 136–138; Ryan 2001), and failed one of the basic requirements of consumer sovereignty: a competitive market which provides consumer choice (Ryan 2001).

Since these constructions of victim as consumer, however, the consumer movement has progressed markedly, resulting in an unprecedented degree of consumer empowerment. Consumers no longer engage in the 'passive' consumption of goods and services. Increasingly, the balance of power is shifting away from the supplier, as the consumer movement has proven to be a powerful social and political force, especially in the Digital Age.

We suggest that recasting victims as 'consumers of the justice system'—in the sense of the contemporary, empowered consumer with which we are today familiar—provides an effective framework for enhancing victims' participatory rights in the criminal justice system. A short history of consumer power is probably in order to understand the changing connotations of this conceptual framework. Despite its apparent lack of success in the 1980s, the longer view suggests that at various times, it has been a transformative force in social relations and power.

The Rise of Consumer Power

Adam Smith first coined the term 'consumer sovereignty' in the eighteenth century (Finch 1985: 23), but it was not until the Great Depression that a grass roots social movement, intent on protecting ordinary people from exploitation by manufacturers and sellers, came into its own. The Consumers' Union was established in 1936 in the US. Initially, consumer activism was denigrated as 'consumerism' by retailers and manufacturers. It met with hostility as an allegedly communist-inspired attempt to derail capitalism.

By the 1950s, the movement acquired legitimacy with housewives leading public campaigns to improve product value and safety for the benefit of women and children (Storrs 2006). One immediate effect was the widespread introduction of 'product testing' (Warne 1973). Innovations in retail, such as self-service stores and large supermarkets, also gave consumers a new level of freedom and control (including 'pre-purchase evaluation' of products) and choice (Davies and Elliot 2006); consumers described 'no longer [waiting] "dutifully" to be served', but taking active responsibility for their own purchasing decisions (Davies and Elliot 2006: 1113).

The growing power of the consumer movement was formally acknowledged in President Kennedy's Consumer Rights Bill of 1962, which declared that consumers were entitled to four core rights—the Right to Safety, the Right to be Informed, the Right to Choose, and the Right to be Heard (Kennedy 1962: 2). In the same set of sweeping consumer reforms, President Kennedy also announced the creation of a Consumers Advisory Council and mandated that heads of 22 nominated Federal agencies appoint special assistants to review consumer interests and concerns in the delivery of their services (Werner 1962).

During this period of social change, the consumer movement formed part of the wider critique of the professions with ordinary people insisting on better information, greater consultation and improved service delivery by manufacturers, sellers, professionals, and by government itself (Laster and Kornhauser 2017). The heyday of the consumer movement came in the 1980s and 1990s, mirroring again the rise of the victim rights movement. Reports critical of the lack of consumer protection led to extensive legislative reforms to better protect the health and welfare of consumers. For instance, in 1987, the Organisation for Economic Co-operation and Development published a report (Organisation for Economic Co-operation and Development 1987) calling on public services to be more responsive to users and the US Federal Bureau of Consumer Affairs was established with a mandate to protect the rights of consumers and prevent 'unfair, deceptive and fraudulent business practices' (Smith n.d.).

The application of consumer rights thinking to victims was less successful during this period probably because it was not robust enough to reshape traditional institutions grounded in protecting an individual defendant from being overborne by the overwhelming power and resources of the state. The 1980s consumer model assumed that a civil law model could reshape criminal justice ideology without a method for achieving such transformative change.

However, the Digital Age consumers have acquired a more powerful tool kit. Technology has provided platforms which readily aggregate comparative data about services of all kinds, providing consumers with hitherto unprecedented information and choice, and with consumers being able to take full advantage of alternative value propositions (Harrison et al. 2006: 975; Pires et al. 2006: 939).

Both commercial and government services are now dealing with increasingly demanding and connected consumers, who are able to navigate complex decision-making processes and 'pull' the information they need, rather than have it 'pushed' to them by suppliers (Deloitte LLP 2014).

Providers of goods and services—and least in the commercial space—were quick to respond and exploit the new technology for their own marketing and other ends. In a highly competitive environment, they have harnessed technology to better inform themselves about individualized service and product needs in a consumer-centric market place. Business seeks to personalize their interactions with individual consumers, and gain earlier and better information about what they are and are not interested in (Pires et al. 2006: 944).

Digital 'department stores' have become crucial to satisfying a key objective of consumer law to enhance informed decision-making, leading to a fairer market (Van Loo 2017). Social media has given new power to consumers to broadcast their concerns in real time. Business (and government) ignores negative reviews at their peril (Busby 2018; Fogel and Murphy 2018). Empowered consumers are more willing to reject value propositions of unsatisfactory quality (Pires et al. 2006: 940).

Social and economic inequalities do, to be sure, leave many from marginalized and vulnerable groups unable to fully assert their consumer rights. Too-great an emphasis on the self-directed victim-consumer risks leaving some behind (Laster and Kornhauser 2017), particularly if it presupposes a level of digital inclusion or literacy are lacking.

While opportunities for empowerment are rapidly increasing as these groups, too, access easily available information, it is incumbent on criminal justice services to recognize barriers and engage with such people in an appropriately targeted way.

For example, in Australia, a website aimed at delivering information to homeless youth about their legal rights was designed having regard to user research which identified a lack of access to information as a barrier to seeking help, but a high level of internet-accessible smartphone ownership (Paper Giant 2014). The result was a plain-language, low-bandwidth, mobile-responsive website produced by a youth legal service which is co-located with a youth homeless service (Youthlaw 2015). And in the UK, the National Health Service publishes information for local health and care organizations to support digital inclusion among consumers of health and care services so as to make digital health services and information more widely accessible and also more accountable (National Health Service 2018).

We have come a long way since Henry Ford's now apocryphal quip when asked about the color choices available to buyers of his (then) new Model T Ford, 'Any color as long as it's black' (Betton and Hench 2002). These days there is no doubting that consumer experience matters and attitudes toward them have changed dramatically. For both consumers and providers, new tools and technologies have proven to be an efficient, and relatively inexpensive, way of meeting changing consumer expectations and needs. Such approaches might be more effectively adopted in the criminal justice system to satisfy many of the criteria noted above for successful victim integration.

Tools and Techniques for Victim Engagement

Technology now provides the justice system with ready and affordable tools to systematically and meaningfully monitor and evaluate victims' experience of justice.

Victim Surveys and Customer Focus

The pioneer of TJ, David Wexler, has argued that victims should be asked to fill out customer satisfaction surveys or 'criminal justice impact statements' at the conclusion of a case (Wexler 2008). The aim of the feedback is to evaluate victims' experiences of the process. Just as victims in many adversarial systems are routinely permitted and expected to submit VIS, detailing the impact of their primary victimization (i.e. the crime), a 'criminal justice impact statement', according to Wexler, would document any secondary victimization they encountered through their involvement in the criminal justice system. Victims' feedback could include details about how proceedings and practitioners' actions, utterances, gestures, or (extra-legal) decisions have impacted them. Feedback would provide court professionals (in addition to victim support services: see Hall, Chapter 10 in this volume) with insights to modify their practice in the future.

'Customer satisfaction' reports would also be an effective accountability mechanism. They could, for instance, be considered in administrative decision-making about professional rewards or promotions, and potentially, as the basis of disciplinary action. While controversial in some quarters—such as student evaluations in higher education (Díaz-Méndez et al. 2017; Pounder 2007)—the use of evaluative 'customer' feedback has nevertheless proven to be an effective tool for changing behavior and attitudes in the public, business, and education spheres.

User feedback instruments have already proven to be effective in civil justice. The Civil Review Tribunal (CRT) in British Columbia, Canada, the first fully online civil dispute resolution jurisdiction in the world, for instance, regularly conducts 'participant satisfaction surveys' and publishes the aggregate results every six months (Rosteck 2018). The data are used for quality control, service improvements, and to monitor 'customer' (parties to disputes) satisfaction. The data also provide an accountability mechanism for government and the public alike. The consistently positive survey results have been a key factor supporting the expansion of the jurisdiction of the tribunal to cover all civil disputes less than $5000, strata property disputes of any amount and, in April 2019, motor vehicle injury claims up to $50,000 (Civil Resolution Tribunal 2019).

On a much smaller scale, Australia's Fair Work Commission, the tribunal charged with determination of industrial disputes, was one of the first legal entities to engage a public value consultancy group to conduct 'user-experience research' in 2017 to 'examine client experiences and ... improve case management practices' (Fair Work Commission 2018). The subsequent report measured user experience and used the data to compile several recommendations for the improvement of the Fair Work Commission's services (Cube Group 2018).

In criminal justice, systematizing the use of evaluative feedback would send a message that victims' sensibilities matter and that decisions and behaviors are being monitored. Potentially, the use of such tools could have a transformation effect on legal culture without, importantly, disrupting any of the existing criminal justice protections afforded to defendants. At a minimum, a new emphasis on finding out what victims want and need should encourage provision of better information including explanations about complex matters such as evidentiary and practical constraints on prosecutors and sentencing guidelines and practices. Victims, in turn, might then readjust their expectations, avoiding some of their current frustrations and unhappiness with the process (Erez and Tontodonato 1992).

An even more effective way of ensuring that victims' perspectives are taken into account though is to actively involve them in the design of system reform.

User-Centered Design

User-Centered Design (UCD) involves users at every stage in the creation and development of services of all kinds. UCD is effectively a co-design process between the intended user/recipient and service provider (van Velsen et al. 2009). Commercial enterprises, like technology companies and banks, have relied on UCD processes for many years, where the emphasis is shifting from 'Customer Relationship Management' to 'Customer Management of Relationships' (Pires et al. 2006: 944).

More recently, government has begun adopting UCD to reform outdated services. For example, the social support e-Service in the Netherlands (van Velsen et al. 2009) and the Australian Taxation Office (Martin et al. 2008) have applied UCD principles to great effect. British Columbia's CRT employed UCD in the development of its online portal to ensure that the new jurisdiction 'puts the user first' (Salter and Thompson 2016–2017: 123).

Leading law and innovation theorist, Margaret Hagan, suggests that legal professionals should embrace a designer's approach to reform of the legal system to focus on 'real, lived human problems to help us think more ambitiously and creatively about how we could address the many frustrations, confusions, and frictions in law' (Hagan 2018). We argue this approach be extended to victims as 'consumers' of the justice system.

Re-orienting conservative professions, like medicine, to put patients at the center of the system has, after initial resistance, ultimately succeeded in changing conservative attitudes. This gives some hope that a 'victim as consumer' mindset could reshape traditional attitudes currently thwarting the acceptance of victim inclusion reforms.

Changing Conservative Cultures and Systems: The Healthcare Experience

As part of the health consumer movement, from the 1980s onwards, the medical profession was persuaded to adopt patient-centered care (PCC) approaches, with decision-making shared between doctors and patients (Gorin et al. 2017). Ethical considerations (Gorin et al. 2017), as well as consistent empirical findings showing significantly improved health outcomes through the new collaborative approach, supported its gradual uptake (for examples, see Greenfield et al. 1985).

Initially, PCC met with strong resistance from practitioners. In health care, paternalism was seemingly ingrained into the system. 'Doctor knows best' was the mantra and patients were regarded as passive participants in their own treatment (Adams and Drake 2006: 89).

Some doctors reasoned that patients do not really want to be involved (Strull et al. 1984) and that sick patients lacked the knowledge and independence to make informed choices (Sherlock 1986). Even those who supported PCC in theory, found it difficult to implement in practice (Adams and Drake 2006; Gwyn and Elwyn 1999). There was significant cultural resistance to change (Gollop et al. 2004) from a traditional and conservative profession.

As the body of evidence about the health benefits, both mental and physical, grew (Bertakis and Azari 2011; Delaney 2018; Herman 2005; Lee et al. 2018; Roumie et al. 2011; Thompson and McCabe 2012)—including in relation to postsurgical outcomes (Lee et al. 2018), better patient adherence to treatment plans (Roumie et al. 2011; Thompson and McCabe 2012), and reduced stress and increased empowerment in diabetes patients (Hermanns et al. 2013)—PCC secured its place as standard policy and practice across the healthcare sector in Australia (Better Health Victoria 2015), America (American Medical Association 2017), the UK (National Health Service n.d.), and elsewhere. Actively involving patients in decision-making is now unequivocally regarded as 'best practice'.

There is no need to labour the parallels between the consumer movement, including the dramatic changes in the healthcare system through the application of PCC approaches.

The success of the consumer movement though does suggest that it is probably time to move beyond legal centricism in our thinking about victim reform. Reimagining victims as 'consumers of justice' is likely to bring significant systemic change not only to benefit victims but also the criminal justice system as a whole.

Conclusion: Relegitimizing the Criminal Justice System?

Despite concerted legislative reform efforts over the last four decades to integrate victims into the criminal justice system, there is still marked resistance to full victim participation. Many victims continue to feel disempowered and disillusioned, or worse, as they experience the 'law in action'. A new approach is required to transform traditional attitudes and disrupt adversarial culture to make room for victim participation.

We now know that there are major benefits of victim inclusion in criminal justice processes, not only for victims but also for the system as a whole.

In reviewing the empirical evidence, Erez and Roberts (2013) and Roberts (2009) summarize diverse findings to the effect that;

- active consumer participation throughout the whole process of decision-making (i.e. bail to parole) makes victims feel safer;
- appropriate sentencing (facilitated by VIS) assists defendants secure appropriate treatment;
- increases in (net) victim satisfaction with justice grounded in perceptions of procedural fairness constitutes a significant element in litigant satisfaction;
- victims experience of justice services significantly increase when principles of customer care (respect, transparency, consultation, explanation of options, rules, constraints, outcomes) are applied; and
- victim advocates do effectively assist with social support, empowerment, and enhanced quality of life for individual victims, thereby reducing reliance on (generally more expensive) community services.

Reconceptualizing victims as consumers of the criminal justice system, could, we suggest, provide this powerful metaphoric shift in thinking. The victim rights movement has not typically aligned itself with the broader consumer rights movement, even if some reform measures, from time to time, have employed the rhetoric of 'consumer rights'. However, we contend that the victims' rights activists have much to gain by associating themselves with the growing power of the consumer movement, especially the enhanced status of the 'consumer' in the Digital Age.

Recasting victims as 'consumers of the justice system' meets the five criteria we have identified as necessary for a fundamental change to criminal justice theory and practice. The model is presently conceptual but could be put into practice and become transformational: the concept is easily understood by everyone and so easily 'marketed'. It imposes little or no additional costs on the system. Consumerist consciousness also affords its own mechanisms for testing/measuring attitudes, including the impact of any changes. Regarding victims as consumers of the justice system does not, in itself, displace defendants' rights. But perhaps most significantly, the new incarnation of the victim as a consumer of justice could provide greater transparency and accountability, not just for victims but for the wider community about the criminal justice system.

At the moment, all institutions in Western democracies, including the courts, are experiencing a crisis of confidence. Observers have noted a steep decline in institutional trust since the 1960s (Blind 2007). The legitimacy of public institutions derives from the extent to which the public trusts them (Hakhverdian and Mayne 2012). 'Institutional trust' is formed when citizens have reliable and affirmative experiences of using societal systems (Blunsdon and Reed 2010). The RAND Corporation, in a comprehensive report on the state of institutional trust in Western democracies, identified lack of transparency as a major contributing factor in the loss of confidence in public institutions. The report suggests institutions that have traditionally taken a conservative approach to information sharing have been slow to meet the expectations of a digitally literate public that treats opacity with skepticism and distrust (Ries et al. 2018). The antidote, according to 'Open Government' and 'Crowd Law' theorist and advocate, Beth Noveck, is for courts to embrace transparency, participation, and collaboration with the community as core values (Noveck 2015).

How victims are treated is, at one level, a barometer of the health of the justice system itself as victims are effectively the proxy for 'the community'. The continuing legitimacy of courts and the criminal justice system as a whole may well depend on how well they learn to accommodate the proxy citizen, the 'victim consumer', in their processes and thinking.

Notes

1. In the US, major pieces of legislation providing victims with various rights include: the Victim and Witness Protection Act of 1982, Pub. L. 97-291; the Victims of Crime Act [VOCA] of 1984, Pub. L. 98-473; the Victims' Rights and Restitution Act of 1990, Pub. L. 101-647; the Violent Crime Control and Law Enforcement Act of 1994, Pub. L. 103-322; and the Crime Victims' Rights Act of 2004, Pub. L. 108-405. The Crime Victims' Rights Act (CVRA) was signed into US federal law in 2004 with the expressed purpose of empowering crime victims, expanding the role of the victim in federal criminal prosecutions, and providing more clearly defined roles for victims in court proceedings.

2. There is no doubt that victim rights have been captured and used by conservatives to bolster their political agenda. Victim rights have been caught up in countervailing ideologies of late modern capitalism: neoliberalism, neo-rationality, and neoconservatism. Each of these ideologies has exploited particular rhetoric about victims to further their distinct political agendas (Laster and Erez 2000).

3. But even for those who have become victims in the course of committing crime—the 'viminals' as victim advocates refer to them (Globokar et al. 2019)—they too, as these advocates have reminded us, have a mother, sister or significant other, who need and deserve help as secondary victims.

References

Adams, J. R., & Drake, R. E. (2006). Shared Decision-Making and Evidence-Based Practice. *Community Mental Health Journal, 42*(1), 87–105.

American Medical Association. (2017). *AMA to Unleash a New Era of Patient Care* [Online]. Retrieved January 16, 2019, from https://www.ama-assn.org/press-center/press-releases/ama-unleash-new-era-patient-care.

Ashworth, A. (1993). Victim Impact Statements and Sentencing. *Criminal Law Review, 1993*, 498–518.

Bandes, S. A. (1996). Empathy, Narrative, and Victim Impact Statements. *The University of Chicago Law Review, 63*(2), 361–412.

Beloof, D. E. (1999). The Third Model of Criminal Process: The Victim Participation Model. *Utah Law Review, 1999*, 289–330.

Bertakis, K. D., & Azari, R. (2011). Patient-Centered Care Is Associated with Decreased Health Care Utilization. *Journal of the American Board of Family Medicine, 24*(3), 229–239.

Better Health Victoria. (2015). *Patient-Centred Care Explained* [Online]. Retrieved January 16, 2019, from https://www.betterhealth.vic.gov.au/health/servicesandsupport/patient-centred-care-explained.

Betton, J., & Hench, T. J. (2002). "Any Color as Long as It's Black": Henry Ford and the Ethics of Business. *Journal of Genocide Research, 4*(4), 533–541.

Blind, P. K. (2007). *Building Trust in Government in the Twenty-First Century: Review of Literature and Emerging Issues*. Vienna: United Nations Department of Economic and Social Affairs.

Blunsdon, B., & Reed, K. (2010). The Effects of Technical and Social Conditions on Workplace Trust. *The International Journal of Human Resource Management, 14*(1), 12–27.

Boateng, F. D., & Abess, G. (2017). Victims' Role in the Criminal Justice System: A Statutory Analysis of Victims' Rights in the U.S. *International Journal of Police and Management, 19*(4), 221–228.

Braithwaite, J. (1989). *Crime, Shame and Reintegration*. Cambridge: Cambridge University Press.

Broadhurst, R., Morgan, A., Payne, J., & Maller, R. (2018). *Australian Capital Territory Restorative Justice Evaluation: An Observational Outcome Evaluation*. Canberra: Australian National University and the Australian Institute of Criminology.

Busby, C. (2018). *Ignoring Negative Reviews Bad for Business Says ServiceSeeking* [Online]. Retrieved January 24, 2019, from https://www.kochiesbusinessbuilders.com.au/ignoring-negative-reviews-bad-for-business-says-serviceseeking/.

Cassell, P. G., & Erez, E. (2011). Victim Impact Statements and Ancillary Harm: The American Perspective. *Canadian Law Review, 15*(2), 150–204.

Christie, N. (1977). Conflicts as Property. *The British Journal of Criminology, 17*(1), 1–15.

Christie, N. (1986). The Ideal Victim. In E. A. Fattah (Ed.), *From Crime Policy to Victim Policy* (pp. 17–30). London: Palgrave Macmillan.

Civil Resolution Tribunal. (2019). *Welcome to the Civil Resolution Tribunal* [Online]. Retrieved January 24, 2019, from https://civilresolutionbc.ca/.

Corns, C. (2000). Police Summary Prosecutions in Australia and New Zealand. *University of Tasmania Law Review, 19*(2), 280–310.

Cube Group. (2018). *Unfair Dismissal: User-Experience Research*. Melbourne: Fair Work Commission.

Daly, K. (2017). Restorative Justice: The Real Story. In *Restorative Justice* (pp. 85–109). New York: Routledge.

Davies, A., & Elliot, R. (2006). The Evolution of the Empowered Consumer. *European Journal of Marketing, 40*(9), 1106–1121.

Davis, R. C., Kunreuther, F., & Connick, E. (1984). Expanding the Victim's Role in the Criminal Court Dispositional Process: The Results of an Experiment. *Journal of Criminology and Criminal Law, 75*(2), 491–506.

Delaney, L. J. (2018). Patient-Centred Care as an Approach to Improving Health Care in Australia. *Collegian, 25*(1), 119–123.

Deloitte, L. L. P. (2014). *The Deloitte Consumer Review: The Growing Power of Consumers*. London: Deloitte LLP.

Delong, C., & Reichert, J. (2019). *The Victim-Offender Overlap: Examining the Relationship Between Victimization and Offending* [Online]. Retrieved January 29, 2019, from http://www.icjia.state.il.us/articles/the-victim-offender-overlap-examining-the-relationship-between-victimization-and-offending.

Díaz-Méndez, M., Saren, M., & Gummesson, E. (2017). Considering Pollution in the Higher Education (HE) Service Ecosystem: The Role of Students' Evaluation Surveys. *TQM Journal, 29*(6), 767–782.

van Dijk, J. (1988). Ideological Trends Within the Victims Movement: An International Perspective. In M. Maguire & J. Pointing (Eds.), *Victims of Crime: A New Deal?* (pp. 115–126). Milton Keynes: Open University Press.

Doak, J., & O'Mahony, D. (2006). The Vengeful Victim? Assessing the Attitudes of Victims Participating in Restorative Youth Conferencing. *International Review of Victimology, 13*(2), 157–177.

Duff, P. (1988). The "Victim Movement" and Legal Reform. In M. Maguire & J. Pointing (Eds.), *Victims of Crime: A New Deal?* (pp. 147–155). Milton Keynes: Open University Press.

Eisenstein, J., & Jacob, H. (1977). *Felony Justice: An Organizational Analysis of Criminal Courts*. Boston: Little, Brown.

Erez, E. (1990). Victim Participation in Sentencing: Rhetoric and Reality. *Journal of Criminal Justice, 18*(1), 19–31.

Erez, E. (1994). Victim Participation in Sentencing: And the Debate Goes On.... *International Review of Victimology, 3*(1–2), 17–32.

Erez, E. (1999, July). Who's Afraid of the Big Bad Victim: Victim Impact Statements as Victim Empowerment and Enhancement of Justice. *Criminal Law Review, 1999*, 545–556.

Erez, E., & King, T. A. (2000). Patriarchal Terrorism or Common Couple Violence: Attorneys' Views of Prosecuting and Defending Woman Batterers. *International Review of Victimology, 7*(1–3), 207–226.

Erez, E., & Roberts, J. V. (2013). Victim Participation in Criminal Justice. In R. C. Davis, A. J. Lurigio, & S. Herman (Eds.), *Victims of Crime* (4th ed., pp. 251–270). SAGE: Thousand Oaks.

Erez, E., & Rogers, L. (1999). Victim Impact Statements and Sentencing Outcomes and Processes: The Perspectives of Legal Professionals. *British Journal of Criminology, 39*(2), 216–239.

Erez, E., & Tontodonato, P. (1992). Victim Participation in Justice and Satisfaction with Justice. *Justice Quarterly, 9*(3), 393–427.

Erez, E., Ibarra, P. R., & Downs, D. M. (2011). Victim Participation Reforms in the United States and Victim Welfare: A Therapeutic Jurisdiction Perspective. In E. Erez, M. Kilchling, & J. Wemmers (Eds.), *Victim Participation in Proceedings and Therapeutic Jurisprudence* (pp. 15–40). Durham: North Carolina Press.

Erez, E., Globokar, J. L., & Ibarra, P. R. (2014). Outsiders Inside: Victim Management in an Era of Participatory Reforms. *International Review of Victimology, 20*(1), 169–188.

Fair Work Commission. (2018). *Client Experience Feedback & Research* [Online]. Retrieved January 11, 2019, from https://www.fwc.gov.au/about-us/consultation/client-experience-feedback-research.

Feeley, M. M. (1979). *The Process Is the Punishment: Handling Cases in a Lower Criminal Court.* New York: Russell Sage Foundation.

Fenwick, H. (1997). Procedural Rights of Victims of Crime: Public or Private Ordering of the Criminal Justice Process. *Modern Law Review, 60*(3), 317–333.

Finch, J. E. (1985). A History of the Consumer Movement in the United States: Its Literature and Legislation. *Journal of Consumer Studies and Home Economics, 9*(1), 23–33.

Fletcher, G. P. (1999). The Place of Victims in the Theory of Retribution. *Buffalo Criminal Law Review, 3*(1), 51–63.

Fogel, J., & Murphy, K. (2018). Intentions to Use the TripAdvisor Review Website and Purchase Behavior After Reading Reviews. *Human IT, 14*(1), 59–100.

Frohmann, L. (1991). Discrediting Victims' Allegations of Sexual Assault: Prosecutorial Accounts of Case Rejections. *Social Problems, 38*(2), 213–226.

Garland, D. (2001). *The Culture of Control: Crime and Social Order in a Contemporary Society.* Chicago: University of Chicago Press.

Giant, P. (2014). *Youthlaw Mobile: User Research.* Melbourne: Paper Giant.

Globokar, J. L. & Erez, E. (2019). Conscience and Convenience: American Victim Work in Organizational Context. *International Review of Victimology, 25*(3), 341–357

Globokar, J. L., Erez, E., & Gregory, C. R. (2019). Beyond Advocacy: Mapping the Contours of Victim Work. *Journal of Interpersonal Violence, 34*(6), 1198–1223.

Gollop, R., Whitby, E., Buchanan, D., & Ketley, D. (2004). Influencing Sceptical Staff to Become Supporters of Service Improvement: A Qualitative Study of Doctors' and Managers' Views. *Quality and Safety in Health Care, 13*(2), 108–114.

Goodey, J. (2005). *Victims and Victimology: Research, Police and Practice.* Essex: Pearson Education Limited.

Gorin, M., Joffe, S., Dickert, N., & Halpern, S. (2017). Justifying Clinical Nudges. *Hastings Center Report, 47*(2), 32–38.

Greenfield, S., Kaplan, S., & Ware, J. E. (1985). Expanding Patient Involvement in Care: Effects on Patient Outcomes. *Annals of Internal Medicine, 102*(4), 520–528.

Greer, C. (2017). News Media, Victims and Crime. In P. Davies, P. Francis, & C. Greer (Eds.), *Victims, Crime and Society* (pp. 20–49). London: Sage.

Gwyn, R., & Elwyn, G. (1999). When Is a Shared Decision Not (Quite) a Shared Decision? Negotiating Preferences in a General Practice Encounter. *Social Science and Medicine, 49*(4), 437–447.

Hagan, M. (2018). *Law by Design* [Online]. Retrieved June 22, 2019, from http://www.lawbydesign.co/en/home/.

Hakhverdian, A., & Mayne, Q. (2012). Institutional Trust, Education and Corruption: A Micro-Macro Interactive Approach. *Journal of Politics, 74*(3), 739–750.

Hall, M. (2010). *Victims and Policy Making: A Comparative Perspective.* New York: Willan Publishing.

Harrison, T., Waite, K., & Hunter, G. (2006). The Internet, Information and Empowerment. *European Journal of Marketing, 40*(9/10), 972–993.

Herman, J. L. (2005). Justice from the Victim's Perspective. *Violence Against Women, 11*(5), 571–602.

Herman, S. (2010). *Parallel Justice for Victims of Crime.* Washington, DC: National Center for Victims of Crime.

Hermanns, N., et al. (2013). The Effect of a Diabetes Education Programme (PRIMAS) for People with Type 1 Diabetes: Results of a Randomized Trial. *Diabetes Research and Clinical Practice, 102*(3), 149–157.

Hudson, B. (2002). 'Restorative Justice and Gendered Violence: Diversion or Effective Justice? *British Journal of Criminology, 42*(3), 616–634.

Jackson, J. (2003). Justice for All: Putting Victims at the Heart of Criminal Justice? *Journal of Law and Society, 30*(2), 309–326.

Kennedy, J. F. (1962). *Special Message to Congress on Protecting Consumer Interest* [Online]. Retrieved January 24, 2019, from https://www.jfklibrary.org/asset-viewer/archives/JFKPOF/037/JFKPOF-037-028.

Kidd, R. F., & Chayet, E. F. (1984). Why Do Victims Fail to Report? The Psychology of Criminal Victimization. *Journal of Social Issues, 40*(1), 39–50.

King, M., Frieberg, A., Batagol, B., & Hyams, R. (2009). *Non-Adversarial Justice*. Sydney: Federation Press.

Kirchengast, T. (2006). *The Victim in Criminal Law and Justice*. Basingstoke, UK: Palgrave Macmillan.

Kirchengast, T. (2010). *The Criminal Trial in Law and Discourse*. Basingstoke, UK: Palgrave Macmillan.

Kirchengast, T. (2016). *Victims and the Criminal Trial*. Basingstoke, UK: Palgrave Macmillan.

Lakoff, G., & Johnson, M. (1980). *Metaphors We Live By*. Chicago; London: The University of Chicago Press.

Laster, K. (2018, 1 June). Designing Digital Justice. *Law Institute Journal, 92*(6), 20–21.

Laster, K., & Erez, E. (2000). The Oprah Dilemma: The Use and Abuse of Victims. In D. Chappell & P. Wilson (Eds.), *Crime and the Criminal Justice System in Australia: 2000 and Beyond*. Sydney: Butterworths.

Laster, K., & Kornhauser, R. (2017). The Rise of 'DIY' Law: Implications for Legal Aid. In A. Flynn & J. Hodgson (Eds.), *Access to Justice and Legal Aid: Comparative Perspectives on Unmet Legal Need* (pp. 123–140). Portland: Hart Publishing.

Lee, J., Seo, E., Choi, J., & Min, J. (2018). Effects of Patient Participation in the Management of Daily Nursing Goals on Function Recovery and Resilience in Surgical Patients. *Journal of Clinical Nursing, 27*(13), 2795–2803.

Lonsway, K. A., & Fitzgerald, L. F. (1994). Rape Myths: In Review. *Psychology of Women Quarterly, 18*(2), 133–164.

Loseke, D. R., & Cahill, S. E. (1984). The Social Construction of Deviance: Experts on Battered Women. *Social Problems, 31*(3), 296–310.

Martin, N., Gregor, S., & Rice, J. (2008). User Centred Information Design Practices and Processes at the Australian Taxation Office. *Information Design Journal, 16*(1), 53–67.

McCold, P. (2006). The Recent History of Restorative Justice: Mediation, Circles, and Conferencing. In D. Sullivan & L. Tifft (Eds.), *Handbook of Restorative Justice: A Global Perspective* (pp. 23–51). New York: Routledge.

Morris, A. (2002). Critiquing the Critics: A Brief Response to Critics of Restorative Justice. *British Journal of Criminology, 42*(3), 596–615.

National Health Service. (2018). *Digital Inclusion Guide for Health and Social Care.* NHS Digital.

National Health Service. (n.d.). *Developing Patient Centred Care* [Online]. Retrieved January 16, 2019, from https://www.england.nhs.uk/integrated-care-pioneers/resources/patient-care/.

Noveck, B. (2015). *Smart Citizens, Smarter State: The Technologies of Expertise and the Future of Governing.* Cambridge: Harvard University Press.

O'Connor, S. D. (2003). *The Majesty of the Law: Reflections of a Supreme Court Justice.* New York: Random House.

O'Hara, E. A. (2005). Victim Participation in the Criminal Process. *Journal of Law and Policy, 13*(1), 229–247.

Organisation for Economic Co-operation and Development. (1987). *Administration as a Service: The Public as Client.* Paris: OECD Publications.

Packer, H. L. (1964). Two Models of the Criminal Process. *University of Pennsylvania Law Review, 113*(1), 1–68.

Pear, R. (2010). If Only Laws Were Like Sausages. *New York Times.* Retrieved September 4, 2010, from https://www.nytimes.com/2010/12/05/weekinreview/05pear.html.

Peterson Armour, M., & Umbreit, M. S. (2006). Victim Forgiveness in Restorative Justice Dialogue. *Victims and Offenders, 1*(2), 123–140.

Piggott, E., & Wood, W. (2019). Does Restorative Justice Reduce Recidivism: Assessing Evidence and Claims About Restorative Justice and Reoffending. In T. Gavrielides (Ed.), *Routledge International Handbook of Restorative Justice* (pp. 387–404). New York: Routledge.

Pires, G., Stanton, J., & Rita, P. (2006). The Internet, Consumer Empowerment and Marketing Strategies. *European Journal of Marketing, 40*(9/10), 936–949.

Pounder, J. S. (2007). Is Student Evaluation of Teaching Worthwhile? An Analytical Framework for Answering the Question. *Quality Assurance in Education, 15*(2), 178–191.

Regehr, C., & Alaggia, R. (2006). Perspectives of Justice for Victims of Sexual Violence. *Victims and Offenders, 1*(1), 33–46.

Richardson, L. L. (2013). Impact of Marsy's Law on Parole in California. *Criminal Law Bulletin, 49*, 1091, 1115–1116, 1119–1120.

Ries, T. E., et al. (2018). *2018 Trust Barometer: Global Report*. Sydney: Edelman Australia.

Roberts, J. V. (2009). Listening to Crime Victims: Evaluating Victim Input at Sentencing and Parole. *Crime and Justice, 38*(1), 347–412.

Roberts, J. V., Crutcher, N., & Verbrugge, P. (2007). Public Attitudes to Sentencing in Canada: Exploring Recent Findings. *Canadian Journal of Criminology and Criminal Justice, 49*(1), 75–107.

Rosteck, T. (2018). *Participant Satisfaction Survey – April to November 2018* [Online]. Retrieved January 11, 2019, from https://civilresolutionbc.ca/participant-satisfaction-survey-april-november-2018/.

Roumie, C. L., et al. (2011). Patient Centered Primary Care Is Associated with Patient Hypertension Medication Adherence. *Journal of Behavioural Medicine, 34*(4), 244–253.

Ryan, N. (2001). Reconstructing Citizens as Consumers: Implications for New Modes of Governance. *Australian Journal of Public Administration, 30*(3), 104–109.

Salter, S., & Thompson, D. (2016–2017). Public-Centred Civil Justice Redesign: A Case Study of the British Columbia Civil Resolution Tribunal. *McGill Journal of Dispute Resolution, 3*, 113–136.

Schafer, S. (1960). *Restitution to Victims of Crime*. London: Stevens and Sons.

Schuster, M. L., & Propen, A. (2011). Degrees of Emotion: Judicial Responses to Victim Impact Statements. *Law, Culture and the Humanities, 6*(1), 75–104.

Sherlock, R. (1986). Reasonable Men and Sick Human Beings. *The American Journal of Medicine, 80*(1), 2–4.

Smith, A. (n.d.). *About the Bureau of Consumer Protection* [Online]. Retrieved January 24, 2019, from https://www.ftc.gov/about-ftc/bureaus-offices/bureau-consumer-protection/about-bureau-consumer-protection.

Spencer, P. (2017). A View from the Bench: A Judicial Perspective on legal Representation, Court Excellence and Therapeutic Justice. In A. Flynn & J. Hodgson (Eds.), *Access to Justice and Legal Aid: Comparative Perspectives on Unmet Legal Need* (pp. 87–102). Portland, OR: Hart Publishing.

Starkweather, D. A. (1992). The Retributive Theory of "Just Deserts" and Victim Participation in Plea Bargaining. *Indiana Law Review, 67*(3), 853–878.

Storrs, L. R. Y. (2006). Left-Feminism, the Consumer Movement, and Red Scare Politics in the United States, 1935–1960. *Journal of Women's History, 18*(3), 40–67.

Strang, H., & Braithwaite, J. (2001). *Restorative Justice and Civil Society*. Cambridge: Cambridge University Press.

Strull, W., Lo, B., & Charles, G. (1984). Do Patients Want to Participate in Medical Decision Making? *Journal of the American Medical Association, 252*(21), 2990–2994.

Sudnow, D. (1965). Normal Crimes: Sociological Features of the Penal Code in a Public Defender Office. *Social Problems, 12*(3), 255–276.

Tapley, J. (2005). Public Confidence Costs – Criminal Justice from a Victim's Perspective. *British Journal of Criminal Justice, 3*(2), 25–37.

Thompson, L., & McCabe, R. (2012). The Effect of Clinician-Patient Alliance and Communication on Treatment Adherence in Mental Health Care: A Systematic Review. *BMC Psychiatry, 12*(87), 1–12.

Tyler, T. R. (2003). Procedural Justice, Legitimacy, and the Effective Rule of Law. *Crime and Justice, 30*(1), 283–357.

U.S. Department of Justice. (2012). *Victimizations not Reported to the Police 2006–2010: Special Report.* Washington, DC: Office of Justice Programs Bureau of Justice Statistics.

Ullman, S. E. (2010). *Talking About Sexual Assault: Society's Response to Survivors.* Washington, DC: American Psychological Association.

Van Camp, T., & Wemmers, J.-A. (2013). Victim Satisfaction with Restorative Justice: More Than Simply Procedural Justice. *International Review of Victimology, 19*(2), 117–143.

Van Loo, R. (2017). Rise of the Digital Regulator. *Duke Law Journal, 66*(6), 1267–1329.

Vanfraechem, I., Pemberton, A., & Ndahinda, F. M. (2014). *Justice for Victims: Perspectives on Rights, Transition and Reconciliation.* New York: Routledge.

van Velsen, L., van der Geest, T., ter Hedde, M., & Derks, W. (2009). Requirements Engineering for e-Government Services: A Citizen-Centric Approach and Case Study. *Government Information Quarterly, 26*(3), 477–486.

Warne, C. L. (1973). The Consumer Movement and the Labor Movement. *Journal of Economic Issues, 7*(2), 307–316.

Wemmers, J.-A., & Cyr, K. (2004). Victims' Perspectives on Restorative Justice: How Much Involvement Are Victims Looking For? *International Review of Victimology, 11*(2–3), 259–274.

Werner, R. O. (1962). Regulation of Product Characteristics. *Journal of Marketing, 26*(3), 84–86.

Wexler, D. B. (1993). Therapeutic Jurisprudence and the Criminal Courts. *William and Mary Law Review, 35*(1), 279–299.

Wexler, D. B. (2008). Crime Victims, Law Students, and Therapeutic Jurisprudence Training. In D. B. Wexler (Ed.), *Rehabilitating Lawyers: Principles of Therapeutic Jurisprudence for Criminal Law Practice* (pp. 323–326). Durham: Carolina Academic Press.

Williams, B. (1999a). The Victim's Charter: Citizens as Consumers of Criminal Justice Services. *The Howard Journal, 38*(4), 384–396.

Williams, B. (1999b). *Working with Victims of Crime: Policies, Politics and Practice.* London: Jessica Kingsley Publishers.

Wilson, D., Olaghere, A., & Kimbrell, C. (2017). *Effectiveness of Restorative Justice Principles in Juvenile Justice: A Meta-Analysis.* Washington, DC: US Department of Justice Office of Justice Programs.

Winick, B. J. (2011). Therapeutic Jurisprudence and Victims of Crime. In E. Erez, M. Kilchling, & J. Wemmers (Eds.), *Victim Participation in Proceedings and Therapeutic Jurisprudence* (pp. 3–14). Durham: Carolina Academic Press.

Winick, B. J., & Wexler, D. B. (2001). Drug Treatment Court: Therapeutic Jurisprudence Applied. *Touro Law Review, 18*(3), 479–486.

Youthlaw. (2015). *Street Smart* [Online]. Retrieved June 22, 2019, from https://streetsmartvic.com.au/.

Zweig, J. M., & Yahner, J. (2013). Providing Services to Victims of Crime. In R. C. Davis, A. J. Lurigio, & S. Herman (Eds.), *Victims of Crime* (4th ed., pp. 325–348). Thousand Oaks, CA: Sage Publications.

14

A Theory of Injustice and Victims' Participation in Criminal Processes

Antony Pemberton

Introduction

A key topic in the short history of victimology concerns the role of victims in criminal proceedings. One of the driving forces behind the study of victims of crime under the heading of victimology is the understanding that criminal justice processes were neglecting victims' interests and that practices and routines of criminal justice could result in serious harm to victims. Much of this is rooted in the practical experiences of different groups of victims as well as those working directly with victims. This realization has led academics, policy-makers and practitioners at the level of national jurisdictions and supra- and international bodies to undertake initiatives seeking to remedy this. Broadly speaking, these initiatives can be divided into three categories. The first keeps a safe distance from interfering with the criminal justice process and its key rationales (e.g. Goodey 2005; Pemberton 2009). It draws on empirical evidence that emphasizes

A. Pemberton (✉)
LINC, KU Leuven, Leuven, Belgium

NSCR, Amsterdam, The Netherlands
e-mail: antony.pemberton@kuleuven.be

© The Author(s) 2020
J. Tapley, P. Davies (eds.), *Victimology*,
https://doi.org/10.1007/978-3-030-42288-2_14

the independent importance of improving the procedural experience of participants in justice processes and transplanting that perspective to victims in criminal justice (Wemmers 1996). It thereby seeks to improve the experience of victims by introducing key constructs of the domain of procedural justice, like respectful treatment, information and voice, maintaining that such improvements do not and should not influence or diminish due process, the rights of the suspect and/or the offender and the prerogative of the state to adjudicate crime and its aftermath. The second merges the rationales of criminal justice with a victimological perspective. Unlike the first perspective, it is specifically focused on the outcome of the criminal justice process, the sentencing of the offender, and considers that the victim has too little say over this outcome, and is particularly impoverished in comparison to the protections the system offers the suspect/the offender (Scheingold et al. 1994). It is the type of victimological perspective that is therefore often invoked in 'law and order' campaigns that primarily focuses on rebalancing the rights between victims and the rights of suspects and offenders.

The third adopts a more critical stance towards criminal justice. Both the process and the outcome should be rethought. A clear, albeit not the only, example is the literature on restorative justice (RJ). In the processes it proposes—mediation and conferencing—and in the outcomes it seeks—a focus on repairing harm done, rather than punishment; it seeks to supplement, change or even transform the societal-institutional reaction to crime (Marshall 1999; Walgrave 2008). It does so with the specific intention of improving the plight of victims of crime, proposing to offer both processes and outcomes that are more harmonious with victims' experiences (Strang 2002; Zehr 1990). In its critical stance, the perspective in this chapter is akin to that of RJ, although as I will develop below, it also offers the possibility to offer—positive—criticism of RJ. It concerns the development of a *theory of injustice*, which will provide the basis for a victimological perspective on justice processes. The first step in this theory is understanding that injustice needs to be viewed as 'an independent phenomenon in its own right' rather than as an opposite/derivative/antithesis of justice, while the extent to which justice can or is even intended to be a reaction to the experience of injustice has inherent limits. This draws heavily on the work of political thinker Judith Shklar (1990, 1964/1986; see also Pemberton 2015; Pemberton and Aarten 2017).

A consequence of viewing justice and injustice as poles of one dimension is that the experience of injustice is framed in constructs that are derived from justice. One of those features is the centrality of rules guiding the relationships between people to justice, and as a consequence, conceptualizing injustice as a breaking of these rules. I will propose that this in particular neglects that what matters most in experiences of victimization is, as J.M. Bernstein put it, not 'broken rules, but broken bodies and ruined lives' (Bernstein 2015: 4). Drawing on Matthew Ratcliffe's (2008) concept of existential feelings and Susan Brison's (2002) phenomenology of victimization, I will argue that this entails understanding first that injustice concerns a relationship of victim with his or her self, rather than a relationship with other persons, and second that this self is only accurately understood if it is understood as being-in-the-world. The experience of injustice then comes into its own, when it amounts to an *ontological assault*: damage, diminishment or even destruction of the way people normally and unreflectively exist in the world.

The theory of injustice has various upshots for the conceptualization of victims' perspectives on justice processes. Countering injustice concerns itself with the *fact of victimization*, which relies upon the first-person interpretation of the situation and can be distinguished from the manner in which justice processes conceive of victimization, which follows the epistemology and logic of the law conception of ethics. This distinction is similar to that between illness and disease in the philosophy of medicine (Pellegrino 1979), and even more pertinent due to the socially constructed and political nature of the law. Like Pellegrino, I will argue the importance of the Aristotlean virtue of *phronesis* in the institutional response concerned with the fact of victimization. In the final section, I will sketch some of the implications for a victimological perspective (on participation) in justice processes.

A Theory of Injustice

In her work, Shklar (1990) criticized the 'normal model' of justice and the way that injustice is portrayed in this 'normal model'. In many theories of ethics and morality, examples of victimization and suffering provide a starting point—but no more than that—for reflection on the key elements of (processes of) justice. Injustice is then viewed, in seeming coherence with its etymology, as a lack of justice, as one pole with justice, as another side of one dimension with justice. Because the normal model understands injustice and justice as one dimension, this makes justice the obvious counterforce against suffering wrongdoing. Moreover, in the 'normal model', justice is viewed as something that should be considered in abstract, which can apply irrespective of people's history and relations, that is, be universal, and upon which reasoned debate will converge, as being a matter of rational thinking. It is a perspective that rules out the context of institutions of justice, and/or of the actual functioning of processes of justice. That processes of justice in reality do not function in such an idealized manner cannot amount to an argument against justice, but amounts to an indictment of reality instead.

In *Legalism*, Shklar already argued against this position (Shklar 1986). Or more to the point, Shklar claimed that the virtue of justice could be strengthened by acknowledging its limitations. That was due to her moral scepticism: her conviction that key moral questions will only emerge in reality and cannot be settled once and for all beforehand (see also Yack 1999). And it was also due to her commitment to pluralism: her belief that many of our fundamental values can and will be at odds with each other. Freedom might conflict with welfare, different freedoms likewise. Disputing these matters will need continuous attention, as they are contingent on the social and political context. The key to our current subject is Shklar's view that systems of justice might intend to counter injustice, but also and more fundamentally focus on order and regularity, as she put it 'well-oiled social functioning'. Systems of criminal justice can be understood in this light. The antipathy to private revenge is a case in point, as in Francis Bacon's dictum: 'Revenge is a kind of wild justice, which the more a man's nature runs to, the more ought law to weed it out'. Processes of compensation, reconciliation through payment to the injured party, pre-dating formal criminal justice and co-existing with private revenge, also served to pacify the victim and any desire to take matters into his or her own hands. The goal of this pacification is to maintain regularity and order. But this system can only truly be understood if what it seeks to restore is not an antecedent condition of justice, but one of social order.

The notion that initially there is a just situation, which is thrown into disarray by injustice and subsequently returned to tranquility by (the outcome of) a justice process, does not stand up to much scrutiny, even though it is the—often implicit—view in the 'normal model' of justice. This is the topic of the Elizabeth Wolgast's (1987) book *The Grammar of Justice*. Following a homicide, sexual violence or the torture of a child, the punishment of the offender might provide some satisfaction, but it cannot be said to restore the situation to the way it was before the offence. The victim does not regain life nor has she become un-raped or un-tortured.

To this, two separate points of critique may be added. The first, notes that the suffering of the offender, even if it was equal to that experienced by the victim, differs because it is his or her just deserts, unlike the victim, who suffered unfairly (Wolgast 1987). In the second—a staple of the restorative justice literature—it is maintained that the suffering of the offender, rather than restoring a prior balance, merely adds his or her suffering to that of the victims or the offender, thereby increasing the amount of pain in the world (e.g. Zehr 1990). Indeed, the notion that at any point in time a fully just situation existed is contradicted by the historical record and the present occurrence of injustices (Shklar 1990). Even a cursory examination reveals the ubiquity of unchecked murder, violence and even massacre and genocide throughout the ages, while any introductory criminology text-book will provide a compendium of the prevalence—the so-called dark figure—of crimes committed with de facto impunity today.

This is not intended to be an argument against (processes of) justice, but does speak against the way they are normally viewed: what is restored or maintained by systems of justice is not an imaginary just situation predating injustice, but social order in society. It is therefore not in first instance intended to rectify the injustice that has occurred, and victimological research has repeatedly confirmed that it does not in practice succeed in such an aim in any case. Instead these outcomes seek to maintain order so that 'we can move on' with our various projects and the 'victims have to learn to live with them', as Shklar (1990) concluded. This applies to systems of retributive punishment, which RJ-thinkers have rightly noted. But it is not restricted to this: it also applies to the more 'constructive' alternatives to punishment that these thinkers often suggest, like apologies, atonement or compensation. I have no doubt in the value of criticising punishment as a means to restoring the situation before the occurrence of injustice. But the most fundamental issue concerns not the means used—punishment or 'infliction of pain'—but the twin assumptions that a previous situation can be restored and that this is what a system of justice truly sets out to do. Instead justice, as Shklar argued, is both narrower and wider than countering injustice. Its central aim of 'well-oiled social functioning' concerns order and regularity and emphasizes rules and universality. Following this perspective, it views the experience of injustice in terms of rule-breaking and seeks to impose norms and solutions to this rule-breaking that apply across situations. But it therefore does not and cannot include a full picture of injustice.

Shklar already assembled much of the materials that a justice perspective on victimization airbrushes out of the picture, which includes much of what matters most to victims: the personal details of what it felt like, their story past and present, the imprints it left on their memory and their body and the particular meaning that the event had in their lives.

Unfortunately, Shklar passed away in 1992, before she could grasp the full scope of the question she posed. Moral scepticism, value pluralism and the inherent limits of justice reactions to injustice already underline the importance of viewing injustice as a phenomenon in its own right, but leave open the possibility that experiences of injustice are still derived from different, competing or more general notions of justice (Nussbaum 1990).

The discrepancy between the system of justice in use and these other notions can be helpfully illuminated by victims' experiences, and this is in itself already a reason to include victims' perspectives. It emphasizes the importance of avoiding equating 'doing justice', with 'countering injustice' (Yack 1999). That would hide the reality that we could meet the requirements of justice, without having much impact on the lived experience of injustice. This would reduce the extent to which such lived experience of injustice could act as a means to legitimately criticize processes of justice. Put more simply, doing justice and countering injustice, both to the extent possible, are overlapping but distinct activities. What countering injustice in a particular situation might require, often can and will run counter to the requirements of what it means to do justice. Separating the two offers the possibility to harness the experience of countering injustice to accommodate the reality that we cannot settle the answers to all moral issues in advance, for the possibility that people will have varying views on the underlying values, also depending on social and political context, and the acknowledgement that justice processes are limited in what they can do to counter injustice, because their prime directive is maintaining order and regularity.

The Relationship with Others and the Relationship Within the Self

Nevertheless, this might be as far as Shklar's critique goes. Bernard Yack (1999) argued: 'murder, and I would say injustice in general, invokes a harm such as killing, plus *the violation of some expectations we have about the behaviour of others*'. The last clause is crucial: Yack equates this with a basic sense of justice, whether it concerns 'moral judgements about the high standards of behaviour we expect from rational and civilized creatures, or…little more than the habits formed by repetitive actions of one sort or another'. In his view, a full-blown sense of a just order of things might not be necessary in order to recognize injustice, but a *sense of justice* is. People might use their experiences of 'broken bones, ruined lives' to amend or criticize systems of rules, but this criticism will at most lead us to adopt a different set of rules. We cannot escape the fact that 'broken rules', in the form of a 'violation of some expectations we have about the behaviour of others' are an indispensable element of such an experience.

This is not the way I would understand Shklar though. I think there is more to the experience of injustice than that can be captured as something that concerns the relationship between people, 'the behaviour of others' as well as includes 'an expectation', a sufficiently intentional experience that it can be seen as an—albeit rudimentary—rule. In my view, both these assumptions arise from viewing injustice in terms relevant to justice, rather than on its own terms, and it obscures the reality that much of the experience of injustice contradicts these assumptions. In particular, I will argue first that we cannot truly understand the experience of injustice if we do not understand its nature as damage to, diminishment of or even destruction of the relationship we have with our selves, rather than with others. And second, much of what this damage/diminishment/destruction entails concerns experience we have of the self that form the taken-for-granted backdrop of our lives. We only become aware of this backdrop in the aftermath of the victimization, rather than as an intentional expectation beforehand. Indeed, even in this aftermath (the consequences of) this experience, it remains difficult and even impossible to put into words.

A first step in understanding can draw on Nietzsche's line of criticism of Christian morality (Nietzsche 1888/1967). He argued that this morality conflates two separate relationships. As Nietzsche-scholar, Clark (2000) concluded: 'In Nietzsche's account of moral guilt, there are two different realms: the relationship of the individual to someone she has injured or faulted in some way and then the self's relationship to the standards she accepts for a good person. Moral guilt makes it easy to conflate these two issues'. A similar issue was raised by Bernard Williams (1993), as Clark (2000) emphasizes 'Williams located morality's confusion between the relationship to others and one's relation to one's own standards of goodness or worth in the conflation between obligations to others and the all things considered judgement of practical necessity. Where the former concerns the expectations that others are right to have of me, the latter concerns the experience of what I must do as a matter of maintaining my own identity'.

In both Nietzsche and Williams' cases, the argument concerns the perpetration of wrongdoing, but it also illuminates a reality that is relevant to the suffering of wrongdoing and for the distinction between justice and injustice. We have obligations in the domain of our relationships to others, and failing them or transgressing them is the concern of justice. But this does not exhaust our relationships. Beyond the realm of relationships between people, there is a realm of the relationship within the self. Justice concerns the ordering of the former relationship, but it does not follow that this then also applies to the experience of injustice. In the next section, I will make the case for understanding injustice as concerning a relationship with the self, although I caution that the self needs to be understood in a particular manner.

An Ontological Assault: The Role of 'Existential Feelings' in Victimization

In recent publications, my colleagues and I have taken to referring to severe forms of victimization as an 'ontological assault', an attack on being (see Pemberton et al. 2019). The phrase 'ontological assault' was coined in the description of the phenomenology of life-threatening illness (Pellegrino 1979). It also maintains the double meaning that the phrase has in this literature. First, it concerns a clear and present threat to the victim's existence, a confrontation with the reality of one's demise, the end of one's being. Second, it also highlights features of being that previously were taken for granted and/or remained implicit. Illness 'transforms the "lived body" in which self and body are unified and act as one in the world to the "object body" where the body is a source of constraint and is in opposition to the self' (Garro 1992: 104, see also Gadow 1980). This makes explicit the extent to which the manner in which the body-self unity is an implicit but necessary backdrop to the way we normally exist.

Severe forms of victimization have a similar potential to 'unmake the world' (Janoff-Bulman 1992, see also Crossley 2000). Victimization not only reveals the reality and possibility of the threat posed by others but also exposes features of one's existence, precisely through the damage it does to them. To understand the nature of this damage, recent work by philosopher Matthew Ratcliffe is key (Ratcliffe 2008, 2012, 2017; Ratcliffe et al 2014).

Ratcliffe (2008) discusses a class of affective experience that concerns ways of finding oneself in the world, which shape all experience, thought and activity. These 'existential feelings' concern 'the intimate association between feeling, how one finds oneself in the world and one's grasp of reality' (Ratcliffe 2012). Examples are experiencing contingency, uncertainty, insecurity and homelessness. When existential feelings remain stable, we are most often oblivious to their role. But in change, particularly where such change is sudden, we experience this change and/or the absence of the way the world felt before. This offers a glimpse of these existential feelings. However, because these existential feelings normally form an implicit taken-for-granted backdrop for experience, they are likely to be difficult to describe. 'These feelings are not usually explicit objects of experience or thought—we tend to be pre-occupied by what is going on in the world, rather than with the backdrop against which those happenings are intelligible' (Ratcliffe 2012). This poverty of vocabulary to describe such shifts in existential feelings is further enhanced because of the lack of interpretative resources to make sense of them. 'If we fail to acknowledge that experience incorporates a background sense of belonging to a world, then we will inevitably misinterpret an alteration of this sense of belonging in terms of something else' (Ratcliffe 2012). Due to this, it is highly likely that the terms used in theories of justice become affixed to victimization experiences, even if that does not fully reflect the reality of these experiences.

Ratcliffe's main source of evidence for the phenomenon of existential feelings is derived from the first-person experience of psychological disorder, including depression and schizophrenia, but it includes victimization and trauma as well (see Ratcliffe 2017; Ratcliffe et al 2014). Three issues are pertinent. First, Ratcliffe's perspective offers an understanding that victimization first concerns (an alteration in) the sense of self, that is, as a shift in existential feelings. Second, it emphasizes the fact that this self can only be accurately understood as being-in-the-world, rather than the so-called modern Cartesian subject, which is still the default model for most work in social sciences. Third, it offers the insight that the nature of the experience of victimization renders it suspect to frame such experience in terms of (transgressions of) expectations, assumptions and beliefs. Existential feelings operate at the 'pre-intentional' level: before intentional states of mind such as expectations, assumptions and beliefs are formed about what should and should not happen in the world, one already has to find oneself in it (Ratcliffe 2017; Ratcliffe et al 2014). The interpretation of what should have been expected, assumed and believed is then retrospectively applied to the experience, as a consequence of meaning and sense-making in the aftermath of experience, rather than something that existed prior to its occurrence.

Narrative Foreclosure and Radical Loneliness: Brison's Phenomenology

Alice Sebold (1999), a victim of rape, succinctly laid out the core of her experience in *Lucky*. She 'was now on the other side of something they could not understand'. And she added, 'I did not understand it myself'.

The experience fundamentally changed the way she experienced life: 'My life was different from other people's; it was natural that I behaved differently'. She related this difference to a sense of ubiquitous ominousness: 'Threat was everywhere. No place or person was safe'.

Sebold's memoir offers many examples of the role of the shift in existential feelings in severe forms of victimization and the difficulty of accurately understanding and verbalizing this experience. This experience receives its most full-blown treatment in Susan Brison's (2002) brilliant *Aftermath: violence and the remaking of the self*. Brison was a victim of rape and attempted murder, and *Aftermath* is the book in which she puts her philosophical acumen to the task of developing a phenomenology of experiencing rape and living through the consequences. In this, she also invokes the testimonies of other survivors of violence, rape and even genocide and the Holocaust. She points to the three different interconnected ways in which her sense of self was impacted by her experience: the damage to her *embodied self*, her *self as narrative* and her *autonomous self*.

The Embodied Self

The first is the embodied self. Before the rape, Brison and her husband were trying to conceive for the first time. Like Pellegrino's perspective on illness, Brison found: 'I was no longer the same person I was before the assault, and one of the ways I seemed changed was that I had a different relationship with my body. My body was now perceived as an enemy, having betrayed my newfound trust and interest in it, and as a site of increased vulnerability'. Victimization here impacts the taken-for-granted relationship with our body. As J.M. Bernstein (2015) analysed Brison's work, at the same time, we *are* our body and we *have* our body. The latter refers to the control we believe to have over our own body, while the former refers to the fact that embodiment is our main avenue of physical existence *in* and interaction *with* the world. Victimization separates these two: we still are our body, but no longer feel to be in control of it. The rapist took over the control of Brison's body, and in the aftermath, her body appeared as alien and even as an enemy. The experience of rape therefore reminds us forcibly of our embodiment, while rendering us extremely vulnerable by diminishing or destroying our sense of control. As Carole Winkler (1991)—another rape victim—described it: 'Our existence becomes like a body on life support'.

The Narrative Self

Such taken-for-grantedness also concerns more abstract ways in which we are in the world. Brison discusses her experience of her self as narrative. Identity is fundamentally storied: we construct our own life stories, while our life stories help us understand ourselves as continuous beings from the past into the present into the future and as connected to our close and distant social surroundings (Ricoeur 1986). Severe forms of victimization pose a threat to such narrative identity: causing a narrative rupture in people's lives, who struggle to make sense of the relationship between their lives before, during and after victimization and the implications of this moving forward into the future (Crossley 2000; Pemberton et al. 2019). Such a rupture also concerns the continuity with our social surroundings. Here the phenomenon of 'narrative foreclosure' is important (Freeman 2000). Brison speaks about the disappearance of the past and the foreshortening of the future, the narrowing of her normal sense of self as being past, present and future all at once, to being a momentary self, a residue of self lingering on even after the life story has effectively ended. 'Like animals, we were confined to the present moment.' Auschwitz survivor Primo Levi (1988) summarized this experience. The difficulty, or perhaps inability, to experience oneself as temporal, forms the backdrop of such narrative foreclosure. But the ability to experience this temporality is key to human existence, which is most crucially distinguished from things and—perhaps more debatably—animals in that the latter instead occur as a succession of 'nows', simply being present at discrete moments in time.

Again, the taken-for-granted manner in which we exist as temporal beings-in-the-world is diminished or devastated in similar fashion to our embodied selves (Ratcliffe 2017; Ratcliffe et al 2014). This similarity also applies to the necessity and difficulty of speaking to others as a means to counter the experience of injustice. Again, language fails survivors in communication of these shifts in existential feelings, of which such temporality could also be an example. It is in this light that Primo Levi's observation: 'our language lacks the words to express this experience, a demolition of a man' can be understood. The Alice Sebold quote above 'on the other side of something they could not understand' reveals the degree to which the absence of what was taken-for-granted is key to understand what victimization entails, while simultaneously revealing the awareness on the part of the victims that others still take-for-granted what the victim has lost. This fact means that they do not expect these others to be able to fathom what they have been through. And that in the victim's social surroundings, all too often others confirm this lack of understanding, thereby exacerbating this experience.

The Autonomous Self

Finally, Brison talks about the damage to her autonomous self. The damage to her embodied self, and her self as narrative, left her with almost insurmountable challenges to understand herself as being able to pursue her own final ends, the goals and the relationships that provide the horizon of her life. We noted the difficulty it raised to her desire of becoming a mother, while narrative foreclosure renders projecting, planning and pressing forward into the future all but impossible. In this section, she also makes the crucial point that her experience revealed and confirmed the relational nature of her sense of autonomy. 'Enhancing the autonomy in the aftermath of my assault reinforced my view as autonomy as fundamentally dependent on others.' In much Westernised social science research, selves are not understood this way; instead a large body of work implicitly ascribes to the modern Cartesian subject, or in other words, a 'Lone Ranger' theory of humans, in which the healthy individual is largely seen as one who is 'self-contained, independent and self-reliant' (see Rimé 2009 for this description). It is the kind of self that is easily incorporated in theories of justice. I would argue this to be generally mistaken: humans are not beings who are selves first and then subsequently interact with a world outside but are better understood as 'being-in-the-world': a self that as Brison summarizes is 'created and sustained by others' (see also Ratcliffe 2008). But in addition, Brison's account reveals that becoming such a shut-off, self-contained individualized, non-relational self is a *consequence of victimisation*, that the victims in the aftermath desperately need to remedy. A self that is 'radically alone': suddenly unable to do what it previously did without reflection, namely, exist in connection to a physical, temporal and social world. This is where I think the ontological assault of victimization comes into its own.

Regaining a sense of self in the aftermath of victimization requires regaining such an experience of 'communion' that in our normal lived experience is taken-for-granted (Bakan 1966, for its application to victimology Pemberton et al. 2017). Again, this is not (primarily) a sense of a relationship between people, as separate selves, but the role of communion with others as a means to become and sustain our own selves. Rebuilding autonomy following victimization requires people to 'remake themselves', and people's own choices and actions are vital to this end. But without reconnecting to others they would remain selves in the radically lonely limbo to which the victimization banished them. It also restricts the extent to which viewing victimization as repair or restoration to a previous self is accurate or useful. Realizing victims' nature as beings-in-the-world can help us avoid adopting metaphors for victimization that see it in bio-medical terms: victims as self-contained, and individual, biological entities that solely need restoring or repair to their previous level of functioning. This view is suspect in medicine itself, see below. The remade self of which Brison speaks is a self that is altered by living through the experience, one for whom the victimization and its aftermath, the manner in which it was situated in time, become part of the fabric of existence. The taken-for-grantedness of the existential feelings will not return, which—I should add—does not have to be for the worse, although it often will.

Taken together, viewing the experience of injustice as an 'ontological assault': entails understanding it as an attack on our selves as 'beings-in-the-world', as embodied, temporal, narrative and relationally autonomous beings, in which the experience of a shift in our existential feelings is important, and indeed makes these feelings explicit: precisely in the breakdown of such feelings of being, we become aware of them.

The Fact of Victimization: The Importance of the Virtue of Phronesis

On these terms, countering injustice involves remaking such a self, an endeavour that is fundamentally bound to people's idiosyncratic experience. There is some more to be learnt from the examination of the 'ontological assault' in life-threatening illness. Here it refers specifically to the (diminishment of the) integrity of self and body, an experience in which body stands opposed to self and which also alters the individual's sense of relatedness to the world of others and of things. Thus, the experience of illness is an experience of *dis*integration and *dis*unity, often accompanied by a frustration and disillusionment that are profoundly 'existential', also given that it can explicitly threaten the individual's existence. *The fact of illness* is the subjective state of the individual experiencing this ontological assault and therefore can be distinguished from *disease*, which concerns a quantifiable disorder of biologic function objectively located in the body. The fact of illness and disease are not unrelated, but the experience of illness can exist in absence of disease and vice versa, while the distinction also suggests that there is more to the craft of medicine than curing disease.

Indeed, Pellegrino (1979) parlayed this distinction into an argument for a conception of healing following illness as the ultimate *telos* of medicine, focused on 'a return to the unity of self and body, although this unity may represent a renegotiation, a newly struck balance, between the self's hopes and the body's capacities'. Given that this sense of renewed unity of self and body is located in the first-person interpretation of the person, the patient suffering the illness, this 'return of unity' cannot be determined in abstract of this experience. Pellegrino (1979) made this explicit in his reference to the distinction Aristotle made in his *Nicomachean Ethics* between the intellectual virtues *episteme, techne* and *phronesis*. The former concerns the acquisition of universal knowledge and the second concerns the craft of applying this knowledge in a particular situation. This is the how curing diseases is conceptualized: a craft that involves knowing what to do, how to do it, and why one does it. The healing of illness instead requires *phronesis*, which is often translated as the practical wisdom of knowing how to act in a particular social and political context. It poses the questions of what ought to be done, while incorporating the meaning and morals of those actors involved in the situation (see also Davis 1997; Flyvbjerg 2001).

I would argue the analogy of the dichotomy of countering injustice and doing justice with healing illness and curing disease, respectively. Following the previous sections, the purpose of countering injustice would then be conceived as a remedy to the damage inherent in the onto-logical assault, in the case of victimization the attack on ourselves as beings-in-the-world, including the resulting sense of narrative foreclosure and radical loneliness. The distinction with doing justice also follows a similar logic: justice pursues an amalgam of an epistemological founda-tion and technical application, abstracted from the particular situation, context and interpretation of the actors involved. Countering injustice, however, necessarily navigates the idiosyncratic experience of victimiza-tion, including the interpretation, meaning and morals of those directly impacted. A similar argument for invoking the virtue of phronesis can therefore also be made in the case of countering injustice. Indeed, the differences between the situation of victimization and life-threatening ill-ness only serve to strengthen the case for this distinction and for *phrone-sis*. First, as mentioned above, justice's primary purpose is not countering injustice, but preserving order. Striving for order might run counter to countering injustice in real-life situations. Part of the prudence of *phrone-sis* in this regard would involve navigating this contradiction. Second, where Pellegrino (1979) remarks that medicine is the 'most scientific of the humanities' (or the most humane of the sciences), given the objective, biological basis for disease, justice is itself instead steeped in socially con-structed meaning and explicitly and primarily political in purpose. Reformulating Shklar's critique of legalism in Pellegrino's terms reveals that the 'amalgam of episteme and techne' to which processes of justice aspire is itself the result of political choice, rooted in an understanding of the social and political context, and in that way draws upon *phronesis*.

The above reveals the extent to which countering injustice is a process in which any outcome is emergent rather than pre-conceived and pre-determined. It is clear when the justice process has come to its conclu-sion, and it is clear when and under what conditions justice may be said to have been done, while neither of these statements hold for countering injustice. Again, the same can be said to be true for healing illness, but the necessity of re-connection to others in remaking oneself in the aftermath of injustice serves to increase its indeterminacy.

Conclusion: A Theory of Injustice and Victim Participation

The issue at stake in this chapter is the manner in which the theory of injustice presented here connects to victims' participation in justice processes. Given the differences discussed between countering injustice and doing justice, their asymmetry, and in particular the idiosyncrasy of countering injustice, might seem to lead to a conclusion that they do not have much to do with each other. All this talk of selves being remade, is that not more the work of psychologists or councillors than of justice processes? To that my answer is no. For one thing, I think we should not let justice get off so lightly. Our justice processes feed on the experience of injustice, and without a sufficient claim to actually be involved in countering the experience of injustice, justice processes would solely exist for their own sake. And the fact that justice is only likely to have a limited potential to achieve any undoing of injustice does not mean that it cannot do anything at all nor does it mean that it cannot be improved either.

I think the previous discussion can help us in such attempts at improvement. Much of the currently existing modes of participation and input for victims can be viewed as attempts to create spaces of countering injustice within the landscape of justice processes. I think that is, for instance, true for victim impact statements and particularly so for processes of restorative justice. The latter's focus on lived experience embedded in the exact context of crime and conflict, its inclusion of the feelings, narratives and relationships of those involved: much of it resonates with countering injustice and can be understood as part of the victims' attempts to remake him or herself.

A key issue is that these spaces could or should be seen as vessels of communion. The separation of the rest of social life, the hedged off, game-like quality of a process of law, in itself poses difficulties for the victim's need for communion, to reconnect. It also clouds our understanding of the nature of the victim's involvement, in which communion and connection-based needs are instead summarily assumed to be oriented towards achieving some outcome, whether that is influencing the sentence or couched in therapeutic language. Victims need to communicate their experience in justice processes, but I increasingly doubt the extent to which this is best understood in terms of reducing their stress symptoms, becoming less anxious, or changing the sentence. Instead, the justice process itself can be an important site for reconnection: of victim experience with society, and with important symbols of shared values. Crucially: victims do not want to be left alone again. Victim input is also important because neglecting it would reinforce the manner in which victims have experienced 'radical loneliness'.

Understanding the role of phronesis in countering injustice can offer a point of departure for academic research, as well as a philosophy of practice relevant to victim participation in justice processes. As to the former, it emphasizes the folly of defining victimological experience in the terms of justice institutions, urging victimologists to understand (criminal) justice processes in the way they are encountered by victims as an element of the unfolding narrative of the remaking of the self (see also Pemberton et al. 2019). It offers a point of resistance against the manner in which theories of justice distinguish process and outcome, the haste to conceptualize victims' perspectives in legal terms, like rights, and attempt to isolate the process of justice from the rest of social life. Here it actively speaks against the conceptions of victim participation that see it as a supportive handmaiden of criminal justice aims but also against the view that the victim can be tacked on to the process by merely procedural means.

The theory of injustice is most similar to the critical position adopted in restorative justice, while restorative practices have a seemingly large potential to offer phronetic inroads to remaking the self. However, the unreflective use of *justice* might mask the reality that will stand in the way of the type of constructive, context-based solutions to which restorative practices often aspire (see also Pemberton and Aarten 2017). Moreover, much of the most vexing, but also most important, issues concerning the remaking the self after an ontological assault, come into view when it is unclear, what, if anything, can actually amount to *restoration*. Indeed, the theory of injustice can enhance the critical potential of restorative justice thinking, as it reveals that difficulties of maintaining a belief in a possible restorative solution in the aftermath of an ontological assault, as well as an a priori definition of what such a solution should amount to. Both are remnants of 'the normal model' of justice, that for all it might contribute to our social life, needs to be treated with much more wariness and caution than is currently the case.

References

Bakan, D. (1966). *The Duality of Human Existence: Isolation and Communion in Western Man*. Boston: Beacon Press.

Bernstein, J. M. (2015). *Torture and Dignity: An Essay on Moral Injury*. Chicago: University of Chicago Press.

Brison, S. J. (2002). *Aftermath: Violence and the Remaking of the Self*. Princeton: Princeton University Press.

Clark, M. (2000). On the Rejection of Morality: Bernard Williams' Debt to Nietzsche. In R. Schacht (Ed.), *Nietzsche's Postmoralism* (pp. 100–122). Cambridge: Cambridge University Press.

Crossley, M. L. (2000). Narrative Psychology, Trauma and the Study of Self/Identity. *Theory & Psychology, 10*, 527–546.

Davis, F. D. (1997). Phronesis, Clinical Reasoning and Pellegrino's Philosophy of Medicine. *Theoretical Medicine, 18*, 173–195.

Flyvbjerg, B. (2001). *Making Social Science Matter. Why Social Inquiry Fails and How It Can Succeed Again*. Cambridge: Cambridge University Press.

Freeman, M. (2000). When the Story's Over: Narrative Foreclosure and the Possibility of Self-renewal. In M. Andrews, S. D. Sclater, C. Squire, & A. Treacher (Eds.), *Lines of Narrative: Psychosocial Perspectives* (pp. 81–91). London: Routledge.

Gadow, S. (1980). Existential Advocacy: Philosophical Foundation of Nursing. In S. Spicker & S. Gadow (Eds.), *Nursing Images and Ideals: Opening Dialogue with the Humanities* (pp. 79–101). New York: Springer.

Garro, L. C. (1992). Chronic Illness and the Construction of Narratives. In M. J. D. Good, P. E. Brodwin, B. J. Good, & A. Kleinman (Eds.), *Pain as Human Experience: An Anthropological Perspective* (pp. 100–137). Berkeley: University of California Press.

Goodey, J. (2005). *Victims and Victimology. Research, Policy, Practice.* Harlow, UK: Pearson.

Janoff-Bulman, R. (1992). *Shattered Assumptions: Towards a New Psychology of Trauma.* New York: Free Press.

Levi, P. (1988). *The Drowned and the Saved.* London: Abacus.

Marshall, T. (1999). *Restorative Justice: The Evidence.* London: Home Office.

Nietzsche, F. (1888/1967). *On the Genealogy of Morals* (R. J. Hollingdale & W. Kaufman, Trans.). New York: Random House.

Nussbaum, M. (1990, 26 November). The Misfortune Teller. *The New Republic*, pp. 30–32.

Pellegrino, E. D. (1979). Toward a Reconstruction of Medical Morality: The Primacy of the Act of Profession and the Fact of Illness. *Journal of Medicine and Philosophy, 4*, 32–56.

Pemberton, A. (2009). Victim Movements: From Varying Needs to Diversified Criminal Justice Agenda's. *Acta Criminologica, 22*, 1–23.

Pemberton, A. (2015). *Victimology with a Hammer: The Challenge of Victimology.* Tilburg: Prismaprint.

Pemberton, A., & Aarten, P. G. M. (2017). Judith Shklar's Victimology and Restorative Justice. In I. Aertsen & B. Pali (Eds.), *Criticial Restorative Justice* (pp. 315–330). Oxford: Hart.

Pemberton, A., Aarten, P. G. M., & Mulder, E. (2017). Beyond Retribution, Restoration and Procedural Justice: The Big Two of Communion and Agency in Victims' Perspectives on Justice. *Psychology, Crime and Law, 23*(7), 682–698.

Pemberton, A., Mulder, E., & Aarten, P. G. M. (2019). Stories of Injustice: Towards a Narrative Victimology. *European Journal of Criminology, 16*(4), 391–412.

Ratcliffe, M. (2008). *Feelings of Being. Phenomenology, Psychiatry and the Sense of Reality.* Oxford: Oxford University Press.

Ratcliffe, M. (2012). The Phenomenology of Existential Feeling. In J. Fingerhut & S. Marienburg (Eds.), *Feelings of Being Alive* (pp. 23–54). Boston; Berlin: De Gruyter.

Ratcliffe, M. (2017). *Real Hallucinations. Psychiatric Illness, Intentionality and the Interpersonal World.* Cambridge, MA: MIT Press.

Ratcliffe, M., Ruddel, M., & Smith, B. (2014). What Is a Sense of Foreshortened Future? *Frontiers in Psychology, 5*, 1–11.

Ricoeur, P. (1986). Life: A Story in Search of a Narrator. In M. Doeser & J. Kray (Eds.), *Facts and Values* (pp. 34–68). Dordrecht: Nijhoff.

Rimé, B. (2009). Emotion Elicits the Social Sharing of Emotion: Theory and Empirical Review. *Emotion Review, 1*, 60–85.

Scheingold, S., Olson, T., & Pershing, J. (1994). Sexual Violence, Victim Advocacy and Republican Criminology: Washington's Community Protection Act. *Law and Society Review, 28*(4), 729–763.

Sebold, A. (1999). *Lucky.* New York: Scribner.

Shklar, J. (1986). *Legalism: Law, Morals and Political Trials.* Cambridge, MA: Harvard University Press.

Shklar, J. (1990). *The Faces of Injustice.* New Haven: Yale University Press.

Strang, H. (2002). *Repair or Revenge: Victims and Restorative Justice.* Oxford, UK: Oxford University Press.

Walgrave, L. (2008). *Restorative Justice, Self-interest and Responsible Citizenship.* Cullumpton, Devon, UK: Willan.

Wemmers, J. M. (1996). *Victims in the Criminal Justice System.* The Hague: The Netherlands, WODC/Kugler.

Williams, B. (1993). *Shame and Necessity.* Berkeley: CA. University of California Press.

Winkler, C. (1991). Rape as Social Murder. *Anthropology Today, 7*(3), 12–14.

Wolgast, E. (1987). *The Grammar of Justice.* Ithaca: Cornell University Press.

Yack, B. (1999). Putting Injustice First. *Social Research, 66*, 1103–1120.

Zehr, H. (1990). *Changing Lenses: A New Focus for Crime and Justice.* Scottsdale: Herald Press.

15

Conclusion: Understanding Victimisation and Effecting Social Change

Pamela Davies and Jacki Tapley

Introduction

The introduction to the volume is subtitled *Victimology: A Conversion of Narratives* and our aim from the outset has been to critically examine the range of complex and competing factors that have impacted upon and altered the criminal justice landscape in terms of how victims of crime are perceived. The narratives underpinning these debates and developments have emerged from the interplay between victimology as an academic discipline and the activism of individuals and special interest groups. Activist-led campaigns have given voice to victims' experiences, sparking

P. Davies (✉)
Department of Social Sciences, Northumbria University,
Newcastle upon Tyne, UK
e-mail: pamela.davies@northumbria.ac.uk

J. Tapley
Institute of Criminal Justice Studies, Faculty of Humanities and Social
Sciences, University of Portsmouth, Portsmouth, UK
e-mail: jacki.tapley@port.ac.uk

© The Author(s) 2020
J. Tapley, P. Davies (eds.), *Victimology*,
https://doi.org/10.1007/978-3-030-42288-2_15

controversial debates about the role of victims in adversarial justice processes, influencing reforms and the impact upon policy, professional culture and practice. Central to this book has been our acknowledgment of and tribute to the role of activism in the development of victimology as an academic discipline. This is reflected in the range of subjects covered within the chapters of this volume where questions about collective and less collective movements, ideological similarities and differences, divergent perspectives, paradigms and wisdoms, as well as divergent cultures and competing rhetoric and discourse are discussed. A common thread running throughout these chapters is a story of relentless activism, campaigning and tales of resilience, revealing the extent to which victimology, as proposed in our introductory chapter, is very much a theoretically informed humanist endeavour. The chapters presented in this volume map out how often courageous and personal endeavours are related to the political and from both personal and collective tragedy can emerge positive social and political change.

The second feature of the book has been to critically examine how victimology has contributed to shaping the political and criminal justice landscape during the last half of the twentieth century and continues to do so in the early decades of the twenty-first century. An important sub-theme to this is the politicisation of crime victims. Combining theory, research and activism, the chapters in this book have explored and heightened our awareness of the significant influence of the humanist and activist wing of victimology upon the politicisation of crime victims and the development of policy and legislation. We feel that it is fair to say that victimology has not been afraid to flaunt its intentions to influence the wider socio-political climate, with many victimologists actively involved in the emancipation of specific groups of victims or forms of victimisation. Whilst activism has championed specific offences and the signalling of new offences created by new forms of technology, academic scholarship has also been undertaken, often directly influenced by those who would not perhaps consider themselves primarily as 'victimologists'. Thus, as an inter-disciplinary endeavour, victimological scholarship draws from a range of sources of knowledge. Whilst victimology was once considered a sub-discipline of criminology, criminologists examining areas of criminality attracting increasing political and public concern find themselves acknowledging the plight of the victims and examining ways to provide support them and prevent further harm. In particular, this can be seen in relation to the policing of domestic abuse and offences of fraud and cybercrime (Button et al. 2013, 2014; Karagiannopoulos 2018).

Following on from the above, we pledged to reflect upon and critically explore the value and contribution of victimology as a theoretically informed humanist movement, utilising activist strategies as a tool to persuade and influence social change. We now weigh up what victimology—given its diversity, mix of ideas and agendas—as a discipline has achieved. Can the discipline help to ameliorate the harms caused by criminal justice processes for both complainants and defendants and victims and offenders? How do we move beyond distracting debates such as those that have set up false zero-sum contests between the rights of the accused and the rights of the victim? How can victimology be the pioneering discipline that informs and influences adversarial justice processes such that they accommodate the needs and rights of all parties? To consider these questions, this chapter identifies and summarises the key themes emerging from this volume. In doing so, we will synthesise the commonalities and review some of the key enduring features emerging from these chapters. Second, we will make some forward-looking and informed yet speculative assessments about victimology as a thriving academic discipline and activist movement. Whilst we are wary of the pitfalls of doing so, we feel that in order to push forward on progressive change, and in our efforts to prioritise the safeguarding of victims and survivors and prevent further harm and victimisation, we feel compelled to set out what we see as some of the obvious and immediate areas that must be given precedence on an agenda for reform.

Activism: Exposing Personal, Private and Public Harms

A contributing factor to the growth and widening influence of victimology has been its activist wing, although historically this has been made up of an unlikely alliance of disparate groups often representing competing interests. This has led commentators to debate for some time whether such alliances represent a 'victims' movement', but as summarised by Goodey (2005: 103), the label 'is at best an inadequate description for what is a diverse international array of academic, activist and politically-based developments'. Despite this, activism by special interest groups has remained a predominant feature of victimology with the intention of influencing social change. This is reflected in the chapters of this volume which, although focusing on diverse forms of victimisation and how they impact upon different groups and communities, have, at their core, ambitions to contribute to significant changes in perceptions of victimisation and aspirations to influence social change and criminal justice reforms. An example of this, since the second half of the twentieth century and continuing into the twenty-first century, are feminist activists and scholars who have been fundamental in linking academic research with activist-led calls for social change and who have made substantial contributions to the growth of victimology during this time (Goodey 2005; Davies 2018). Such feminist campaigns reveal social and political inequalities that sustain specific forms of victimisation. They challenge the political institutions that condone them and the criminal justice agencies that undermine them.

Savage et al. (2007: 84) critically examined the role of campaigns in exposing miscarriages of justice, whether based on 'wrongful convictions' (doing the wrong thing) or failures to act in response to victimisation (not doing anything or not doing enough). Whilst they are unlikely to style themselves as victimologists, these authors identified a number of significant points relating to who, how and why campaigns aimed at addressing perceived injustices, rely on victims, families and advocates to achieve success in terms of influencing social and criminal justice change. In particular, they highlight the criminological importance of what such campaigns can reveal about the criminal justice policy process and, more specifically, the role of victims in miscarriages of justice campaigns based on 'questionable actions' caused by police malpractice and/or incompetence, the poor treatment of victims, failures to investigate, or inadequate prosecution processes and unaccountable prosecutorial decision-making (ibid.: 99). Their research identifies the 'critical success factors' (ibid.: 90) behind the campaigns and concludes that:

> two factors have been the key to successful campaigns against miscarriages of justice: on the one hand the ability of campaigns to access the social resources and social capital associated with campaigning networks; on the

other hand the ability of victims and families associated with injustices to provide the resilience and cohesion which campaigns typically need to achieve goals. (Savage et al. 2007: 83)

These authors argue that individuals and agencies, acting as pressure groups, play a key role in the 'distribution' of justice, as they have been important engines of criminal justice reform, therefore, who they are, how they operate and with what effect, constitutes important questions to understanding the distribution of justice within the criminal justice system, as 'they act (at least up to a point) as "extra-judicial", "extra-legal", "non-governmental" or "unofficial" sources of influence over the machineries of law-enforcement and criminal justice' (ibid.: 85).

A key question yet to be explored under the victimological agenda concerns which campaigns achieve the greatest social resources and social capital, and why? Who the victims are, and who the individuals and groups supporting them are, can be key to the success or otherwise of the campaign. As previous campaigns indicate, those individuals, families and interest groups representing 'ideal victims' are able to more effectively mobilise social resources and capital, the significant backing of the media, and the authorities (Greer 2017: 49). This feeds in to the creation of a 'hierarchy of victimisation' (ibid.), with those most deserving of our sympathy (because they conform to the ideal victim stereotype) at the top (qualifying for resources and support) and those considered most blameworthy and undeserving placed at the bottom (less likely to be acknowledged as victims and less likely to receive resources and public support). We witness this scenario being played out in the media often in the editorial choices made as to which campaigns are given coverage and those which are not. This becomes especially important in determining what experiences influence the development of new legislation (as examined by O'Leary and Green in Chapter 7). Savage et al. (2007: 94) argue that the media can be pivotal in the success or otherwise of campaigns, as they can offer a range of social resources, in particular, publicity, influence and the power to investigate. Victims and/or their families are often in a vulnerable and powerless position when seeking to expose the wrongdoings of powerful institutions such as the police, the CPS or the magistracy/judiciary, so an ability to access social resources and gain the support of the media and the public can play a crucial role in whether a campaign achieves its aims. Up until recently, the media has acted as a key filter in determining which campaigns are given prominence, but as demonstrated by Sugiura and Smith in Chapter 3 of this volume, the advent of social media has enabled previously marginalised and powerless groups to mobilise their own campaigns and gain significant support to influence the development of legislation, often assisted by high profile individuals and celebrities. Social media, therefore, can be seen to be breaking the monopoly of the traditional news media where victim myths and stereotypes have been perpetuated. Such new media illustrates the additional harm that outdated and entrenched views and misconceptions can have with significant consequences in respect of who and what qualifies as victim (see Tyson, Chapter 8; Tapley, Chapter 9; White and Weis, Chapter 12; and Erez, Jiang and Laster, Chapter 13).

Given the persistence of the powerful concept of the 'ideal victim' and the associated myths and stereotypes around victim culpability and blameworthiness, the next part of this chapter traces the influence of victimology on the politicisation of crime victims and how this has contributed to shaping the political and criminal justice landscape. As well as acknowledging the achievements, it also identifies those areas that have been neglected and marginalised, drawing upon what have become key concepts within victimology— vulnerability, risk and resilience.

Victimology and the Criminal Justice Landscape

In our efforts to conceptualise victimology as an academic discipline and an activist movement, the reader—whether a student, academic scholar and/or practitioner— has been encouraged to 'think critically about' the contributions. As editors, we encouraged authors to 'write critically about…' and having done so we are now in a position to begin to offer our own overarching thoughts on victimology and its (re)shaping of the criminal justice landscape. Whilst it is near impossible to separate out each of the components of research, discourse, policy, legal and practice developments, that is, features that in various combinations typically comprise a discipline, whether academic or activist driven, we make some observations on each of these below. In particular, we highlight how whilst an activist-led agenda can expose previously hidden vulnerable groups at risk of victimisation, it can also result in the neglect of other groups. With respect to the latter, feminist activists and scholars have revealed the extent and range of victimisation suffered by women and initiated the development of grassroot support services to assist survivors where none had previously existed. However, for some, this agenda overshadows the victimisation of other groups, including children, men and LGBTQ+ communities. Whilst organised, determined, persistent and resilient activist-led groups are able to get their voices heard eventually, other groups lacking collective representation, solidarity and advocacy can be neglected and remain on the periphery of agendas for social change. Feminist activism has been underpinned by a collective ideology (equality for women), though informed by a range of different and competing theoretical—including intersectional—perspectives.

Research: What Counts as Victimological Research?

First, if we were to review what constitutes victimological research and how it is variously executed we find a vast range of empirical inquiry and theoretical insight that might constitute such research. Some of this is clearly presented, badged and understood as victimological. Some, though not couched as victimological, would certainly meet any criteria that might qualify the empirical inquiry and findings and/or theoretical insight as victimological. Such criteria do not exist. And, we rarely see much in the way of an exchange of views or debate about what does and does not constitute victimological research. Indeed, this may not be a worthwhile exercise. The early chapters in the volume, in particular, refer to several studies into victimisation, yet we contend that the authors of these would not self-refer as victimologists. Examples of studies of victimisation come from a variety of different disciplines and perspectives. Several emerge from the realms of health with insight from the fields of mental health and well-being. A large body of work emanates from the practice-based fields of child protection and child and family social work, with contributions also from social psychology. Our point is not so much that there might be few who badge themselves as victimological researchers, but that the strength of the discipline lies in our ability to mine data and scour a plethora of robust and ethical research—and indeed theoretical traditions and philosophies—to produce new knowledge.

Much criminological and victimological research, as is very well documented, draws on reported incidents of criminal victimisation, and two sources of data are often cited as key in this respect. These are incidents reported to and recorded by the police and data derived from victimisation surveys. In many jurisdictions, it is generally accepted that, by aligning these two sources of information, a more 'accurate' dataset is obtained. This evidence base has become the staple way in which levels and trends in victimisation are captured. It has given rise to generic patterns of victimisation and this, largely quantitative data, has fed into our ways of assessing risk and vulnerability to victimisation, which in turn has provided 'evidence' to mobilise and steer resources towards certain types of victimisation and victim groups. As we consider further below, these broad patterns tend to obscure nuanced gender patterns for example and reproduce simple rather than complex representations of who is victimised and what support might be most appropriate.

The problem of what is known about, what is counted and how problems are measured remains an area of research that requires much more victimological imagination. A number of recent studies are drawing on mixed-methods approaches and more imaginative research strategies including co-produced research and tools to assemble evidence about the lived experience of those suffering harm and victimisation. This includes visual and photographic techniques and imagery, as well as qualitative narrative approaches that lend voice through storytelling to those who are not often heard from, listened to or acknowledged (see Cook, Chapter 5). New and vast pools of quantitative big data are emerging too, all producing evidence attesting to harm and suffering experienced by populations across the globe (Bennett Moses and Chan 2018). These, however, are very recent developments and the value of mining such data is yet to be exploited in victimological contexts. Questions about the origins of big data and its relevance to northern or southern continents are just beginning to emerge. The implications of the knowledge garnered are yet to be systematically explored in the context of a discipline that purports to have victims, victimisation, harm and injustice at its heart.

Challenging Dominant Discourse

Though the overall thrust of the book has been informed by an ambition to 'think critically about', individual chapters have different starting points and underpinning perspectives. The chapters thus engage with different theoretical frameworks, though there is a common feminist-influenced strand which connects several chapters where activism is focused on gendered forms of violence and abuse. Another common theoretical strand is the impact of the neo-liberal agenda and the influence of this upon matters of crime and justice. Particular theoretical frameworks appear to have shaped and framed dominant discourse and some policy developments. Tracing the history of the problematic discourse of the present, we have already pointed towards stubborn preconceptions around victim-blaming and enduring rape myths. The victim typologies developed by Von Hentig and Mendelsohn in the 1940s and 1950s remain theoretical touchstones in this respect. Von Hentig identified some people—women, children the elderly and the mentally subnormal—who were more prone to becoming victims, whilst Mendelsohn's typology was underpinned by the underlying legalistically influenced concept of 'victim culpability'. Later contributions in the 1970s introduced the concept of 'risky lifestyles' together with a focus on public spaces—as opposed to homely private spaces—as locations for criminal victimisation (Spalek 2017), after Amir (1968) had extended the repertoire of controversial concepts in victimology in claiming evidence of victim precipitated rapes. The idea of inviting rape continues to plague women seeking justice as rape victims today, despite evidence to the contrary and challenges from feminist and critical perspectives (Walby et al. 2015; Davies 2018). These contributions capture the essence of the fundamental assumptions in early victimological thinking and bear the traditional hallmarks of positivist traditionalism. Such perspectives have a strong hold over our understandings of how victimisation is researched, how it occurs, what form it takes, how often it happens, why it happens, when and where it takes place and who it happens to. The contesting of this legacy underpins much of the content of this volume. Dominant and stubbornly embedded conceptualisations and understandings of victimisation appear to have facilitated victim blaming and serve to undermine and negate the ways in which victimisation is resisted. As observed by Sugiura and Smith in Chapter 3, practices of victim blaming continue in the digital world, with old misogynistic attitudes being transposed to new media and new technology facilitating new forms of sexual violence. These attitudes and ill-informed stereotypes continue to permeate professional practices and those involved in criminal justice processes, including the public who serve as jurors (see Burman and Brooks-Hay, Chapter 6 and Erez et al. Chapter 13). The persistence of these myths and in whose best interests and convenience they serve also requires deeper critical victimological inquiry.

Our point about theorising is that progressive theoretical developments are evident and these emerge from an abundance of disciplinary traditions. However, the most dominant and enduring theoretical influences in victimology appear stubbornly wedded to traditional and positivist perspectives. Although feminist thinking has made inroads, they appear fleeting and short lived. Despite the introduction of new policies and reforms, professional cultures and practices act as a barrier to the successful implementation of reforms and behaviours revert to default (see Tapley, Chapter 9 and Erez et al. Chapter 13).

Policy, Legal Developments and Practice

Several contributions in this volume have acknowledged the plethora of progressive and innovative practices and legal and legislative reforms that over half a century have been pioneered and secured at national and supranational levels. Whilst these piecemeal developments have been welcomed, several contributors lament the blind faith that persists in expecting solutions from mandated criminal justice interventions. Others couch this in terms of there being an implementation gap. The evaluation of the MATAC, discussed by Davies in Chapter 11, reported on the under use of criminal justice and other civil sanctions and Davies, together with the authors of several other chapters, has observed the limits of criminal justice sanctions alone in impacting on the safety of victims.

The most controversial legal development in the UK in recent years is that the dynamics of domestic abuse are now recognised as being connected to the concept of coercive control. The latter concept captures both the psychological and physical aspects, the on-going nature of abusive behaviour, and the extent to which the actions of the perpetrator control the victim through isolation, intimidation, degradation and micro-regulation of everyday life (HMIC 2015). The offence of 'controlling or coercive behaviour in an intimate or family relationship' was introduced under Section 76 of the Serious Crime Act 2015. This development is the subject of much current debate (see Fitz-Gibbon, Walklate and McCulloch 2018, Special Issue *Criminology & Criminal Justice*). Walklate et al. (2017) observe that the implementation of this offence in England and Wales has been patchy and, based on their gendered analysis of coercive control, they conclude that more law will not improve responses to intimate partner violence, as also commented by Robinson (2015). Others are also wary of the wholesale adoption of coercive control as an approach that seeks to explain variations in domestic violence (Walby and Towers 2018). In Brisbane, Australia, Douglas (2017) reports that legal engagement can be an opportunity to extend an intimate partner's coercive control. Coining the phrase 'legal systems abuse', Douglas cites survivors' comments as evidence of how the legal system continues to be harnessed by perpetrators as a tool to extend coercive control beyond separation.

A very recent case example illustrates the complex issues at stake in respect of implementing the new law on coercive and controlling behaviour:

Sally Channon

At the court of Appeal in London in 2019, Sally Challen's case made headline news when her conviction was quashed and a fresh trial was ordered in light of new evidence about her mental state at the time of the killing. Challen was jailed for life after a murder trial in 2011 for killing her husband in a hammer attack in 2010. Sally had experienced decades of abuse and pleaded not guilty to murder. She admitted manslaughter and the Crown accepted her plea to the lesser charge. In this case, it was the tireless campaigning of her two sons, who had witnessed the abuse, that helped to keep the story in the news and bring to bear pressure for a re-trial.

The prospect of Sally Channon facing a retrial was seen as a key test of the new laws on domestic abuse and coercive control, and this case has opened up a series of legal challenges linked to other women who are in prison for murdering their abusive partners. The lack of understanding of how to recognise coercively controlling behaviour and how to evidence it and operationalise the law in practice continues, although some progress has been made in developing training to assist police officers in this regard (Brennan and Myhill 2017). Recent developments thus all reinforce the longstanding concern that there is a miss-match between the letter of the law and practice. The implementation gap remains very real for those seeking protection and justice from domestic abuse and coercive control.

Looking to the future, as politicians consider the introduction of further legislation in the form of a victims' law in England and Wales and victim advocates propose the development of a professional victim's service, readers of this book may now have a more refined view about the complex interplay between *theory, policy, legal developments and practice*. As noted above, we have encouraged the authors to draw upon and critically reflect upon the evidence base that underpins their arguments, the theoretical perspectives they are leaning towards or indeed pioneering, the policy developments they are both supportive and critical of, and the experiences of victimisation they are at pains to foreground. In reality, each contribution collapses the key hallmarks of an academic and activist endeavour, as explored above, together, in a complex array of weightings. Nevertheless, a number of key themes appear to rise to the surface, and we pull these to the forefront and examine these next.

The Politicisation of Crime Victims

Literature that adopts a critical perspective on victimology and the criminal justice landscape tends to be sceptical about the extent to which legislative changes and criminal justice policy and practice have moved the victim centre stage in matters of criminal justice (see Tapley, Chapter 9 and Hall, Chapter 10 in this volume). The authors of such views query the extent to which change has been affected with the real interests of victims at the forefront. For example, politicians who draw on the political rhetoric of 'putting victims at the heart of the criminal justice system' in their campaigns may be exploiting them for political gain, using victims as vote-winners and political pawns (Duggan and Heap 2014). Whilst these observations remain useful reminders of the value of a critically informed and edged approach to assessing the changing criminal justice landscape, there are a number of key issues that have emerged during the foregrounding of victims' experiences that will continue to be core to the victimological agenda. We promised to synthesise some commonalities and review a limited number of key features or 'continuity themes' that we feel stand out as enduring. We headline these as follows: vulnerability and resilience, evidence—what works, digital communications and socio-technological trends, the global political economy of crime, victimisation and local agenda setting. In various combinations, these concepts and issues are to be confronted via research, policy and activism if social change is to be achieved to reduce harm and prevent victimisation.

Vulnerability and Resilience

The topic of 'vulnerability' forms a major theme in terms of common content. This underlying thread is explored in relation to new types and conceptualisations of victimhood, as well as victim groups who are already identified as vulnerable. Specific protections have increasingly been afforded to those who qualify as vulnerable whether as victims or offenders in the criminal justice process. Those deemed vulnerable are eligible for special protective measures when they encounter police, for example, enhanced entitlements under the Victims Code of Practice and for special measures in court (Ministry of Justice 2015). Those classed as vulnerable include anyone under the age of 18; those who suffer from a mental disorder (as defined by the Mental Health Act 1983), or who have a significant impairment of intelligence and social function and well as those who have a physical disability or disorder. Following the Youth Justice and Criminal Evidence Act 1999, vulnerable witnesses (and intimidated witnesses) are eligible for 'special measures'. These allowances can include screens in the courtroom to prevent the defendant and the witness seeing each other and allowing the defendant to give evidence via a live video link from somewhere outside the court room. The *Code of Practice for Victims of Crime* is a key document that outlines the entitlements all victims have and in particular those of vulnerable victims (Cook and Davies 2017). These protections and special measures have been variously discussed as more or less adequate by critical commentators in this volume and elsewhere, especially in relation to those experiencing sexual victimisation and rape where attrition rates remain problematic (Hester and Lilley 2017). Safeguarding the vulnerable is a key priority for Police and Crime Commissioners and Matthew Hall in Chapter 10 explores how, under these new commissioning arrangements in England and Wales, PCCs measure their own performance and report on it in their annual reports. The concept of vulnerability is also considered in other contexts, including in Chapter 12, where the authors explore the failure to provide environmental protections for those who are already amongst the most vulnerable.

Vulnerability is an oft used term in criminological and victimological discourse. As the victim has become more central to achieving justice over the last forty years, 'vulnerability' has been used as a means of securing improved support for some victim-witnesses seeking justice through the courts. Vulnerability, however, is more broadly applicable to matters of harm and criminal justice. Measures are in place (but are points of contention) for vulnerable suspects, defendants, offenders and, as those engaged in activities, research and teaching around professional policing will attest, vulnerability is a recurring and dominant theme in policing priorities and on syllabus for the education of police recruits. Despite the term's ubiquity, however, both in academic and professional discourse, there has been little systematic effort to define this as a concept or to trace the emergence and operationalisation of 'vulnerability' across a range of settings and contexts.

Whilst policies and reforms outline the key entitlements for those victims and witnesses deemed as vulnerable, a barrier to ensuring such victims and witnesses are afforded such entitlements is the lack of a clear and operational definition. Professionals working in statutory and third-sector organisations within criminal justice and social care will now be very familiar with the terms 'vulnerable' and 'vulnerability', but may face challenges in knowing how to work with partners according to joined up understandings of how to identify the vulnerable or how to make sure measures are put in place to ensure the vulnerable are safeguarded. Too often vulnerable victims are not identified sufficiently early in the criminal justice process and denied access to the services and support available to them (Wedlock and Tapley 2016). The term 'vulnerable' has become widespread and is now used in a range of contexts, applied to individuals, groups and communities. To such an extent perhaps, that criminal victimisation has now become synonymous with being 'vulnerable'. Some have examined the relationship between vulnerability and victimisation (Green 2007) and the impact of this upon an individual's fear of crime, perceived risk and their actual risk of becoming a victim (Lee 2017), but further critical examination and clarity is required and this might emanate from a more ambitious victimological research agenda. Certainly it seems to us, conceptual clarity of vulnerability in crime prevention, community safety and justice contexts—from the global to the local—is beginning to seem overdue, as is a clearer understanding of peoples' abilities to recover and move on from victimisation.

The concept of resilience is often linked in antithesis to the concept of vulnerability, but this is overly simplistic in the context of experiencing and surviving victimisation. Walklate (2011: 180) has observed that whilst the concept of resilience has been the focus of studies from a range of disparate disciplines, including child development, psychopathological developments and social policy, and could also include theories of desistence, economics and politics, very few studies have focused on resilience and criminal victimisation. Resilience has been defined as 'the capacity to do well despite adverse experience' (Gilligan 2000: 37, cited by Walklate 2011: 184). Dutton and Greene (2010) examined existing research to explore the individual differences and responses to criminal victimisation and to explain why some people are able to adjust well despite criminal victimisation, whilst others do not. In particular, they proposed that a better understanding of resilience could help to inform new approaches for 'enhancing pathways to positive outcomes following victimisation by crime' (ibid.: 215) and to consider what resources might be integrated into those institutions with whom victims are likely to come into contact, for example, health and social care services, third-sector support services and criminal justice agencies, which might enhance resilience in both the short and long term.

Dutton and Greene (2010) explored resilience from three different approaches; resilience as protective factors; as a process of adaptation; and as positive outcomes. Psychological studies have indicated that individual personality factors have been identified as protective factors and that resiliency is also associated with an individual's biological characteristics, including genetic markers. Dutton and Greene (2010: 216) also found a range of social and cultural factors associated with resilience, including gender, age, race and ethnicity, social support networks and prior history of trauma. In an earlier study focusing on the psychological consequences of crime, Norris, Kaniasty and Thompson (1997, cited in Tapley 2003: 228) found that the primary moderators of the more distal or lasting effects of victimisation were formal and informal sources of support, and that victims of more violent crime were more likely to have contact with health professionals. An important finding was the positive correlation between informal support and the use of services, indicating that the greater the informal support provided by family and friends, the more likely victims of violence were to seek help from professionals. Whilst this may simply reflect some people's ability to mobilise help from all available sources, Norris et al. (ibid.) suggested this could also indicate that responsive social networks facilitate use of services by encouraging or enabling victims to seek the care they need.

The importance of informal social networks was also found to influence the decision-making processes of crime victims. Greenberg and Ruback (1992, cited by Tapley 2003: 128) found that whilst individual difference variants were not a significant predictor of the decision to report an offence to the police, social influence (i.e., those with whom the victim spoke to directly following the offence), together with the perceived seriousness of the crime, were important predictors of decisions to report the offence and seek help. Importantly, these earlier studies indicate the influence of informal social networks in the help-seeking behaviour of victims, which may provide pathways of support to enhance their resilience.

As acknowledged by Dutton and Greene (2010: 216), 'resiliency has not only been attributed to individuals, but also to communities and social networks that can promote resilience in individuals. When considering the role of the criminal justice process and the crucial importance of the initial response to victims by the police as first responders (Wedlock and Tapley 2016), it seems that both the health and criminal justice systems play an important role in determining resilience in the immediate and longer term aftermath of crime. Dutton and Greene (2010) suggested the need for a longitudinal perspective to measure resiliency factors across time. Such a study has been undertaken in Canada, with the preliminary findings discussed at the World Society Victimology Symposium held in Hong Kong (Roebuck 2018). This mixed-method study focuses on resilience and the experiences of victims of violence. It examines victims' navigation and negotiation of the criminal justice system, victim assistance services and informal support networks. The study demonstrated the importance of victims being afforded specific rights within the criminal justice process. The findings also illustrate what support services victims found most helpful and found evidence of the existence of post-traumatic growth in some participants. The study has also found that trauma can lead to personal growth and that whilst it does not negate post-traumatic stress, positive change can be measured beyond baseline levels. Growth domains were found to include improvements in relating to others, new possibilities, personal strength, spiritual change and an appreciation for life (Roebuck 2018). This is similarly demonstrated by Cook in Chapter 5 of this volume, where she explores the resilience of families impacted by violent death through public campaigns to effect change and how this has impacted upon further changes in their own lives.

In summary, the research examined above provides links between the concepts of vulnerability, risk and resilience and demonstrates how definitions and perceptions of these concepts have been applied (or not) to criminal victimisation. The research begins to explore how criminal justice responses to victims can determine not only their ability to attain the legitimate status of victim and their perceived level of harm and vulnerability but also how this may impact on their ability to receive protection and support and assist in building their resilience. This is also an important area when considering the commissioning and funding of support services, as the distribution of funds is starting to be increasingly linked with outcomes achieved instead of the previous measure used of numbers contacted (see Hall, Chapter 10), thereby placing an emphasis on which interventions can be shown to work.

Evidence: What Works?

Under this headline theme, we are thinking about more than an instrumental and objective 'what works' evidence base. The problem of 'transfer failure' is widely noted in the policy literature, and in criminal justice and policing in particular. As Fleming and Rhodes (2018: 22) have observed in the context of evidence-based policing, much of this takes place:

> in charged organisational and political contexts that ensure that the data are always incomplete, always uncertain, and always ambiguous, so, the meaning of evidence is never fixed, it must be constantly won.

We feel it is useful to acknowledge this as a given starting point so that a forward momentum might be established. We are keen to explore what might work better. The agenda for effecting change is as much dependent upon robust research as it is about context and local implementation and practice. Empiricist evidence, devoid of social context is doomed to fail in terms of preventing victimization and with respect to meeting the needs of, and support for, victims.

The authors who have contributed to this volume have drawn upon their own collaborative research endeavours and have drawn on a wealth of other research to support their arguments. Many have focused on research that relies on partnership working, and they explicitly or implicitly suggest there is a need to develop a deeper and richer understanding of how to make things work better. An understanding of what the enabling circumstances are is key. Though some contributions have showcased new developments and mechanisms that are innovative, there is common agreement on the need to focus on *how* processes unfold, what works most effectively, when and where. It seems to us that it is the combination of various elements that is important and success may be dependent upon: interventions having a clear and delimited focus; collaborations and multi-agency working that comprises complementary partners and skill sets; swift and shared access to data and organisation, leadership and management (Rowe et al. 2018).

A further point, under the headline of research, concerns 'politics'. One of the most dominant themes of this book has been the politicisation of crime victims. At local multi-agency and partnership level and at the point of service delivery, the politics of what works in preventing victimisation and supporting victims often surfaces (Wedlock and Tapley 2016). The question of what works, or what might be made to work through a more comprehensive understanding of the problem, is nowhere more important than in the context of domestic abuse. Coercive control has been discussed at various junctures in the pages of this volume. Legislative developments, as we have seen, have not always been operationalised and implemented in ways that have effected positive change. Whilst multi-agency working is well established as the dominant way of tackling such forms of harm, progress has been slow, and within these collaborative partnerships, stakeholders need to be keenly aware how perpetrators may begin exchanging physical violence for more subtle and coercive forms of abuse, worsening the situation for the victim/survivors and their children. Increased victim intimidation by an abuser who blames their partner for the more intense surveillance and/or interventions they are now experiencing could put victims at greater risk. Increased self-censorship by a victim who feels responsible for 'bringing trouble' to their partner's door does not represent an effective way of tackling serial perpetrators, preventing victimisation and safeguarding victims (Davies 2018).

The wide-ranging approach inherent in the new formulation of domestic abuse as coercive control is controversial and this too is perhaps only heightening the tensions about what should be done and how. Robinson et al. (2017) have reported on the extent to which the work of practitioners is informed by a sound understanding of coercive control and find that the absence of a clear understanding when making judgements about victims and perpetrators has serious implications for the efficacy of current approaches to domestic abuse. These tensions come to the fore in local multi-agency partnerships that are tackling domestic abuse and more broadly in the context of feminist activism and resistance to violence against women and girls. In the context of domestic abuse, innovations in digital communications have been used for the surveillance and monitoring of victims and in ways to further abuse (Woodlock et al. 2019) but are also being explored in important ways to increase safety and protect victims.

Innovative Digital Communications and Technologies and Broader Socio-Technological Trends

Innovative digital communications and technologies and broader socio-technological trends are creating new forms and experiences of victimisation and a proliferation of victims. Sugiura and Smith in Chapter 3 focused on responsibilisation and resilience in online sexual abuse and harassment. Their chapter began by stating that an unintended consequence of the expansion of digital technologies has been the growth of criminal activity shaping traditional offences in new and diverse ways. However, the chapter also considered the positive role of digital technologies in mobilising online feminist activism and advocacy to challenge and raise awareness of not only online sexual abuses but also wider societal sexually based harms. Such campaigns have extended the reach of feminist activism and given voices to those previously silenced by more traditional forms of media and communication.

Furthermore, technological and social changes associated with consumerism and shifting patterns of leisure activity mean that the domestic sphere—understood to be a complex and shifting category—is a site, and a place, associated with a wide spectrum of crime and social harm. As such, there are new avenues for considering how broader socio-technological trends are shifting how we conceive of 'the domestic' sphere. The latter has long been an area of contention brought to the fore by feminist-influenced thinking about the inappropriate separation of the public and private in matters concerning intimate partner violence and the gendered nature of patterns to sexual abuse more broadly. As technological and social change, for example, in relation to leisure and consumption, have made boundaries between public and private space ever more fuzzy, criminological research needs to pay greater attention to domestic environments in which both offending and victimisation occur

(Davies and Rowe 2020). Technology has made the distinction between public and domestic environments considerably less clear-cut, and, it might be found that the underlying sense of security and safety associated with 'the home' applies less strongly in the future. Our traditional assumptions about risk may need reconceptualising, especially in respect of young people's online activities. While this might mean that there is less of an additional impact in terms of individual experiences of crime, it would represent a highly problematic outcome if this reflected a more fundamental rise in insecurity. There is also a need for criminal justice agencies to embrace new digital technologies to improve their communication with victims, in particular, to use digital technologies to improve how they provide information and timely and accurate updates to victims and witnesses (Wedlock and Tapley 2016).

The Global Political Economy of Crime and Victimization and Local Agenda Setting

The global dimensions to the problem of crime and victimisation are increasingly being recognised even as they are discussed at the very local level. The politicisation of crime victims has been a central focus of this book, and many contributors to the volume overtly acknowledge that, in the last forty to fifty years a shift has taken place seeing increased preoccupation with security at individual, local, national and global levels (Johnston and Shearing 2003; Mythen and McGowan 2018). Some have explored the ways in which this translates in to a knotty problem of who should be held to account for (in)security, victimisation and perpetration. In Chapter 11, Davies examines the problems of responsibilising serial perpetrators of domestic abuse, all against a backdrop of strategies and politics that have seen an increasing emphasis upon prevention and individual responsibility on both victims and offenders. The conundrums and dilemmas this poses for victim safety and safeguarding surface in the form of authors' reporting on friction, tensions, trade-offs, compromises and debates about 'rebalancing' and focus on victims, as opposed to focus on offenders and perpetrators and subtle, yet important, differences between victim-focused and victim-oriented approaches.

As several of the chapters in the volume point out, violence against women and girls is now recognised globally as a significant harm, with estimates published by the World Health Organisation (WHO) suggesting these harms affect large proportions of women with potentially devastating consequences. As Wiper and Lewis note in Chapter 2, since the late 1980s, dominant approaches to VAWG at the international level have been set within the context of human rights. Whilst this might be a unifying theme in global context, there are significant differences in justice systems around the world. This is well illustrated in Chapter 4 by Mukungu and Kamwanyah, who explore gender-based violence, activism and victims' quests for justice in the context of Namibia's dual justice system—the statutory system and the traditional system—where victims may engage with neither, either or both systems. Little is known about such justice systems outside of Namibia and this is just one illustration of the bias in our knowledge about crime, victimization, harm and justice around the world.

We have pulled these 'continuity themes' to the forefront in this concluding chapter and set them out as part of an agenda for victimological attention into the next decades. They form part of our prelude to the future. There are of course overlaps between what we have termed 'continuity themes'—digital technological trends and vulnerability, for example. We therefore leave room also for the reader to ponder their own predictive reflections about future agendas for victimological inquiry.

The Social Science of Victimology: Research, Policy and Activism

The next part of this chapter moves us towards a further level of future-oriented reflection. Thinking about the contribution as a whole, we now pause to think critically about the contribution of victimology: its contributions, omissions, successes and future potential. For us, victimology is a social science. At its simplest, victimology involves the study of the suffering of those who have experienced wrongdoing. Victimology has previously been described as a sister or sub-discipline of criminology. The latter has been described as a rendezvous discipline, an interdisciplinary, multi-disciplinary, applied, social and behavioural science. The same hall-marks apply to victimology. In the same way that criminology, crime and justice are not easily harnessed or described, neither is victimology, victimisation and harm. The subject matter of victimology is wide, deep, varied, contested and debated. However, here we put forward some of our own thoughts about the historical development of victimology and its claims to being an academic endeavour and a social movement, but more importantly we contemplate how the agenda for change might be progressed under an umbrella discipline called victimology.

Despite many contributors being sceptical about the extent to which there has been progressive developments in respect of understanding the plight of victims of crime and social harm, there is much evidence contained within the chapters of this volume that suggests (although gradual) significant improvements have been made. Several legal and legislative milestones signify the progressive potential of the law, for example, and (notwithstanding the implementation gap) the nature and extent of support for victims of crime has changed dramatically over the last forty years or so, such that victims survive their experiences and sometimes witness their perpetrators being held to account for their offending behaviour in ways that sometimes satisfy victims conceptualisation of justice. Other initiatives point towards a future where various forms of victimisation, including domestic abuse, is being prevented through approaches that tackle serial perpetrators, challenge cultural understandings about violence against women and girls, and support victims through to survivor status. There are numerous examples of how reform has been animated throughout this volume.

Formal policymaking has sometimes been an important spur for change, though in the case of domestic abuse, policy and legal developments in isolation have failed to prevent on average two women a week from being killed by their abusive partner (Long et al. 2017). Grassroots activists, on the other hand, have, in key social and political moments in time, been instrumental in bringing invisible crimes and victimisations to the fore and rendering private violence's public problems. Progressive victimological ideas have only rarely coincided with political movements such that moments of real change can be identified. Examples of effective victim-oriented and victim-centred innovations are rarely unequivocally identified by evaluative research projects and the complex interplay between research, theory, policy and practice, as well as different working practices and multi-agency partnership approaches, illustrate the complex ways in which reform and change in the very real-world context of crime and social harm can be brought about. Some things work, under certain circumstances and conditions and in particular contexts, much of the time.

Lifting our gaze out of the UK context, we find similarly complex routes and cul-de-sacs to social change. In the US, years of activism by community-based organisations and coalitions helped lay the groundwork for the more recent protests around police violence towards young people of colour. Grassroots organisations and social media prompted mobilisations and campaigning such as the Black Lives Matter movement which gathered momentum since 2012. This movement captures the outrage arising from police killings of unarmed African-Americans. The sustained national protest against unaccountable police actions has played a major role in bringing racially defined roles back into the limelight. The Movement for Black Lives wants not only to end anti-Blackness but also to end the marginalisation for others as well, such as gay, lesbian, and transgender people. In many urban conurbations and rural areas around the developed world, activism and mobilisation is taking place. Anti-fracking movements have emerged as a grassroots direct action against unconventional gas and oil extraction. Extinction rebellion activists are engaging in 'slow cycle rides' and 'die-ins' as a protest against climate change and as a platform from which to demand reform. The variety of victim responses to harm is well illustrated by Vegh Weis and White in Chapter 12, where they explore this very issue in the context of environmental victimisation.

Concluding Thoughts

Victimology is a relatively new social scientific enterprise. If, at the core of this enterprise the aim is to study the suffering of those who have experienced wrongdoing with a view to establishing a more just existence then in terms of progress so far, there are gains and losses. Gradual, significant progress has been made to many criminal justice systems and processes across the globe. In some jurisdictions, victims are now firmly on the criminal justice agenda with reforms having been introduced, albeit the nature of the change is far from institutional or systemic. New forms of individual and collective suffering continue to come to light from various corners of the globe. Further step changes are needed at institutional and systemic levels as well as at global to local and personal levels. Professional evidence-based responses to victims have yet to become embedded as core practice and greater resources are required to help agencies achieve this. In England and Wales, austerity measures have overstretched services to the point where they are struggling to undertake their day-to-day roles. Victims are not the central responsibility of any one agency and victims' needs, as a consequence, are not prioritised. Reforms to date have been partial, piecemeal and lacking in coordination despite cross-government strategies. More incremental change might yet benefit those who have experienced wrongdoing and are suffering. As proposed by Tapley in Chapter 9, the introduction of professional advocates tasked to represent victims' needs and concerns and help them navigate the complexities of the criminal justice system might be one such improvement. However, fundamental change demands a re-writing of the dominant and flawed discourse about victims, victimhood and victimisation. Activism and activists will remain central to the challenge of doing this. This volume forcefully illustrates the power of individuals and collective groups, in particular, feminist activists and scholars, who have been fundamental in linking academic research with activist-led calls for social change, who have made and will continue to make substantial contributions to the growth and worth of victimology into the twenty-first century.

References

Amir, M. (1968). Victim Precipitated Forcible Rape. *Journal of Criminal Law and Criminology, 58*(4), 493–502.

Bennett Moses, L., & Chan, J. (2018). Using Big Data and Data Analytics in Criminological Research. In P. Davies & P. Francis (Eds.), *Doing Criminological Research* (3rd ed., pp. 251–270). London: Sage.

Brennan, I., & Myhill, A. (2017). *Domestic Abuse Matters 2.0: Evaluation of First Responder Training*. College of Policing (college.police.uk).

Button, M., Tapley, J., & Lewis, C. (2013). The "Fraud Justice Network" and the Infra-structure of Support for Individual Fraud Victims in England and Wales. *Criminology & Criminal Justice: An International Journal, 13*(1), 37–61.

Button, M., Lewis, C., & Tapley, J. (2014). Not a Victimless Crime: The Impact of Fraud on Individual Victims and Their Families. *The Security Journal, 27*(1), 36–54.

Cook, I. R., & Davies, P. (2017). Supporting Victims and Witnesses. In J. Harding, P. Davies, & G. Mair (Eds.), *An Introduction to Criminal Justice* (pp. 388–407). London: Sage.

Davies, P. (2018) Tackling domestic abuse locally: paradigms, ideologies and the political tensions of multi-agency working, *Journal of Gender-Based Violence 2*(3), 429-446.

Douglas, H. (2017). Legal Systems Abuse and Coercive Control. *Criminology & Criminal Justice, 18*(1), 84–99.

Duggan, M., & Heap, V. (2014) *Administrating Victimisation: The Politics of Anti-Social Behaviour and Hate Crime Policy*. Basingstoke: Palgrave Macmillan.

Dutton, M. A., & Greene, R. (2010). Resilience and Crime Victimization. *Journal of Traumatic Stress, 23*(2), 215–222.

Fleming, J., & Rhodes, R. A. W. (2018). Can Experience Be Evidence? Craft Knowledge and Evidence-Based Policing. *Policy & Politics: An International Journal of Research & Policy, 46*(1), 3–26.

Goodey, J. (2005). *Victims and Victimology: Research, Policy and Practice*. Harlow: Pearson.

Green, S. (2007). Crime, Victimisation and Vulnerability. In S. Walklate (Ed.), *Handbook of Victims and Victimology*. Cullompton: Willan.

Greer, C. (2017). News Media, Victims and Crime. In P. Davies, P. Francis, & C. Greer (Eds.), *Victims, Crime and Society: An Introduction* (2nd ed.). Sage: London.

Hester, M., & Lilley, S.-J. (2017). Rape Investigation and Attrition in Acquaintance, Domestic Violence and Historical Rape Cases. *Journal of Investigative Psychology and Offender Profiling, 14*(2), 175–188.

HMIC. (2015). *Increasingly Everyone's Business*. London: HMIC.

Johnston, L., & Shearing, C. (2003). *Governing Security: Explorations in Policing and Justice*. Abingdon: Routledge.

Karagiannopoulos, V. (2018). *Living with Hacktivism: From Conflict to Symbiosis*. London: Palgrave.

Lee, M. (2017). Fear, Vulnerability and Victimisation. In P. Davies, P. Francis, & C. Greer (Eds.), *Victims, Crime and Society: An Introduction*. London: Sage.

Long, J., Harper, K., & Harvey, H. (2017). The Femicide Census: 2017 Findings. The Annual Report on UK Femicides 2017. Retrieved from www.femicidecensus.org.uk.

Ministry of Justice. (2015). *Code of Practcie for Victims of Crime*. London: Ministry of Justice.

Mythen, G., & McGowan, W. (2018). Cultural Victimology Revisited: Synergies of Risk, Fear and Resilience. In S. Walklate (Ed.), *Handbook of Victims and Victimology*. Cullompton: Willan.

Robinson, A. (2015). Pie in the Sky? The Use of Criminal Justice Policies and Practices for Intimate Partner Violence. In H. Johnson, B. S. Fisher, & V. Jacquier (Eds.), *Critical Issues on Violence Against Women*. London: Routledge.

Robinson, A. L., Myhill, A., & Wire, J. (2017). Practitioner (mis)understandings of Coercive Control in England and Wales. *Criminology & Criminal Justice, 18*(1), 29–49.

Roebuck, B. (2018). Resilience and Victims of Violence. Plenary Address Presented at the 16th International Symposium of the World Society of Victimology, Hong Kong.

Rowe, M., Davies, P., Biddle, P. and Brown, D-M. (2018). *Innovation in Policing Domestic Abuse: Understanding Success to Build Capacity*. N8 Policing Research Partnership.

Savage, S., Grieve, J., & Poyser, S. (2007). Putting Wrongs to Rights – Campaigns Against Miscarriages of Justice. *Criminology & Criminal Justice: An International Journal, 7*(1), 83–105.

Spalek, B. (2017). *Crime Victims: Theory, Policy and Practice*. London: Palgrave.

Tapley, J. (2003). *From 'Good Citizen' to 'Deserving Client': The Relationship Between Victims of Violent Crime and the State Using Citizenship as the Conceptualising Tool*. Unpublished PhD Thesis, University of Southampton.

Walby, S., & Towers, J. (2018). Untangling the Concepts of Coercive Control: Theorizing Domestic Violent Crime. *Criminology & Criminal Justice, 18*(1), 7–28.

Walby, S., et al. (2015). *Stopping Rape: Toward a Comprehensive Policy*. Bristol: Policy Press.

Walklate, S. (2011). Reframing Criminal Victimization: Finding a Place for Vulnerability and Resilience. *Theoretical Criminology, 15*(2), 179–194.

Walklate, S., Fitz-Gibbon, K., & McCulloch, J. (2017). Is More Law the Answer? Seeking Justice for Victims of Intimate Partner Violence Through the Reform of Legal Categories. *Criminology and Criminal Justice*, 1–17. https://doi.org/10.1177/1748895817728561.

Wedlock, E., & Tapley, J. (2016). *What Works in Supporting Victims of Crime: A Rapid Evidence Assessment*. London: Victims' Commissioner. Ministry of Justice.

Woodlock, D., McKenzie, M., Western, D., & Harris, B. (2019). Technology as a Weapon in Domestic Violence: Responding to Digital Coercive Control. *Australian Social Work*. https://doi.org/10.1080/0312407X.2019.1607510.